Jim Tully

Jim Tully

American Writer,

Irish Rover,

Hollywood Brawler

Paul J. Bauer and Mark Dawidziak

Foreword by Ken Burns

Commonwealth Book Company
St. Martin, Ohio

Copyright © 2011, 2023 by Paul J. Bauer and Mark Dawidziak

All rights reserved. No part of this book may be reproduced in any form or by any means without the prior written consent of the publisher, excepting brief quotes used in reviews.
Printed in the United States of America.

ISBN: 978-1-948986-48-9

Frontispiece photograph: Jim Tully, 1886–1947. Authors' collection.

For brothers

Gregg, Thomas, Steven, David

and sons

Justin Pierce, Michael Pierce, Samuel Bauer

—PJB

For Sara and Becky, who also traveled this road

—MD

Contents

	Selected Quotes	ix
	Foreword by Ken Burns	xi
	Acknowledgments	xvii
	Introduction	1
1	Coins for a Dead Woman's Eyes	11
2	Six Years of Imprisonment	25
3	Hearts Ignorant of Homes	33
4	Big Rock Candy Mountain	49
5	The End of the Road	66
6	The Fire and the Ring	76
7	Troubled in Heart	94
8	Write or Starve	102
9	*Emmett Lawler*	121
10	Hollywood Writer	126
11	The Road-Kid and the Little Tramp	135
12	*Beggars of Life*	148
13	One More Illusion	155

14	*Jarnegan*	168
15	*Circus Parade*	176
16	*Shanty Irish*	184
17	*Shadows of Men*	196
18	*Beggars Abroad*	204
19	*Blood on the Moon*	214
20	*Laughter in Hell*	228
21	*Ladies in the Parlor*	241
22	Return to the Ring	252
23	*The Bruiser*	264
24	*Biddy Brogan's Boy*	275
25	The Last Division	287
	Epilogue	299
	Appendix	302
	Notes	305
	Index	340

Selected Quotes

If Tully were a Russian, read in translation, all the Professors would be hymning him. He has all of Gorky's capacity for making vivid the miseries of poor and helpless men, and in addition he has a humor that no Russian could conceivably have.
—H. L. Mencken

If there is a writer in America today who can lay hold of mean people and mean lives and tear their mean hearts out with more appalling realism, his work is unknown to me.
—George Jean Nathan

[Jim Tully] has fathered the school of hard-boiled writing so zealously cultivated by Ernest Hemingway and lesser luminaries.
—Rupert Hughes

. . . a refreshing fountain of wisdom and wit.
—Charlie Chaplin

As for American writers, I think yourself and Jim Tully are the only ones whose work will endure; among the writers now living, I mean.
—Robert E. Howard to H. P. Lovecraft

Tully should be taken in large doses for the reduction of Hollywood head-swellings.
—W. C. Fields

... the most intelligent and human man in Hollywood.
—Charles Laughton

Jim Tully is a strange and compelling writer. His work may delight you or it may shock and disgust you; but it will never, never bore you. . . . There is more red blood in him than in a dozen run-of-mine novels.
—Bruce Catton

Genet's pederasts, Burroughs' junkies, and all the minor scarecrows—Selby, Rechy, Schneck, LeRoi Jones—are all schoolboys alongside old Tully. And at least he has the virtue of absolute honesty, of innocence.
—Gerald Green

Jim Tully has slugged a typewriter from obscurity and poverty since hanging up the gloves. . . . He has become a greater writer . . . one of the finest in America. We will put him among the first five anyway.
—Damon Runyon

That Jim Tully wrote at all is a miracle; that he wrote so well is a gift to the world.
—John Sayles

Foreword

Ken Burns

Shelby Foote once shared an apt description of Mark Twain and Abraham Lincoln that has always stuck with me. He said that they both wrote "with the bark on." They both spoke American English. They spoke to Americans in a language they understood because it was of them and from them. I'm not sure if that is a description directly attributable to Shelby or whether he was just passing it along from some other keen observer, but, clearly, what we also have in the work of the remarkable Jim Tully is a distinctly American writer who wrote with the bark on.

Tully is a diamond in the rough, untrained as he is both structurally and narratively. But it doesn't matter. His gifts so far outweigh his limitations; there are no doubts that the reader is encountering an American original. There are echoes of Twain, to be sure, but this is not an imitation of that great writer or anyone else for that matter. This is a unique American voice, born in unspeakable poverty, shaped by hardships, and illuminated by enormous compassion. Jim Tully has been nothing less than a revelation to me—an amazing and extraordinary discovery. I love his books, and I loved getting to know him in the pages of this wonderful, hugely important biography. Here is a writer who not only deserves to be rediscovered, he needs to be rediscovered.

Although his books are accounts of a bygone America, they have a timeless quality about them. The elasticity of his narrative amazingly puts his bailiwick somehow between the Great Potato Famine and the Great Depression; the effect is like getting a remedial course about whole parts of America that heretofore have been excluded for the obvious reason that they are embarrassingly unfit for our sanitized Madison Avenue view of the past. He opened up a whole world that has been conveniently airbrushed over the decades. It is incredibly valuable to have this view of our past, mined as it is from its darkest corners. Whether he is remembering the brutalities of the hobo world or the boxing ring or the circus, Jim Tully never flinches from showing us something more decrepit and more dangerous and more depraved than we possibly could have expected. Consider what he does in his 1927 book, *Circus Parade*. We think of the circus as a source of joy and wonder and eternal childhood, so we are shocked but nonetheless fascinated by the savagery and dissipation he is describing. This is not a sentimental work but rather an artistry born of the excruciating facts of his own experience and suffering. Tully does this again and again in his books. He shows us real life, at the beginning of the American century when we like to think that we are at our best and emerging into an industrial worldwide power, and he stands there, alone almost, listening, watching, insisting that attention must be paid to this gigantic, "Yes, but. . . ." Yes, we are this way, but there are all these other parts of American life that have been largely kept from view. Yes, we are this way, but there are also these marginalized lives, and we must know about them too.

These are lives filled with authentic tragedy, not the inconvenience of divorce and scandal, disgrace and loneliness, but the real human tragedy of abject poverty, cruelty, death, and even starvation. These people knew things. Tully knew them too, and he fashioned them into an art, drawing on his unflinching recollection of what he saw and heard—and what he experienced firsthand. One of the great joys of reading Tully is realizing how fantastically he noticed everything, observing nuances of speech, behavior, and personality. Then he set these people down on paper without judgment or denunciation.

You feel a kind of authenticity here that reaches back into the last half of the nineteenth century and moves clear up to the Second World War, when there is a sense that America has somehow been united. Jim Tully digs in and says to us, "Maybe, but don't miss this part." He constantly exposes us to those brutal realities and inconvenient truths often scrubbed clean by history, but what makes this a universal and transcendent experience is that he does this with an unerring eye for detail and with a great capacity for compassion. The human transcendence that comes from his art, when it comes, is diffused with a remarkable sympathy, and that is a blessing. It somehow mitigates the suffering he is describing. It is a wonderful thing to behold, leaving us with a sense of brotherhood and fellowship that transcends race, ethnicity, and economic station. His common humanity, the heroism of so-called ordinary people, is always spectacularly in evidence.

This is on prominent display in *Beggars of Life, Circus Parade,* and, my personal favorite, *Shanty Irish*. If I had to choose one passage from this great American writer, I would draw it from *Shanty Irish*. He is with his grandfather, Old Hughie, waiting for his father to return—an indifferent father who has condemned him to six years in an orphanage after his mother died young—a death young Jim Tully blamed himself for all his life:

> I spent hours with him at the different bars.
> Still a child, I learned quickly to drink and to observe, and to remember.
> I developed early a capacity for remembered sorrow. It is possible that I have remembered too much.

That is Jim Tully. It is the burden of remembering. There is, no doubt, a fatalism in his observations, born of a poetic Irish upbringing—a fatalism that would make the Frank McCourt of *Angela's Ashes* shiver. And if Frank McCourt did shiver when, as a young man, he read *Shanty Irish*, I'm sure it was the shiver of familiarity with Tully's excavation of remembered pain. In all of his books, you're hearing this without any varnish and without any kind of the expected sentimental poetry. Old Hughie is so capacious a figure that there attends to him a kind of mythic sentiment, but it doesn't exhibit a shred of sentimentality. His depiction of Old Hughie has the same kind of cold-eyed, hardscrabble sense that you get from *Angela's Ashes,* but more so.

I found the descriptions of his parents in *Shanty Irish* lingering in my memory like the lyrics of Stephen Foster's "Hard Times Come Again No More," which has so much resonance in an American experience we always want to whitewash like Tom Sawyer's fence, always want to soft-pedal: "Hard times, come again no more. Many days you have lingered around my cabin door. Oh hard times, come again no more." Tully knew hard times. His sympathy is with the people who know hard times.

Under Tully's direction we are drawn to irony, fairy tales, cleverness, simplicity, and, most of all, stories, but without an underpinning of advancement, good chance, wealth, achievement. It is what it is—no happy endings or rags to riches. This is no Horatio Alger stuff. He is Horatio Alger in the sense of what he himself accomplished through sheer determination and against such daunting odds, but none of his stories brims with that treacly brand of optimism. He is very much in the tradition of Twain, but without the celebrity to maintain or the need to soften any blow. Although Tully can be wryly humorous, the humor always is an integral part of the shanty, the boxcar, or the barroom. No matter what homes or position Tully's wealth can temporarily buy, he seems to still have one foot in that old saloon, with the ghost of his grandfather hovering, haunting all future proceedings—our inescapable past. He is the guy in the boxing ring. He is the kid in the orphanage. He is still—and always—the boy in the saloon waiting with his grandfather for his father to come and take him home.

There is also Tully's wonderful and revealing description of Charlie Chaplin, the screen vagabond for whom this real vagabond worked: "Having learned to observe men during seven years as a road-kid, and later as a wandering bruiser, I was soon aware that success had put a polish on the screen vagabond. If manners were a cloak to hide feelings, he wore a gorgeous garment."

The great saving grace of Jim Tully is that he never had to hide behind the masks and garments of conventional society. Everything remained raw until the end, and raw meant realizing he was not going to be published at the end. Raw meant he was going to get those bad reviews. Raw meant he was going to sell one house, retreat to another, only to sell that one. He is always reminding us of the sordidness and deprivation, and he is doing this, always, at great cost to himself. He loses so much after he gains, because he is unwilling to compromise. He's going to be who he's going to be. That is extraordinarily refreshing and, yet, not without dangers, dangers he willingly confronted all of his pugnacious life.

It is also not without greatness. While there is this diffusion of Irish pathos in his works, he is utterly American. The similarity to Twain is mostly in the choice of words. Twain's famous maxim is, "The difference between the right word and the almost right word is the difference between lightning and the lightning bug." Tully doesn't choose too many wrong words. His writing is full of "lightning." Tully's youth may have been framed by abandonment and poverty and alcohol, yet it nevertheless somehow loosened his tongue and permitted this great but nearly unremembered tributary of writing to flow, as this magnificent biography suggests, into the larger ebbing and flowing river that is our English language.

With Tully there is a sense that a piece of the jigsaw puzzle that has long been missing has been found. You may not have even known it was missing, but there it is, and it fits in, and it connects with everything around it. There is a piece, maybe it's in the left corner, that connects to Twain and looks ahead to Steinbeck. It straddles both the Civil War and the Second World War. It is a view of an America we suspected had to have been there. We've glimpsed bits and pieces of it in novels and movies, but that world hadn't been fully illuminated and brought back so vividly to life. Having it thus resurrected, Tully has connected us all to a continuum that flows a little more clearly. We understand a little bit more. We might be left a little bit shocked and more than a little bit embarrassed by this understanding, but we're also exhilarated by this ride he's taking us on.

Acknowledgments

We remember the late Mort Krahling, who set things in motion two decades ago by walking into a bookshop and stumping the proprietor with his request for a copy of *The Bruiser*.

The bulk of Jim Tully's literary remains is scattered in libraries from New York to California. Unearthing them has been a long and sometimes difficult task. Jim Tully had a special fondness for librarians. So do his biographers. We gratefully tender our thanks to Charlotte Brown, Simon Elliott, Lilace Hatayama, Octavio Olvera, and Jeff Rankin of the Department of Special Collections, Charles E. Young Research Library, UCLA; Alex Gildzen, Jeanne Somers, and Michael Cole of the Kent State University Library; Geoffrey D. Smith of The Ohio State University Library; Linda Koons, Joy Johnson, and Beth Keuneke of the St. Marys Community Public Library; Kate Templeton Hancock, Beth Poley, and Linda Hengst of the Ohioana Library; and Kathy Steele Gaivin and Pam Simones of the Kent Free Library. Mencken's letters are quoted by kind permission of the Enoch Pratt Free Library in accordance with the terms of the will of H.L. Mencken.

John T. Hubbell was both generous and wise in helping us work out a delicate point of history. We appreciate the bits of Tullyana unearthed and supplied by John Carson; Hank Schmid of the Davey Tree Expert Company; Father Tom Grilliot of St. Patrick's Church in Glynnwood, Ohio; John Francis Glynn of Modesto, California (great-grandson of John Glynn, who lobbied the Lake Erie & Louisville Railroad to place a "stop" outside of St. Marys that would become known as Glynnwood); Robert Howard of St. Marys City Schools; Rachel Barber of the Auglaize County Historical Society; Lu Albers of Holy Rosary Church in St. Marys, Ohio; Geoffrey Drew of the

Historical Archives of the Chancery of the Archdiocese of Cincinnati; Roger Bruns of the National Historical Publications and Records Commission of the National Archives in Washington, D.C.; Nora Guthrie of the Woody Guthrie Archives; Leo Grin, writer, filmmaker, and founder of the literary journal *Cimmerian* (2004–8); Roger Di Paolo of the *Kent-Ravenna Record-Courier;* David Stilwell of the *St. Marys Evening Leader;* and Sandra and Henry Halem of the Kent Historical Society. Tullyphiles C. Franklin Bauer, David Bianculli, Tony Bill, Bob Burford, Louise Warren, Edythe Zimmerman, Doris Lawler, and Ned Lawler have been in our corner from the start.

Dan Moldea answered all our questions about the Freedom of Information Act and the FBI. Mary Elaine Chase found a copy of Alton Tully's missing birth certificate. Jim Richards kindly shared several of H. L. Mencken's letters. Denise Vogel shared many of the photos and letters given to her mother by Myrtle Tully. Sharon Touchton passed along a copy of a letter Tully wrote to her grandfather, Jim's cousin. Michael Hatherly compiled an extensive genealogy of the Lawler and Tully families and was very generous in sharing it with us. Jim Perkowski helped digitize our many photos. And Bill Freeman's assistance during the stretch run is most appreciated.

We are also grateful to Kentites Francis Kline, Ruth Greer, and Titus Jackman for sharing their recollections. Crime historian Albert Borowitz kindly shared his knowledge of the Orpet case. Maura Wahl read the early chapters and suggested improvements. Joseph C. Dawidziak researched Tully's will. Michael Dawidziak was dogged in seeking out copies of Tully's work. Samuel Bauer tracked down incomplete citations at the Ohio State University library. And we thank Gregg Bauer for illustrating the dust jacket.

A very pleasant afternoon was spent at the home of Pam and Robin Beamon while we visited with Robin's mother and Jim's daughter, Trilby Tully Beamon. We appreciate their hospitality and support. Indeed, few things could be less pleasant than having two strangers poking around your family history and generally disrupting your life for years. Robin couldn't have been more patient and understanding. We are in his debt.

Our path to the Kent State University Press was, let's say, indirect. Will Underwood, Joanna Hildebrand Craig, Mary Young, and the Press staff made it well worth the trip. Sonia E. Fulop was everything one could hope for in an editor: sharp-eyed, meticulous, and professional. Her hard work has made this a much better book.

Lastly, our wives, Francine Bauer and Sara Showman, were unfailingly patient and enthusiastic during our two-decade odyssey. We can't imagine completing this book without them.

Jim Tully

Introduction

In the parlance of the boxing ring, Jim Tully was a bruiser. His build was hardly athletic. His sawed-off, chunky frame forced him to depend on a straight-ahead style that required him to absorb punishment in order to land his own punches. A relentless warrior from the small western Ohio town of St. Marys, he kept moving forward—often when more cautious men would have retired from the field. Certainly less skilled than many of his contemporaries, he was always dangerous.

His resilience and determination had been forged in the wretched poverty of his youth. He had honed his fighting instincts by surviving more than six years as a "road-kid" (a young vagabond, and not, Tully explained, "in the strict sense of the word, a hobo. . . . The road-kid is more cunning and daring").[1] His muscles had been hardened during stints as a chain maker ("my only chance to get away from the road").[2] It was the ideal preparation for a bruiser, a fighter who keeps throwing leather round after brutal round.

The term describes Jim Tully the boxer, who, in the first decade of the twentieth century, fought his way through the ranks of promising featherweights. But it also is an accurate description of Jim Tully the writer, whose books first appeared when the aptly named Roaring Twenties started to roar. Having decided to pound a typewriter instead of other prizefighters, this son of an Irish ditchdigger tenaciously applied his ring style to the literary trade.

Tully had been nurturing the dream of becoming a writer ever since his sister Maggie (later Virginia) put the idea in his head. "Some day I would show the world—she was sure of that," he wrote fourteen years after her death in 1926. "She did not know the long road I had to travel."³ She also didn't know how difficult the road would be. Her kid brother, a teenager when she so grandly named his destiny, had about as much chance of becoming an Oxford don. His formal education had ended when he left a Cincinnati orphanage at the age of eleven.

"I had none of the usual illusions of youth," he declared in *Blood on the Moon*. "I knew that I would never become President of the United States. I came, on both sides, from drunken barbarians who groveled in superstition and were as illiterate as geese. All the vast realms of knowledge and beauty were closed to me. Nearly all of my mother's brothers were half mad. Most of my father's people were witty Irish morons. My mother had moods which lasted for days. . . . I inherited her moods and silences along with the wild blood which flowed in two rivers of half insane Irish."⁴

Somehow, though, Virginia's dream for her youngest brother endured. Others, too, left their mark on this fledgling American writer. From his father's father, the colorful Old Hughie, he had learned the value of a good story well told. His father, also named Jim Tully, kept a small library of books by everyone from Gustave Flaubert, Thomas Hardy, and George Eliot to the Victorian occult writer Marie Corelli.⁵ Young Jim inherited his father's love of books. A nun at the Catholic orphanage where he spent six lonely childhood years "taught him how to modulate his voice and speak words correctly" and encouraged him to read Dickens, Shakespeare, and Hugo.⁶ A librarian in Kent, Ohio, where he worked at a chain factory while looking for boxing matches, gave him the key question of his life: "What's the use of whipping the whole world and ending up a bartender?"⁷

When he took to the road, he discovered a new set of writers and made them his constant traveling companions. Haunting libraries, he searched the stacks for works by Twain, Balzac, and Dostoyevsky. "The road gave me one jewel beyond price," the former "library bum" wrote in *Beggars of Life*. "The leisure to read and dream. If it made me old and wearily wise at twenty, it gave me for companions the great minds of all the ages, who talked to me with royal words."⁸ He was largely unschooled but hardly uneducated.

And every step of the way, he carried with him pictures of three one-time drifters who had become internationally known authors: Jack London, Maxim Gorky, and John Masefield.⁹ If they had made it, so could he. After reading Joseph Conrad's *Almayer's Folly*, he made his decision.¹⁰ "The chance was worth taking," Tully declared. "I would never be happy at anything else." He decided he would "write or starve."¹¹

He gamely jabbed at the keys of his typewriter, knowing that the ranks of contenders were swarming with prospects with college degrees and far more polish. When Jim Tully decided he'd rather be a writer than a fighter, few would have given the awkward plodder a chance to achieve much more than stumblebum status. Yet Tully knew that he was better prepared for this fight than many a college-trained scribbler raised with all the "advantages." Poverty had been his earliest and harshest trainer. While his punishing youth had left its share of deep psychological scars, it had also "equally twisted and strengthened me for the sadder years ahead."[12] The Spartan existence of a struggling writer couldn't be worse than the hunger and squalor he'd already survived.

The road, too, proved a great teacher. The legends and myths of the road told in rattling boxcars and around hobo campfires swirled about him. "I fraternized with human wrecks," Tully recalled. "I learned the secrets of traitors and crawlers and other fakers. . . . Fortunately for me, there had always been some chemical in my nature that had kept my mind active so that I was not allowed to rot in hives of congested humanity. Tramping in wild and windy places, without money, food, or shelter, was better for me than supinely bowing to any conventional decree of fate."[13]

Few writers possessed such a curious array of talents. He could bring tears or laughter to the country's toughest critics—bar patrons—and cadge drinks in the process. He possessed a right powerful enough to deliver a devastating punch, and a chin sturdy enough to take one. He had the ability to hop on moving freight trains while eluding the railroad bulls who hunted for hoboes. And he could stand between a furnace and anvil, pounding out links of chain.

By the time his first book, the semiautobiographical *Emmett Lawler*, was published in 1922, Tully had worked as a dishwasher, chain maker, boxer, railroad laborer, newspaper reporter, tree surgeon, and circus roustabout. He also had stockpiled most of the experiences and characters that would fill the pages of his best work. He mingled with prizefighters and prostitutes. He was tutored in the low arts by hoboes and yeggs. And he absorbed the hard ways of con artists, carnies, criminals, and drifters. Many journalists and authors of the period tried to write about people at the edges of society. None knew them better than Tully. He had lived with them. He had been one of them. "It's a long fight. . . . I have beaten the writing racket mainly because I am barroom smart," he said.[14]

"All I know of human nature was learned in a saloon before I was twenty," he recalled. "I learned to distinguish between a laugh from the head and one from the heart. I gauged sincerity by the intonations of speech. . . . I have since found that men and women in far places of the world and in different social strata are fundamentally the same as those I first met in my formative years."[15]

With the publication of his breakthrough second book, *Beggars of Life* (1924), the account of his road years, Jim Tully achieved the widespread literary recognition he had been pursuing with a bruiser's tenacity since leaving the ring. He was thirty-eight and more than a dozen years into his writing career.

Tully's raw staccato style in many ways provided the hard-boiled link between London's literature of the "strenuous life" and Ernest Hemingway's muscular prose. Like Hemingway, Tully wrote of rugged sorts in crisp, understated sentences. Like John Steinbeck, he was more interested in society's outcasts than in high society. Like Dashiell Hammett, he had a gift for depicting violence in realistic tones. "My belief is that anything that has been lived should be written about without equivocation," Tully wrote.[16] As early as 1927, *New York Times* critic Edwin Clark declared that Tully "has been the novelist of the hard-boiled." Author and journalist Frank Scully agreed, crediting Tully with being "the leader (and the founder) of the hard-boiled school of writing."[17] And George Jean Nathan—dean of Broadway critics and coeditor of the *American Mercury*—once flatly stated to Tully, "Jim, you really started the hard-boiled school."[18] Little wonder, therefore, that both Tully's literary champion, writer-editor H. L. Mencken, and the *New York Times* compared him to Gorky. By 1932, Nathan was looking over America's literary heavyweights and ranking Tully with Sinclair Lewis, Eugene O'Neill, and Theodore Dreiser.

Critical opinion aside, Tully's influence in the 1920s and 1930s was enormous. One morning in 1932, years away from becoming a film noir, a young Robert Mitchum hopped a southbound freight train to live out his wild daydreams of the open road. He left behind not Hemingway's *A Farewell to Arms* or Dorothy Parker's *Laments for the Living*, but a copy of *Beggars of Life* so heavily worn that the type was smeared and the pages loose.[19] Jim Thompson, Nelson Algren, Charles Willeford, John Steinbeck, Charles Bukowski, Ralph Ellison, William Kennedy, Jack Kerouac, William T. Vollmann, Frank McCourt, Woodie Guthrie, Bukka White, Blind Willie McTell, Furry Lewis (who lost a leg hopping a railroad car[20]), Harry Partch, Merle Haggard, and Tom Waits are just a few who have followed in Tully's dusty footsteps. Some spent time on the road, all worked the same dark end of the American street.

If ahead of his time from a literary standpoint, however, Tully was the ideal celebrity writer for the Roaring Twenties. Perhaps no other decade produced more bigger-than-life American characters. Almost everywhere one turned in those heady days of Charleston-crazed flappers and bootlegged gin, there was a headline-making celebrity ready to grab your attention and seize your imagination. Everyone knew that Babe Ruth was the mightiest slugger ever to swing a baseball bat. Few questioned that Jack Dempsey, Tully's pal and fellow road-kid, was the mightiest heavyweight champion of all time. No one doubted that Bobby Jones was the finest golfer to stride down a fairway or that Red Grange was without equal on the gridiron.

The newspapers and press agents proclaimed the news. Hype had become an American art form in the 1920s, and no prior period had so effectively packaged its heroes and villains for popular consumption. Al Capone grew in legend until he actually symbolized the American gangster. Clarence Darrow became the model of the crusading lawyer. Charles Lindbergh almost defined the word "hero." Hollywood, meanwhile, was telling the public that Rudolph Valentino was the world's greatest lover, that Charlie Chaplin (to whom Tully dedicated *Beggars of Life*) was the greatest comedian, and that Mary Pickford was "America's Sweetheart."

Jim Tully was a literary star tailor-made for the era. Although he stood only five foot three inches tall, the stocky road-kid from St. Marys was the kind of bigger-than-life character the decade craved. He grinned at the passing parade from beneath an unruly mop of brick-red curls. By the time Wall Street crashed and silenced whatever roar remained of the 1920s, Jim Tully was established as one of the country's best-known writers. *Beggars of Life*, which told of his six years as a road-kid, was turned into a Broadway play by Maxwell Anderson (with a young James Cagney as Tully), and a movie by director "Wild Bill" Wellman (with Louise Brooks among its stars). *Jarnegan* (1926), the first critical novel about Hollywood, also was adapted for the Broadway stage. *Circus Parade* (1927) described his time with circus and carnival people. *Shanty Irish* (1928) brought his family in St. Marys back to life.

Tully used his status as a major American author to launch a parallel writing career—that of a Hollywood journalist. Between 1924 and 1944, he contributed hundreds of articles on movie stars and directors to magazines and newspapers. While these Hollywood pieces certainly proved lucrative to Tully, they were perplexing to even his staunchest admirers. What intrigued Scully, for instance, was "how a man who made a fortune out of writing for motion-picture fan magazines . . . could gain a world-wide reputation as" the man who put hard-boiled writing on the literary map. "How could one lobe of his brain turn out stuff that made him the highest-priced peddler of a picture star's passions and kitchen recipes, and the other lobe of his brain make him, currently a best-seller in the U.S.S.R. for such non-political portraits of Americana as *Jarnegan, Circus Parade, Beggars of Life, Ladies in the Parlor, Shanty Irish, Emmett Lawler, Laughter in Hell, Shadows of Men, Blood on the Moon, The Bruiser,* and *A Dozen and One?*" How, Scully wondered, could the same writer produce both "this mass of bilge and enduring literature"?[21] It's a question this biography attempts to answer. It's also a question that, in all probability, Scully was wise enough never to pose directly to Tully.

"People are enamored by his speech or his reputation," Scully said of his friend,

and almost break their necks in their efforts to meet him. In all too short a time he has broken the rest of what's left of them and tossed it back to their humbler relations for a decent burial. . . . His right arm weaves across your vision, feinting like a fighter leading you into the final blow which will leave you slug-nutty for life, and you either take it and stagger from the salon a stumble-bum, or you scram for your car and scream all the way home that the guy's impossible, an army tank let loose among civilized people in a drawing room. The bigger you are the harder you fall. There isn't a mind in all Hollywood that can stand up to him in a finish fight.[22]

Maybe that's why Tully was called the most feared man in Hollywood—indeed, some regarded him as a reputation-devouring minotaur let loose on Sunset Boulevard. Or maybe it was because he was one of the very few journalists covering the movie industry honestly at a time when studio-generated publicity was swallowed whole by columnists all too willing to let press agents write their copy. Or maybe it was because he never lost that tremendous right (something matinee idol John Gilbert found out when he foolishly attacked Tully in the Brown Derby restaurant).

Tully's Hollywood pieces fell into two categories: serious profiles (published in magazines like *Vanity Fair* and *Esquire*) and lighter features (published in such fan magazines as *Photoplay* and *Screen Play*). Then, as now, the press made a convenient target, and as might be expected, the harder-hitting pieces made Tully plenty of enemies in Tinseltown. Chaplin, for whom he worked as a writer and publicity man in the mid-1920s, was fearful enough to pressure a New York publisher into dropping Tully's completed biography of the great comedian. It never saw print.

Still, despite his reputation and despite the break with Chaplin, Tully kept a loyal and diverse circle of friends. The closest included Mencken, Scully, Dempsey, Nathan, and producer Paul Bern. Other notable Tully pals were directors James Cruze and Frank Capra, columnists Walter Winchell and Damon Runyon, actors Clark Gable and Wallace Beery, and kings of laughter W. C. Fields and Mack Sennett. Traveling through Europe in 1929, he was welcomed into the homes of George Bernard Shaw, James Joyce, and H. G. Wells.

By the time he died in 1947, declining sales and poor health had already conspired to put his reputation into eclipse. His books slipped out of print as Tully slipped off the cultural landscape. The postwar boom of new writers completed his disappearing act. Today, one can find little evidence that this Irish American storyteller was one of the country's leading authors.

Many other writers of the 1920s and 1930s experienced a similar loss of favor during and after World War II. A group of exciting young authors led by Norman Mailer and James Jones temporarily blasted away the old guard. Some, like Faulkner and Hemingway, wrote themselves back into prominence. Others, like Fitzgerald and Wolfe, received posthumous boosts thanks to academic champions.

Tully mounted comebacks in 1936 and 1942. Both novels were commercial failures. And his champion, Mencken, suffered a massive stroke in 1948, just seventeen months after Tully's death. Although the Sage of Baltimore lived another seven years, he was unable to read or write. When the 1950s gave way to a new decade, not one of Tully's fourteen books was in print. This would not have surprised Jim Tully. He put little stock in fame, which he described as "merely the prolonging of neighborhood gossip."[23] His celebrity, fueled by the success of *Beggars of Life*, spread quickly, raged for two decades, and burned out. Many readers of his obituary in 1947 who recognized his name were undoubtedly surprised to learn that he hadn't died years before.

London, Tully's boyhood hero before he decided that his idol was something of a "fake," once declared, "Life that lives is life successful."[24] It could have been an epitaph for Jim Tully, who had several times tramped his way across the country, had boxed to victory with blood clogging his nose and one eye nearly closed, had costarred in a Hollywood movie with a future

Oscar winner, had broken bread with Langston Hughes, had used his influence to save death-row inmates from the electric chair, had won drinking contests in San Francisco and Baltimore, and had swapped jokes with W. C. Fields and written them for Charlie Chaplin.

It has been argued that the greatest character Samuel Clemens ever created was Mark Twain. A similar claim could be made for Jim Tully. If he had never written a single book, Tully's life would be worthy of attention.

Little has been written about Tully since his death in 1947. A brief entry by Paul Chapman in *Ohio Authors and Their Books* appeared in 1962 and was followed by two decades of silence until David D. Anderson contributed two studies of Tully to the *Society for the Study of Midwestern Literature Newsletter*.[25] One of the first to rediscover Tully was himself a former vagabond. Ray Hinkle was a young hobo from Polk County, Missouri. Passing through Memphis in 1935, he discovered a copy of *Beggars of Life*. Fifty years later he self-published *The Hobo from St. Marys: A Tribute to Jim Tully*, a brief appreciation of Tully drawn mostly from his books.[26] Many book collectors were first introduced to Tully by Maura McMillan's fine profile of him in *Firsts: The Book Collector's Magazine*. And Charles Willeford introduced Tully to hard-boiled mystery fans in his essay, "Jim Tully: Holistic Barbarian," which appeared in his 2000 book, *Writing & Other Blood Sports*.[27]

Tully has also surfaced in several literary histories. H. Bruce Franklin's landmark study, *Prison Literature in America*, considers Tully's literary forays into crime.[28] Those interested in Tully's place in Irish American fiction are encouraged to read *The Irish Voice in America*, a comprehensive survey by Charles Fanning.[29] Fanning describes two cycles of Irish American fiction. The first occurred in the nineteenth century, and the second commenced with the 1932 publication of James T. Farrell's *Young Lonigan*. Ron Ebest's *Private Histories* largely focuses on Irish American writers, including Tully, who were active between Fanning's two cycles.[30]

In a prefatory note to *Old Mr. Flood*, his collection of evocative New York stories, Joseph Mitchell wrote, "I wanted these stories to be truthful rather than factual, but they are solidly based on facts."[31] Tully's best work shares this goal. While biographers also seek truth, their roads must be paved with fact. The source for much of Tully's early life has, by necessity, been Jim Tully. Tully's books range from straight fiction to autobiographical novel to memoir and nonfiction. How does one distinguish between the true and the factual in Tully's work? Tully tells us. In a 1930 letter to the editor of an encyclopedia, Tully notes that "*Emmett Lawler* is an autobiographical novel. My other books—*Beggars of Life, Circus Parade, Shanty*

Irish, and *Shadows of Men,*—depict various phases of my own life."[32] (*Blood on the Moon,* which covered another phase of Tully's life, would not be issued until the following year.) This, however, was not Tully's final word on the subject of the true and nearly true in his books.

During the late 1930s, Tully made several attempts to write a comprehensive autobiography. These drafts, titled "Out of My Heart" and "I Passed by Here," along with an untitled manuscript about a former sweetheart, are rich in detail, covering his life from childhood to the present.[33] Tully's account of his life after *Emmett Lawler* made him famous is easily corroborated by newspapers, magazines, and other contemporaneous sources. But what of his early years?

To the extent that Tully's unpublished autobiography of his life before 1922 can be verified, he was where he said he was, doing what he said he was doing. Newspaper accounts, for instance, verify most of his boxing career, and the records of the Davey Tree Expert Company confirm his travels as an arborist. To offer two further examples, both from Illinois, his eyewitness accounts of the 1903 collapse of the Dowie cult in Zion City and the 1916 Orpet-Lambert murder case in Waukegan are entirely consistent with the facts. Not everything, of course, could be verified, but it seems clear that when Tully set out to write his autobiography, he intended it as purely nonfiction, not another exercise in autobiographical fiction. He said as much in a 1939 letter to H. L. Mencken: "I've been pounding out, as you know, for months a story on my own life called *Out of My Heart.*"[34]

There is, however, a significant gap in Tully's unpublished autobiographical work. In the manuscript titled "I Passed by Here," he explains, "The years as a road kid, though they wrote with heavy and terrible hand upon me . . . can have but little space in this story, being detailed in other books."[35] It is clear then that by the late 1930s, Tully intended the true record of his life to be found in his unpublished memoirs and his books devoted to his years as a road-kid, *Beggars of Life* and *Circus Parade.* When Tully's publisher added the subtitle *A Hobo Autobiography* to *Beggars of Life,* Tully objected not to the word "autobiography" but to being identified as a hobo.[36] Indeed, when the pioneering scholar of vagabondage, sociologist Nels Anderson of the University of Chicago, reviewed *Beggars of Life* in 1924, he regarded the book as "autobiographical material."[37] And the *New York Times* began its review of *Beggars* by noting simply that "Jim Tully's book is autobiography naked and unashamed."[38]

When a critic attacked *Circus Parade* for factual errors, Tully went to great lengths to defend the book's veracity to Mencken.[39] And when censors attacked a chapter in *Circus Parade* depicting the abuse of a young girl by a gang of carnies, Tully defended the chapter, noting that it was written from memory with "little embellishment."[40] Another "embellishment" would appear to be the character Blackie, which Tully conceded was based on a road-kid he traveled with after his circus days.[41]

Still, *Shadows of Men* (1930), which also chronicles Tully's road years, requires a degree of caution. Some passages are clearly true and can be verified by outside sources, while others reflect the hand of Tully the novelist. For example, Tully's description of a drug-induced dream world is clearly fiction, while the events of the final chapter of the book, which describes the adult Tully's visit to San Quentin, are well documented. Tully maintained that *Shanty Irish*, his book about his childhood, is truthful about all the members of his family except his grandfather Hugh Tully. In his foreword to *Blood on the Moon* (1931), Tully notes that "I have thought it best to change names and situations."[42] As it's apparent that *Blood on the Moon* is a mixed bag of fact and fiction, it is safest to consider it an autobiographical novel. For the purposes of this biography, then, we have come to regard two of Tully's books, *Beggars of Life* and *Circus Parade*, as well as his travel book, *Beggars Abroad* (1930), as sound and reliable sources. *Shadows of Men*, *Shanty Irish*, and *Blood on the Moon* strike us as having an autobiographical framework but with passages that display embroidery or outright fiction. For this reason, these three of Tully's books have been cited sparingly and with caution.

Frank Scully, who knew Tully better than anyone, had a warning for any biographer so foolhardy as to attempt to capture Tully in print: "Obviously such a hammered-down Titan needs a Boswell as good as himself, and the pity of that is there is none. I have met many of the great men of our time, both in Europe and America, but none has fetched me with the force of his personality as Tully has. And none has pulverized my confidence to portray them as Tully has."[43]

We can't say we weren't warned.

1

Coins for a Dead Woman's Eyes

In the cool of the western Ohio barroom, young Jim Tully sat with his father, also Jim, and his father's father, Hugh. The men drank whiskey. The boy sipped beer. As the elder Jim drank silently, young Jim looked up from his glass and studied his grandfather's face for a moment. It was a face that, by the closing years of the nineteenth century, had seen decades of hard work and hard drink. It was a face framed by a thick head of light gray hair and a beard beginning at his chin with a tuft of dark hair that quickly ran to gray as it followed his jawline back. In his dark moments, he looked like an Old Testament prophet. He had few dark moments. On the contrary, no one knew better than his young grandson that Old Hughie could be counted on for a good story, one full of drama, humor, and not a little blarney—and never more so than when a full bottle sat in front of him. Unless it was a half-full bottle. The tales grew taller as the whiskey grew shorter. "You must have had a lot of fun in Ireland when you were a kid," young Jim remarked. Hughie's response surprised young Jim. "There was niver any fun in Ireland, me lad—It was always a wailin' and a weepin' country. Hearts full of the great sadness and stomicks empty of food—fools prayin' to God, and starvin' on their knays.... There was niver nothin' like the famine of '46—an' the boy here talks about a lot o' fun."[1]

Old Hughie's tale of his childhood, elegiac and angry, punctuated by the sound of glass and bottle on the wooden table, fills the opening chapter of Jim Tully's autobiographical novel *Shanty Irish*. While Tully's account of his grandfather's days in Ireland is certainly more imagined than real, the dire conditions that Hugh Tully describes are certainly true.

The first reports came from the Isle of Wight in the cool, damp August of 1845.[2] Farmers were alarmed to find that the tops of their potato plants "had been transformed into a black, evil-smelling slime."[3] They saw, upon digging up the tuber, that it too was rotten or would rot quickly when removed from the soil. The collapse of the potato crop, staple of the Irish diet in the nineteenth century, would lead to famine and disease on a staggering scale and result in the deaths of a million-and-a-half people and the migration of another million, nearly all peasants.[4]

Amid the unfolding tragedy, life went on. Young men still courted young women, marriages were made, and families started. One such union took place in 1847 in the parish of Inverness,[5] County Donegal, between twenty-three-year-old Hugh Tully and Catherine Byrn. The groom was the son of Andrew Tully and Margaret McGrorty, his bride, the daughter of Anna Gaitens and Charles Byrn. She was educated; he was not.[6] Both families were from County Donegal, and according to family lore, "about half way between Mount Charles and Dunkenalia, all west of Donegal."[7] As there is no Dunkenalia, it is likely that the families were from the area between Dunkineely and Mountcharles on Ireland's northwest coast. The newlyweds settled in the area and produced three babies over the next half-dozen years.

The young family's financial position, tenuous from the start, strained with the addition of each hungry mouth. Like so many of his countrymen before him, Hugh Tully looked across the Atlantic for a better life and sailed to America, most likely in 1854. He left his wife and small children behind.[8]

Having survived the privations of the eight-week voyage, which almost certainly included overcrowded living quarters and primitive cooking and sanitary conditions, and often typhus, he landed, probably in New York or Boston.[9] Unlike many of his countrymen, he did not settle in the bursting slums of either of these port cities. Instead, beginning in 1857, he spent the next three years traveling across the South, selling Irish linen and lace.[10] If Hugh Tully thought he had seen the depths of human suffering in Ireland, he soon learned otherwise in the antebellum South. He watched as black slaves, stripped naked, were auctioned like livestock to the highest bidder.[11] It was a sight he would never forget.

One foray north of the Mason-Dixon line took Hugh Tully to Clinton County, Ohio, southeast of Dayton, where he took up farming.[12] He sent for Catherine in 1860, and together they worked the land. Their three children—James Dennis, Anna, and Maria—remained in Ireland in the care of aunts and uncles. With the death of her father, Catherine inherited twenty acres of land, which she sold to her brother, using some of the proceeds to bring the children to Ohio in 1864.[13] The children were thirty-eight days, thirty-four of them at sea, in reaching their parents.[14] The family kept the farm another two years before one last move, north to St. Marys, a town of about 1,500 people located in Auglaize County.

The town of St. Marys, Ohio, not yet fifty in 1866, had grown from a Shawnee village and trading post alongside the St. Marys River to a shipping and milling center for corn, lumber, and wheat.[15] Three developments spurred this growth. The first was the expulsion, by treaty, of the Indians in 1831. As one local historian dryly noted, "At last, we secured every foot of their land and sent them into the far west."[16] The second factor in St. Marys's growth was the completion in 1845 of the Miami and Erie Canal and the creation of the St. Marys Reservoir, which supplied the canal with water. Finally, the sodden land began to drain. The digging of ditches in the fertile but flat muck had been undertaken by the early pioneers and farmers with mixed success. The ditch that drained one farmer's land often flooded his neighbor's. Such disorganized and chaotic attempts led to the enactment of ditch laws, with the first government ditch in Auglaize County being dug in 1868. By the end of the nineteenth century, more than a million feet of ditches would be dug at a cost of more than $200,000.[17]

The arrival of the Tullys in Auglaize County coincided with these organized efforts to drain the land. Indeed, it might be said that the history of the Tully family in Auglaize County is largely writ in mud. First Hugh Tully and, when he was old enough to operate a shovel, his son, Jim, dug ditches. Hugh Tully was said to be able to dig a ditch a mile long across a meadow and keep his line within a foot of true.[18] As his son, Jim, recalled, "It was all woods, no gravel roads anywhere not even in St. Marys. . . . My boyhood was spent in the country clearing land and ditching. We had to build roads and clear them. We used to use poles called corduroy and put them across the roads and cover them with dirt. We had to do that in summers or we couldn't get out at all in the spring."[19]

The first school did not open in Hugh and Catherine Tully's part of the county until their son was eighteen. It was open for two months in the summer and three months in the winter, bypassing the spring planting and fall harvest. Jim's attendance was limited to winter days when no work was possible.[20] By the time he was twenty-one, he had saved enough money to move to Wisconsin, where he took a job as a railroad brakeman on the run between Racine and Savannah, Georgia. Homesick, he returned to Ohio after a year. He married Bridget Lawler, eighteen years old and the daughter of Irish immigrants, in February of 1875.[21]

The Lawlers had come from County Kildare, close to the rolling greensward of the Curragh, Ireland's pastoral horse country.[22] Family lore has it that when Thomas Lawler sailed for America in 1852, he too left his wife and small children behind.[23] His wife joined him three years later, but their three children remained in the care of relatives in Ireland. Two of the children later started the voyage to America but died aboard ship. The oldest child, John, stayed behind.

Her full name was Maria Bridget Lawler, but to her family she was simply Biddy. Born in Butler County, Ohio, in 1856, a year after her brother Dennis, she was soon joined by younger brothers Tom, Jim, and Pete, and a baby sister, Maud or Moll.[24] The Lawlers moved to Preble County, Ohio, where they were eventually joined by seventeen-year-old John.[25] Biddy Lawler's childhood was hard and short. A week before her twelfth birthday, Biddy had to quit school and work at fifty cents a week as a house servant for "an old doctor woman."[26] She worked there for a year before moving to the home of a couple of schoolteachers, doubling her salary.

When Biddy was fourteen, her mother, Margaret, took over a boardinghouse near a short line and, together, mother and daughter baked bread, pies, and cakes; prepared meals; and saw to the laundry of two- to four-dozen boarders, most of them laborers, but also a handful of small children.[27] Biddy's father worked on a road crew. In less than two years, Biddy's mother managed to save $1,500, enabling the Lawlers to move to Auglaize County, where they bought a 160-acre farm in 1872.[28]

The farm would not remain intact for long. Since joining his family in America, John Lawler had worked on a farm and stayed out of trouble, but when he was twenty-two, a young woman came forward, pregnant with his child. She sued him and was awarded $300, which John got from his parents. He reconciled with the woman long enough to get the $300 back from her and flee to Illinois.

Passing from the simply immoral to the positively criminal was the work of but three years. When John Lawler determined that the coast was clear, he returned to Preble County. After a month in Ohio, he hit upon a nearly foolproof scheme. He stole an old team of horses and drove them back to Illinois, where he surreptitiously swapped them for a good team. He covered his tracks by burning the barn containing the old horses and returned to Preble County, where he sold the new team at the desired profit of 100 percent. Things came a cropper when the Illinois owner observed that the shoes on the charred horses in the ruins of his barn did not match the ones obtained from his blacksmith. Once again, John Lawler laid low for a while. When the heat had died down, he repeated the scheme in Preble County, leaving behind another burning barn filled with panicked horses. He returned to Auglaize County to sell the new team but this time was caught redhanded. While he awaited trial in Preble County, the Illinois authorities traced the first theft back to him but were forced to wait until the state of Ohio was through with him.[29]

In her efforts to keep her oldest child from the penitentiary, Mrs. Lawler sold some of the farm acreage to raise money for John's defense. The land was sacrificed in vain as, in 1878, John received a fifteen-year sentence. In a rare bit of good fortune for the Lawlers, the remaining property stayed in the family at Margaret's death when the high bidder for the remaining eighty acres at a September 1892 auction was the wealthy German Axe family, whose daughter Sadie married Biddy's brother Tom.[30]

If life was hard for Biddy before her wedding, it scarcely improved after. The young couple's first home was a few miles outside St. Marys, deep in the woods at the end of what was, for most of the year, a glutinous mud road. Jim had cleared a small plot, building a log cabin and stable.[31] The location of the cabin proved to be a mistake, as the damp woods bred clouds of mosquitoes "as big as chickenhawks," and the young couple suffered repeated bouts of malaria and yellow fever.[32] After three years in the woods, they moved out, poorer than on their wedding day.

For the next two years, Jim dug ditches. His boss's son recalled that Jim "was the best ditch digger in the country" and "had a great reputation of being able to lay tile in the spring or summer even when there was no water running to indicate the fall."[33] Hoping to pull down a little more money, Jim tried his hand at farming for a year. The couple, now with two children, Hugh and Margaret, called Maggie by the family, moved again, this time to Geneva, Wisconsin, where another son, Tom, was born.[34] While in Wisconsin, the family lost most of what little they owned to a fire, and after a year and a half, Jim bowed to family pressure and returned with his family to work on the family farm in Auglaize County. It was on this farm that Biddy bore two more sons, Charles on February 9, 1884, and James (no middle name given) on June 3, 1886.[35] (There has long been uncertainty about Jim Tully's age, stemming from Jim's own apparent confusion over his birthday. Hoping to finally clear up the matter in 1936, Jim wrote his eighty-six-year-old father, who erroneously replied that Jim was born on June 3, 1891.[36] Baptismal records confirm the earlier date.) Jim, as he was called by his family, was baptized three days later at Holy Rosary Church in St. Marys, with his uncle and aunt, William and Anna Tully Danaher, serving as godparents.

Jim, who resembled his brother Tom, would be the baby of the family for the next five years, doted on by both his mother and sister.[37] His father recalled Jim as a solitary child who preferred to play alone or with Monk, a purebred Collie puppy given to Biddy by the parish priest. Indeed, Jim recalled that his first steps were taken with Monk at his side.[38] One time, Jim's father recalled, he was working in the stables when his three-year-old namesake, not wise in the ways of dogs and bodies of water, burst in to announce that Monk had jumped into a water hole and would surely drown without immediate rescue.[39]

When Jim was four, the family moved to neighboring Van Wert County, where his father paid half on a house on a few acres at a place called Jennings Prairie.[40] Here Jim's idea of a suitable pet took a frightening turn when his father spotted him trying to catch a rattlesnake that had slithered under a rock. When the elder Tully lifted the rock, he found, much to his surprise, not one rattlesnake but two. He killed both.[41]

Had a family portrait been taken at this time, it would have shown James Dennis Tully, 190 pounds, "a gorilla-built man . . . squat, agile, and muscular," with stooped shoulders; long, crooked arms; and a mustache, the ends of which touched his shoulders, giving him a ferocious look that masked his laconic personality,[42] with his wife, Biddy Tully, her golden hair braided and reaching her knees; her eyes deep brown, large, and sad; her mouth puckered, almost pouting, and their children: Anna, the baby (her twin brother did not survive), held by her mother; Hugh, the eldest, with curly red hair and freckles;[43] Maggie, hair straight and brown; Tom, with curly red hair and freckles; Charlie, also with curly hair but brown, nearly black; and Jim, also with a mop of red hair and a face full of freckles.

Their home was, as might be expected of any household dominated by young boys and a dog, noisy and full of adventures and misadventures. With her husband working most daylight hours, Biddy had to ride herd over four high-spirited boys. Her one ally in this campaign against anarchy was Maggie, whom friends remembered as "a little mother."[44] Both would come to occupy a special place in Jim Tully's heart.

If the Tully house was the domain of the women, the outdoors belonged to the men. Sometimes Jim would tag along with his father, splashing in one of his dad's freshly dug ditches. The childhoods of father and son were similar in at least one respect. As the younger Jim Tully observed decades later, "It was a muddy world we lived in. It seemed as if my childhood contained nothing but mud and water."[45]

Jim's greatest childhood adventures, however, occurred away from the watchful eyes of father, mother, and sister. There were the usual boyhood fights, although his father recalled that young Jim got along well with his brothers.[46] Never picking on smaller boys, he wouldn't hesitate to scrap with a bigger boy. One playmate recalled that when Jim was teased by other children, he would walk up to them, double up his fist, and say, "You smell my masser."[47] Decades later, another boyhood pal recalled Jim as a

> freckle faced chubby boy and one of the best natured fellows I ever knew. You were always smiling and several times each week we would wrestle and box, that is we called it boxing but we really went at it bare-fisted and usually kept at it until the bell rang and called us in after the noon hour. Often a good hard blow would glance off and strike one or the other square in the face but we always seemed to enjoy it and thought we had a good time. Up until that time you were the first boy I had met that I couldn't handle, it just seemed to be about nip and tuck.[48]

Often with one of his brothers at his side, almost always with Monk darting ahead, Jim explored the fields, woods, ponds, and ditches of the surrounding countryside. One such adventure, described in his unpublished memoirs and retold in *Shanty Irish*, found Monk venturing too near a rattlesnake. "It struck him on the shoulder with enough force to knock him backward. He ran yelping away." Jim and his brother trailed after the dog, following him to a large ditch in front of the house. They watched as the dog quickly buried himself up to the neck in mud and refused to be coaxed out. This, their father explained, was a dog's way of getting the poison out and would take four or five days. "Each night before going to sleep," Jim wrote, "I would think of Monk, alone, out in the mud." Offerings of meat and water were left untouched. Attempts to stroke Monk's fur were met with growls. After several days, starved and limping, Monk returned home. "The Prodigal Son was not treated with greater kindness," Jim recalled.[49]

One of Jim's favorite adventures was to walk several miles to a culvert underneath some railroad tracks.[50] There, in the shade of the culvert, with the tracks overhead, he could sit and wait in eager anticipation for the distant thunder of a coming train. As the ground began to tremble and the rumble built to a roar complete with smoke and whistle noise, he found himself overcome with an exhilarating sense of danger. On one such trip with Tom and Monk, the brothers decided to tease the dog. This time they crawled into the culvert without Monk and wouldn't let him in. As the train bore down on the culvert, the boys were horrified to see Monk barking at the approaching train and running up and down the tracks. The boys yelled to Monk to get away, "but Monk, feeling that we were in danger, dashed along the rails."[51] Jim and Tom scrambled out but their calls were drowned out by the train, and their view obscured by clouds of dust. As the noise faded and the dust settled, with mounting dread the boys anxiously searched for Monk, but he was not to be found. Trying to reassure his younger brother, Tom predicted that Monk had gone home ahead of them and would surely be waiting for them in the kitchen. The boys started home. Jim recorded the next scene in his unpublished memoirs and in *Shanty Irish*:

> Tom fell on the ground a short distance further.
> "Monk—Monk—Monk! Please look, please, please. We didn't mean it Monk, please, PLEASE."
> Monk's eyes were partly open. His legs were bent under him. His body still quivered. He tried to open his eyes. They went shut.
> We placed him in an easier position.
> He moaned; and moved no more.
> We laid him upon a board. Murderers could have felt no worse.[52]

Biddy was heartbroken. In the weeks that followed, her singing filled the house as in days past, but an already guilt-ridden Jim couldn't help but notice the dampness of her eyes.[53]

Greater disaster was just weeks away. The family had been in Van Wert County for about a year when the blow fell. Jim's father later recalled being about a quarter of a mile from home, ditching in a nearby field late one afternoon, when he noticed flames shooting from the roof of the house. As he knew that Biddy and the children were not at home, his only thought was to rescue what few possessions could be salvaged. He was met at the burning house by Biddy and a few neighbors. Amid the chaos of eye-stinging smoke, hot cinders, and consuming flames, they set to work grabbing anything they could. A crock of eggs waiting to be fried for supper was scooped up by a neighbor and thrown from the structure, smashing against a fence. Jim's father bolted upstairs to save the family's clothes, threw handfuls of them out the window, and followed them out the window when he found his return route down the stairs blocked by flames. The clothes burned anyway. Biddy grabbed a clock and carried it outside. She clung to it, refusing to put it down. It was the only thing she saved.[54]

Rain, too late to quench the fire, but in plenty of time to add to the Tullys' misery, began to fall. It slashed over the ruins, mingling the ashes of the family's home with the sticky Ohio mud. The children returned shortly to find their house burned to the ground; their father poking at the scorched and soggy ground, soaked to the skin but stoic and unflinching as always; their mother sobbing over the charred clock that hours before had been gilt, a thing of beauty and pride in her small household.[55]

Jim, not yet five, rescued from the mud a sign that had hung above the cabin door and handed it to his father. It proclaimed that the cabin had been insured by Ohio Farmers. "It's no good now," his father said.[56] Their coverage had lapsed. Young Jim clung to his father's leg and began to cry. The father rested his calloused hand on his son's head and gently, almost absentmindedly, stroked the little boy's hair.

The neighbors drifted away. The Tullys were alone, owners of the clothes on their backs and the mud on their shoes, at least, those of the children who had shoes. Jim's one pair of shoes was reserved in the warm months for Sundays, leaving him barefoot. The family decamped to a leaky old schoolhouse. Jim's father, without bitterness, recalled that only one person, a neighbor named William Dannakersand, stepped forward that day and unceremoniously reached into his pocket to help. Dannakersand gave the family five dollars.[57] Later, pride would keep the family from accepting the charity of other neighbors.[58] Seeing it as yet another childhood adventure, young Jim enjoyed his stay at the schoolhouse and the family remained there for several weeks before another house on Jennings Prairie was found and rented.[59]

The fire, Jim came to believe, was typical of the bad luck that followed his father. Jim observed that for all his father's hard work, the family never prospered.[60] Self-pity—indeed, sentimentality of any kind—was not the stuff of James Dennis Tully. While Biddy's eyes would grow wet with tears at the loss of all they owned or the death of Monk, not so her husband. He was, by his son's recollection, "a man without tears."[61] Nor did he share his wife's faith in God. He was "a pagan all his life, and never inside a church, unless by force of circumstances."[62] Jim recalled that despite his modest education and severe nearsightedness, his father read anything he could get his hands on but was especially fond of newspapers and dime novels, which he held two inches from his face because of poor vision. Constantly in debt, he would borrow and lend money with equal indifference. Jim Tully saw in his father a certain backhanded dignity. "Aware of the trap in which life had caught him, he bowed to his peasant futility like a gentleman."[63] That life was cruel and unfair was obvious to the elder Tully. The notion of sheltering his children from this harsh reality seemed never to have occurred to him.

Second only to Monk in the affections of the Tully children was a pet mare named Old Nell. Totally blind, she could, to the children's amazement, navigate the trails in the surrounding woods without so much as touching tree or shrub. A year or so after the fire, she grew lame, and what had been put off could be delayed no longer.[64] Years later Jim recalled the scene in *Shanty Irish*:

My father seized a revolver. I followed him. He crashed a bullet through her skull.

She went to her front knees, as if in prayer for the dying. Her hide was bare as a glove. She twitched once—and was still.[65]

After Jennings Prairie, the family returned to Auglaize County, this time to work on Mrs. Lawler's farm. When Biddy and her mother couldn't get along, the family moved one last time, in early 1892, to an area known as Glynnwood a few miles outside St. Marys.[66] For Jim, the family's return to Auglaize County also meant a return to the Tully and Lawler grandparents, aunts, and uncles he loved so dearly. "Supposedly peasants," Jim later wrote of the Lawler men, "they were more like Irish brigands with verve and grandiloquence."[67] He observed in *Shanty Irish* that they "were all devout Catholics during mass on Sunday." Otherwise, they were "roisterers, drunkards, braggarts, picturesque men and poor farmers."[68] The Lawlers "believed in ghosts, in fairies and in witches. In their hearts, ready to germinate at any moment, were the wild seeds of fanaticism and bigotry."[69] Years later, Jim wrote one correspondent that "there was a streak of madness in my mother's people. There seemed to be something desperate caged in them that needed outlet."[70]

The wildness of the Lawlers was perhaps best illustrated in a story Jim picked up from his father. Writing in 1927, the elder Tully recalled the time when Biddy's younger sister, Moll, who had been working as a domestic, did the unthinkable. She stopped attending Sunday Mass and, worse, astonished the family when she was sighted at the Walnut Grove Methodist Church.[71] Jim retold the story, embellished and with a comic touch, in *Shanty Irish*. The Lawlers, he wrote, discussed the situation over dinner. The question of a possible motive fell to Biddy's older brother, Dennis. Turning the thing over in his mind, he spotted the devil's fingerprints all over it. After all, "they say he likes to steal the souls of good lookin' girls," and with her dark hair and flashing eyes, Moll was certainly beautiful.[72] Not given to half-measures, Dennis and his father hit on a plan as simple as it was inelegant. They hitched up a buggy and headed for the Methodist church, where evening services were in full cry. Dennis and his father listened from outside as the preacher whipped the revival to fever pitch. When they could listen no more, they burst through the front door and stormed the church. What they saw stopped them in their tracks. "Moll, their Catholic pride and joy, was being caressed in the name of religion by a group of fanatic farmers."[73] Their Irish blood now at full boil, they sprang into action. As Jim recounted in *Shanty Irish*, Dennis grabbed his sister, thrust her into the arms of her father, and carved a path to the door. "Methodists fell to right and left, nursing bruised jaws." As they headed home in the buggy, their quarry safely in hand, Mr. Lawler laughed, "Ah, Denny, . . . it's proud of ye I am this night—for ivery time ye stuck out yere fist a Mithidist fell down."[74]

The real end to the story was, however, somewhat more ignominious. In the noise and excitement, Moll slipped out, and her father and brother were forced to leave empty handed. Not only were they denied the hero's welcome they surely felt they deserved, but to make matters worse, when word arrived the following day that his arrest might be imminent, Mr. Lawler was forced to leg it.[75]

Over time, Moll, who married outside the church, was forgiven her apostasy and welcomed back to the family by all but one of the clan. Biddy would not be reconciled. When, one winter's day, a sled carrying Biddy's relatives pulled up in front of her house, Biddy met the group in the front yard and dramatically informed them that all were welcome but Moll, who need never darken her door again.[76] The others left with Moll, and as Biddy watched the sled disappear down the road, she wept, "Moll, Moll—my baby sister, Moll."[77] Jim later recalled that his earliest memories were "of my mother gazing down roads."[78] Whatever sadness Biddy felt over the breach, the fact remains that the woman who had wept in the ashes of her home, wept over the death of her dog, even wept over a bed of pansies and violets claimed by frost had, in the name of religion, turned away her sister.[79] In her husband's view, Biddy "was high tempered but had no moods."[80] In contrast, Biddy's youngest son thought of her as mercurial and felt that "I probably inherited my moodiness and my incapacity to fit into conventional life from my mother."[81]

In 1891, after serving thirteen years of his fifteen-year sentence, John Lawler was released from the Ohio Penitentiary and returned to Auglaize County. Still wanted for the thefts in Illinois, John's reunion with his family was necessarily brief.[82] He was spirited off to Canada with the aid of his brothers and his brother-in-law, Biddy's husband (a man not given to sit in judgment of others).[83] There, if *Shanty Irish* is to be believed, John Lawler married a banker's daughter and died owning the bank.[84] What is known is that when he died of a stroke in 1905, he left behind a wife, two daughters, and two sons—all well provided for.[85]

Despite the deaths of pets and the loss of his home to fire, the first six years of Jim Tully's life, hardscrabble though they were, were not so different from the early lives of other boys of his age and background. If his was a childhood spent in poverty, it was a rural poverty that allowed him a certain lack of self-awareness. Going barefoot, because his family lacked money for shoes, would surely have invited comment and ridicule in a city. In the country, it passed without notice. Not that lack of shoes was a hardship to be lightly dismissed. Jim recalled some mornings so cold that when he hiked to the barn to lead the cows out to pasture, he had to pause to warm his feet in the hay where the cows had slept.[86] Still, Jim's early childhood years were largely happy ones.

All that changed in 1892. In February of that year, Grandfather Lawler died, followed by Grandmother Lawler on March 2 at the age of seventy-two.[87] Whatever grief the young boy felt over the loss of his grandparents was tempered somewhat by the sight of his mother's swollen belly and the knowledge that he would soon have a baby sister or brother.

The final blow was not long in coming. As Jim Tully wrote in *Shanty Irish*:

> She died on a rainy April night.
> She had been ill for several days.

The little baby, as if in a hurry to leave the dreary Ohio country, died too.

My uncle Tom awoke me. The kerosene lamp threw weird shadows over my attic bed. The rain rattled on the roof.

My uncle tapped my shoulder and said, very slowly, "Jimmy—your mother's dead."[88]

Numb and uncomprehending, Jim and his brothers silently dressed, climbed down the ladder from the attic, and filed into their parents' bedroom.

The chilling tableau that awaited him that Sunday morning, May 1, 1892, would haunt him for the rest of his life.[89] In his unpublished memoirs, Tully recalls that his eyes first fell on his twelve-year-old sister, Maggie. Sobbing, "Mother, mother," she stroked Biddy's long hair.[90] With dread he looked at his mother's face. Her hazel eyes, partly open, stared at the ceiling from beneath two silver dollars that had failed to keep them closed. He then noticed the baby, silent, by her side. Hanging on the plastered log walls, as if silently gazing at the sorrowful scene below, were color pictures of Jesus, Mary, and Joseph, and St. Patrick driving the snakes from Ireland.[91] Horror and panic welled up inside him as he searched the room, full of Tullys and Lawlers, for Aunt Moll. He spotted his father standing at the foot of the bed, silent, head bowed, dry eyed. Moll was not present, and his cries for her left his throat and filled the tiny room. Tom Lawler went for her.

The week before had certainly begun badly enough. Jim's father recalled that all the Tully children except Anna had been sick with the mumps.[92] And by Wednesday morning, Biddy, too, perhaps because of her advanced pregnancy, wasn't feeling well. Her husband, as he recalled, had left early that morning to deliver a load of potatoes to St. Marys, and Biddy was trying to rest when she heard a knock at the door. She rose and found a neighbor seeking a meal, which she prepared. The exertion made her feel worse, and by the end of the day, she also had the mumps. A doctor was summoned, but by Saturday night, Biddy had not improved and she was in labor. The baby was stillborn. By dawn, Biddy had joined her child in death. She was thirty-five years old.[93]

The children left the crowded bedroom and gathered around the kitchen table. A fire burned in the stove nearby. Maggie, regaining her composure, placed a jar of cookies on the table. The cookies, they all knew, were the last batch Biddy had baked, and Jim's thoughts drifted to how proud he had been to hear his mother called "the best bread baker in Auglaize County."[94]

This reverie of his mother baking bread in her kitchen was pushed aside by other horrible thoughts. An incident the day before haunted him. Between sobs, he spoke of it to the other children.

Biddy's doctor, Jim had learned, had told everyone but him that Biddy was absolutely not to be given water. When Jim had gone into her room, she had asked for water, and Jim had returned with a dipperful. Tom and Hugh reassured their younger brother that Jim couldn't have known. Still, the awful thought that his mother might be alive but for a drink of water troubled him until the kitchen door opened. It was Moll. Jim ran to her. She took him in her arms and held him tight for a moment. She spoke softly to the children. She made coffee and sat at the table with them. As Moll and Maggie quietly talked, Jim noticed how much the two, not separated by more than ten years in age, looked alike. Mostly, though, he would remember their sad and beautiful eyes.

Aunt Sadie, Uncle Tom Lawler's wife, walked in and softly told the children that they would be going home with her and Uncle Tom. Aunt Moll chose to stay behind with the body of her sister. The children, grief stricken and silent, climbed into Uncle Tom's rig. Along the way, Jim heard his Uncle Tom complain to Aunt Sadie that the two silver dollars that he had loaned Jim's father were for food, not to weigh down Biddy's eyes. Tom Lawler did not speak to his brother-in-law again for twenty-five years.[95] Money was tight, but as Jim Tully later concluded, "My father had intended no harm."[96]

When the time came to take Biddy's body to St. Patrick's Church in Glynnwood, where she would be buried next to her mother in the little cemetery across the road, it was decided that the children did not have clothes fit for the occasion and should be left behind. Maggie, who had climbed into Uncle Tom's surrey and refused to stay behind, was finally permitted to leave with the older relatives. Jim and his brothers stood in the middle of the road and watched the hearse bearing their mother's body disappear, the clip-clop of the horses fading in the distance.[97]

2

Six Years of Imprisonment

Prior to his mother's death, Jim was seldom alone. A noisy assortment of Tullys and Lawlers seemed to constantly pass in and out the door. In his immediate family alone, there were three older brothers to show him the woods, hills, and train tracks around St. Marys. And Maggie, his older sister, doted on him like a second mother. Everything, however, revolved around Biddy. Her voice had a musical cadence, and the first sound Jim heard most mornings was his mother singing in the next room, her lilting brogue filling their small home.[1] The quiet that settled over the household after her death was a palpable reminder of all that had been lost.

Biddy's death shattered Jim's world. She had held the family together through hunger, disease, and fire while his father, often following ditch-digging jobs in neighboring counties, was absent. After his wife's death, he would never again provide a home for his six surviving children. Not only did young Jim lose his beloved mother, but he would find himself cut off from everyone and everything that represented happiness and security.

The two oldest, Hugh and Maggie, could find work in St. Marys. The youngest, Anna, could stay with Maggie and relatives. Biddy's brother Tom Lawler offered to take the children into his home. He believed "Biddy's boys" should be kept together in St. Marys.[2]

He was opposed, with equal passion, by the Tullys' pastor, Father John S. Singleton. The respected and well-liked priest at St. Patrick's in Glynnwood successfully argued that the three other children—Tom, Charlie, and Jim—should be sent to St. Joseph's Orphan Asylum, a Catholic orphanage in the

Cumminsville area of Cincinnati. There they would at least learn to read and write. They also would be well trained in the Catholic faith so important to their mother.[3] Acceptance at St. Joseph's was by no means automatic. As Jim Tully later observed, "Money was scarce and orphans were plentiful."[4] Yet, having made his case, the sympathetic pastor busied himself securing admission for the boys.

The family's sorrow was in no way assuaged during the month following Biddy's death. One sunny morning, Jim, Maggie, and Tom headed down the road, bound for the cemetery. They quickly spotted the Lawler headstone of their grandparents and their gaze fell on the fresh grave nearby that they knew belonged to their mother. Heads bowed, they did not speak, the silence complete but for Jim's quiet sobbing. Their solitude was broken by the approach of Father Singleton. He exchanged a few words with Maggie and led them to his house near the church. His housekeeper brought out cookies, and with Jim's tears dried, the priest took the children home in his surrey. Decades later, Jim would fondly recall this kind man: his brogue, which reminded Jim of his mother, and the smell of his ever-present cigar. Mostly, he would recall the priest's gentle spirit—a spirit that sustained his mother's faith and her steadfast belief that better days were ahead, if not in this world, then in the next.[5]

So it was that on a morning a few days after his sixth birthday, Jim, distraught and disoriented, found himself saying good-bye to Maggie, Old Hughie, Aunt Moll, and St. Marys. When the priest's ancient surrey pulled off the dirt road in front of the Tully home, a hush fell over the family. The three boys, accompanied by their father and dressed in new suits, silently squeezed into the rickety carriage. Their older siblings, Maggie and Hugh, were in the front yard with Aunt Moll. Father Singleton drove slowly to the St. Marys station, where Tom, Charlie, and Jim would board the train taking them from their childhood home to Cincinnati, a distance of slightly more than a hundred miles.

Jim was determined not to cry. He had promised Maggie he would be brave. His resolve crumbled when the rig, pulled by two aged mules, passed the Forty Acre Pond, a favorite haunt of the Tully boys. The sight of the morning sun shimmering on this "lonely water" triggered memories of happier days.[6] He gave way to the overpowering sense of loss and grief. His father said nothing. It was Tom who tried to calm his sobbing brother. As the priest tried to hurry the worn-out mules to the station, Jim could hear a farmer singing on the sunny June morning:

The boat is comin' around the bend,
Good-bye, old Grover, good-bye,
It's loaded down with Harrison men,
Good-bye, old Grover, good-bye . . . [7]

Jim had heard his father and grandfather speak approvingly of President Grover Cleveland. While he never saw the farmer, the song became etched in his memory.

Uncle Tom wanted to accompany the boys, but Father Singleton urged that the sons be joined by their father. Biddy Tully's youngest son again tried bravely to keep his emotions under control while they waited at the station. When the train pulled into St. Marys, Jim tried to run away. Tom caught him. It was a trip filled with fear. Jim was terrified by the sight of the stocky conductor "in his blue suit and brass buttons."[8] He again burst into tears. He filled the third-class coach with his wild sobs. The movement of the train mercifully lulled the distraught boy to sleep.

The bustle of Cincinnati also frightened him. From the train station, they caught a streetcar that deposited them some blocks from the orphanage. They completed their journey on foot. On their arrival, the heavy yellow doors of the orphanage swung open, and from its maw emerged a woman wearing a "black costume" and "heavy glasses." Her face was "red and sharp."[9] Jim clung pathetically to Tom and Charlie. Crossing the threshold, Jim couldn't have known that he was passing through a gate of sorrows that would haunt him for the rest of his days. Their father was ushered into another room. He left without a parting word. Just like that. Gone. Despite work that sometimes took him far from St. Marys, not once in Jim's entire six years at the orphanage did his father visit or even write.[10]

The three Tully boys were then led to the clothing room, where they surrendered their new suits. Purchased with money the family could ill afford, they were never again worn by Jim and his brothers.[11] Each boy was issued an orphanage uniform and a number. Shaking violently, Jim then had his unruly red curls clipped by another nun. He would describe the scene both in his unpublished memoirs[12] and in faithful detail in his autobiographical 1942 novel, *Biddy Brogan's Boy*. "A dreadful homesickness followed," he wrote. His "mother and sister had been his entire life," and "with one gone and the other not with him," he "was very lonely."[13]

Although surrounded by children, Jim spent the next six years forlorn and bereft of his family in St. Marys. The homesickness gradually faded as the people and places of his childhood receded in memory. In its place, a profound sense of abandonment took root. "I cannot recall that period of imprisonment without a feeling of overwhelming sadness," he wrote in *Shanty Irish*.[14]

Compounding this desolation and misery was the notion that somehow he deserved the punishment. The doctor had forbidden her water, yet when his feverish mother begged, he filled the dipper and handed it to her. The cool water, he came to believe, killed her just as surely as if he had given her poison. He could not shake the idea of the saintly mother dead at the hands of her wicked son. All he did was obey his mother. In keeping that commandment, he'd broken another. What hell surely awaited him? In a nineteenth-century Irish Catholic child's understanding of guilt, the sin could not go unpunished. "Never did a criminal put in six more terrible years of torture," he recalled in *Shanty Irish*. "And often I felt that I too was a convict. I had given my mother water to drink."[15]

Much that went on behind the orphanage walls was indeed reminiscent of prison. The orphanage was run with a ruthless efficiency that would have been the envy of any gulag chief. A network of spies was maintained, and the word of a snitch always taken. The system provided the nuns with a steady supply of sinful boys. "It's the thing that made the nuns whang hell out of me at the orphanage," he remembered, "for not telling on other kids."[16] One nun, weary of reaching for the whip at all hours, devised the time-saving method of keeping a list of offenders and meting out punishment only at day's end. With a flair for the dramatic, she would stand before her charges, the day's list in one hand, rawhide whip in the other. Fear was palpable as guilty and innocent alike suffered through the reading of the list, not knowing if they would be called to step forward and receive a lash across the hands. In an effort to toughen their hands, the boys tried rubbing them on the ground or against old pipes, but to no avail. The whip never failed to sting "like the pricking of small hot needles."[17]

Jim refused, however, to depict his years at St. Joseph's in strictly Dickensian terms. Indeed, he readily acknowledged the benefits of life at the Cincinnati orphanage. "What academic education I have was received in St. Joseph's Orphan Asylum," he wrote to a friend in 1930.[18] A few years later, he told a Chicago reporter that he didn't know what would have become of him had it not been for the orphanage.[19] The nuns not only taught him to read, they instilled in Jim a love of words both spoken and written. Within two years of his arrival at St. Joseph's, he was reading to the nuns as they knitted or sewed. When he came across a word that stumped him, one of the nuns would provide the proper pronunciation.[20]

Knowing of his growing love for reading, Tom would bring him books whenever possible. By the time he left the orphanage, Jim knew the works of Charles Dickens, Victor Hugo, Oliver Goldsmith, and William Shakespeare.[21] He became fascinated with the deeds of Napoleon and Alexander the Great, so much so that he wavered between the two before choosing Alexander as his confirmation name (based on his suspicion that there was no St. Napoleon).[22]

He soon acquired a reputation among the nuns for his writing. They rewarded him with penny candies.[23] "Blasphemic on most issues, he was forever grateful to the nuns who had given him that much," old pal Frank Scully later observed. "They taught him to write sentences as short as a prison haircut. He kept them that way."[24]

The short redheaded boy from St. Marys also realized that he possessed a powerful memory. He excelled at what the nuns called memory tests. Every Monday morning, for instance, the students were asked what they could remember of the priest's Sunday sermon. Jim could spew it back at his astonished teachers, almost word for word.[25]

In preparation for the sacraments of Holy Communion and confirmation, about forty-five children embarked on three rigorous months of catechism and Bible study. They were quizzed regularly. Jim never missed a question. Only Laura Gilfoil, a girl with an equally impressive memory, matched his accomplishment.[26] As a reward, each was given an imitation-pearl rosary. Jim treasured his prize and was fascinated by the "glass imbedded in the cross," which contained a scene of "children receiving communion."[27] Curiosity made Jim keep track of his chief rival in catechism classes. Years after leaving the orphanage, he learned that Laura was a kitchen drudge. It taught him how much "luck is a factor in life, and that really intelligent people do not always get a fair chance."[28]

He certainly could see that good and bad luck wrapped themselves around his years at St. Joseph's. Decades removed from the experience, Jim Tully could recognize the orphanage as a vital link in the chain of events that led him to literary success. It was where his passion for reading blossomed. It was where his interest in writing was first nurtured. It was where he learned to rely on his keen memory. Absent one of these, perhaps he would never have become a writer.

By his own recollection, while Jim excelled in his classes, he was no angel.[29] He was, for example, a key figure in the Bedbug Scam. The bloodsucking insects were a constant nuisance in the dormitory. Each Sunday, the nuns placed a bounty on the tiny vermin. Boys who caught the required number were free to play. Pinned insects were taken to Sister Benedictine, who recorded each boy's score as the insect was deposited in a bottle of water. Aged and nearsighted, Sister Benedictine proved the perfect mark.

One enterprising lad noticed that chips of the dull-red paint on the wooden beds could, in the hands of a skilled craftsman, be made into something resembling a bedbug. The counterfeit didn't have to be perfect, just good enough to fool an elderly, half-blind nun. Sister Benedictine could be forgiven for believing that the simple bedbug infestation had suddenly transformed into an Old Testament plague. Bugs were being found at such a pace that a shortage of paint chips hit the dormitory. Only the shoddy work of one boy saved the beds from being completely stripped of paint. Sister spotted a fake and all that remained was the inevitable punishment of the guilty. The mother superior was summoned and pronounced a sentence of three days' time spent under guard in bed. Any blood lost to the remaining insects was simply divine retribution.[30]

Jim understood retribution but was growing doubtful about the divine. By the end of his stay at St. Joseph's, he no longer held fast to the religion that had meant so much to his mother. He was slipping into an agnosticism that lasted the rest of his life. "I never did believe in God," he explained in a 1923 essay. "I had it all figured out when I was still quite young. . . . I have been a pagan all my life. Yet—I like Christ, the Agitator. The cross must have hurt His shoulder. . . . I have always felt sorry for Christ. Out of twelve chosen friends—two doublecrossed Him. And the rest of them probably garbled His words. One should not choose friends among fishermen."[31]

His break with Catholicism did not stop him from remembering some of the more understanding priests and nuns with great affection. And he would always credit certain nuns with recognizing and developing the promise they saw in him. In his books, he depicted both the kind and the cruel. In *Blood on the Moon,* for instance, he describes Archbishop Elder, "the ruler of our immediate Catholic universe," as a "heavily wrinkled" old man with "a kind, beaming, and bright face like Pope Leo XIII. . . . Christ was a living man to him. . . . Across the decades I can hear the saintly old man's voice. . . . Outside the school room, Sister Mary Edward whipped me often."[32] Such matter-of-fact juxtaposition is as typical of Jim Tully the writer as is the lack of denunciation. He would no more judge the nuns who dominated those orphanage years than he would his own father. He'd been judged harshly enough in life to know that he wanted no part of it.

Another priest he would recall fondly was Father Eugene A. Davis, who "had succeeded two other priests whom the orphanage children loved." About thirty, tall, and broad shouldered, he was described by Tully as "gentle and kind": "I was to remember him through the years with love."[33]

And when the children were called to chapel to pray for the soul of the mother superior as she lay dying, Jim recalled a litany that was rote and devoid of feeling. The news, after an hour, that Sister had died was greeted with indifference. "There had been no love" on either side, Jim recalled. Yet, to his surprise, his eyes began welling with tears as he remembered a time when she'd placed "a wrinkled hand upon my head." In his unpublished memoir he concluded, "Thus the crumb of affection which she had carelessly cast upon the water had come back to her when her heart had ceased to beat."[34]

After three years at the orphanage, Tom Tully was taken by a farmer to work in Kentucky. Though barely in his teens, Tom soon ran away, traveling a hundred miles to see Jim back at the orphanage. Tom just missed Charlie, who had been taken by another farmer to work in Indiana. After Tom's visit, Jim went another three years without seeing family.[35]

With his twelfth birthday only weeks away, Jim was becoming more and more terrified of a new danger: if neither farmer nor family came for him, he would be sent to reform school.[36] He had exhausted the largesse, such as it was, of both church and state. But the second Sunday after his Holy Communion and confirmation, Jim later recalled, he was told he had a visitor. Being summoned to the parlor reserved for visitors was a momentous occasion. Now, with the threat of reform school hanging over him, a curious Jim was met in the parlor by Maggie and his oldest brother, Hugh. They had made the trip from St. Marys with news that Jim was, at last, going home.[37] A letter had been sent by the orphanage superintendent to one of Jim's uncles. Maggie, then making a dollar and a half a week as a servant girl, learned of the reform school threat and, with Hugh, planned Jim's rescue. Neither Maggie nor Hugh had ever been more than ten miles from St. Marys.[38]

Jim's departure seemed to be delayed by "an endless amount of red tape."[39] His pals, Willie Faulkner, Gabe Sullivan, and Billy Ross, were led in by Father Davis to say good-bye, not knowing if they would ever see him again. The last good-bye was reserved for his friend Father Davis, who told him that he should always keep his bright mind in the service of God, and that his sainted mother was watching over him in heaven. Father Davis watched as Jim walked away from the orphanage with his brother and sister. Looking back at the man who had shown him so much kindness, Jim thought of the image of the crucified Christ in the priest's study.[40]

Leaving the grounds of the orphanage for the first time in six years, Jim couldn't help but be struck by the contrast. His nose had grown accustomed to its smells: incense and beeswax in the chapel, the pungent odor in the dormitory of too many humans in too small a place, and the smell of the various soaps and disinfectants arrayed against those odors. All gone. In their place were the myriad smells of the city and her river. And with every breeze, the sweet smell of the Ohio spring—and freedom.

3

Hearts Ignorant of Homes

Jim's flight from captivity hit an immediate snag at the train station. Maggie and Hugh, themselves only teenagers, discovered they didn't have enough money for their brother's fare to St. Marys.

The Sunday excursion train was crowded with small-town men returning home from a day in Cincinnati. Many of them were drunk and only too happy to hide Jim under a seat each time the conductor passed through the car. It was after midnight when the three Tully children reached St. Marys. The city lights of Paris could not have been more dazzling to Jim than the darkness that had settled over St. Marys. Hugh vanished into the night, bound for the Union Dairy, Uncle Tom's farm, where he worked. Maggie led her little brother off to her room and put him to bed.[1] Hugh returned Monday morning and took Jim to the farm, where he spent his first week of freedom. Jim was not allowed to join his family at Mass the following Sunday, because his clothes were deemed too shabby.

With no real home of his own, Jim was moved from one relative to the next. Maggie, no doubt hoping that their father might provide Jim with some semblance of stability, borrowed a few dollars and took Jim to their father, who was thought to be working a ditch-digging job in a town forty miles away.[2] The reunion would have to wait. Jim and Maggie arrived at the pine-board hotel near the train depot in Haviland, Ohio, where Maggie had been told to look for her father. They were met at the door by a large, friendly woman with a mustache. She informed the children that they had missed him by a day. Worse, Maggie lacked the return train fare to St.

Marys. Moved by the children's plight, the kindly woman loaned Maggie money for the fare.[3]

After several more months of being shifted from one relative to another, Jim was finally reunited with his father in the second half of 1898. Jim had gone half his young life without seeing his father and knew him only from distant memory. The elder Tully, perhaps realizing that his peripatetic labor was hardly the stuff of fatherhood to a twelve-year-old boy, promptly placed his son in the home of an illiterate Ohio farmer named Solomon Boroff. The Boroff farm was located about four miles north and one-and-a-half miles east of Convoy, Ohio, in a part of Van Wert County known to early settlers as Bear Swamp.[4] Indeed, Bear Swamp and all of the northern part of Van Wert County lay in a 1,500-square-mile area known as the Great Black Swamp. It spawned clouds of malarial mosquitoes so thick that both Indian and white settlers were repelled until well into the nineteenth century. By late 1898, when Jim arrived at the Boroff farm, the swamp had largely been drained to reveal rich, black soil ideal for farming.[5]

Any notion Jim had that he had at last found a home, somewhere that he belonged, soon evaporated. If the strict, even cruel, discipline of the orphanage seemed like a bad dream, the farm quickly proved a nightmare. Jim was expected to earn his keep toiling at any number of grueling farm chores. Indeed, one would be hard pressed to distinguish Jim's experience from the slavery that his grandfather witnessed forty years earlier in the American South. He had, quite simply, escaped the orphanage only to find himself again in bondage. Caring for livestock wasn't so bad, but he disliked shocking wheat, as the wheat stubble jabbed his bare feet and ankles. Most of all, he hated the lonely work of husking corn.[6] "From early morning until late at night," he wrote in *Blood on the Moon*, "I would take the corn stalks from the shocks, place them on the ground, and peel the husks from the corn. A weak sun would melt the frozen mud between the rows of stubble as I worked."[7]

Farm life was nothing new to Jim. He'd spent most of his early childhood before the orphanage on or around farms. But in the past he'd been able to explore and play with his brothers once his work was done. No more. Play was for children, and Jim's childhood, such as it was, ended when he left the orphanage.

One winter's night when the temperature hovered near zero, Jim's father was summoned to the farmhouse. Boroff informed the elder Tully that Jim had no warm clothes and that he did not intend to provide them.[8] A long discussion ensued. As Tully later observed, "Financing a vast corporation was never given more consideration by two men."[9] Jim's father left with the promise that he would send money for underclothes and a pair of felt boots. The money never came.[10] In the year and a half that he lived at the Boroff farm, this visit to quibble about warm clothes was the only time young Jim saw his father. This despite the fact that the elder Tully was himself living in Van Wert County the entire time.

It was Jim's great misfortune to be ill clothed that particular winter. On Wednesday, February 8, 1899, bitterly cold air from the Canadian arctic swept across the eastern United States. By Thursday the freeze was shattering records for low temperatures from Florida to New England and as far west as Montana. Many of the record lows, including Ohio's state record of thirty-nine below on that Friday, still stand.[11] Jim, clad in a thin shirt and overalls padded with newspapers, shivered through his farm chores, "raw with cold."[12] In *Beggars of Life*, he recalled the temperature at the farm plummeting to twenty-eight degrees below zero, his body turning a "frozen blue."[13]

And it wasn't just the work and harsh living conditions at the Boroff farm that Jim found disheartening. It was the lack of companionship. Only the Boroffs' daughter, Bee, near Jim in age, extended him any kindness.[14] Boroff and his wife, first cousins, were God-fearing rustics and, Jim believed, "slightly mad."[15] Jim spent his evenings in a room that contained little more than the Boroffs, a few pieces of furniture, a ticking clock, a couple of kerosene lamps, and exactly three books, two of which were not the Bible. Jim read them all several times over. Sometimes, according to *Emmett Lawler*, Jim was asked to read aloud, especially if neighbors had come to call. Bunyan's *Pilgrim's Progress* was always a hit, and the Book of Revelation never failed to set the Boroff jaw agape. Hung on either wall, as if watching this country gothic scene, were color portraits of various Boroff ancestors.[16] Jim thought them "demented."[17] He recalled looking about the room "with wet eyes. No kind word had been said to me within its walls."[18]

One incident, which cannot be verified in Tully's unpublished autobiographical writings, is described in *Blood on the Moon*. True or not, it does give an impression of life with the Boroffs. When the Boroffs' cat gave birth to a litter of kittens, Boroff stuffed the kittens into a sack and handed the bundle to Jim with orders to drown them in the creek. By the time he reached the banks of the stream, Jim's sympathy for life's waifs had overcome him. He set the kittens loose and threw the empty sack in the water. When he returned to the barnyard, Boroff looked up from some wood that he was about to saw and asked if the job had been done. Jim's lie that the kittens had been dispatched unraveled a short time later as the kittens reappeared at their mother's side. Enraged, the hulking Boroff lumbered after them with an ax. Only his daughter's desperate pleas convinced him to spare them.[19]

Joseph Blosser was sort of a rustic shaman and known throughout Paulding and the neighboring counties as the "Faith Healer." His nickname was a misnomer, as his large practice relied more on natural medicine and a vegetarian diet than on religion. Farm families traveled miles to be treated at his home. Blosser was a "giant in stature," was relatively well educated, and had a keen sense of intuition. Although beloved by most of his rural neighbors, he struck many of them as an odd and mystic figure.[20]

While it's not clear how they met, according to *Emmett Lawler*, Jim stopped by Blosser's home often to visit and borrow books from his library.[21] Blosser had been disturbed by Jim's tales of abuse at the Boroff farm and had promised him a place to stay should he decide to leave.

In the spring of 1900, after a year and a half on the Boroff farm and having endured his second winter in threadbare clothes, Jim could take no more. For the first time in his young life, he took his fate into his own hands, or, more accurately, his feet. He collected the few belongings he had brought from the orphanage, some worn clothes and a cigar box full of poems clipped from newspapers, and ran away. He found his way to the door of a kindly farmer named Pete Davidson, where he was allowed to spend the night. The next day Boroff and his daughter appeared at the gate to Davidson's farm. Boroff demanded his charge be handed over at once. Jim feared the worst. The only adult he'd ever trusted to save him from disaster had been his mother. To his immense relief, Davidson stiffened. Angry words were exchanged and Boroff backed down. Hand in hand, Jim and his newfound protector watched the Boroffs turn to leave when, to Jim's surprise and Boroff's chagrin, Bee sprang from her father to give Jim a farewell kiss.[22]

Years later Jim would remember his time at the Boroff farm and wonder "why people were so mean to kids." His experience was not unique. "Nearly every kid I knew who had been sent to farmers from the orphanage had run away because they could not stand the treatment." Orphans were, quite simply, cheaper than farmhands and could be worked harder.[23]

From the Davidson farm Jim found his way to Joseph Blosser's home, three miles to the north. In *Emmett Lawler* Jim changed Boroff's name to Soaroff and recalled showing up at Blosser's door.

> The old Healer . . . saw the blue veins swell in the boy's forehead, and the tears fall in his sad eyes.
>
> He gathered the orphan in his arms, and the young sailor and world-roving fighter of other days spoke in words of tense passion.
>
> "Listen, lad, Soaroff and his nine brothers and John L. Sullivan and Jim Corbett can't take you from here till you want to go."[24]

Jim was overcome with emotion and remained with Blosser for several months. When many years later Tully was asked by a reporter who was the greatest man he had ever known, he replied, "The Faith Healer of Paulding County."[25]

With Pete Davidson's help, Jim got a job driving a team of horses for a man named Frank Ralston. Although Jim was now a teenager, "he was not tall enough to curry or harness the horses," so Ralston prepared the team each morning.[26] Jim's job was to drive the team from a quarry, where he picked up a load of crushed stone, hauled it to the road being built between Lima and Fort Wayne, and then returned to the quarry for more. He was provided board and paid three dollars a week, most of which he saved.

His sole extravagance, if *Blood on the Moon* is correct, seems to have involved a visit to Van Wert, the county seat, when the circus came to town. There was much for a farm boy to see, but the young woman in tights telling fortunes especially thrilled him. Jim returned to the farm that evening lighter in the wallet, but with a dozen photographs of the sightly fortune-teller and the stuff of every thirteen-year-old boy's dreams: a deck of pornographic cards. The steamy combination of photos and cards fueled Jim's daydreams, helping him pass the hours atop the quarry wagon.[27]

News from St. Marys of the death of Jim's seventy-six-year-old grandfather, Hugh Tully, on August 9, 1900, apparently did not reach him in time to attend the funeral.[28] Jim's contact with Old Hughie after the death of Biddy, which is to say after the age of six, seems to have been limited to whatever time they might have shared prior to his being sent to the Boroff farm. Old Hughie's wife, Catherine, would outlive him by nine years, dying in August 1909.[29]

When Jim's work hauling stone ended in the fall, his savings amounted to twenty-four dollars, a sum so large that he became slightly confused by the larger denominations of bills. With some regrets at leaving Ralston, Jim took his savings and set out for St. Marys.[30] Jim quickly found that the problem of too much cash had a way of resolving itself when he was among family. His father borrowed ten dollars, which was never repaid.[31]

After the death of Jim's mother, his father's life had fallen apart. The strength that had seen him through fire, flood, and myriad other disasters was washed away in a river of whiskey and beer.[32] Since his Lawler grandparents, Old Hughie, and his mother were dead, and his father absent, Jim sought out the only responsible adult relative left in his life, his sister Maggie. She was then working in a laundry, making five dollars a week, three dollars of which paid her board at the home of Mary Hardy. She made an extra dollar a week by helping around the house on evenings and Sundays.

Upon hearing that Tom Tully was laid up and unable to work after being thrown from a horse on a farm, Jim proudly set upon a course to aid his older brother. With a dollar of his hard-earned savings, he rented a rig from a livery, picked up Maggie, and drove out to the farm. As they pulled up to the farmhouse, Tom limped out to meet them. Maggie playfully "introduced" the brothers, addressing each as "Red-head." Jim, unable to restrain himself any longer, pulled out the ten dollars he had pocketed for the occasion and pressed it into his brother's hand. Tom held the money, weighed his financial situation against that of his brother, and decided he couldn't accept. When he tried to return the money, Maggie, moved by the gesture, stopped him. The Tullys must always stand by one another, she admonished. It was advice that Jim took to heart. Tom kept the money, which he later repaid, and limped back into the house while Jim drove his sister home, pleased with his role as family provider.[33] It was a role that he would often fill, with less pride and more pain, in the years to come.

The labors of Jim Tully's father's generation to lift St. Marys out of the mud were evident to his son. The St. Marys that Jim Tully found upon his return at the dawn of a new century was

> An old town, a strange town, a completely original town. A canal and river flow through it within a few hundred feet of each other. The bridges over each arch across Spring Street, and the natives often pause in their walks to look down at the yellow waters flowing lazily below. . . .
>
> Spring Street stretched east and west, the paved bricks touching the

open country at each end. A brick hotel, with a fountain near it, loomed majestically on the river. It allowed a loitering place for actors and traveling men, bartenders and preachers, and all the procession of men who wore white collars and labored not with their hands.[34]

The country at the close of the nineteenth century was moving from horse power to oil, and St. Marys found itself with a front-row seat to the transformation. The first oil well in town was drilled a few weeks before Jim was born in 1886, and in the ensuing years, oil derricks dotted the landscape. To their consternation, the oil men realized that the largest oil reserves in the county had, only decades before, been flooded by the St. Marys Reservoir.[35] Area schoolchildren, already taught to repeat that the St. Marys Reservoir was, as Jim recalled, "the largest artificial body of water in the world," soon learned that it was also "the site of the world's first off-shore oil wells."[36]

And while oil did spur growth, it would be wrong to characterize turn-of-the-century St. Marys as an oil town or a boomtown. The population of St. Marys and the surrounding township was stable and numbered 6,729 in 1900.[37] A young man looking for work and not wishing to follow in the muddy footsteps of his father and grandfather had much to choose from. There were sawmills, a large wheel and spoke factory, a manufacturer of woolen blankets, a foundry, carriage works, machine companies, grain mills, lumber yards, stores selling everything from dry goods and hardware to drugs and feed, banks, hotels, grocers, butchers, haberdasheries, taverns, blacksmiths, liveries, restaurants, an undertaker, a bakery, a jeweler, an optician, and even an art studio and gallery, as well as many other small concerns. And saloon work was always enticing.[38] Jim later recalled "that I used to . . . gaze longingly through the big front window of Charley Koch's saloon. . . . There was a kid in there that I envied. He had a swell job, polishing brass and washing dishes. The only music he had to listen to was a perfectly grand mechanical piano. . . . That kid was also privileged to listen to the swellest of dirty stories, retailed for all to hear by the drummers who stopped for a foaming glass of Wooden Shoe lager."[39]

Much of this existed not because of the canal, which had all but ceased operation by the end of the nineteenth century, but because of the growth of the railroads in Auglaize County.[40] First to arrive was the Dayton & Michigan (later the Cincinnati, Hamilton & Dayton Railroad) in 1858, followed by the Lake Erie & Western in 1872, the Ohio Southern in 1892, and in 1900 the Columbus & Northwestern.[41]

Indeed, one St. Marys industry, the chain works, founded in 1887, could not have existed without the railroads to bring it steel and then take the finished chain, coil, and cable to market.[42] Like many St. Marys boys, Jim Tully walked down Oil Street to apply for a job heating links at the chain factory. "On quiet days," he recalled, "the roar of the factory could be heard above everything else for miles around. It was a steady, continuous roar, as incessant as the sea upon a silent shore."[43] Decades later, Tully pal John Ford, directing *The Quiet Man,* had John Wayne, playing an Irish American boxer and steelworker, describe such a furnace as "so hot a man forgets his fear of hell." Jim got the job in late 1900. His pay was fifty cents for a ten-hour day, with two dollars of his weekly pay going to his board.[44]

In *Emmett Lawler,* Tully described the 5 A.M. start of a typical working day.

> The boys would file through the silent streets on their way to the factory. Many were clad thinly, and without overcoats, as they faced the winter winds.
>
> Arriving at the factory, they would dip pieces of waste in crude oil, and light them, and place the burning pieces on the furnaces to enable them to see. In a short time the factory would be full of the smoke from burning rags and a dim, uncertain light. When the boys had finished the blast would be turned on . . . and the roar of the factory would commence for the day.[45]

Jim found the work satisfying and, more important, given Ohio winters, warm. He also grew to respect a chain maker who knew his business.

> The chainmaker's art is the poetry of motion. The furnace is built in the form of a square stove of firebrick, with holes in the top the size of the links to be welded into chain. The link-heater's duty is to hang the open end of the links downward in the fire, out of which the chainmaker takes them as they are heated, in endless rotation, one after another.
>
> The link is shaped upon the die, after it is skillfully attached to the red chain lying on the anvil plate. The heavy trip-hammer comes down many times and shapes the link upon the die into the finished chain. While it is doing so the maker's hand hammer is beating a swift tattoo upon the hot link, between the strokes of the trip-hammer. His blow must be timed to the fraction of a second, for, should the trip-hammer strike his small

hammer, link, die hand hammer, and perhaps the chainmaker's hand are mixed in a frightful welter.[46]

So Jim spent the winter at the chain factory, befriending a boy three years younger. Charles Makley was, in Jim's view, well off.[47] Makley lived with his parents and was able to hang on to some of his meager salary. Jim was a frequent guest at the Makley home, and Charley and his mother made a point of passing along old clothes.[48] Charley's father, hardworking and kind, saw Jim as just another boy like his son, only poorer.

The following summer of 1901, Jim again drove a team for Frank Ralston. With winter coming on, he stopped by the Makley home for a few days. With Makley's help, he landed a job with Ed Berger, one of the better chain makers at the factory. Also with Makley's help, he bargained for and received a dollar and a half a week plus his board. This was a great improvement over the previous winter, when a chain maker might lay him off for a couple of days, forcing him to scramble for his board money.[49]

One evening, for the first time since her death, Biddy's family came together in St. Marys. The occasion was a rare visit by the Tully children's wandering and detached father. Maggie had called the children together to spend an evening with their father before he again passed from town and their lives. Brother Charlie was back from the farm in Indiana. Tom, who had lied about his age and joined the army, also found his way home.[50] Maggie was determined that for one evening they would be like other families, and to that end she warned her four brothers and young sister "to be nice" to their father. "He's suffered enough," Jim recalled her telling them, "in losing our mother." Such was Jim's respect for his older sister that "from that day my father was no longer a roving ditchdigger and drunkard—he was the man my mother had loved."[51]

It would be their first and last reunion. Tom, probably AWOL, was headed to Mexico. Young Jim, perhaps out of wanderlust, or maybe just fearing that he was on course for a lifetime trapped in a chain factory in St. Marys, Ohio, was anxious to tag along. Maggie begged Tom not to take him. Realizing that Jim was too young, Tom agreed. He put his arm around his youngest brother and exhorted him to make something of himself. If life had already trapped the older children, there was still time for Jim. Maggie, too, viewed Jim as the special one, the last, best hope of Biddy's children. Jim later described the scene in a piece for *Esquire*.

Our father heard the dialogue. I can still see him gazing out of the window across the bleak town in the direction of our early home. After some minutes he came to us.

There was a long silence. To break it, Tom said quickly, "Good-bye, Dad—good luck to you all."

He looked quickly at those he was never to see again and was on his way to Mexico.

Our father returned to the window.

After a while he said, "Let's take a walk, Jim."

We went in the direction of the railroad yards. A long freight was just leaving. My father heard the last rumble of the caboose before he moved.

Then he said, "Tom's gone—it doesn't seem like you and him are my sons," and walked on with me in silence. Long after I became known the scene still haunted me.[52]

Gone. Just like his uncle, John Lawler, Tom left, never to return. He hadn't been much of a father, the elder Tully acknowledged, but still he worried that Tom and Jim were untamed, impulsive, and emotional. In short, they weren't Tullys. They were Lawlers.

"During idle hours, I loitered near the railroad yards of an Ohio town from which I launched upon my tramping career," Jim Tully wrote in the opening of *Beggars of Life*.[53] All the necessary ingredients, save courage, had been in place for up to a year. St. Marys, by Jim's account, was home to more than two-dozen saloons, and despite Maggie's lectures to stay out of them, Jim had learned to drink, on occasion heavily. He gravitated to the cheap saloons near the train yards.[54] Here railroad men came to wash the smoke and dust out of their throats. In addition to brakemen, engineers, and firemen, Jim also met hoboes who rode in empty boxcars or, if none could be found, "rode the rods," strapping themselves to the irons rods beneath the cars, riding inches above the tracks.[55] They tutored Jim in the art of jumping a moving car without falling beneath the steel wheels. And they described in unforgettable detail the fate of those who failed. To a boy beaten down by the monotony of heating links in a chain factory, such stories sounded wild and romantic.

Jim befriended one of the old hoboes, a former tramp printer named Jack Raley, and his rambling reminiscences never failed to enchant the wide-eyed young factory worker. Frail and elderly, Raley used a thin valise strap to hold up his tattered corduroy pants. Only two of his front teeth remained, and streaks of blood ran through his yellowish eyes. Yet Raley endeared himself to Jim because he gladly shared his knowledge of books with the inquisitive St. Marys youth: "Though a poverty-stricken drunkard, a cadger of drinks, a cleaner of cuspidors, a mopper of bar-room floors, he was still the wealthiest man I knew in that town;—for he carried a tattered volume of Voltaire in his pocket, and he talked to me about it."[56]

When drunk, "which was nearly every day," Raley also talked about his years traveling from town to town. He "bragged of his past, a tortuous, winding road, full of many a weary bog."[57] It was heady stuff for a boy who'd seen little of the world beyond western Ohio and the walls of a Cincinnati orphanage.

While Maggie was making little headway in her campaign to keep her younger brother out of the buckets of blood down by the tracks, she was having a bit more success convincing Jim that he should become a writer. Ever since Tom had told her of Jim's compositions at the orphanage, she had been his biggest fan. She would remain so for the rest of her life. This, despite the fact that neither she nor Jim, in Jim's exaggerated recollection, knew a comma from a period. If Maggie realized how poor she and Jim were, she managed never to show it. Jim would contend that he never considered himself or his family inferior in any way.[58] And in one important way he *was* superior to most other boys his age. He was an intellectually curious child who, like his father, devoured books. As St. Marys was without a public library, Maggie made a deal with a newsstand owner who allowed Jim to borrow his magazines.[59]

Maggie's plan to make a writer out of her younger brother by keeping him well supplied with reading material had an unintended consequence. Fueled by stories of life outside St. Marys borne by magazine and hobo, Jim grew restless. His brothers and father had drifted away, leaving him with his sisters, Maggie and ten-year-old Anna.[60] The three of them, according to *Shanty Irish,* lived in two rooms above a grocery store. They were, in Jim's words, "children with hearts ignorant of homes."[61]

Maggie, twenty-one, had drawn the attention of would-be suitors. Though she had fallen in love with one of them, she turned down his proposal. Her first responsibility lay with her motherless younger sister and brother. The thought that he might be a hardship to his beloved sister increased Jim's desire to be out on his own. The hobo and magazine stories, the desire not to be a burden to his sister, poverty, boredom with St. Marys, and wanderlust saturated Jim's thoughts.[62] The particle that crystallized his resolve took the form of a one-eyed drifter named Billy. The brawny, sunburned traveler wore a black leather patch over the vacant red socket. With pride he related how he'd lost the eye in Arkansas, drifted out to California, and done two months in a western jail on a vagrancy charge. "He made me ashamed of my humdrum life in a humdrum town," Tully recalled more than two decades later in the opening chapter of *Beggars of Life*. "He was flippant in manner, and spoke of far off countries with careless gesture instead of reverence."[63]

Sitting on a trestle over the St. Marys River, the boys talked and threw stones into the water. "Hell, I wouldn't be found dead in a joint like this," Billy told him. "It ain't a town; it's a disease. A guy's only in the world once. He may as well lamp it over while he's at it, even if he has only got one lamp." Now ashamed of where he lived and worked, Jim decided to change the subject. Did Billy like the road? "Sure I likes it," Billy said. "I wouldn't give it up for nothin'. They ain't nothin' in workin'. Only boobs work. Them old whistles blow ev'ry mornin'—an' they piles out like a lotta cattle. Not for Yours Truly. . . . Chuck it, Kid, chuck it. Gosh, you can't do no worse."[64]

While it is impossible to determine if Tully's recollection of this pivotal conversation is precise in every detail, it does indicate Jim's state of mind as he was making the decision that would forever change his life. Jim was susceptible to this brand of reasoning. Tully and Lawler men were forever disappearing down country roads. He'd spent much of his life watching them fade into the horizon. Now, listening to Billy extol the road, Jim recalled the tales told with such sweeping grandeur by Raley and the other hoboes he'd met. He resolved to leave his hometown as soon as possible. "I'll beat it out of here, all right," Jim told one-eyed Billy, "but I hate to leave some of the people." It was the last shackle holding Jim in place. Billy quickly broke it. Jim recalled his reply: "Well, you can't take 'em wit' you. Forgit all that stuff."[65]

Before jumping on a train headed for Lima, Billy offered one last piece of advice: "If you ever go on the road, Kid, don't you never let no old tramp play you for a sucker. You know, them old birds're too lazy to scratch themselves when they're crummy. So they gits young kids and teaches 'em to beg. They know people'll feed kids quicker'n they will them, so they make the kids do all the beggin'. Lotsa people pity kids at back doors. The old tramps call the kids their punks. There's lot of punkgrafters on the road. Lotsa things I could tell you."[66]

His discourse was interrupted by the sound of an engine's whistle. The boys heard the familiar rumbling of boxcars. The tracks started to vibrate. With a wave of a nicotine-stained hand, Billy was on the train and gone.

A few weeks later, with the winter of 1901 still hanging on in the Midwest, Jim's independence came in the form of a westbound freight train. It was a decision that changed everything. "The atmosphere was murky green and neither cold nor warm," he wrote of this first journey. "The animals huddled in the fields, as though reluctant to break the warmth-giving habits of winter.... What did it matter though.... I was going somewhere. ... I, a throwback to the ancient Irish tellers of fairy tales, was at last on the way to high adventure."[67]

Jim had seen nothing of the other forty-four states in the union (Arizona, New Mexico, and Oklahoma would be admitted in his lifetime) and little of his native Ohio beyond the western counties. In many of these states, local police officers, railroad detectives, and judges viewed tramps and hoboes as little better than vermin. Notions that the hobo was a "subspecies" had been in the air since at least the 1880s. By the time of Tully's first trip, public campaigns against hoboes and tramps widely fell under the banner of public health. Such crusades borrowed the fervor and trappings of campaigns to deal with rats and insects.[68] Sometimes the similarities were more than superficial. As early as 1877, the July 12 edition of the *Chicago Tribune* went so far as to advocate the distribution of strychnine—or arsenic-laced meat—to tramps.[69] Nor did a fresh-faced road-kid need only fear the local police armed with vagrancy laws and brutal railroad bulls armed with saps and guns. He, and occasionally she, had no way of knowing if the stranger at the other end of the dark boxcar was simply an itinerant laborer or one of the many "blowed-in-the-glass-stiffs" who, in the words of one road-kid, "soaked themselves in booze when they could get it and ... were always out to snare kids to do their begging and pander to their perversions."[70] But this part of the road was not yet a cruel reality to the young teenager watching the Midwest pass by from the door of a boxcar. "What a picture I must have made," Tully later wrote, "a heavy-jowled red-headed youth with a crooked smile and a freckled face, and clad in the cast-off clothing of more fortunate working boys."[71]

Jim's first tramping trip took him to Peoria, Illinois, and as far as St. Louis. He was gone no more than a month, but when he returned, "I was a different fellow."[72] There was nothing tentative or cautious about Jim's first tramping trip. He reckoned he had journeyed a thousand miles; he had ridden the rods, been alone for days at a time, and survived.

Penniless and exhausted, he returned to Maggie. She gave him fifty cents and took him to Hugh, who was working in George Rapp's livery barns, just south of Spring Street, near the canal bridge. He stayed in one of the barns, picked up odd jobs and meals when he could, and slept in the hay.[73]

If Maggie hoped that her brother's hobo trip to Illinois and Missouri had shattered his romantic illusions about the road, she was to be disappointed. Jim had seen firsthand the hardship of hobo life on his trip to St. Louis, but it was not enough to extinguish the burning desire to break away from his hometown. The teenager could only appease his restless spirit by traveling far from everything he cherished and despised in St. Marys.

Several weeks later, Jim found a freight train with an open boxcar and, with several other boys from the livery, headed for Lima in the next county. Less than ten miles outside town, at a speck on the map called Buckland, the boys were caught and put off the train. They could either walk back to town and face the likely taunts of their associates or hop the train again. Jumping the train again did present one small problem. The train had come to rest a few hundred feet from a long trestle. Jump too soon, and they'd be caught again; jump too late, and they would risk being thrown from the trestle. To a boy, they decided to jump. As the train built speed, the boys ran alongside and jumped into the open boxcar. Jim, waiting near the trestle, ignoring the moral of nearly all the hobo stories he had heard, jumped at the passing boxcar from a standstill. His hand caught the iron ladder and began to slip. Feeling his body sliding under the wheels, he panicked. He shoved himself away from the car. "The heel of my shoe," he recalled, "caught under the edge of a wheel. Dazed with pain, I rolled down the embankment."[74] Seeing what had happened, the other boys could only wait until the train had crossed the trestle. Once across, they jumped off and ran back to help. They found the leather heel of Jim's shoe torn away and his foot swollen but intact. Money was collected and Jim rode legally—"on the cushion"—back to St. Marys. He limped for days.

Back at the livery stable, Jim's job was to deliver horses to customers around town and walk back to the stable. Often he would accompany traveling salesmen on their rounds aboard one of the rented rigs. As he had with the hoboes down by the tracks, Jim soaked up their stories of life outside Auglaize County. At the livery he came in contact with St. Marys society, high and low.[75]

High society was foreign to him and heightened his sense of alienation. He realized at an early age he could never be part of that world. It was just as well. Low society was much more interesting. It would have been about this time that Jim began hanging around Rabbit Town, the St. Marys neighborhood along the Lake Erie and Western tracks where a dollar could buy most anything, including the favors of a young prostitute with "yellow corn-silk coloured hair" that fell down to her white shoulders. Jim recalled how she told him of one night when she earned the unbelievable sum of forty-eight dollars. She also passed along the happy news, or so it must have been to Jim, "that women liked red-headed guys."[76] On this point anyway she was as good as her word. She took his virginity but never his money. She even gave him her last dollar when she discovered that he had stolen four dollars from her while they were both drunk.

Jim's days were no less interesting. In fact, he had the most exciting job at the stables, and one for which he had scant competition. He rode with the "shooter" for the Standard Oil Company who boarded his horses at Rapp's livery. Together they would hitch up a team to a wagon loaded with nitroglycerin. With Jim holding the reins, they would bump along with enough nitro to leave nothing but an unexplained dip in the road for future travelers. At the well site, the shooter would load a go-devil, a torpedo-shaped cylinder with a cap at one end, with explosives and drop it into the drilled hole. After a journey of several thousand feet, the go-devil would detonate and the ground begin to rumble. Rock, earth, and sometimes oil would rocket to the surface. If they had a gusher on their hands, they would spend the next few hours capping it until equipment could be hauled in.[77]

After one three-day trip with the shooter, for which he was paid three dollars, Jim concluded that the U.S. Navy might prove safer and more lucrative without any appreciable loss of excitement.[78] To this end, probably in the summer of 1902, he set out for the nearest recruiting office, in Chicago. From the railroad yards in Lima, he hopped a Chicago-bound freight train "as easily as if I'd paid my fare."[79] He marched down State Street, impressed but undaunted by the big city, to the recruiting office in the Masonic Temple. He sat in a waiting room, staring out the window at Lake Michigan. It was so blue and so large. His thoughts drifted. He was finally led into another room and told to strip for his physical. As Jim told him of his life, the physician, a gentle old man with red whiskers, looked him over and found him in excellent shape, even his teeth, which had never been brushed. After explaining basic dental hygiene to Jim, he sighed and delivered the bad news. At four feet eleven and eighty-five pounds, Jim would not be going to Newport News with the other recruits.

Knowing that rejecting Jim for service meant consigning him to life on the streets, the doctor said, "I'd make a new rule to have you in the navy, but I can't."[80] Crushed, Jim walked the lonely miles back to the railroad yards.

After a few days, he was back in St. Marys. He again took up residence in the hayloft at the livery. He passed a sleepless night watching the lazy water in the canal, inhaling the pungent and distinctive odor of horse, listening to the freight trains come and go, and thinking about his life.[81]

At some point, probably in early 1902, Maggie, having had her heart broken one too many times, decided to make a fresh start. She changed her name to Virginia, and with a small tin trunk, a large color portrait of Biddy, and her sister, Anna, she moved to Chicago, where she found work waiting tables in a greasy spoon.[82] Hugh had left the livery to apprentice at the chain works, but when Jim tried to follow him, he was turned away. He was too old to heat links but too young to apprentice. And with Hugh gone from the livery, Jim knew that his days living in the barn were numbered. He could, as in the past, wash dishes at Charlie Koch's saloon, but kitchen work was drudgery of the worst kind.[83]

Although Charley Makley still had a place to stay at his parents' house, he too was without a job or any hope that better times were around the corner. He and Jim decided that their fortunes followed the steel rail out of town. They hopped a freight and jumped off in Cincinnati. Along the banks of the Ohio River they met up with other road-kids and spent several carefree days swimming in the swirling yellow water. When Charley decided to move on, leaving Jim behind in Cincinnati, no reporter took down their good-byes; no newspaper marked their parting.[84] Yet their next meeting, more than three decades later, would make headlines across the country.

Up to this point in his life, Jim had regarded St. Marys as his home. He might hop a train and disappear for weeks at a time, but he always returned. Now the siren's song of the locomotive whistle called him to join the ranks of hoboes and road-kids who left their homes and families, more or less, for good.

4

Big Rock Candy Mountain

The "thrill of adventure," as he later wrote, seized fourteen-year-old Jim Tully's imagination when he made his first hobo trip in 1901.[1] By the time he left St. Marys for good in 1902, however, his romantic notions about life on the road had been severely tempered by illusion-shattering experiences. "My wanderlust was a fever that burned deeply," Jim recalled.[2] And the fever was not cooled by these early trips. But he learned that it was dangerous to romanticize the hoboes he encountered. "Petty men themselves," Tully wrote in *Beggars of Life*, "they expect pettiness from others, and find it, as they deserve. The vast crowd of them are liars, ingrates, and thieves.... The road writes with heavy hand its lines of degeneracy, brutality, and all-around wretchedness on their faces and body."[3]

The fledgling wanderer also learned that, in the words of hobo historian Kenneth Allsop, "in reasonable times as well as bad there has always been a cold harshness shown by small town America to the wayfaring stranger."[4] And men whose only crime was having no home proved irresistible targets for law enforcement. Tully saw "that innocent vagrants were often punished for crimes they did not commit."[5] This was particularly true in the Deep South, where hoboes, jailed as vagrants, might sweat out months or years as chain-gang laborers.

No state was more feared by the hobo than Mississippi. Under the "terrible Mississippi vagrancy law," Tully wrote in *Circus Parade*, "an officer is given two dollars and a half for every vagrant he captures alive.... Once captured, he is given a fine of seventy-five dollars. Having no money, he is made to work the fine out—at twenty cents a day! This comes to about eleven months and twenty-nine days, allowing a few days for good behavior."[6] But most Mississippi jail terms, Tully noted, stretched far longer than this. Prisoners were charged for their clothing: three dollars for a fifty-cent pair of overalls and seven dollars for brogans. These expenses also were worked off at a rate of twenty cents a day. If these items needed to be replaced or state property was damaged, the expense was translated into increased jail time. "It is no uncommon thing for a friendless man to spend several years as a peon in Mississippi," Tully observed.[7]

Small southern and western towns particularly hostile to hoboes kept alive the ugly tradition of the Sapping Day. Men and boys judged to be vagrants were forced to run a harrowing gauntlet past law-abiding citizens armed with stones, whips, and clubs. The runner unfortunate enough to stumble might be stoned and kicked into insensibility.[8] In later years, Tully recalled an exception to southern inhospitality.

> Mobile was always regarded as a "good town" for hoboes. As soon as we would scurry to the woods from the railroad yard we would spread out and go in different directions to gather up food for a feed.
>
> In a few minutes the jungle kettles would be simmering, loaded down with food donated by generous Mobile housewives.[9]

While Tully remembered Mobile's railroad bulls as particularly tough, one of Mobile's cops left a different impression.

> I had just arrived on a freight train and was making my way up town to get something to eat.
>
> A policeman stopped me, which is nothing unusual in the life of a hobo, but it seems something had happened that day and the officers were making a roundup.
>
> In my coat he found some religious cards.
>
> The sight of the pictures cut the Irish cop's heart.
>
> "Here, me boy, put these back in yer pocket," he said, "ye can't do much wrong carryin' them pictures with you."
>
> It just happened that day that another hobo had given me the cards.
>
> "Take them with you, you may need them someday," the bo told me.[10]

Henceforth, Jim made a point of keeping a prayer card to soften up Irish cops.[11]

Generous housewives and soft-hearted Irish cops were the exception. The Jim Tully who cut his final ties with St. Marys in 1902 had learned that death stalked the vagabond in many forms. The rider of the rails literally took his life in his hands when he jumped for a moving freight car. As another chronicler of hobo life, historian Roger A. Bruns, explained, "Hoboes and tramps suffered a grisly slaughter on the tracks . . . mangled by sliding boxcar doors; crushed by shifting loads on gondolas; suffocated or frozen . . . ; rolled off decks of passenger cars; pitched from rods and gunnels to the track bed and the grinding wheels; beaten, and killed by fellow drifters and train dicks."[12] Dead hoboes seldom merited an inquest. Indeed, railroad men often never bothered to report them. As an old railroad man observed in 1907, one would be hard pressed to find a railroad line that didn't have "private graveyards on its own right of way."[13]

Still, even with the road's harsher aspects fresh in his young mind, the boy from St. Marys couldn't resist the ways of a rover. Starting with his earliest trip in the spring of 1901, Jim Tully's road-kid trips spanned six years. The number is significant. He had spent the first six years of his life in St. Marys. He had spent the next six in a Cincinnati orphanage. Now, after a period of drudgery in St. Marys, Tully declared his independence from others' modest expectations of work with horse and chain. Something better must be out there, and out there he would go.

For these six years, he tramped around the country, occasionally leaving the road to work as a newsboy, dishwasher, link heater, or circus hand. No other period of Jim Tully's raucous life yielded as much raw material for his writing. Three of his best books—the autobiographical *Beggars of Life* (1924) and *Circus Parade* (1927), as well as the mostly autobiographical *Shadows of Men* (1930)—were based on these six crowded years. Significant parts of six other books—*Emmett Lawler* (1922), *Blood on the Moon* (1931), *Laughter in Hell* (1932), *Ladies in the Parlor* (1935), *The Bruiser* (1936), and *Biddy Brogan's Boy* (1942)—were also drawn from experiences from this period.

Tully would always feel a special kinship with writers who, by choice or necessity, had experienced even a little taste of the road. Any author who had put in time catching boxcars, laboring aboard ships, or merely tramping from town to town would be considered a spiritual brother. This fraternity would grow to include Maxim Gorky, Cervantes, Joseph Conrad, John Masefield, Jack London, Mark Twain, Oliver Goldsmith, and Eugene O'Neill. They knew what it meant to spend their days not knowing where they would find supper or bed. It was the price they paid for freedom.

Jim Tully felt liberated as a road-kid in the company of hoboes and yeggs. Several years later, writing in the third person for a small newspaper, he recalled "that the young tramp, outside the time he spends in jail, was a free individual. There was no one to tell him that if he worked hard he might become President of the United States."[14]

A road-kid could be described as a young hobo, although such a description is not entirely accurate. The hobo "is a migratory worker," Tully explained, while the road-kid, with the yegg, "is the most relentless and ruthless species of the roving vagabonds of America."[15] The yegg, according to Bruns, was an "itinerant criminal," maybe a safe blower, maybe a stick-up artist.[16] Ben Reitman, hobo king and whorehouse physician, put America's vagabonds in three basic categories: the tramp, the hobo, and the bum. Popular culture has made the terms synonymous, but they describe three different types of wanderers. A tramp, Reitman said, is constantly traveling and "apparently doesn't want to work." A hobo is a laborer "looking for work." And a bum is someone "who hangs around a low-class saloon, and begs or earns a few pennies a day in order to obtain a drink."[17] A road-kid, then, could at various points in his travels fit in any of these three categories, so it is perhaps best to think of a road-kid as characterized by youth and wanderlust.

Each of these three major categories contained several subcategories, and the lines between them were not always clear. There was the "bindle stiff," a hobo who carried his belongings in a bundle and seldom hopped trains. A "dingbat" was an itinerant beggar. A "stew bum" was a tramp devastated by years of heavy drinking. A "fly-by-night" was a young tramp who boldly favored fast trains.

Hoboes, tramps, and bums may be symbols of poverty, yet they are identified by a rich variety of low and lofty names: "rovers," "rounders," "vags" (short for "vagabonds" or "vagrants"), "turnpikers," "knights of the road," "wastrels," "ragmen," "swagmen" (Australian), and "schnorrers" (Yiddish).[18] In the company of such men, young Jim Tully learned how to "beat the train" (board a moving freight). He learned that the "blind baggage," a spot between the mail car and the express coach, was an ideal place to avoid detection while boarding a train. He learned that riding the rods underneath the railroad cars could be especially dangerous. And he learned that vicious railroad employees would sometimes string iron weights to wires dragged under the cars, killing any hoboes who might be on the rods.

He learned that a mastery of hobo jargon was equally necessary for survival on the road. The local policemen were the "John Laws." A detective was a "bull" or a "dick." A railway detective was a "cinder dick." An inept detective was a "mail-order dick." A place to sleep was a "flop." A hobo camp was a "jungle." The stew cooked in these jungles, out of almost anything that looked edible, was known as "mulligan." "Hitting the stem" meant begging for money on the street. "Hitting the back door" meant begging at private homes, usually at the kitchen door. A "sit-down" was a meal served to a tramp allowed to remain seated. A "handout" was a meal wrapped in paper or tossed into a bag. A doctor was a "croaker." A mortician was a "man-planter." A farmer was a "clover kicker." A train was a "rattler." The conductor was the "con." The brakeman was the "brakie." To be "ditched" or "red-lighted" meant being thrown off a train. A "glim" was a kerosene lantern. Hands were called "grab hooks." Eyes were called "lamps." A kindly area for bums was labeled "good hitting." A dangerous area for hoboes was termed "hostile." The euphemism for blood was "red ink." Death was "the last division."

Among themselves, hoboes addressed each other as 'Bo, and the opening line in most railyard conversations was "Which way, 'Bo?" They also assigned fanciful nicknames to fellow vagabonds. Tully, for obvious reasons, was called Red, never Jim, by other rovers. For the rest of his life many knew him as Red Tully, even in Hollywood.

If he began his traveling as a road-kid, near the end of his six wandering years Tully certainly fit the hobo definition. There were times when he was looking for work. There were other times, however, when he fit the tramp definition. He didn't want to work and wasn't looking for it. There were even times when he was "on the bum," using his boyish appearance to "batter the back doors" (beg for food door to door).

Red Tully, though, always was quick to say that for most of the six years, he was simply a road-kid. He was proud of the fact that many road-kids became great boxers, including Jack Dempsey (later a close friend), Charles "Kid" McCoy, and Stanley Ketchel. Some road-kids, he noted, became yeggs, while others became clergymen. And the "names of many road-kids may be found in the records of men who dangled through the traps of gallows."[19]

Tully never put together an accurate chronology of his travels. It's clear, however, that the break from St. Marys was not a clean one. During his first year as a road-kid, he returned to his hometown several times, lured back by the assurance of a job and a place to stay. But by the spring of 1902 he was gone for good. During those spring months he "hoboed about Kentucky and Indiana," temporarily leaving the road to work for Amy, the lead attraction with the One and Only Street Fair Company.[20] His job was every bit as unusual and hazardous as his stint hauling nitroglycerin along rutted roads. Billed as "the Beautiful Fat Girl," Amy weighed almost five hundred pounds. She would "dance upon a heavy glass stage while she held a long piece of white gauze across her shoulders," which "was supposed to make her represent an angel."[21] Jim was hired to crawl under the stage and change the colored filters on lights that illuminated Amy's dance. In a 1940 letter, Jim recalled passing through Elwood, Indiana, with the troupe. "I was . . . a red-headed pug-nosed freckle-faced kid driving a shetland pony hitched to a wagon on which there was a gilded wooden statue of Robinson Crusoe, and before him kneeling Friday."[22]

The traveling show never stayed more than a week in each town. The now fifteen-year-old Jim learned about carny folk from Amy and her "spieler," expert side-show barker Happy Hi Holler, who "could have talked a ghost into seeing its shadow."[23] When the caravan reached Sioux City, Iowa, Jim was given sixty dollars to procure a week's ration of liquor for Amy, who "would swear terribly at me when the strain of her angel dance was upon her."[24] Falling in with some men who had just left the caravan, he became drunk and was relieved of his money. Fearful of Amy's wrath, he left for Chicago.

Any road-kid passing through the Midwest, and especially central Indiana, would feel the gravitational pull of Chicago. All road-kids "eventually wound up here, the railroad center of America," Tully told a Chicago reporter in 1936.[25] He would return to the city several times during these roving years, making the Windy City his winter headquarters at least twice. He peddled newspapers at the corner of Roosevelt Road and Wabash Avenue. And he haunted Michael "Hinky Dink" Kenna's saloon on South Clark Street, getting the free meal that came with "a schooner of beer." The beer cost a nickel. With it, he would enjoy bread, soup, and sausage (sardines on Friday). Tully would always remember the bar's sawdust floor and the "little trough of water under the brass rail where the hoboes could spit."[26] Tully had especially warm memories of November in Chicago. "When I was a lad," he wrote George Jean Nathan, "it was possible to get three dollars a vote and at that time I helped Hinky Dink and others, often earning twenty-one dollars and more a day in the cause of human rights."[27] And when the spring weather again heated up his wandering spirit, he could easily catch a freight train out of town.

During an early visit to Chicago, he was reunited with Billy Ross and Gabe Sullivan, his buddies from the orphanage. They were trying to bum money on Sixty-third Street when Jim got lucky. He slipped a dime in his pocket and headed for the Loop, where he planned to meet up with Billy and Gabe. Not so lucky, Billy and Gabe were picked up for "plinging," or panhandling, and sentenced to sixty days.[28] The role of stupid, illogical fate—one kid is handed money and another a jail sentence—made a great impression on Jim, and years later he recalled the event and wondered what course his life might have taken had *he* been sent to jail at so young an age.[29]

After Billy was released, on a spring night shortly after sunset, Jim and Billy boarded a mail train just outside the Northwestern station. They were heading for Omaha. They reached DeKalb, where they boarded another train. Almost immediately they were pinched by a railroad detective. The bull intended to take them to Clinton, Iowa, where they'd easily "get the rock pile for a couple o' months."[30] Although handcuffed together, Bill and Jim overpowered the pistol-wielding detective and threw him off the train. Or, as Tully put it in *Beggars of Life*, Billy "kicked the majesty of railroad law in the south as he looked north."[31] Before the train could pull into Clinton, the boys jumped from the train, the handcuffs tearing at their wrists. Finding a rock, they battered off the metal restraints.

They made a formidable duo. Although short, Jim already knew how to throw a punch and make it count. The heavy-set, blond-haired, blue-eyed Bill had a square chin and powerful shoulders. "He had no morals at all," Tully remarked, "and was as irresponsible as the wind. . . . He was quick in movement and daring in resolve."[32]

When the two youthful drifters wandered into a hobo jungle near Clinton, they learned that more trouble was on the way. There were six vags in the camp, and one rover had already heard talk of a railway detective being kicked off a train. Clinton, a hostile town, would be considerably unfriendlier now. Sure enough, the next day the hobo jungle was invaded by two bulls—one of them the detective recently humiliated by the two road-kids. A quick diversion, and the two bulls were overpowered. The lawmen were left handcuffed to a tree, unconscious.

About an hour later, Jim and Billy were on the Number 1, a mail train out of Clinton. They reached Omaha, but not before being put off another train. They drifted for several months, getting as far as California, where they spent the winter at a hobo jungle in Santa Monica. Returning to the Midwest, they got to within thirty miles of Chicago. Bill opted for returning to the city. Jim decided to hop a freight for the wheat country near Davenport, Iowa. Standing on the bumpers between two cars for four or five hours, he finally reached Rock Island, across the Mississippi River from Davenport.

It was here he met a hobo who told of being forced to run a Sapping Day gauntlet in Clinton.[33] It seems the town was up in arms about two railway detectives being left handcuffed to a tree "wit' their own bracelets."[34]

A few days following this encounter, Jim Tully, by now sixteen, wandered perilously close to "the last division." He had taken a job in the camp of a grading outfit. He drove a team of mules for ten hours a day under the hot summer sun. On the fourth day, he tried to get out of bed and failed. Dizzy and feverish, he was sent to a doctor, who suspected typhoid.

With a dollar and fifty cents in his pocket, he hopped a freight for Chicago. "My throat burned and my jaws ached," he recalled. "My head was in a vise, and spikes were being driven through it. . . . The train rattled on through the hot day. . . . I reached for water, and grabbed but empty space."[35] Delirious with fever, he jumped from the train, desperate for water. Had the train not been slowing down for a scheduled stop, he might have been killed.

How long he remained motionless near the tracks is uncertain. Gathering the strength to stagger to a saloon, he gulped down water and felt queasy. He boarded a cattle train that night, and only the kindness of a brakeman kept him from being tossed. Jim was allowed to sleep on a bed of hay. He awoke burning with fever. "My throat ached from thirst," he wrote in *Beggars of Life*, "and my tongue was as dry as a withered leaf. My lips stuck together, and my eyelids burned as though matches were being constantly lit under them."[36]

Leaving the train at the edge of Chicago, Jim was determined to find Bill. Like many paper peddlers, Bill stayed at the Newsboys' Home. Jim had not stayed there during his earlier visits to the city but hoped that Bill would intercede on his behalf. Jim knew "that any inmate of the Home would be given a bed in St. Luke's Hospital and the best medical attention in the city."[37]

Jim, like most vagabonds, was terrified of county hospitals. Even in the orphanage, he had heard the legend of the infamous "Black Bottle." The frightening Black Bottle was said to contain a fast-acting poison. Hobo lore held that doctors and nurses would use the Black Bottle to clear a ward bed occupied by a sick or elderly vagrant. Superstition? Perhaps, but Jim feared that "its root may be planted in fact."[38] His only hope was Bill and the Newsboys' Home. Through parched lips, he described his plight to a bartender who was so moved that he made certain that Jim would be taken to the faded red-brick building at Fourteenth and Wabash, near the shores of Lake Michigan.

"Boys of all sizes romped in the cement yard that fronted the Newsboys' Home," Tully remembered more than twenty years later. "Bill was among the number. . . . Bill ran up the stairs to the Matron of the Home, and quickly pleaded for my entrance."[39] Touched by the boy's story, the silver-haired matron, Josephine G. Post, entered Jim's name on the home register, thus making him eligible for expert medical care. "Ever impulsive," he later wrote, "and unused to the touch of gentleness, I cried in her arms."[40]

A doctor was summoned. The physician followed his examination with an inexact but serious diagnosis: "Typhoid—malaria—advanced. Call the ambulance." Jim was taken to St. Luke's Hospital. From his white bed, he could see the blue waters of Lake Michigan. Although near death several times during the next two days, Tully remembered them as "the very happiest in my life."[41] He was surrounded by nurses who lavished kindness and attention on him. Doctors and interns always had words of encouragement for him. There were no concerns about the next meal. Boys from the home, many bringing fruit, were frequent visitors. The matron treated him like a son.

And, to top it all, there were books and magazines. From his hospital bed he read Rudyard Kipling's *Kim*, Thomas Hardy's *The Mayor of Casterbridge* and *Tess of the D'Urbervilles,* and Emily Brontë's *Wuthering Heights.* It was yet another difficult period when books provided company and comfort. Unlike the orphanage, though, and unlike the lean times in St. Marys when he was bolting down his father's paperback library, these days were viewed in a golden haze. When life got stormy for the adult Tully, he often found himself wishing "for a haven like St. Luke's Hospital."[42] He remained hospitalized for forty-seven days.[43]

Issued new clothes and shoes upon his release, Jim took up residence at the Newsboys' Home. Several weeks later, the matron asked the boys to write compositions for an upcoming visit by a wealthy and influential woman. Jim read his aloud. The gray-haired blue blood told Josephine Post, "There's literary talent displayed here," and asked for the teenager's name. "It was my first literary triumph," Tully commented, but he never heard from the society dame.[44]

He stayed at the Newsboys' Home through the winter of 1902–3, deciding in the warmth of May to again try life as a road-kid. After those long winter months in Chicago, less than two months away from his seventeenth birthday, he discovered something about himself: "I had been cured of typhoid and malaria, but the fever of the wanderlust still burned fiercely in my breast."[45]

The warm weather of 1903 found him on the blind baggage of a mail train. With him was a heavy-set road-kid named Dutch Vander. Jim and Dutch hopped trains until they reached Cincinnati, the city where Jim had spent six years at St. Joseph's Orphan Asylum. He had no desire to see the building. "When a boy leaves an American orphanage," he stated, "he leaves it forever."[46]

Splitting up in downtown Cincinnati, they agreed to meet later on the Kentucky side of the Ohio River and hop the *Fast Flying Virginian* to Washington, D.C.[47] Sliding across the river, Jim waited for Dutch and the train that would roll by at about seven o'clock the next morning. As night fell on his secluded spot in the Kentucky hills, he could see a large white boat making its way downriver. The lanterns in her windows splashed flecks of yellow light across the water.[48]

> Some negroes lolled on boxes in the steerage and chanted an indistinct song, inarticulate dark poets, weary with the labour of the world, sailing back to rest on their wonderful river of dreams. With well-modulated voices, their words glided over the water in a weird and beautiful cadence. Forgetful of the fascinating road of the young hobo, I gave myself up to listening to unknown minstrels, singing to relieve their snarled and wretched lives.... The boat glided onward, and the voices became more indistinct. They at last died away, softly, like a June breeze swaying shamrocks over far-off Irish graves.[49]

Jumping aboard the *Fast Flying Virginian*, Jim and Dutch were determined to cover the several hundred miles to Washington by the next afternoon. It would mean clinging to the train for about twenty-one hours but, as he later reasoned, a "test of endurance is a wonderful thing when the blood flows swiftly and the years are young."[50]

The only thing to gain from such a feat was the right to brag about it. Huddled around a campfire in a hobo jungle, he would be able to boast about an accomplishment as foolish as it was daring. The goal was met, but he and Dutch were arrested in Washington as vagrants. Dutch was philosophical. "Oh, well, let's flop," he said, stretching out on an iron cot. "They may not hang us."[51] The next morning, the cells were unlocked at seven and the prisoners were marched to a breakfast of "wieners, rye bread, and weak coffee." "It was Sunday morning," Tully wrote in *Beggars of Life*, "and, perhaps out of courtesy to President Roosevelt, who believed in the strenuous life, the cell doors were left open so that the derelicts might exchange social gossip."[52] After spending the day in jail, the two road-kids were released and given until nightfall to leave the city. Jim wouldn't always be so lucky.

Hopping trains and begging for food, the two teenagers made their way through Virginia, Maryland, Pennsylvania, New Jersey, New York, Connecticut, and Rhode Island. Dutch was arrested in New Haven and invited to stay for ninety days as a guest of the city. Jim moved on to Manhattan, riding most of the way on the top of a mail car.

He stayed in New York for two weeks then headed west. In Pittsburgh he made his way to the Newsboys' Home. Poking around in their dingy library, he found a copy of a book titled *The Story of an African Farm*. Neither the book nor its author, Olive Schreiner, was known to him, but the book transported the teenager to a place unlike anything he had ever seen. He came to regard Schreiner as "one of the greatest women of the nineteenth century . . . South African dreamer of beautiful dreams . . . a Jane Addams with a genius for writing."[53] He was so taken with the book that he stole it and read it aloud to a yegg traveling with him. Years later in an article about female writers, he ranked Schreiner alongside Jane Austen, the Brontës, and Willa Cather.[54]

From Pennsylvania he drifted on to Missouri, Kentucky, and Illinois. Moving into Tennessee then Arkansas, Jim made the acquaintance of Dublin-born Oklahoma Red, the powerfully built tramp and yegg he would immortalize in *Beggars of Life*. Although ruthless in a fight, Oklahoma Red had a generous nature. He took the considerably shorter Red under his wing, mixing stories of his life with valuable advice. "He gave me all he had and asked nothing in return," Tully explained.[55] Jim watched the brawny veteran hobo die when both of them tried to board a train. Oklahoma Red's foot slipped through the iron rung of a ladder hanging low from a freight car. His upper body was thrown backward, his head crashing on the railroad ties. Pulled in this position for several yards, he was dead before Jim could pull him free from the ladder. His arm had been cut off at the elbow, but death "had ironed his habitual leer away."[56] After mourning for his friend, Jim searched the dead man's pockets and found two dollars and a blue pistol. He sold the gun in Dallas for four dollars. Jim later met many hoboes and crooks who had known Oklahoma Red, yet he told none of them about how the mighty yegg had died. He believed "that Red would not have cared for them to know."[57]

And from Dallas he hoboed his way across Texas. Stranded in Del Rio, Jim was sickened by the sight of his first lynching. He recalled the scene in *Beggars of Life*, where he described how a mob dragged a black prisoner from his courthouse jail cell and burned him to death in the town square. Jim put Del Rio behind him, finally making it all the way to Los Angeles.[58]

The following winter found Jim back at the Newsboys' Home in Chicago. In December of 1903, the *Tribune* chose Jim and three other boys known for their salesmanship and toughness and sent them to nearby Zion City, the Christian utopian community founded by John Alexander Dowie, a charismatic Australian immigrant and healing minister. Dowie hoped that Zion City, modeled after Salt Lake City, would be the first of a number of communities free of the evils of alcohol, tobacco, pork, newspapers, and medicine.[59] The cult's Armageddon came in that most secular of places—a bankruptcy court.[60] Years later Tully recalled that December day.

> We got five dollars and the profits on the papers and carfare and food. We were arrested—and let go in an hour—for the damned town belonged to the receivers that day.... We passed a school house yelling our wares—"All about the big failure—John Alexander Dowie in the hands of receivers." The teachers brought all the children in the front yard and yelled in beautiful rhythm..."Hurrah for John Alexander Dowie—hurrah for John Alexander Dowie" and as we trudged on down the road the refrain took on a great tinge of sadness for me. When we passed old Dowie's house the mighty fanatic sat at the window in ceremonial robes—and I rather felt sorry for the poor old devil.[61]

It was probably in the summer of 1904 when Jim again returned to Cincinnati, this time to work as a busboy at the Gibson Hotel. He and the other boys would labor all week for a few dollars just so they could work the barroom on Saturday night. That was when the whiskey and tips flowed like the nearby Ohio River.

Jim also worked at the Queen City Club. One night a large banquet at the club was hosted by a cardinal, who presented each of the guests with a little red hat autographed by His Eminence. Smelling favorable markups and brisk sales, Jim and the other boys pinched as many of the hats as they could. The next day, when they tried to peddle them, they found that each of the hats bore not only the cardinal's signature but the name of the recipient. If the market for autographed little red hats was thought to be healthy, the market for hot autographed little red hats was nonexistent.[62]

When he wasn't busing tables or trying to make a killing in the commodities market, Jim could be found in bars with names like the Blue Moon or the Silver Moon or a saloon on Fifth Street that served both black and white patrons. It was in such Cincinnati and Chicago saloons that Jim further developed the "gift of gab" he had inherited from Old Hughie. Like his grandfather, the young Irish rover would spin a heartbreaking tale or recite a poem in exchange for drinks. No actor could have had a sterner test of his skills. Certainly a theater packed with hardened New York critics would have been an easier audience than the barflies who found themselves handing over some small part of their drinking money to the redheaded boy with the lyrical tall tales.

In Paddy Croan's Chicago bar, where he met boxer Joe Gans, Jim had ample opportunity to hone his storytelling skills. "I soon became useful to Paddy Croan," he recalled in *Blood on the Moon*.

> I knew how to make drunkards spend money at the bar. I knew, through long training, how to make the tempo fit the occasion. If a man drank to forget trouble, I too, had trouble. If he were hilarious, I fitted his mood. . . .
>
> I knew many poems by heart, and made others up to suit the audience. If the crowd were listless, a catchy tune, a swiftly recited verse, a dramatic tale made them more alert.[63]

The tall, purple-faced Paddy's favorite story was "Ostler Joe," the tragic tale of a man "who bore up bravely under the blow" of being deceived by a woman. "It never failed to get an attentive audience," Tully remembered fondly. "Even the head bartender cried."[64] Paddy Croan himself might well have become the subject of a tragic tale. He was later found beaten to death, the murder weapon his heavy buckthorn cane.

November of 1905 found Jim crouched in an open railroad car behind the locomotive tender, his damp clothes stiffening with the dropping temperature. He hopped off in Adrian, Michigan, about a dozen miles north of the Ohio line. A "harness bull" gave him directions to the livery where his brother Hugh had been working. Hugh was not to be found, but Jim stayed on in Adrian, working on and off at the livery and at the Page Fence Company factory. Two decades later he was recalled in the local paper as "good-natured, carefree and irresponsible." It was further noted that Jim had been fond of one Adrian resident in particular. That person was one William Luck, then manager of the Springbrook Brewery. Luck "found Tully a frequent caller and a staunch admirer of the Springbrook product when drawn in big copper dippers from the cooling vats."[65]

With the entire country open to him, it is difficult to imagine why Tully spent the winter of 1905 traveling along the frigid shores of lakes Erie and Ontario. And although even the hardiest Buffalonian has entertained thoughts of retreating from a Buffalo winter, it is difficult to understand Jim's decision to flee western New York in the manner he chose. In what must surely rank as the most punishing trip of his life, he caught a fast mail train to New York, "riding on the coupling between the tender and the first mail car."[66] When, penniless, stiff with cold, and "covered with coal dust and soot," he jumped off at 125th Street, he was immediately caught and interrogated by railway workers. Astonished, they took up a collection and handed him sixty cents. Anyone who had "held" the fast mail that far deserved a little something for his trouble.[67] "I wanted to wash up," Tully told a reporter in 1922. "I knew you could wash up in any saloon without charge, and I hadn't any trouble finding a saloon."[68] The saloon, alas, had neither hot water nor mirror.

He made his way to Chatham Square and the Newsboys' Home near Forty-fourth Street. Before he could settle in, he was told, he would have to bathe. Only when he saw his sooty face in the mirror did he understand his odd reception. While in New York, he learned the rudiments of boxing, begged for money on the Bowery, and stood with derelicts in the nightly Herald Square bread line waiting for a cup of coffee and a scrap of food from a wagon. He won a bed at the Salvation Army headquarters on the Bowery by testifying with "hypocritical eloquence" during services. He avoided being thrown out of the Duane Street bullion (a dormitory-style flophouse) by winning the job of dishwasher.[69] He did whatever he could to stay warm and fed. "And when work interfered with reading," "he gave up work."[70] Books, as always, were a refuge. "Why, I opened and closed the Peter Cooper Library in New York one whole winter.... It kept me off the streets and made me forget hunger. It gave me an environment I couldn't find elsewhere."[71]

From New York he tramped to Boston before returning to St. Marys. Back home, having learned that his brother Hugh had taken a job in Meridian, Mississippi, he hopped a southbound train. It appears that from

Meridian he made his way west in November 1905, getting as far as Canton before being arrested for vagrancy. He spent thirty-eight days in jail, some of that time in cotton fields, attached to a ball and chain.[72] Jail was the price to be paid for freedom. He'd spent ten days (probably also in 1905) in a Syracuse jail for vagrancy, in addition to his stint in Washington, D.C. And two years later he would be jailed in Cincinnati for fighting three other young men.

Tully said that he spent time in five jails during his six years on the road. His longest incarceration was the four-month sentence he served with another road-kid, nicknamed Blink, in a western county jail. The colorful inmates they met during this stretch populated the book Tully believed was his best, *Shadows of Men*. Brother Jonathon Maloney was an elderly and eloquent medicine man who "spoke of the ancient prophets as though they were personal friends."[73] Nitro Dugan was a feared yegg known for his expertise with dynamite "soup," nitroglycerin. And there was the thin, gray-haired Dippy, a pyromaniac facing a twenty-year stretch for, of course, arson.

Tully had met Blink Thomas at the Chicago Newsboys' Home, probably in 1903.[74] A year younger than his redheaded friend, the handsome, dark-haired Blink was then called Bright Eyes. Bright Eyes, a well-liked, gentle boy, worked in a print shop while Tully sold newspapers and toted luggage for travelers. Some printer's ink infected the boy's left eye, and it was removed. Bright Eyes became Blink. Many years and many roads later, their paths would cross again.

Although he associated with famous yeggs, Jim resisted the many offers to make a career of crime. There was no shortage of willing teachers on the road. He might have given into these temptations were it not for a promise he made to his sister. Having seen the devastating effect of Uncle John Lawler's jail sentence on their mother, Virginia extracted from Jim a solemn vow. "Two things worried her," Tully wrote. "I might get killed as a road kid, or, what seemed worse to her, become a criminal. I promised faithfully to do nothing that would involve me with the law."[75]

When the road became too hard or too dangerous, Jim found other ways to make money. It was during what he called his "second hobo journey through Mississippi," probably in early 1906, that the teen rover decided to take a break from the vagabond life. "Half dazed from loss of sleep," he wrote, "weak from hunger, and irritated by vermin-infested clothes, I resolved to leave the road for a spell."[76] After reaching Louisiana, he took a job with Cameron's World's Greatest Combined Shows. He traveled with the circus for about four months through Texas, Oklahoma, Missouri, Arkansas, Georgia, and Florida. He recalled those days in *Circus Parade*.

Bob Cameron, the circus owner, was tyrannical, cheap, and brutal. Tall, red-haired, and muscular, Cameron "always wore plaids or loud checked clothes. A gold watch chain, with links an inch long, was stretched across his vest. Two immense green elk teeth dangled from it. His hair was long and straggly. He wore a broad-brimmed Stetson hat. He was never without a heavy gold-headed cane. It was loaded with lead at the top. The cane had served as a weapon in many a circus battle."[77] His wife, a greedy crone nicknamed "the Baby Buzzard," weighed about a hundred pounds and looked about ninety years old. She was as mean and petty as Cameron was miserly and ruthless.

The Cameron circus traveled through the South packed into ten railroad cars. Jim did a little bit of everything during his tenure with the colorful outfit. He was hired to help tend the animals, and that remained part of his duties. But he also helped the roustabouts unload equipment and cages. He drove the stakes that secured the ninety-foot "big top" tent. He ran errands for the performers and freaks. He took part in the circus parades through small towns, wearing a long red coat with brass buttons and driving a team of Shetland ponies. His duties, he later claimed, included wrestling a trick mule.[78] After about a month he was making seven dollars a week. His income was periodically boosted by the four half-dollars the Baby Buzzard slipped him for reading to her. "Adventure lurked around every corner then, and life was wild and free," he wrote in *Circus Parade*. "I often went to my canvas bunk with muscles that ached and legs that dragged wearily. But each morning opened on a new world—and many tales were told."[79]

The first circus friend he made was Denna Wyoming, the somber lion tamer. It made no difference to the young man from St. Marys that Wyoming was black. Encountering all types on the road, Jim had learned the foolishness of prejudice. On the subject of race, he was of the same mind as one of his literary idols. Mark Twain wrote in 1898 that he was quite sure he had no race, color, caste, or creed prejudices: "Indeed, I know it. I can stand any society. All that I care to know is that a man is a human being—that is enough for me; he can't be any worse."[80]

While it is not likely that Jim knew those lines from a Twain essay, it is entirely likely he would have endorsed the sentiment with a rueful smile. A social outcast who had known abuse, abandonment, and persecution, Jim was not one to dismiss a society matron or a stew bum on the basis of race, religion, or income (or lack of it). His acceptance of people was almost as keenly developed as his sympathy. "There are so many people who are hated," he told a reporter in 1929. "I suppose nearly everybody hates somebody else. A lot of whites hate the negroes. . . . The Westerners hate New Yorkers, the intelligentsia hate the Babitts. I'm shanty Irish, and there are people who hate us. I've met quite a number of people who don't like New Englanders. When I go to Europe, I'll find more people hating and considering themselves superior to other peoples. Is there, anywhere, a group of people that nobody hates and cherishes prejudices against? Is there somewhere a perfect race?"[81]

More impressed by character than color, Jim also made friends with two other black circus stars: William Jay Dickson, the jumpy elephant trainer known as Goosey, and John Quincy Adams, the guileless former stake driver who found success as Whiteface the clown. Trap drummer Rosebud Bates trusted Jim enough to admit what many suspected: the talented musician was a homosexual. Rosebud's trust was not misplaced. Jim decided the secret was "Rosie's own business" and continued to be his friend.[82]

Others in the troupe included Slug Finnerty, the stoop-shouldered chief spieler, who had lost an eye in a brawl; Lefita, "the favorite dancer of the Sultan"; Alice Devine, the Moss-Haired Girl, who bathed her long locks in a mixture of stale beer, herbs, and wildflowers; and Lila, the four-hundred-pound Strong Woman billed as "the Female Hercules." Before Jim left the circus, Wyoming the lion tamer would be mauled to death by a blind bear in Texas, Lila would commit suicide after being cruelly swindled and jilted by a con artist, and John Quincy would die after being tarred and beaten during a race riot in Florida. Jim, who had tried to hide his friend from the mob, watched John Quincy die. He approached the body, holding the gentle clown's cat, Booker T. Washington. "The white paint on his face was streaked with tar and blood," Tully wrote in *Circus Parade*. "I knelt beside him while Booker T. Washington licked his face."[83]

Not yet twenty-one, Tully had tramped through at least thirty states and Washington, D.C. He had seen a lifetime of death and brutality.

5

The End of the Road

"**D**etermined to get away from the road, I made many futile attempts," Jim would later recall. "The wanderlust is a fever that burns deep into the soul."[1] Several events in 1906 cooled that fever.

He drifted into Cincinnati that summer and discovered an untended covered wagon in an alley near Sixth and Sycamore. He'd bunked on its hard floor for several weeks when another young man also took up residence there. The floor mates were fine at first, but Tully soon found himself unable to discourage the newcomer's sexual advances. The threat of rape lurked around every dark corner of a road-kid's life, and Tully's first instinct was, as always, self-preservation. Tully wrestled with his assailant before getting his hands wrapped around the aggressor's throat. As Tully throttled him, the man began to scream. With a beat cop approaching, Tully released his grip, scrambled to his feet, and disappeared into the night. He made his way to the river and set up camp. Three days later, Tully ran into the young man and two of his friends. In the ensuing fight, Tully kicked the man in the groin but the other two pounded him. Tully's nose was broken, his eyes and face a bloody mess. Someone in the crowd that had gathered yelled a warning that the cops were coming. The three men escaped. Tully, nearly blind, did not and was hauled off to jail. He faced a six-month sentence of hard labor.[2]

At police court the following morning, dreading the worst, he came before Judge William Lueders. He was no longer a boy and had no expectation of mercy because of his age. Lueders, stern by reputation, looked down on the physically and emotionally beaten young man before him and decided to try something different. He encouraged Tully and expressed confidence that he could turn his life around.³ Tully never forgot the mercy of this judge and for the rest of his life would take a strong interest in the welfare of young prisoners, passionately arguing for rehabilitation over punishment.

It is noteworthy that Tully's first response upon his release was *not* to find the first freight train out of town. Instead, he remained in Cincinnati and befriended Dan Sullivan, a porter at St. Xavier's College. Sullivan, who would remember Tully as a friendly fellow, not big, but very muscular, helped him get a job as dishwasher in the school's kitchen. Tully received twenty dollars a month plus his room and board and "worked from early morning until eight at night."⁴ "What I remember best about him is the fact that he used to recite poetry while doing the dishes," Sullivan said. "His performances lightened many an hour of scrubbing and dishwashing for both of us. Tully was here about four months."⁵

Tully recalled the school fondly. "I remember washing all the pots and pans, also kettles, and of scrubbing the floors and halls while at Saint Xavier College. The priests, and, in fact, all there were fine to me. I was never treated better anywhere."⁶ Father Francis J. Finn often visited the kitchen, where he was entertained by Tully's doggerel. In appreciation he gave Tully a copy of Tennyson's poems. The small book became one of Tully's earliest acquisitions in a library that would grow to many thousands of volumes.

But dish washing hardly seemed like a promising career. Searching for the job that would keep him off the road, he hopped a northbound freight. The train stopped in St. Marys. Curious, he decided to look around. "I walked from one end of it to the other several times and met no one whom I knew," he recalled. "Everything looked different."⁷ He had left as a young teenager and returned a young man far older than his years.

The chain factory burned to the ground in July of 1906 and the embers had scarcely cooled before rebuilding commenced.⁸ For six weeks, Jim helped clear away the bricks and debris at a rate of fifteen cents an hour. Having learned to heat links on this site, Jim got an idea. Several chain makers he knew, including his brother Hugh, had gotten jobs at a foundry in Racine, Wisconsin. Late in 1906, with thoughts of eventually joining his brother in Racine, he caught a train headed for Lima.⁹ From there, "via the brake-beams," he rode to Chicago to visit Virginia.¹⁰

He picked up a Chicago newspaper, and the name Josiah Flynt jumped off the page. His thoughts turned to a trip through Michigan during which he had camped in an abandoned house. In a stack of old magazines he found a few copies of *Scribner's* and started leafing through them. He couldn't believe his eyes. There, in a serious magazine, were several articles about hoboes.[11] The author was Josiah Flynt, a hobo turned writer and early muckraker.[12] At last Tully had discovered someone writing about the world he'd come to know.

Now, in Chicago, Tully read in the paper that Flynt was gravely ill and staying in one of the city's more fashionable hotels. Tully resolved to meet his hero but reasoned that proper arrangements would have to be made by letter. And as Flynt was a famous writer, nothing short of a formal typewritten letter would do. Not owning or even having any idea how to operate a typewriter, Tully found a store on State Street where a young saleswoman demonstrated its use. Would she mind typing a letter to a famous man? She would not mind at all and even helped compose the letter when Tully became flustered at finding the proper wording. Letter in hand, Tully made his way to Flynt's hotel but lost his nerve in the ornate lobby. Tully swallowed hard and launched himself in the direction of the desk. He nervously asked the desk clerk for Flynt's room number. The bewildered clerk eyed the bedraggled young man and paused. Sensing that he was about to be turned away, Tully waved the letter, hoping to impress the clerk with the gravity of the request. A few minutes later, he found himself at Flynt's door. Flynt looked up, noticed the young stranger's confusion and red hair, and said, "Come and sit down, Red."[13]

Tully recalled their meeting in a 1922 newspaper article.

> "Been on the road long?" he asked.
> "All my life I've been on the bum, Mr. Flynt."
> "Can the mister stuff, Red. Call me Cigarette. That's my moniker."
> His faded eyes closed as he looked at me, "Orphans' Home or Reform School," he asked.
> "Orphans' Home," I replied. "I got away before they shipped [me] to the Ref."
> "Lucky dog," he said. "A Home's bad enough. Half the young tramps I know come from a Home or Reform School."[14]

They spoke for a long time, with Flynt, his face sunken and his frame withered, pausing to take a drag on a cigarette or compose himself after a spasm of coughing. Flynt continually returned to one point.[15] Tully recalled Flynt's sober words in *Blood on the Moon*. "'Get off the road, kid,' he gasped. 'They're all snakes who crawl over it.'"[16] It was, at least initially, unreceived wisdom.

As their conversation drew to a close, Flynt grew wistful. "Tramping like we've both known it, Red, will soon be a thing of the past."[17] He passed Tully a five-dollar bill and they parted. It might well have been a torch. A few weeks later, two days short of his thirty-eighth birthday, Flynt was dead.[18]

Just as all the necessary factors had come together to lead Tully to the road, now, six years and thousands of miles later, elements were gathering that would end his wandering. He'd been thinking about Judge Lueder's encouragement to make something of his life. Now visions of the dying Josiah Flynt and his crawling snakes came, like Marley's ghost, to haunt his nights.

His sister Virginia and one of her friends would supply the missing piece. Virginia was then working as a waitress and living in a dingy apartment strewn with mattresses for the use of whatever road-weary beggars washed up at her door. The mattresses, like her kitchen, seldom went unused. And if, at month's end, her tip money proved insufficient for her bills, she practiced a brand of economics that "consisted in withholding from the grocer to pay the butcher, and reversing the procedure when necessary."[19] When times grew *really* hard, she did what poor and desperate people have done for centuries—she paid a visit to the local pawnbroker.

It's not known how Virginia Tully met Mary Lygo, as they moved in decidedly different circles. Mary Lygo was a glamorous Follies showgirl who, at age twenty, was recognized in papers from coast to coast as one of the twenty best-dressed women in the country. That they became close friends when their disparate paths did cross is perhaps less surprising, because Mary Lygo, like Virginia Tully, did not grow up among the rich and famous. Born Mary Goodall, she grew up near the giant rubber factories of Akron, Ohio. She disdained books, school, and boys but learned to dance at a young age. With smokestacks belching the smell of curing rubber into the air and adult conversation centering around which factory was cutting wages, young Mary resolved to exchange this gray industrial world for the bright lights of show business. Whatever her merits as a dancer, her physical appearance certainly favored her aspirations. "A brunette with brown eyes and perfect figure, she was," in Jim Tully's words, "as lovely as Barbara LaMarr and as languorous. Her unconscious sensuality, and her extreme shyness made her always seem ready to yield. It was her most deceiving quality. She was, in spite of everything, virtuous."[20]

Leaving Akron, her mother, and her birth name behind at age seventeen, Mary Lygo hitched her star to a carnival company. Her duties consisted mainly of dancing on a small platform outside the tent while a barker touted the wonders to be found within and separated the gaping suckers from their cash. She stuck it out for five weeks, going as far as Chicago before heading to New York. When she returned to Chicago the following season, it was as a Follies girl.

Shortly after her return to Chicago, she fell in love with a millionaire named Gordon Thorne. He was something of a social butterfly and, most significant, already married. If Mary Lygo knew the circumstances of Thorne's marriage, she didn't let them give her pause. Thorne had wagered another playboy $2,000 that he could marry a Chicago heiress in six months. Thorne wooed the unsuspecting woman and collected his winnings at the altar. He then became enamored of Mary Lygo, and she of him. By her account, Thorne promised to wed her as soon as he could legally dispose of the current Mrs. Thorne. After resisting Thorne's blandishments for several months, Lygo finally succumbed and moved into his mansion overlooking Lake Michigan—a mansion Thorne shared with his mother. The older woman deeply resented the presence of an interloper not her current daughter-in-law and, because of her working-class background, not about to become her daughter-in-law. The two women quarreled incessantly.

In short order, Mary Lygo moved out of the mansion and into the West Side apartment of Virginia Tully—and, as wronged women are wont to do, hired a lawyer. She filed two $100,000 lawsuits: one against Thorne for breach of promise, the other against his mother for libel. Both made headlines across the country.[21]

It was while Mary Lygo was living at Virginia Tully's that Jim first fell in love with her. His love for Mary would survive, by fits and starts, for two decades and as many marriages. And while Virginia would quickly come to oppose their romance—indeed, forcefully so—she may have unwittingly broken the ice by inviting the two of them to come look at a certain objet d'art she was thinking of buying from a local shop. It was a three-foot-tall bronze gypsy. "It had a green coat, a red hat which barely sat on its disheveled head, and in its hand a long rod with which it poked a red electric-bulb fire."[22] As they took in the statue, Mary—and, uncharacteristically, Jim—struggled to find just the right words. Mary, as tactfully as possible, asked Virginia if she was *sure* she wanted the statue. With longing in her eyes, Virginia replied that she was *very* sure and, recognizing a heart's desire, Jim and Mary offered to help her carry it home.[23]

If Virginia entertained certain fixed ideas of what her brother should do with his life—get off the road and become a writer—she was less sure of her own place in the world. Hustling for tips in a succession of diners and hash joints was not the way she wanted to spend the rest of her life. Recalling Old Hughie's stories of peddling linen and lace in the antebellum South, she decided to follow in her grandfather's footsteps and, over Mary's objections, open a small linen shop. She found a storefront and, on credit, stocked it. In four months, her entire stock was gone—not sold but given away. Mary observed that Virginia never so much as mentioned the shop's failure.

Like her mother, Virginia's soft heart could, on occasion, turn to stone. To Jim's dismay, his budding romance with Mary Lygo was such an occasion. Citing Mary's pending breach-of-promise case against Thorne, Virginia cautioned her younger brother to be wary of such a woman. Jim's persistence, at least early on, usually managed to wear his sister down and Virginia would retreat, ashamed of her mistrust of her best friend.

One evening, as Jim and Mary strolled through Garfield Park, the subject of their future came up. Everything, Mary argued, depended on Jim getting off the road. Furthermore, Mary argued, nothing would make Virginia happier than seeing her brother settle down. When it became clear that doing something he had been considering doing anyway would please *both* of the women he loved, he conceded.

Mary could hardly wait to get back to the apartment and deliver the news. Virginia was delighted and immediately began phase 2 of the master plan for her younger brother. It was time for Jim to stop all the talk of becoming a writer and begin to write. After all, didn't they have a mutual friend who was writing short stories for magazines? If she could do it, why not Jim? Why shouldn't Virginia see her brother's name in print down at the newsstand? And Jim's first piece of writing should be a letter announcing his intentions to their brother Tom, still prospecting in the Mexican mountains.

That letter had scarcely been mailed when a telegram arrived. Tom had been killed in a construction accident. Virginia dabbed her eyes, reading the awful words over and over. Her worst fears for Jim, a lonely death in a faraway place, had come true for his look-alike brother. His death was not just another blow for Virginia to endure; it was one from which she never fully recovered. While she never spoke of Tom's death to others, Virginia spoke of little else to Mary, who listened for hours, hoping to comfort her grief-stricken friend.[24]

A week later, Jim left to join Hugh in Racine, without good-byes, as was his custom. He was hired at the Racine chain factory as a day laborer at nine dollars a week, of which he pocketed two after expenses.[25] His job "was to stand at a forge in Wisconsin with a huge Dane and twist into rings the straight pieces of iron which he handed me. At the end of six months, the foreman gave me a chance to make chain."[26] He was, by his later account, very lonely in Racine.[27] He poured out his unhappiness in weekly letters to Virginia and Mary. Mary wrote back. His sister did not, but she would happily add a line or two to Mary's letters.[28]

He tried seeing another girl. She was young, attractive, and vibrant and, he thought, she understood him. As he walked her home one snowy night, he was surprised when she left him standing on the porch with nothing more than a curt good night. The wind swirling in off Lake Michigan seemed particularly cold on the walk back to his room, the crunching of the snow under his feet the only other sound. Back in his small room, he stared at the pictures of actresses he had cut from magazines and glued to the lid of a tin trunk.[29] He had been lonely before, but his loneliness in Racine was especially bitter. The Danes at the foundry struck Jim as clannish, and he made but one friend in Racine—Hugh's black-and-white fox terrier, Mac. Jim took the dog on long Sunday walks along Lake Michigan, returning at night to his small room. Exhausted, Jim would collapse into bed while Mac would settle into an old coat in the corner. Jim would awake Monday morning to find the dog in bed with him.[30]

In the spring of 1907, Mary came to Racine for a visit. Mary was lovelier than ever—a fact, Jim later noted with some pride, not lost on his neighbors. They walked along the shore of Lake Michigan with Mac scampering ahead, clearing the way of gulls. Jim would never forget her eyes, which sparkled like the sun-flecked water that lapped at their feet. They walked, pausing occasionally to retrieve a shell and examine it in the sunlight.

When it seemed to Jim as if the heady, sublimely perfect intoxication of young love might last forever, Mary spoke. How, she wondered, could she ever leave this? *Leave?* Jim was jolted back to reality. Why, he asked Mary, did she have to leave? Why must they ever be apart? She looked into his eyes and said, "This is all we'll ever have."[31] She pulled him close and held him tight. Jim saw the sun slip behind a cloud, heard the dog barking, the water slapping the shore, gulls crying, and a distant train whistle. It was as if he was watching himself with a young woman, her arms wrapped around him.

At last Mary turned the conversation to Jim's writing. Jim, still numb, mentioned that he'd been working on a story. She pressed him for details, and he spoke of a young road-kid who, on a bitterly cold night, was taken from a train by an old man. The old man took the boy to his home, where his wife had prepared dinner. They ate and afterward, as the kindly couple and the young boy sat in the living room, the boy noticed a picture on the wall. The boy recognized the picture as that of another road-kid and spoke his name. "Yes," the old woman half-smiled. "He was our son."

Mary praised the story, noting that it sounded as if it had actually happened. "It did," Jim replied, telling her when and where. As she begged him to keep on writing, a breeze caressed her hair. As she brushed a wisp of hair out of her face, Jim remarked that he had never seen her more beautiful. She let the remark pass but returned to Jim's writing: "There's something to live for."

The couple spent the next few days together, much of that time in the public library. Mary found a magazine with a picture of "the brilliant tramp writer" Jack London and brought it to the table where Jim was seated. He looked at it for a long time. "I'll get there someday," he remarked a little too loudly, drawing a glare from the gray-haired librarian.[32]

Mary left the following day, and loneliness again pressed in on him. But he continued to write. The days passed—no longer the solitary, adventurous days of the road, but the gray days of a working man. The whistle that called him came from the factory, not the train.

At last Tully had found work that would keep him off the road, provide a warm place to sleep, and keep food on the table. There was, however, a price to pay for such security. There was no room in this workingman's world for literary endeavors, and the dream of becoming a writer wilted under the blast of the forge's intense heat. "It was my only chance to get away from the road," he recalled. Looking over the first twenty years of his life, Tully could say he was "proud of but one achievement—the unyielding determination with which I left the way of the vagabond."[33]

What had started as a grand adventure to a fourteen-year-old boy had turned into a bitter struggle for a young man. There was no glamorizing what he had found: "I lived in many a brothel where the dregs of life found shelter. I fraternized with human wrecks whose hands shook as if with palsy, with weaklings who cringed and whined at life, with degenerates and perverts, greasy and lousy, with dope fiends who would shoot needles of water into their arms to relieve the wild aching."[34]

Still, many years later, he was not unmindful of what his six years as a vagabond meant to his literary personality. Perhaps the hardships of the road "gave me the courage to endure the keener mental tests that met me at the yearly stations ahead, when I learned to write without knowing the simplest rules of punctuation. Indeed, the endurance learned on the road abided with me on many a sixteen-hour day during which I fumbled at a typewriter with the knuckle-cracked hands of the hobo and the pugilist."[35] The road and the nation's public libraries were links in the chain that would lead him to write, but not yet twenty-one, the aspiring chain maker recognized that he wasn't ready to support himself with a typewriter.

One Saturday, a payday, Jim approached Hugh and announced he was quitting. Hugh, who had been a jockey for a while prior to working in the factory, knew firsthand how factory life could grind dreams to dust. Like his father, Hugh also recognized that Jim was, at heart, a wild Lawler and unsuited to factory life. With resignation in his voice, Hugh looked at the brother he had long ago rescued from the orphanage and said, "Okeh kid ... get the hell out. You ain't got nothing to lose but your chains."[36]

Jim instructed his brother to collect his remaining pay and keep it to settle an outstanding debt. When, Hugh asked, did Jim think he would leave? Jim, with his aversion to good-byes, simply responded that when he didn't show up for work, it meant he was gone. With twenty dollars in his pocket, he headed back to Chicago, thinking of Hugh and his dog all the way.[37]

He arrived at Virginia's to learn that Mary had left the night before. Virginia, her own heart having been broken countless times, did her best to comfort Jim. She had spoken to Mary about Jim. Mary had agreed it was best that they go their separate ways. Mary believed that she was in love with Jim but, Virginia now cautioned her brother, Mary had been convinced she loved Thorne, a man she was now facing in court. Still, Jim countered, Hugh had just told him he'd be a fool to walk away from Mary. Virginia paused, not fully believing that Hugh would give his younger brother such unsound advice. Finally, Virginia embraced her brother and told him that Hugh must have forgotten that Jim was a Lawler. Hugh, a Tully to Virginia's way of thinking, could walk away from a Mary Lygo–like disaster. Jim, a wild, untamed Lawler, could not. Indeed, hadn't Mary voiced her doubts about the combination of two such untamed hearts? Furthermore, Virginia wondered aloud, wasn't Mary a woman of means with more than five hundred dollars a week to spend? The sum staggered the near-penniless Jim into silence. He was, Virginia continued, the embodiment of her own hopes and dreams. She couldn't lose that. Not to Mary, not to anything.[38]

Jim, his head swimming from his sister's barrage, retreated by train to Rochester, Indiana. He was so distraught, he paid his fare. He then wandered the railroad yards, finally jumping an eastbound freight. As he rolled by the farms and small towns of the Midwest, he fished out a book that Virginia had purchased at a secondhand bookstore and insisted he read. The author, she explained, was an adult before he was taught to read and write by a compassionate young woman. And, Virginia continued, if Owen Kildare could write *My Mamie Rose,* then Jim, who had learned to read and write as a child, could write a book too. She was sure of it. And by the time Jim had reached the end of the book, where the young woman dies and the author's book becomes a success, Jim was sure of it as well.[39]

His plan in the spring of 1907, despite his unhappiness in Racine, was to land a job as a full-fledged chain maker. To this end, he jumped off the train in Columbus, Ohio, and found work at the Hayden-Corbett chain works. After a few months at the Columbus shop, he'd achieved an important goal: a union card. When the late spring heat made working in the factory unbearable, he cut back his hours, spending more time in the dusky cool of saloons, at the library near an open window, or under the shade of trees on the grounds of the insane asylum. A photo of Mac arrived in the mail, sent by the Polish laborer who had adopted him from Hugh. Jim held on to it for a few days before destroying it, unable to endure the painful memories of Wisconsin it evoked.

Although Jim was not nearly as lonely in Columbus as he'd been in Racine, he decided to move on and one afternoon jumped a freight train.[40] This time he was bound for a chain works near Akron in northeastern Ohio where another brother, Charlie, had found work after leaving the Indiana farmer. "I arrived in Kent," he wrote, "one early June morning. It is situated on the banks of the Cuyahoga River. A fall of thirty feet in the river could be seen from the depot, from which, a mile away, could be heard the familiar roar of the chain shop. Down a street of symmetrical hard maple trees I walked toward the factory."[41]

6

The Fire and the Ring

Jim Tully's travels across the United States in the first years of the twentieth century took him through dozens of cities, hundreds of towns, countless jerkwaters and whistle-stops. After all that, as Jim walked the streets of Kent, he must have quickly realized that if he hadn't found his way home, he'd found a place that sure looked a lot like home. Indeed, despite the two hundred miles that separated the flatlands of St. Marys and the gently rolling hills of Kent, the two towns hardly could have been more alike.

With a population of more than 4,000, Kent was roughly the same size as St. Marys.[1] Kent, too, was bisected by a river, the Cuyahoga. Kent also had once been a canal town; the Pennsylvania-Ohio ran alongside the river. And, as in St. Marys, the spread of railroad tracks in the middle of the nineteenth century had choked off the canal's business.[2] Of particular interest to Tully, Kent, like St. Marys, had a large chain works. Perhaps in Jim's mind Kent was as close as one could get to St. Marys without being in St. Marys. As he wrote in *Blood on the Moon*, when his travels took him near St. Marys, "My one resolve was not to go near that place."[3] Kent was familiar, but without the ghosts and painful memories of his hometown.

The Kent that Tully found in June 1907 was only beginning to join the twentieth century. Parts of Main and Water streets in the downtown area had been paved, and a few other city streets laid with gravel, but most of the streets in the city, and 80 percent of the county roads, were mud. In good weather, an automobile trip to Cleveland, some thirty-odd miles northwest, took about three hours. While some basic utilities, such as water, electricity, and telephone, were more or less established, others, like natural gas and sewers, were nonexistent.⁴ The sewage system, if it may be called that, consisted of outhouses and "open ditches into which evil-smelling refuse drained."⁵ Stagnant water filled the old canal.⁶ And with more than thirty saloons to serve the tough railroad and factory workers, Kent was anything but a Norman Rockwell painting of an American small town.⁷

Yet there was much reason for optimism. Civic pride still swelled at mention of the library, donated by Andrew Carnegie and opened in 1903. And a 1906 moving picture show at the Opera House proved so popular that three movie theaters had opened their doors by late the following year.⁸ Downtown seemed prosperous, dotted with dry goods, hardware, clothing, drug, and furniture stores as well as banks, grocers, jewelers, photographers, and other merchants.⁹

A shopper strolling through downtown could not help being reminded of two important pillars of the town's economy. Many of the trains rumbling by the Main Street area were bound for the southside Erie Railroad repair shops or the roundhouse at Breakneck Yards north of downtown. Together they employed several hundred men.¹⁰ Nor could a window shopper have missed the towering grain elevator at the Williams Brothers flour mill, visible from many downtown vantage points.¹¹ But perhaps no business elicited more enthusiasm in the growing town than the Seneca Chain Company. Founded in 1900, the chain works had, by the time of Tully's arrival in 1907, grown to do an annual business of more than $300,000. With about four hundred union employees, Seneca's $120,000 payroll represented a significant chunk of the Kent economy.¹²

From downtown Tully set off for the chain works, walking west on Main Street. He started across the town's stone bridge, and there, across the river, he spotted it. "I had seen the library on leaving the freight. It over-looked a water-fall in the Cuyahoga River, along which the railroad ran. I passed it on the way to the chain factory, and immediately had the feeling that I would like the town."¹³ Tully must have happily noted the words "Free to the People" chiseled across the front of the Carnegie library. When in a new town, he always made a point of locating the library. In a library he could always be safe from the police, forget his hunger, warm up, read of worlds he had never known, and discuss books and ideas with other readers. On the road, he'd heard Andrew Carnegie cursed: "You can't eat his damned libraries." Tully disagreed. Books "were more to me than food—my very life—my rope to the shore in the surging waters."¹⁴

Passing in front of the brick library, along West Main Street, lay the tracks of an interurban.¹⁵ Tully followed the tracks up the street, passing through a residential neighborhood. The familiar roar of the furnace grew louder. At last he saw a pine building, one hundred feet long and three hundred feet deep, covered with corrugated zinc, the glow of the furnace fires plainly visible from a patch of woods one hundred feet away. Alongside ran the tracks of the Wheeling and Lake Erie Railway.¹⁶

As Jim walked into the factory, he was immediately recognized by chain makers he had worked with in other towns. "Chainmakers," he later wrote, "are the gypsies of manual labor. It is unusual to find one who has not worked in a half-dozen states."¹⁷ Yelling over the roar, he asked to see the foreman and was pointed to a large, muscular Irishman with jet-black hair. Jack Bracken, who had limped off the pitching mound of the 1901 Cleveland Blues (the American League forerunner of the Indians) with a bad ankle and a 4–8 record, directed him to an office.¹⁸ Tully recalled their meeting: "I had heard of him. The term 'mister' is not known in the chain world. . . . I said, 'I've been seven years hoboing around the country, Jack, and eight months in Racine among a lot of clannish Danes. I've only worked a fire two months, but I worked a long time in Saint Marys as a kid. I want to get away from the road.'"¹⁹

Bracken started Tully with three-eighths log chain, and because he could not find a link heater, Tully heated the links himself and made the chain. In the summer heat, his sweat streaked his clothing with salt and rotted his shoes. His hard work did not go unnoticed. It wasn't long before Bracken promoted Tully to a better grade of chain, a grade beyond Tully's experience. When Tully's chain failed to pass inspection, Bracken returned him to the less demanding grade with the promise that as long as Jim kept trying, he would work with him to improve.²⁰

Chain makers, Tully maintained, like their brethren steelworkers, believed strongly in the restorative powers of beer. At the end of a hot day's work, a man could wander back downtown to Gibson & Otts, at least until the dry vote carried the county in 1908.²¹ While a thirsty and discreet fellow could still find a drink at the little restaurant,²² Tully and the other chain makers would usually climb aboard one of the electric trolley cars that ran along West Main Street and ride across the county line to "wet" Cuyahoga Falls, disembarking at Jackman's saloon.²³ There, the men could spend the evening getting drunk, talking, and, not infrequently, fighting. "It was," Tully claimed in *Blood on the Moon*, "our club."²⁴ As one Kent historian wrote, "The last trolley car coming from the Falls on Saturday nights usually carried a number of men who had imbibed unwisely, or were in belligerent moods and some lively times resulted. Often the motorman had to come to the conductor's assistance with a controller handle in his hand."[25] Tully was no stranger to such "lively times." And while Kent State University alumni may regard the keg party as a fairly recent innovation in the town's rich cultural history, in fact the tradition predates the university and goes back at least as far as the Taft administration, when Tully was busy collecting keg money from other working men.[26]

Tully, who had written much hobo doggerel during his years on the road, was now writing regularly in Kent. After a day of handling a heavy pair of tongs and swinging a large hammer, Tully often returned to his dreary boardinghouse, lit a kerosene lamp, picked up a pencil stub, and scratched out poetry late into the night. Jim's brother Charlie had also moved to Kent to work at the Seneca factory and, having been elected secretary of the chain-makers' union, maintained a journal for the rank and file. Much of this writing fell to Jim. His hands, scorched from the forge's fire, stiffened and cramped over the course of the night. Not all nights were productive. His attempts at prose, often hours at a sitting, produced nothing of value.

Charlie arranged for Jim to take a room in the much more pleasant boardinghouse where he stayed. Located on West Main Street, just a few blocks from the chain factory, the green-and-white gabled house was home to a half-dozen of the better chain makers and was run by the wife of a night-shift mechanic at the Erie Railroad roundhouse. Never having learned to dance, swim, shoot pool, or play cards, Jim mostly kept to himself. He read or helped the landlady's children with their schoolwork, even writing a composition for the oldest daughter. He took great satisfaction when it earned her the praise of her high school teacher. Family life suited him and he appreciated that it kept him out of the saloons, where he and his modest paycheck parted company much too quickly.

At a time when an evening's entertainment often meant curling up with a book, Jim enjoyed selecting books from the Kent library for his landlady's family and the other boarders to read.[27] On the evenings when he wandered into the library, he could usually be counted on to pull books and magazines off the shelves and pore over his selections until closing. And like the bartender who comes to know his customers by their preferred beverage, the young librarian knew her customers by their taste in books. The redheaded stranger's literary tastes were decidedly catholic, but she noted a distinct preference for Jack London. Jim always had a genuine affection for librarians, as they were a reliable source of two commodities lacking on the road: compassion and books.[28]

Her name was Nellie Dingley. She had an olive complexion, black hair, dark eyes, and a figure that not infrequently diverted Jim's gaze from the printed page. She was single and twenty-six years old and had grown up in Painesville, Ohio, in the care of a wealthy grandmother. She'd attended exclusive schools and, upon completing her education, had to decide what to do with her life. In 1903, she impressed the Kent library board with two important qualifications. She knew and loved books and, given her independent means, she would require little in the way of a salary. She was hired as the new library's first librarian.[29]

Their talk, not surprisingly, was bookish at first, but each came to learn things about the other. She learned that he, too, was an outsider, having moved to Kent from elsewhere in Ohio. He also was single, albeit five years her junior. He was, despite his interest in books, essentially unschooled and decidedly working class. Indeed, he had only recently been a drifter and was now working up the street at the chain factory.[30]

Jim concluded that Nellie was a snob. She regarded him as a roughneck. Contempt, at least within the confines of a small town, breeds familiarity. As they warmed to each other over the coming months, Nellie Dingley, normally reserved and private, found herself telling Jim Tully things she had never told anyone in Kent. She spoke of living with her reclusive grandmother on a stretch of high ground along the Lake Erie shore and how she would watch winter squalls roar across the water. On calm summer days, she would take a few books to a large rock at the water's edge and spend the day reading, watching boats glide across the water, and daydreaming.[31]

For his part, Jim overcame his shyness and allowed that his great desire was to write. While it was a dream he had not dared mention to his fellow chain workers, Nellie was different. His dream would be safe with her. It was, to his delight, not just safe but welcome. Her interest was sincere and enthusiastic and she even made the bold assertion that Jim might someday write like Jack London. She was so supportive that he worked up the courage to show her a poem about John Keats he had been working on. She read it carefully and suggested an improvement to one of the lines.[32] She even suggested the title, "Out to Old Lake Brady," for another poem that would eventually find its way onto a local postcard.[33]

Virginia Tully's confidence in Jim's plan to become a writer may, in large part, be written off as the love of a doting sister for a younger brother.[34] The source of Nellie's enthusiasm is less clear. She must have been struck by the sheer implausibility of this unlettered—many would say crude—nomad turned chain worker becoming a writer. Still, she rallied to the idea, however preposterous. Perhaps she was simply coming to the aid of another outsider, for Nellie too was a loner. Although she was highly regarded by the library board, she remained aloof from the townspeople and had no friends her own age.[35] Aware of her small library salary but unaware of her independent means, town gossips, Tully wrote, "attributed her fine clothes to men who paid."[36] Nellie, like Jim, found sanctuary in the library.

With a push from Nellie, Jim managed to get himself hired as a reporter at the *Akron Press*.[37] It was a job for which he was ill prepared and he was let go after two weeks. Reporters, like chain makers, Jim was happy to learn, also believed in the restorative powers of drink. At an alcoholic session with another *Press* reporter, Tully looked back over his brief career in journalism. Given Jim's years on the road, the other young reporter wondered, why not write a few articles on hoboes for their editor? Jim felt such an idea couldn't miss and wasted no time in presenting it to his former editor. It missed. His friend at the *Press* then suggested he try the competing Akron paper, the *Beacon Journal*. He further counseled that Jim not tell the *Beacon* that he'd been fired from the *Press*. To Jim's surprise, he was hired at twelve dollars a week. This time he lasted almost five weeks before being fired. The *Beacon Journal* editor softened the blow by pointing out that many men fail in one area only to distinguish themselves in another.[38] Tully returned to Kent to face some hard questions about his life.[39]

Having watched his father's spirit slowly crushed by a life of long, hard, backbreaking work, his sturdiness and stoicism gradually replaced by despair and alcoholism, Tully realized that he was sinking into the same trap. He was done with the road and, at least temporarily, writing. Having little formal education and being the son of Irish immigrant parents didn't afford him the option of working in Daddy's firm or marrying the banker's daughter and being installed a vice president. Instead, he chose a path favored by immigrants and drifters. He would put on boxing gloves and enter the ring.

Tully's boxing training amounted to little more than sparring in a gym. But like most road-kids, he had learned to depend on his wits and, failing that, his fists. As he later recalled, writing of himself in the third person,

"Environment seemed bound to make him a pugilist. He fought so many brakemen, yeggs, and railroad detectives (he lumps them altogether) that he subconsciously became a trained fighter. Drinking rotgut whiskey, he battled galore in box cars and saloons. He learned the elemental lesson of the survival of the fittest. For in tramp life the struggle is primal and the weak are used as door mats while the strong are respected."[40]

A plan took shape. He'd heard of a boxer named Chicago Jack Tierney, who had opened for business in Lima, Ohio, about twenty miles from St. Marys. He was beating all challengers. As a St. Marys boy, Tully would have no trouble convincing the promoter that he could boost the gate in a match with Tierney. The problem would be convincing the promoter that he could survive the first round. The solution, courtesy of a pal who worked as a printer for a local weekly, came in the form of a manufactured newspaper clipping listing his many ring triumphs. The deception worked and Tully was booked for ten rounds with Chicago Jack Tierney.[41]

He next paid a visit to the tailor's shop at 140 North Water Street, just a few blocks from the Seneca chain works, to be measured for a new suit.[42] John Evans, a Welsh immigrant in his early sixties, a Mason, and one of Kent's most respected citizens, agreed to fit him.[43] Like his last Evans suit, it would go on the tab, five dollars down and five a month. Evans, whose own children were about the same age as Tully, had taken an interest in the young redheaded chain worker, and Tully clearly looked up to the older man. Indeed, Jim was a frequent visitor to his shop. He'd spend hours thumbing through fashion books and watching Evans in his thick glasses as he sat cross-legged at his bench. He'd observe the tailor meticulously working his needle and thread, sometimes lifting his gaze to watch the trains coming and going at the station.[44] It was not lost on Jim how different he was from Evans and his usual clientele of businessmen and professionals. Many Kent businessmen, such as Emmet Kline, who ran the grocery downtown, regarded Tully as a "big talker" and dismissed him as the sort of time waster whom small-town merchants dread seeing walk in the door.[45] But if Evans heard one of his respectable friends comment on his disrespectable friend, he would, without fail and with a touch of Wales in his voice, reply, "Chimmy's all right."[46]

So it was with some pride that, as Evans measured Tully with his tape, Tully announced that he was going to be a boxer.[47] Evans couldn't believe his ears. "I'm getting a hundred dollars down in Lima," Jim told Evans, "if the fight goes the limit it'll be only a half hour's work."[48] The tailor stepped back, put his hand still holding the tape to his chin, and considered the thing. Respectable men might *watch* boxers, but they did not *become* boxers. Were it his own son, a bucket of cold water would have been in order, but he was not in the habit of telling other men, even young men, how to order their affairs. "Well," he finally said, "you know best."[49] It was the same response Jim had received from his brother Charlie.[50]

The lack of enthusiasm was a blow. Tully chose the material for the suit, agreed to pick it up in a week, and left, the words "You know best" echoing in his head. On the train bound for Lima in December 1908, Tully stared glumly out the window in a vain effort to silence those words.[51] Evans just didn't understand. But thoughts of Mary Lygo pushed Evans aside.[52] His mood, which often followed the weather, darkened. Snow swirled around the cattle in the fields. They seemed forlorn. He watched for birds and saw none. Only the blast of the engine's whistle cut through his thoughts.[53] He knew an ex-boxer from St. Marys named Joe Strade who ran a saloon in Lima. He went there from the train station. He had scarcely gotten in the door when he saw his name, along with Tierney's, on a placard advertising their fight. Joe looked up and greeted Tully, mentioning the upcoming bout. Tully somewhat sheepishly acknowledged his newfound status as prizefighter then came quickly to the point of his visit: he wanted a scouting report on Tierney. While Tierney was good and fast, the old boxer declared, Jim could beat him. As he had presumably never seen Jim box, Joe's confidence in Tully might have been a bit hard to justify, but Tully welcomed it just the same. He also welcomed Joe's offer to train him and work his corner.

Strade sent for a welterweight pal of his by the name of Happy Davis, who was to fight on the same card.[54] Davis arrived, prematurely bald, leather skinned, and hawk faced with a nose that had stopped many a glove. The three men headed up the steps to a small gym above the saloon. Tully, twenty-two years old and weighing 122 pounds, reasoned that if he could hold his own for half an hour with Davis, who was twenty pounds heavier, he should be able to handle Tierney. Tully and Davis put on boxing trunks and gloves and climbed between the ropes. Joe held a watch. Davis proved to be a "vicious hitter." But after fifty-one minutes, when Joe called "time," Jim realized he was neither hurt nor winded. He began to share Joe's confidence.

Joe instructed Happy to get Jim a room. The two men changed clothes and set off for a hotel. They stopped along the way in a poolroom where, Davis explained, Tierney could usually be found loafing and entertaining the pool-hall cowboys. He wanted Jim to meet his adversary. Davis introduced the two men. Tierney asked Tully about his health. He would, after all, hate to beat a sick man.[55]

Tully recalled the advice he'd been given by the great lightweight champion Joe Gans, whom he'd met on the road. While they worked out together at a gym, the black legend had advised Tully: "Don't pay any attention to the fellow you fight—just act like he's not in the world."[56] It proved difficult advice for a rookie to follow. Whatever confidence Tully had walking into the poolroom was gone when he walked out. He spent the afternoon in his hotel room trying to nap and, failing that, shadowboxing in front of the mirror. He ticked off points in his favor: brawls and fights on the road had toughened him, taught him not only how to take a punch but how to jab quickly, move his feet, and punch hard. He'd also learned that he was not a bleeder; working with hot chain and swinging a hammer had left him in great physical shape; somehow he'd never taken to tobacco, so his wind was excellent; he'd endured everything the heavier Davis had thrown at him. His confidence began to return.

The knock at his door at four o'clock was Davis. It was time. As the men walked to the weigh-in, Davis, a veteran of the Philadelphia leather wars, then considered among the toughest in the country, coached his young charge. If, Davis cautioned, Tierney came out of the opening gong swinging, it was crucial that Tully not allow him to get his feet set and slug it out. If Tully could keep moving and punching, he could outbox Tierney.

The men arrived at their locker room and changed clothes, and Davis left for his bout. A short time later, Tully heard the crowd roar, and Davis walked back into the locker room. In the hall outside the doorway, Tully saw men carrying Davis's opponent. In the second round, Davis related, he had thrown a left at his opponent's chest with such force that what looked like the man's heart was popping out of his mouth. It turned out to be his tongue, but one look at the man's eyes told Davis he had scored the knockout.[57]

Tully had scarcely absorbed this when a voice from the hallway announced that the time had come. He followed Davis and Strade out the door. The trio trailed Tierney into the low-ceilinged hall and toward the ring. As Tully climbed through the ropes, loud cheers cut through the smoke-filled air. Tully looked out to the crowd and spotted a large knot of fans from St. Marys, many of whom he had known as boys from the chain factory. They saw not the boy they remembered but a sawed-off stub of a man with a pile of unruly brick-red hair.[58]

The gong sounded and Tierney was instantly across the ring, knocking Tully back with a fusillade of blows. Tully instantly suspected he was outgunned. Fear quickly trumped strategy. It was a fight for survival and his only hope was to slash back, blow for blow, just as the black boxer Eddie Simms had done in a fight with Tierney three weeks before. Perhaps a furious assault could overwhelm Tierney. Tully's confidence in this plan of attack was quickly shaken when he further recalled that Tierney put Simms, undefeated to that point, down in five rounds. Still, there was no other choice. He sprang at Tierney, throwing everything he had at Tierney's midsection in an attempt to push Tierney back to the center of the ring. They clinched. He felt Tierney's muscles tighten as he tried to ride Tully into the ropes. Tully pushed back, and as Tierney gave ground, Tully realized he was the stronger man. They separated and resumed the fight. After one furious exchange, Tully recalled, the silence of the awestruck crowd was palpable. Tierney, however, was seldom silent, trying to lull Tully with admonishments to "go easy" or grunting and falling against the ropes with the hope of catching Tully unawares. They fought on.[59] Tully described the action in *Blood on the Moon*.

> I missed a right that whizzed by the spot where Tierney's head had been a second before. He worked in close, and threw blows upward. I heard Tierney grunt. It gave me a cue. I tried to knock his heart out of his breast.
> He broke ground.
> I pounded his heart....
> For the next four rounds we volleyed rights and lefts to heads and bodies. I staggered from an over hand right and rattled the teeth in Tierney's jaw in return. I tried to get under the eaves. Tierney was wise. His rigid arm met my attack. Our gloves were now blood and water soaked. My kidneys ached with pain.[60]

From the first round, Tully believed he was winning, so he and his corner were surprised when the gong sounded to end the tenth and the referee called it a draw. Davis consoled Tully with the news that he was the first not to be beaten by Tierney. He was further consoled by the *Cincinnati Enquirer* report that awarded him the fight, while a Cleveland reporter "called it the best bout he had ever seen in Lima."[61]

Tully suddenly found himself a leading featherweight on the Ohio boxing circuit.[62] The ring, he later maintained, was the only place where he could forget all his troubles. Tully might have appeared boisterous and carefree, but the backhanded assurance "You know best" continued to nag. Although he aspired to something beyond the ring, he quickly found himself addicted to the easy money of prizefighting. Rather than wean himself off boxing money, he weaned himself off a chain factory paycheck.

Quitting the factory relieved him of the obligations of a schedule. In the past, he might have followed the wind out of town. In Kent, the wind took him no farther than a local pool hall, where his status as a rising boxer made him a celebrity to the small-town sporting men, idlers, and hustlers who maintained regular hours there. He was, like his father, not given to moral judgments. Yet he found the "cheap shallow minds, the low, and yet less honorable approach to life," disturbing.[63]

Tully found another Kent boxer, Web "Spider" Kelly, to serve as a trainer. He started lining up bouts around the state. When charged with whooping up the fight but constrained by Tully's meager record, a reporter noted that Tully was "a clever fellow and has done lots of good work in the ring. He should prove a worthy opponent for the Akron boxer."[64] The "Akron boxer" was Eddie Conway, and the two fought six rounds to a draw at Akron's Sawyerwood Athletic Club on February 4, 1909.[65] With Kelly fighting on the same card, a large contingent of fans from Kent packed the hall. "Conway," the *Kent Courier* reported, "expected a walkaway, but Tully surprised him and made good with the crowd."[66]

Also on the card that night was another Irish American featherweight, a twenty-year-old from Cleveland named Johnny Kilbane. The possibility of a Tully-Kilbane match was discussed in the spring of 1909, with Tully going so far as to offer a winner-take-all purse, but Kilbane declined to schedule Tully before July.[67] While the two never fought, they became lifelong friends and traveled together when sharing cards around the state. Had such a fight come off, win or lose, it almost certainly would have been Tully's high-water mark in the ring.[68] Kilbane, already the best of his class in the state, would reign as featherweight champion from 1912 until 1923. He was eventually enshrined in boxing's hall of fame.[69]

While A. J. Liebling famously called it "the sweet science," in more prosaic terms, the very act of stepping into a boxing ring at the risk of severe injury and even death is a mark of economic desperation. And no boxer is more desperate than one who throws a fight in front of his hometown fans. The fight that Tully lost in St. Marys for "business reasons," as he recalled years later, was a wild affair. The bout was organized by Tully and a once-great boxer named Artie Simms. Tully and Simms bet all their money on another local boxer, with the plan that Tully would stay even for a few rounds before finally taking a dive. Early in the first round, it became apparent to Tully that he would have to work hard to earn his easy money. His opponent, to Jim's surprise, was an awkward, frightened rookie. To keep up appearances, Jim worked in close for a few rounds but, sensing the restlessness of the crowd, shot a glancing blow at the greenhorn's jaw. Jim watched in horror as his opponent sank to the canvas. Simms, who was working the greenhorn's corner, rushed in at the six-count and dragged his man back to his corner. Jim was forced to carry his wobbly opponent until the greenhorn was able to muster a punch strong enough to make a knockout seem feasible. The loss in St. Marys saddened Jim's father but, no stranger to loss himself, he said simply, "It's all right Jim, I understand."[70]

After a disastrous fight at the Cleveland Athletic Club, most likely in 1909, in which Tully received a one-round beating at the hands of "Young" Tommy McGlynn of Buffalo, Tully approached Henry P. Edwards, sports editor of the *Cleveland Plain Dealer*. Their conversation about boxing took an unexpected turn when Tully casually mentioned that he was writing a book. If this news surprised the veteran newspaperman, he managed not to show it. Edwards regarded the young boxer for a moment and tactfully suggested that he start with something shorter. Tully recalled the exchange.

"I don't know anything short," was my reply.

Edwards stood up. "Jimmy," he said, "don't take last night's beating to heart. You may never be the featherweight champion, but you'll be heard from."

Edwards would have been no more surprised had I struck him on the jaw. "Sure, Mr. Edwards, I know that."[71]

Typing with two fingers on an old, bulky Oliver, Tully's progress on his first book was halting and tentative. His reservoir of youthful confidence would be tapped but never drained, even though it would take more than a dozen years to see his book in print.[72]

In the late spring of 1909, Tully was in Findlay, Ohio, getting in shape for a June 2 main bout at an Eagles convention in Lima. As part of his training, Tully was sparring with a local fighter named Cloyce Yeager, who was to be Kilbane's opponent for a May 31 fight in Findlay.[73] Sharing the card with Kilbane and Yeager that night in Findlay was a boxer named "Young"

Terry McGovern (nicknamed so as to distinguish him from the recently retired "Terrible" Terry McGovern).[74] When McGovern's opponent failed to show, the promoter asked Tully to take his place. Tully told the promoter that he knew McGovern to be a dangerous fighter. He feared a loss would jeopardize both his headliner status and the extra money it would bring in Lima two days later. The promoter assured Tully that McGovern would "be good."[75]

At the opening gong, McGovern stormed across the ring, raining blows at his surprised opponent. Surviving the round, Tully realized he had been double-crossed and was in deep trouble. Kilbane, working Tully's corner, immediately recognized that McGovern was the superior boxer. Between rounds, he calmly advised Tully that McGovern was fighting to replace Tully on the Lima card and that his only chance was to outpace McGovern and keep him back on his heels. When they met at the center of the ring, Tully let loose a furious barrage of punches. The crowd roared. The exchange, which Tully later recalled as the most intense of his career, lasted a full thirty seconds before McGovern backed off. The break was momentary. McGovern, his lips pressed tight, came right back at Tully and the fight raged anew.[76]

Jimmy Dunn, Kilbane's manager, had replaced Kilbane in Tully's corner while Kilbane prepared for his own fight. Between rounds, Dunn instructed Tully to stay in close, avoid McGovern's right, and pound away at McGovern's midsection. As the gong rang, Dunn threw ice water at Tully. It felt like an electric shock, sending Tully charging across the ring, where he caught McGovern in the corner and hammered him into submission.[77] Tully never again entered the ring against a boxer he'd been told would "be good."

Working on just two days' rest, Tully knocked out Eddie Conway in the sixth round of their rematch in Lima. The luster of Tully's knockout was dulled by the charge in an Akron paper that Conway, the favorite, broke his hand in the fight.[78] The Kent newspaper rose to the hometown boy's defense by noting that the presumably neutral Lima paper reported no such injury to the Akron boxer.[79]

Despite being outweighed by ten pounds, Tully won a six-round decision in Toledo against Jack Gill on July 1.[80] While Tully's ring success had drawn much notice, at least one person failed to be impressed. After one of his fights, he received a telegram from Nellie Dingley. "What's the use of whipping the whole world and ending up a bartender?"[81]

His next fight, the main bout at the Twentieth Century Club in Toledo on September 21, matched him against local favorite, Johnny "Battling" Schultz.[82] It was as close as Tully would get to a shot at Kilbane, as Schultz had drawn with another boxer who had in turn drawn with the great Kilbane. The semi-windup for the Schultz fight matched Curly Gerhardt and Eddie Foster. Tully, dressed in his robes, sat at the end of an aisle and watched the fight. He came to the conclusion that, while not spectacular, Gerhardt and Foster were better boxers than he and Schultz. He watched Gerhardt take a vicious blow to the head in the fifth round and drop to the canvas. Suspecting that Gerhardt's skull had been fractured, Tully knew the fight was over.[83]

> The dying pugilist was carried by. His mouth was wide open, his eyes glared.
> The promoter followed him. Seeing my expression, he said to me, "He'll be all right, just out a little too long."
> I had seen men die. I knew better.[84]

Certain that he had just witnessed a man's death, Tully climbed into the ring. His grim train of thought was broken by the clanging of the opening gong. It was a sound that had a way of focusing a boxer's attention, but Tully couldn't get Gerhardt's battered face out of his mind. The sight of Schultz, muscular shoulders hunched forward, gloves raised, and moving toward him, didn't fully register. And he was scarcely aware at all of the third man in the ring, referee Ollie Pecord, who, ten years later, would officiate the Jack Dempsey–Jess Willard fight for the heavyweight championship in Toledo. Schultz tested Tully with a left, looking for an opening. Tully, in a panic that he might follow Gerhardt out of the ring, threw a desperate right and left. It was Schultz who hit the canvas. Then, as if by an act of an angry God rendering judgment on the evening's entertainment, the power failed, plunging the club into darkness. The outage was brief and when the lights returned, Schultz was back on his feet, pounding away. The fighting, furious and brutal, continued several more rounds, pausing occasionally as the lights continued to flicker and go out. Sitting in his corner waiting for the lights to return, Tully overheard a voice near ringside say that Gerhardt had died on the way to the hospital. The news, which Tully had suspected, stunned him and he found it impossible to focus on Schultz, whose punches started to do damage. The next two rounds passed in a fog. Pecord, seeing that one of his boxers was dazed, stopped the fight and raised Schultz's hand.[85]

That night Tully, along with Happy Davis, who had attended the fight, sought out Pecord at an Irish saloon where he tended bar. Pictures of boxers and burlesque girls clipped from the *Police Gazette* decorated the walls.

The three men drank whiskey and exchanged hushed regrets about Gerhardt. Davis changed the subject, asserting that Tully had Schultz beaten in the first round. Pecord agreed but wondered about the point of dwelling on such matters.

Davis saw Tully off at the railroad station the next day. As the train pulled away, Tully regarded the solitary figure on the platform. Happy Davis, honorable and generous, enjoyed a simple life of violence and loose women. Tully never saw him again.[86]

The train ride to Toledo had been gloomy. The return trip to Cleveland was worse. Gerhardt's death was awful, but deaths in the ring were uncommon. Much more likely was another fate that befell boxers. Tully was reminded of it every time the gong ended a round. He had paid an ex-fighter only a few years removed from boxing headlines five dollars to work his corner in Toledo. Now broke and punch-drunk, the old boxer's fate seemed worse than Gerhardt's.[87] Other boxers, Tully later wrote, "are left with clear brains and sightless eyes."[88] Wet gloves soaked in resin when the referee wasn't looking could blind an opponent. In the worst cases, "resin eyes" were permanent.

When the train pulled into Cleveland, Tully got off and wandered Public Square in a daze. A few days later he received a letter from Stanley Ketchel warning him to stay away from prizefighting. Ketchel even asserted that Jim's loss to Schultz was "the best thing that ever happened to you."[89] Ketchel had also been a road-kid. Indeed, he and Tully had met on the road, and Ketchel also had turned to boxing, winning the middleweight crown in 1908. Then at the pinnacle of his career, the Michigan Assassin, despite being outweighed by nearly fifty pounds, was preparing for an October 1909 fight with heavyweight champion Jack Johnson.[90] While Tully could reject an admonition against boxing as proffered by John Evans, a small-town businessman from a different world, Ketchel was not so easily dismissed.

As for Toledo, Tully could convince himself that death in the ring was unlikely and any stupor he might suffer from blows to the head was still several years in the future. He could not, however, escape the baseness of the entire enterprise and those associated with it. It was honest money. It was not honorable money. He resolved to get out of boxing. It was a sincere determination, but, as with his earlier desire to quit the road, he tarried.[91] It must have been at about this time that Jim's brother Hugh, then working as a jockey, was scheduled for a race in Akron but took ill and missed the event. Hugh was surprised to read in the following day's sports page that he had not only ridden but won the race. He learned that Jim had ridden in his stead and suspected that Jim had doped the horse.[92]

Mostly because he needed the money, but also because he wasn't quite ready to quit boxing, Tully returned to the ring on October 29.[93] His opponent was a Clevelander named Johnny Sinclair, who made the trip to Akron in a special railroad car packed with rooters. Tully was expected to win, and things began well enough, but Tully began bleeding heavily when Sinclair cut him to the bone over the eye. By the end of the bout, both eyes had swollen shut.[94] The *Cleveland Plain Dealer* gave the fight to Sinclair.[95] Tully got a rematch with Sinclair on December 6 in Akron and fought Sinclair to a draw in six rounds.[96]

With his boxing career stalled, Tully decided the time had come to retire from the ring. He walked into the chain works and, to mask his wounded pride, swaggered up to Jack Bracken and asked for his job back. The foreman agreed. To Tully's surprise, the distance from hero to bum was a short one, proving the universal truth that the only itch greater than the one compelling a sports fan to jump on a bandwagon is the one compelling him to jump back off.[97] Tully's return to the chain factory was seen as an act of cowardice by workers who shared but could not live the dream of escaping the factory and fighting their way to the top. Many refused to speak to him. Not even the boy who heated Jim's link was immune from scorn. In a fight with some other boys, he was called yellow, "just like his boss."[98]

Discouraged, Tully went to see John Evans but couldn't seem to get around to telling the older man what was on his mind. Instead, he made small talk, fiddled with the fashion books, and stood at the window, watching the trains come and go. He considered going to the library then decided against it. His years on the road had taught him to go it alone.[99]

On payday, he went to Jimmy Diamond's saloon in Akron. There, he ran into the *Akron Beacon Journal* editor who had fired him many months before. Tully mentioned that he had quit the ring and returned to the chain factory. Tully bought a round and was rewarded with a lecture about success following hard work. Furthermore, the editor continued, he had been to one of the Sinclair fights and wondered why a fellow who could box like Tully would want to waste his time writing in the first place. Tully could not explain.[100]

The question facing Tully was the question everyone faces in childhood and again, soberly recast and with more urgency, on the cusp of adulthood: What are you going to be now that you're grown up? Boxing was out. Writing didn't pay. Not that he was prepared to abandon either pursuit, but neither looked promising in the long haul. Although he later claimed to have considered playing professional baseball, there is no evidence that he ever pursued such a plan.[101] Instead, he resigned himself to the chain works. That Tully in 1909 didn't, like so many other working men, simply vanish in the drudgery of factory life, his ambition and dreams slowly crushed by an unending cycle of paycheck, bills, rent, paycheck, owes much to his determination—and also to blind fate.

In the early morning hours of December 10, 1909, a couple of night watchmen at the Seneca chain works were making their usual rounds when they spotted flames in the dolly shop. They sounded the alarm and did their best to contain the fire until help arrived. Firemen pulled up to find the shop completely engulfed. The decision was made to concentrate on saving the surrounding buildings. They were thwarted by a whipping southwest wind. Ashes fell like snow. Kent residents awoke to find the town blanketed in charred pieces of paper, cinders, and soot. The loss was nearly total, and four hundred men, Tully among them, were thrown out of work.[102] Tully found work in a machine shop at one of the rubber companies in Akron. Five nights a week he made the monotonous twelve-mile trip from Kent to pull a grueling twelve-hour shift.

It was at about this time that Tully met a pretty seventeen-year-old high school girl named Florence Bushnell.[103] Hoping to make a good impression, she presented him with her photograph for Christmas 1909, inscribing it simply, "To Jim, From Florence."[104] He kept the photo. He did not ask her out.[105]

With a new decade about to begin, Tully decided to quit the machine shop and make a fresh start in boxing.[106] This was not to be merely a return to the ring. This time things would be different. Tully realized that he had gone as far as possible on the crude fighting style he had learned on the road. To advance, he would need formal training. He moved to Cleveland, the center of the Ohio boxing world, and started looking for a trainer. In early January 1910 he told the *Cleveland Plain Dealer*, "I have never taken a boxing lesson . . . and kept right at my trade when I have been fighting. I have worked all day, fought the same night, and then gone to work again early the following morning."[107]

It was another false step. After just a few weeks, he again abandoned boxing and moved back to Kent. A man Tully had worked with at the chain works had been put in charge of a gang of car washers at the railroad shops in Kent and offered him a job. Tully accepted and was assigned to the lower grade of passenger cars. His job was to swab them down with a concoction of hot water, soap, lime, and other ingredients. When he proved he could be trusted not to streak the paint or varnish, he was promoted to cleaning the Pullmans. By the end of his shift, his clothes were often soaked and, on the colder winter days, frozen. The work was dreary and he found his thoughts once again returning to the quick money of the ring.[108]

7

Troubled in Heart

The courting of Nellie Dingley hit a snag. While she still enjoyed talking about books with Tully and encouraged his writing, she had pulled back from any romantic involvement. Early on, Tully had attributed her lack of interest to her natural aloofness. But by the spring of 1910, he had concluded that she was often ashamed of him. He was trapped, unable to either win or forget her.[1]

> There was, in her every movement, something graceful. Her step was light. Her legs, perfectly modeled, were always in silk stockings.
> Strongly sexed, vibrant and vital, she troubled me in heart and head.[2]

Tully's physical troubles were not long limited to heart and head. And if he expected that shifting his social orbit from the library to the saloon would help him woo her, he was to be disappointed. While coming to the aid of a friend, as he later maintained, Tully broke his leg in a drunken barroom brawl. He spent the next two months at a small hotel with his leg elevated and in a plaster cast. His expenses were paid by some of his old chain-maker pals who held a public dance for his benefit. He passed the time reading, often late into the night. He thought about Nellie. She did not visit or even ask those supplying him with library books about him. He suspected that the rumor going around town that he had broken his leg in a brothel had reached her ears.[3] It would have confirmed her suspicion that he was not a gentleman but simply an enlightened rogue. Indeed, she often described her favorite things as having "a sense of delicacy."[4] Jim

Tully was many things, delicate not being one of them. Years later Jim came to understand that her loneliness was greater than his. He could get drunk, fight, and rage against his demons. Nellie could not. "Her life," he later wrote, "was a voluptuous repression."[5] Mary Lygo, too, was much on his mind. His happiest hours had been spent at her side, and he longed to go to her. But she had moved to California following a $25,000 judgment in her breach-of-promise suit. Tully was again desperately lonely.[6]

When he finally got back on his feet, Tully headed downtown and, at the urging of an aspiring young businessman named Martin L. Davey, applied for a field crew job at the family business, the Davey Tree Expert Company. For someone whose resume might have included the phrase "willing to relocate," a more suitable job could scarcely have been imagined. He was told that the work, which involved the pruning and care of trees, would be physically demanding and occasionally dangerous and would require weeks of travel at a time. It would also require the ability to get along with other members of the crew both in the field and, during inclement weather, in the close quarters of their lodging. Lack of meaningful experience in the care of trees was no obstacle, as few applicants in the fledgling industry had done little more than swing an ax. Tully was hired and told to report to training classes conducted by Martin Davey's father, John, and held in a hall over the Kent National Bank.

After working at an old orchard on the outskirts of Kent for a few days, the class was judged fit for service and sent to the estate of a millionaire, J. V. Thompson, near Uniontown, Pennsylvania. Tully caught a freight train and arrived in two days, joining forty-six other tree surgeons who had assembled for the job. Few of them, as Tully recalled, knew one tree from another, but armed with chisels, mallets, ropes, and saws, they set to work. The men were not permitted to talk to strangers, except on the subject of tree care. Thompson paid the Davey company six dollars a man per ten-hour day, of which the crewmen got half.[7]

Thompson also gave the men the run of the place when they were off the clock. They collected around the bowling alley and gymnasium, where Thompson's young black chauffeur displayed his handiwork with a pair of boxing gloves by whipping all comers. Matt Muldowney, a former pitcher for the Class D Uniontown Coal Barons and one of the Davey crew, knew of Tully's experience in the ring and approached him with a proposal.[8] Tully agreed to the plan: he would put on gloves and allow himself to get roughed up by some of his friends. The chauffeur, thinking he had exhausted the possibilities within the Davey ranks, grew restless as he watched men he had just pummeled easily beat the young redhead. As Tully was knocked to the ground, Muldowney sidled over to the chauffeur and shook his head. Imagine, he said in wonder, that short redhead thinking he can whip you. With the hook firmly planted, only the reeling in remained.

By the night of the fight, large sums of money, a considerable amount of it put down by Thompson on his chauffeur, had been wagered. As Tully entered the crowded gym, he noted one end of the gym packed with the chauffeur's black friends. The millionaire's friends sat in a separate section, with the Davey crew making up the rest of the crowd. Muldowney, who had managed to scrape together the three hundred dollars he'd put down on Tully at five to one, cautioned Tully to put on a good show and fight like a tree surgeon, lest he be spotted for the ringer he was.

At the gong, the long-limbed chauffeur rushed across the ring and started punching. By turning slightly away from the blows, Tully was able to take the punches without real damage. Tully looked to Muldowney, whose hand was level with the rope—the signal to take it. The chauffeur grew careless, but Tully continued to absorb the blows. The black section of fans roared as the gong sounded. The second round continued in the same vein until they clinched and Tully whispered to go "easy." The chauffeur froze for a second and Tully used the opening to land an uppercut with each hand. Furious at being tricked, the chauffeur ripped into Tully. The money, Tully realized, might not be so easy after all. It was time to fight. The gong sounded.

Muldowney, who sensed that winnings exceeding a year's wages were about to swirl down the drain, agreed. It was time. As the gong opened the third round, the chauffeur again charged across the ring and pounced on Tully. This time Tully lashed back, but the chauffeur was unfazed. Savage blows shot back and forth. In close, Tully pounded at his stomach and noticed him wilt slightly. Taking that as his cue, Tully left the chauffeur's head alone and burrowed in with body blows to finish the third round and begin the fourth. As soon as they broke, Tully would move right back in and start pounding at his midsection. During some intense infighting, Tully landed a solid right. The blow dropped the chauffeur's head onto Tully's shoulder. That was it. Tully quickly stepped back and cracked two solid shots to the chin. The long, hard, angular chauffeur softened slightly, sank to his haunches, and slowly melted to the floor.

Most of the crowd sat stunned, the realization slowly dawning that they had just witnessed, in the words of Ralph Ellison's *Invisible Man,* "the smart money hit the canvas."[9] Tully helped his opponent to his corner and climbed out of the ring. Later, when he had a chance to reflect on his evening's work, he was struck by the financial implications of his victory. Life as a ringer had possibilities. By carefully choosing his matches, he could fatten his wallet with a few months' work. Then, free of money troubles, he might finally settle down to the business of writing.

Muldowney, too, was quick to assess the world of possibilities open to a ringer, or one managing a ringer. He was eager to match Tully with a Pittsburgh boxer. Tully briefly considered the offer, but he wanted to be a writer, not a boxer. Loath to relinquish the modicum of respectability and financial security that would come with writing, he declined. He would stick to his plan of saving enough money during the summer to write during the winter.[10]

His next assignment came in June 1910. He and a young college dropout turned drifter named Robert Bruce Earl were sent to Ballwin, Missouri, a small town just a few miles west of St. Louis. The contract stipulated that the job of pruning a long row of forty-year-old maples along a farm lane be completed within a certain period of time. At their room, Earl opened a window and gazed out at the countryside. The land seemed bleak, their task daunting. After one day, all of Ballwin knew the pair as the tree doctors. After four weeks, the job was complete.[11] Ballwin's lack of nightlife worked to Tully's advantage. He spent the long evenings writing, mostly of his experiences on the road and also, haltingly, of his time in the ring.[12]

Following the Ballwin job, the pair waited hours for a train to their next assignment in Danville, Illinois. Earl, the son of an insurance agent, spent the time napping, using his expensive monogrammed valise as a pillow. Hot and dusty, they finally found their way to the job site, the home of "Uncle" Joe Cannon, the autocratic Speaker of the U.S. House of Representatives and leader of the Republican Party. (Cannon would in fact become so powerful that at the time of his retirement, he was featured on the cover of the inaugural issue of *Time* in 1923.) Cannon took an immediate liking to the two tree surgeons sent by the Davey company. And Cannon struck Tully and Earl as more like an affluent and canny old farmer than one of the most powerful men in Washington. When they finished the job of trimming the elm branches threatening Cannon's house, Martin Davey recalled them to Kent.[13]

Only a couple of years Tully's senior, Davey was polished, sophisticated, and charming where Tully was rough, unschooled, and moody. Neither had met anyone quite like the other. Davey invited Tully for a ride in his car, and as they bumped along the county roads, Davey extolled the power of salesmanship. Eager to please Davey and suspecting that sales might be his ticket to respectability, Tully agreed to promote Davey's tree service.[14]

Davey next sent Tully on a small job to Richmond, Indiana, in August 1910. Tully arranged for John Davey to speak at the local YMCA before a select group of Richmond's landed gentry. Davey passed around stereoscopic slides of trees in various stages of Davey care, and whenever he became confused about where the slide had been shot, Tully bounced to his feet with the name of the correct town. By doing so, he grabbed a share of the spotlight, which proved a great asset when he later solicited area property owners for work. He parlayed a simple four-day job into three months' work for a field crew of seven, signing up so many customers that by September, he was begging the home office for help.[15] "For heaven's sake," he wrote, "send somebody if you have to send the office girls."[16]

More important, Tully's initiative caught the attention of Martin Davey back in Kent. He asked Tully to write up his Richmond experience for the company newsletter. Tully happily obliged.[17] Davey may have expected a straightforward retelling of the taking of Richmond, but the opening lines describe a different battle.

> All students of history will remember what Wellington said on the field of Waterloo, when the tide of battle seemed turning, "Oh that Blucher, or night would come." Victor Hugo, the French novelist, called the Battle of Waterloo, a great battle, won by a second class officer and no doubt after a great many foremen read this they will say, like Hugo did of Wellington, a great battle won by a second class foreman. But Wellington produced and so did the second class foreman.[18]

And, Tully continued, just as Blücher arrived at the last minute to save Wellington, John Davey arrived just in time to save Tully. If the analogy of the defeat of Napoleon and the selling of tree pruning in a small Indiana town is a bit grandiose, it marks the work of a writer—a *well-read* writer—spreading his wings for the first time. Historical comparisons aside, Tully was not without practical advice for his fellow tree surgeons. He found "that it is five times easier to talk big business with a big man, than it is to talk about $30 jobs with a small man."[19]

The one-page letter in the September 24, 1910, issue of the *Davey Tree Surgeon's Bulletin* was Tully's first credited appearance in print, and if Martin

Davey had his way, it would not be the last. Davey, who marveled at Tully's use of language, requested that Tully write more for the publication.[20] Tully responded in November with a letter to the editor suggesting that the company lower its payment to a worker's family upon his accidental death in favor of adding a benefit for a worker's loss of limb. "I do believe, though, that the money should be equal to the one who suffered death and the one who suffered a living death."[21] More prosaic than his earlier effort, it was signed, like the first, James A. Tully. Seeing his name in print was the first tangible evidence that he might indeed realize his dream of becoming a writer.

When he was fired from the Akron newspaper and doubting his ability to write, it was Nellie who consoled him. "It's a matter of finding yourself," she told him.[22] Coming from Nellie, the idea of self-discovery explained everything. "In many ways," he wrote years later, "she did more for me than all the others."[23] At last Jim had found someone who really understood him. Now published, employed, and convinced that they could overcome their differences, Jim went to the library and proposed. For what seemed like an eternity, the only sound he heard was the ticking of an ancient clock.[24] Jim recalled the scene in both his unpublished autobiography and *Blood on the Moon*.

> She stood still for a second; then switching the lights off and shutting the heavy door, she put an arm about me.
>
> I could feel the contour of her breast against my side. A delicate perfume was about her. No word was said by either for a long time. I held her body close, my hand resting on her lovely figure.
>
> Her breath came quickly.
>
> "I've never had anything in my life—. I've never wanted anything very bad before. I'll work hard," I pleaded.
>
> Turning me about until her breasts pressed against me, she pushed my head back and ran her hand through my hair.[25]

She kissed him. She could not marry him.

So it may be that Tully was on the rebound in the summer of 1910 when he found the photograph of Florence Bushnell and paid her a visit on one of his trips home. Although he was still not prepared to completely abandon the golden dream of a romance with the thrilling but extravagant Mary Lygo or the thoughtful but unattainable Nellie Dingley, Jim began a whirlwind romance with Florence. While Florence possessed neither the sexual allure of a Follies dancer nor the intellectual fascination of a librarian, she struck Jim as down to earth. For her part, Florence was flattered by the attention of the full-time tree surgeon, sometimes-boxer, and would-be writer.[26] When he briefly returned to Kent in October, they married. He was twenty-four; she was eighteen.[27]

He was almost immediately beset by doubts. He wrote Virginia, informing her of the marriage. She responded with the longest letter, ten lines, she had ever written. She had, he read, every confidence that they would be happy together. He did not share her sunny prediction.[28]

As Jim had to get back to work, there could be no honeymoon. Florence returned to her parents' home at 120 Oak Street while her new husband returned to the Richmond, Indiana, job.[29] He remained there the rest of the month before moving on to Bowling Green, Kentucky.[30] December found him in Birmingham, Alabama, where several weeks of rain halted the crew's work.[31] Tully, now earning a salary of five dollars a week, tried to help his crew pay for their lodging, but he was soon running short of cash himself. He wrote Davey of the problem. When Davey replied that the company could not be responsible for their personal debts, Tully packed up his toolbox for the season and returned to Ohio.[32] He and Florence took a small apartment over a wallpaper store in Kent, where Jim spent much of the winter in front of a rented typewriter, trying to write.

Marriage and a career in sales were but first steps in Tully's bid for acceptance. At a time when one's social standing, especially in a small town, was largely determined by which lodge or fraternal organization one could claim membership in, Tully chose to apply to the Masons. He'd heard that the group was very old and that all U.S. presidents except Lincoln had been members. Convinced that it was the one group most likely to confer instant respectability and open doors, he placed his application in the hands of a prominent local member, his friend John Evans. After waiting several anxious weeks for their decision, Tully stopped by the tailor's shop. He had been blackballed. Evans sewed and counseled patience. Next time things might be different. Maybe keeping his name out of the sporting pages would help. After all, Evans continued, one applicant had been blackballed for twenty years and had finally gained admission when a member, apparently the one who had been voting him down, died. Tully replied that there would be no next time. When he passed along the news of his rejection to Virginia, he was surprised by her delight. The Masons, she wrote, are a *Protestant* organization. The very idea was enough to awaken their poor mother from her long slumber beneath the Ohio sod.[33]

In early April of 1911, Tully and two other Davey crewmen were sent to an estate near Cleveland. They worked there for several weeks, but when a storm destroyed some hemlocks, the owner blamed them for the damage and fired them. Tully did not like being unfairly dismissed—nor did he like losing a job for Martin Davey. Confident that he could make it on his own, he left the Davey company.[34]

Free time always had a way of being filled by the road. And this time he agreed to travel with Johnny Kilbane to Vernon, California, to work Kilbane's corner in his May 6 fight against Joe Rivers. Tully and Kilbane were shocked when the referee gave a twenty-round decision to Rivers. The discouraged pair made the long journey home to Ohio.[35]

Jim Tully, May 1932. For a few brief years Tully was on top of the world. The years of youthful struggle behind, the indignities of old age ahead. Authors' collection.

Jim Tully's paternal grandfather, Old Hughie, a lace peddler and ditch digger "capable of turning death into an Irish wake and pouring liquor down the throat of the corpse." Family of Trilby J. Tully Beamon; Jim Tully Papers (Collection 250), Dept. of Special Collections, Charles E. Young Research Library, UCLA.

Downtown St. Marys, Ohio, as it appeared about the time of Jim Tully's birth on June 3, 1886. Auglaize County Historical Society.

An al fresco supper in a hobo jungle. Authors' collection.

The dangers of life on the road are dramatically depicted in this 1905 photograph of a hobo caught between boxcars by a club-wielding railroad worker. Library of Congress, Prints and Photographs.

Tully rode the rails into Kent, Ohio, in 1907, hoping to work at the Seneca Chain Company. Hearing the roar of the chain works, he crossed this stone bridge over the Cuyahoga River, passed the town library, and got hired as a chain maker. The baggage chutes had been removed by the time Tully arrived. In Kent, Tully's days as a road kid ended and his life as a writer began. Kent Historical Society.

The man standing far left is believed to be Jim Tully. Taken on Main St. in downtown Kent, Ohio, around 1907, this would be the earliest known photo of Tully. Kent Historical Society.

Left: Nellie Dingley, the Kent librarian who encouraged Tully to write but broke his heart when she declined his marriage proposal. "Her life was a voluptuous repression." Authors' collection. Right: Florence Bushnell of Kent, Ohio, gave this photograph to the sometimes-boxer and aspiring writer she would marry in October 1910. She was eighteen. He was twenty-four. Family of Trilby J. Tully Beamon.

Living in California and working on the manuscript of his first book, Tully poses with his wife, Florence, and their two children, infant Trilby and Alton. Family of Trilby J. Tully Beamon.

Not many tree surgeons could boast an endorsement by Jack London. Family of Trilby J. Tully Beamon.

The silent screen's Little Tramp hires the genuine article, a former vagabond working on his second book. Both had known heartache and hardship in childhood, but, as Tully would observe, "The same winds of environment had shaped us differently." Family of Trilby J. Tully Beamon.

Tully between 1920s screen stars Richard Dix and Raymond Griffith. Authors' collection.

The inner circle gathers to watch Lita Grey sign her contract for *The Gold Rush* on March 2, 1924: left to right, Eddie Manson, Lillian McMurray, Chuck Riesner, Charlie Chaplin, Jim Tully, Grey, Henry Bergman, Eddie Sutherland, and Alfred Reeves. Authors' collection.

Margaret "Marna" Myers Tully, 1929. Family of Trilby J. Tully Beamon; Jim Tully Papers (Collection 250). Dept. of Special Collections, Charles E. Young Research Library, UCLA.

H. L. Mencken, trusted editor, loyal friend. Authors' collection.

Their wedding and their breakups made headlines. Tully's marriage to his second wife, Marna, lasted five tempestuous years. Authors' collection.

Jim Tully and director-producer Edwin Carewe both found life in Hollywood after years on the road. They met shortly after the publication of *Beggars of Life* in 1924 as guests at a hobo luncheon staged in the Sante Fe railroad yard in Los Angeles. Authors' collection.

Left: *Beggars of Life* (1924), Tully's breakthrough book. Authors' collection.

Below left: *Circus Parade* (1927). Authors' collection.

Below right: *Circus Parade* advertisement. Authors' collection.

Top left: *Shanty Irish* (1928), with a cover sketch of its author. Authors' collection. Top right: *Shanty Irish* advertisement with other noteworthy books from the publisher. Authors' collection. Lower left: *Shadows of Men* (1930), the book Tully considered his best. Authors' collection. Lower right: *Beggars Abroad* (1930), with a caricature of the author by the great Peter Arno. Authors' collection.

Blood on the Moon (1931). Authors' collection.

Laughter in Hell (1932). Authors' collection.

The Bruiser (1936). Authors' collection.

John Decker, who would die the same month and year as Tully (June 1947), drew this sketch of the writer. Their mutual friends included W. C. Fields, John Barrymore, Gene Fowler, and Lionel Barrymore. Authors' collection.

8

Write or Starve

Two events in the summer of 1911 shaped the rest of Jim Tully's life.

In the first half of the twentieth century, before it became largely the domain of academics, poetry was a small but significant part of popular culture. Whether slim volumes or fat anthologies, books of poetry lined bookshop shelves and later, with the advent of the mass-market paperback, filled the spinning wire racks of drugstores and newsstands. If the consumption of poetry was a popular pursuit, so too was its production. Literary aspirants who were daunted by the length of a novel could fiddle with rhyming a dozen usually mawkish lines of verse the way one might tinker with a crossword puzzle—with results about as artistically pleasing. (Indeed, Tully maintained that his grandmother Catherine Tully had written verse. And Jim's father-in-law, Lester Bushnell, wrote poetry that appeared in the local paper.)[1]

Some of this output found its way into the newspapers, appearing in the literary pages or popping up as filler whenever an editor found a spare couple of inches. Occasionally it would even surface on the front page. Ted Robinson of the *Cleveland Plain Dealer*, who regularly featured poetry in his "The Philosopher of Folly" column, no doubt spoke for literary editors everywhere when he lamented in a June 27, 1911, column, "A great many people send us a great deal of poor poetry. It is only once in a blue moon that anyone sends a real poem." The poem he ran that day, "On Keats' Grave," was by one James Alexander Tully (Alexander being Jim's confirmation name).[2] It was a poem that Tully had been toying with for some time.

Earth wearied nature, beneath this
lonely stone,
Sleeping ever so sound.
Great-hearted dreamer left to dream
alone
In sacred ground.
Storm-beaten soul, that vainly clutched
through life,
At high ideals; how blissful it must
seem
To leave the burden of stupendous
strife
For one long dream.

Tully, who just a few years before had lived in a hobo camp behind the David Round Company chain works in Cleveland, now saw his work published in the city's leading newspaper.[3] Just as Tully built on his early success in the ring to forge a boxing career, he now used his success with the *Cleveland Plain Dealer* (and the *Chicago Daily News, Youngstown Vindicator,* and *Kent Courier,* all of which reprinted the poem) to launch his literary career.

Over the rest of 1911, the *Kent Courier* published more of Tully's poetry: "The School House on the Hill" (Oct. 11), "To Geo. W. Austin, on His 103rd Birthday" (Oct. 20), "A Message of Cheer" (Nov. 3), "The Porter's Estimate" (Nov. 10), "To a Dead Atheist" (Nov. 17), "A Thanksgiving Meal on the Farm" (Dec. 1), "Samuel Gompers" (Dec. 8), "An Advertising Poem" (Dec. 15), "One Christmas, Years Ago" (Dec. 22), and "The Old Glad Hand" (Dec. 29). While most of this was the sort of sentimental verse much in favor at the time, it did serve to boost the confidence of a young writer. Robinson, Tully's champion at the *Plain Dealer,* even paid a visit to Tully in November for a story about Kent poets that ran the following month.[4]

When the *Kent Courier* printed "Samuel Gompers" in December, Tully mailed a clipping of the poem to Gompers and asked the cofounder and president of the American Federation of Labor for a job. Since the poem paid homage to Gompers, with Tully likening the father of American labor to George Washington and Jesus, Tully anticipated a favorable response. When, at last, a special delivery letter arrived from Washington, it contained a letter of appreciation, but no mention of employment.[5]

In addition to the publication of "On Keats' Grave" and the first flush of literary success that followed, the other big event of 1911 was the birth on August 3 of a son, Thomas Alton Tully, to Florence and Jim.[6] While Jim was thrilled to be a father, he was braced by the realization that Alton, as the child came to be called, represented another mouth to feed. Finding a better-paying job became a priority.

Late in 1911, Tully apparently got a second chance with the *Akron Beacon Journal* before moving to the rival *Akron Press* by year's end.[7] His work for the Akron papers did not deter John Paxton, editor of the *Kent Courier*, from publishing more of Tully's poetry in the spring of 1912.[8] The combination of reporter by day, poet by night would seem to have been an ideal situation for a young writer. But for unknown reasons, Tully and the *Press* again parted company. Perhaps it was because he was no more a reporter in early 1912 than he had been during his previous stints with the Akron papers more than three years before. Perhaps he was simply restless. With Jim contemplating a return to the road after being fired by the *Press*, the ever-supportive Virginia reassured him, "Why, Jim, Dad didn't become a hobo because he lost a ditch contract."[9]

It appears that it was at this point that Tully again returned to a chain factory—this time the Seneca chain works in Mansfield, near the reformatory. While in Mansfield, Tully went to watch a fellow chain maker named Grady box a local hero named Henry "Kid" Sperry.[10] When Grady had to withdraw from the bout, Tully rashly volunteered to take his place, despite giving up thirty pounds to Sperry.[11] While the beating Tully received from Sperry that day would not dissuade him from again climbing into the ring, he did gain a greater appreciation for the simple elegance of boxing's weight divisions.[12]

To the old question of "What next?" Tully supplied an old answer with a new twist. He decided to return to the road, not as a hobo, but as an itinerant tree surgeon. As most tree work requires at least two people, one high in the tree setting ropes and sawing limbs and one on the ground pulling the ropes, Tully needed a partner. His choice was Vernie Smith, another former chain maker, tree surgeon, and St. Marys native. After sending Florence, Alton, and Florence's parents ahead to Los Angeles in the spring of 1912, Tully and Smith started across the country, planning to work their way to California, where Tully would be reunited with his family.[13] Because Smith's mother had moved to a farm near Marion, Ohio, they began soliciting work there. They had traveled as far south as Canton, less than thirty miles, when they hopped off the train to look up a pal who had also exchanged his chain maker's tongs and hammer for a tree surgeon's saw and mallet. The trio repaired to a saloon near the train station for refreshments. Captivated by the convivial Irish owner and his comely barmaid-wife, Tully and Smith sat for hours as their ambition and capital sank to perilous levels. Only after being wrongly accused by another patron of stealing her watch did they finally push off for Marion, traveling through the night.

Exhausted, nearly broke, and, if the activities of the previous day are any clue, hung over, they found the sight of downtown Marion by dawn's first light somewhat less than agreeable. They walked down the main street until the shops and buildings gave way to farms and fields, finally arriving at the farm of Vernie Smith's mother. There they rested and planned. They collected the names of Marion's leading citizens. They read every book on trees at the Marion public library. They wrote the forestry department in Washington for brochures on tree care. They assembled a scrapbook of photos showing off Davey jobs. And then they set off in search of a high-profile client.

A visit to the Marion Board of Education secured them work on the trees at the high school. They had scarcely begun when reporters angling for a your-tax-dollars-at-work story arrived for interviews. Smith worked the trees while Tully worked the press. The resulting story garnered them more attention, and Tully easily signed up a number of Marion's leading citizens embarrassed by the specter of unsightly tree growth. When the publicity of the high school job began to ebb, Tully paid a visit to the *Marion Star*, where he met with the newspaper's owner and editor, Warren G. Harding. The future United States senator and president warmly greeted him, responding to Tully's pitch with an invitation to drop by his home that evening. Later, Tully looked over the trees, quoted a price, and got the job.

The job, Tully later admitted, was a modest one and should not have taken one man more than a week. Instead, Tully and Smith milked every last drop of publicity from being seen on the grounds of Marion's leading citizen. They made it their base of operations for several weeks. Even as other work came in, including an important referral from Harding to work on the grounds of the nearby Sawyer Sanitarium, they were sure to spend part of the day at the Harding residence. While it was in their interest to see that the Harding trees displayed their best work, they appreciated Harding's warmth and kindness. When darkness ended one day's work, they joined Harding on the front porch. As fireflies hung pinpoints of yellow in the still Ohio evening, they entertained the future president with an account of their curious path to tree surgery. It was late when they left, and Tully later recalled looking back to see the future president, illuminated by a shaft of street light, still seated with his hands resting across the arms of his chair.[14]

Tully finally arrived in Los Angeles during the summer of 1912. He moved in with his wife and child, living in a place near Florence's parents. Despite his difficulty finding work, the young family appeared to be the picture of domestic bliss. The weekly arrival of the *Kent Courier* occasioned Wednesday evening visits from Florence's father to hear Jim read the news from home. Other nights, Jim worked on his poetry. His attempts to read these compositions aloud were certain to cause "the King of Ireland," as Jim had dubbed his redheaded son, to start crying.[15]

As money grew short, Jim decided, against Florence's wishes, on a return to boxing.[16] Not that Tully had any illusions about his prowess in the ring. He realized he was a great fighter but one minute in sixty. But he also knew that in that one minute, he could whip a champion. This time, the lesson of Uniontown still fresh, things would be different. Gone was any pretense of sport. Gone was any notion of following Johnny Kilbane up the ranks of contenders. This time it was about money. Using assumed names, he would fight his way across the country, cleaning up against bums, local heroes, has-beens, and greenhorns. There was no disgrace in such a scheme, he reasoned, as many great boxers had started out as ringers. Whereas they had gone on to distinguish themselves in the ring, he would live off his winnings and distinguish himself as a writer.

He drifted as far east as Missouri before arranging a suitable match. He laid down a large chunk of his savings, two hundred dollars, at three to one on himself. The fight took place in a ballpark under a blazing sun. By the tenth round, Tully had put his opponent on the canvas three times only to have his uncooperative foe climb to his feet each time on the Nine count. The counts, Tully felt, had been long—closer to fifteen than ten—but he still estimated his lead to be insurmountable. He was therefore stunned to receive a draw. It revealed the fundamental risk in boxing hometown heroes: hometown referees. To make matters worse, he was stiffed out of much of his purse. Discouraged but undaunted, he turned back west, determined not to be burned again.[17]

Tully drifted into Salt Lake City in 1912. The talk of Commercial Street, the oasis of gentile pleasure in the Mormon desert, was of a gangly teenager fresh out of the mining camps and hobo jungles. The youngster would walk into a tough saloon and brashly announce in his high-pitched voice, "I can lick any sonofabitch in the house."[18] Most barroom toughs saw the skinny build, heard the boyish voice, and began counting their winnings. They might overlook the broken nose, but after seeing the jackhammer arms do their business, none would mistake Jack Dempsey for a mere whelp. Tully and Dempsey would become close friends in the years ahead. From their first meeting in Utah, Tully was impressed with Dempsey's ambition. He was therefore not surprised when Dempsey claimed boxing's heavyweight championship before the decade was out.[19]

In one large western town, probably Salt Lake City, Tully became a fan favorite. His popularity with local boxing fans did nothing to advance his pursuit of cashing in on an "upset," but as the purses got fatter, he found it tougher to move on. As in the past, he lingered in the public library. When the glances of the librarians made him uncomfortable, he drifted off to the pool halls. When he could no longer take the idle chatter there, he finally retreated to the railroad yards.

There, at the depot lunch counter, he befriended a young red-haired waitress named Ellen Renew. She was from a small town in Missouri. Jim gave her his ringer name and did not bother to correct her guess that he was from Kansas City. One evening she pointed out one of the regulars at the restaurant. He was a railroad brakeman who had been a fighter. Ellen volunteered that he was a little crazy, probably from taking too many blows to the head. That night Jim suffered a stabbing headache. He knew it was probably nothing, but he couldn't stem the rising tide of fear that he would share the brakeman's fate. Ellen began accompanying Jim around town but voiced her disapproval of the boxing people she met and boxing in general. They were together on Ellen's Sunday afternoon off when the brakeman was put on the afternoon train bound for the insane asylum. Neither Jim nor Ellen mentioned the brakeman that night. Jim was gone by morning.[20]

After a stop in Reno, Jim arrived in San Francisco, most likely in November of 1912. In earlier years, San Francisco had been a wide-open town when it came to boxing (and most everything else). A young fighter could get a match with nothing more than a fistful of newspaper clippings from his previous fights. This came to an end when one young hopeful was beaten nearly to death. Instead, Tully and other unknowns were forced to audition by going a few rounds with a trial horse chosen by the promoter. Tully withstood the barrage and was awarded one of the two main bouts, a week away. Having apparently abandoned his plan of upsetting a heavy favorite, Tully instead hoped to put together a string of victories and come out under his real name.

The noise of the crowd swelled with the opening gong, the pair met in the center of the ring, and Tully sized up his opponent: lean, broad shouldered, big jawed, slow witted, strong puncher.[21]

> It was in the fourth round—I learned later.
> A right caught me. I was unconscious until the next afternoon.
> All events which preceded the fight, and everything which happened in the ring has been in eclipse all these years. I do not even remember dressing for the fight.
> My opponent, fearful that I had been killed, called upon me while I was still unconscious. A kindly note scrawled with pencil begged my forgiveness.
> Some minutes after I opened my eyes I vaguely grasped the situation. The note began, "You were knocked out last night—"
> Still shaky, I went to the lobby, and from there to the street.[22]

When the concussive pounding in his head dulled to mere throbbing and he was able to refocus his eyes, he caught a southbound train. The knockout worried him all the way to Los Angeles. He had hoped to return with enough cash to support his small family while he wrote. He had fallen well short of that goal. Frightened as he had become of boxing, he couldn't pass up an eighty-dollar payday for climbing into the ring one more time. Christmas was coming.

Entering a gymnasium to train, Tully was immediately assaulted by the odors of boxing, leather and sweat, he had grown to hate. A while later the door opened and in strolled a man wearing an expensive suit. A large diamond decorated his tie, another his finger.[23] All eyes in the gym recognized Ad Wolgast, the lightweight champion of the world by virtue of a legendary forty-round knockout of Battling Nelson in 1910.[24] Wolgast, the Michigan Wildcat, walked up to Tully. Would he mind getting dressed and going someplace quiet to talk?

Johnny Kilbane, himself now the champion of the featherweight class, had sent him. After some small talk about their mutual friend, Wolgast got to the point. Wolgast had heard from Kilbane about Tully being knocked unconscious in San Francisco. And now they had heard that Tully intended to fight again. Just as Josiah Flynt had warned Tully to get off the road, Wolgast now echoed Stanley Ketchel's warning to get out of the ring. Tully resisted. Wolgast offered to put Tully on his payroll as a trainer. He could give rubdowns to the champ or maybe do a little sparring, but no blows to the head. After extracting a promise from Tully that he would not take the fight, they made arrangements for Tully to join the Wolgast camp in nearby Vernon, California.

Each afternoon, the trainers and camp followers gathered to watch Wolgast step into the ring against a Japanese boxer named Togo. It was always the same. Wolgast would sledgehammer Togo's soft, blubbery jaw with left-right combinations that Togo seemed to absorb with little ill effect for the first round. Tully always hoped that Togo would go down in the second or third round, which he sometimes did. If he lasted into the fourth or fifth round, by which time Wolgast had worked himself into a fury, the beating became almost too terrible to watch. For his services, Togo was paid seventy-five dollars a week. Next it was Tully's turn. After Togo, Wolgast's bloodlust seemed sated, and Tully had the champ's promise that he would go easy. If rage overtook Wolgast, however, Tully knew he would have to last until the end of the round. The gong sounded and Wolgast and Tully began pounding away at each other. But, true to his word, Wolgast never hit Tully in the jaw and once when Tully slipped, Wolgast caught him, making it look as if they were in a clinch.

If Wolgast's words had made Tully think twice about continuing a boxing career, his savage beating of Togo drove the point home. Tully's nights were already haunted by his own knockout in San Francisco, Curly Gerhardt's death, the brakeman in the insane asylum, and other nameless, shuffling, punch-drunk zombies. The Togo nightmare, replayed every afternoon, was too much. Tully quit Wolgast and never again put on the gloves.[25] Jim wrote his father with the news that he was quitting the ring. He received a letter agreeing with his decision. In all the years of separation from his children, it was the first letter the elder Tully had ever written.[26]

Tully spent the next ten years as a tree surgeon, first working for a few months at the estate of railroad baron Henry Huntington. He then was hired by the Los Angeles Parks Department, which assigned him for several months to a laborers' camp in Griffith Park. There he read Marx and Engels but found that he was ill prepared to grasp the problem of human greed and their recommended solution for it. Rather, he preferred to while away the peaceful nights in his bunk, writing verse with a pencil. When the Parks Department no longer required his services, he was "loaned" to

King Gillette. After a week at the razor tycoon's estate in Santa Monica, he was sent to a nearby camp overlooking the Pacific Ocean.

Unable to find permanent work in the area as a tree surgeon, Tully tried talking a Hollywood producer into hiring him to work on a boxing story. The producer declined and Tully once more returned to the road, crisscrossing the country as a tree surgeon, at least some of that time with wife and son in tow. It was during these travels that Jim began committing scenes from his life to paper. Despite a schedule that sometimes required him to begin work as early as two or three in the morning, Tully tried to spend part of each day at his typewriter. Over the years, he began assembling these scenes into what would eventually become his first book, an autobiographical novel about a road-kid bearing his mother's maiden name, Lawler.[27]

Tully thought his big break might have arrived through an old pal, hotel porter Joe Bertucci. They had met as road-kids in Chicago. Joe mentioned something that had happened at work. He had delivered a famous writer's trunk to his room. Joe told the writer he had a friend who was working on a book. Harold Bell Wright, now largely forgotten, was then riding a crest of popularity, having turned out a string of sentimental novels. Tully recalled enjoying one of those books, *That Printer of Udell's,* in his youth. When Joe offered to introduce him to the famous writer, Jim eagerly accepted. Led into Wright's room, Jim was greeted by a slight man with intense eyes. Wright's earnest demeanor reminded Tully of a small-town preacher. The aspiring writer dutifully listened to Wright's lengthy discourse. He was dismayed when it became apparent that Wright's area of expertise was limited to the subject of Harold Bell Wright. When, after three hours, the master had exhausted himself and got around to the secret of great writing, Tully brightened. The trick, Wright revealed, was to have a message, specifically Wright's message of inspiration and moral uplift. Tully had no grand message and was wary of people who did. He excused himself, leaving behind the bulky draft of *Emmett Lawler* for Wright's critique. "I should advise you," Wright concluded, "if you continue as a writer, not to use the first person."[28] The ever-faithful Joe Bertucci assured Jim that Wright, while popular, was a hack. Still, Jim worried, Wright had sold a lot of books and his opinion mattered. Several agonizing weeks later it came in the form of a scolding thirteen-page letter. Tully, not mature enough to hoot at bad advice, rewrote *Emmett Lawler* in the third person.[29]

A reading of Jack London's memoir of his drinking days, *John Barleycorn,* moved Tully in September 1913 to write his literary hero.[30] Two years earlier, London had become, in the words of one biographer, "the highest-paid author in the United States, earning around one thousand dollars per story and publishing everything he submitted."[31] Yet despite his enormous popularity and hefty income, London was coping with a miserable year in 1913. His nearly completed twenty-three-room house burned to the ground, and he suffered a host of health problems, including appendicitis, inflamed gums (requiring all his upper teeth to be pulled), and a double fistula so painful that London was becoming increasingly dependent on morphine and heroin for relief.[32] It is a wonder then that London troubled himself to reply to an unknown at all. The ailing author responded that he was weary of writing letters but graciously invited Jim and his wife to visit him for a few days at his ranch in northern California. At the ranch Tully could "work, if you want to work—at writing, at letter-writing, at recreation, at loafing, at enjoying yourself, at doing anything you please. And then you and I can talk. We have some fine trails up the mountain here; we have hunting, if you desire it. On afternoons when I can get you out on horseback, I can tell you all I know about the writing game. I shall not say a word about how much I appreciated your letter."[33] An invitation to Mount Olympus couldn't have been more welcome, and yet their eventual meeting in 1914 took place not at London's ranch but at a hotel bar.[34]

Plying his trade as a hotel porter, Bertucci heard of a job opening for a taxi starter near a nightclub. He mentioned it to Jim, who got the job and was issued a cap with the name of the cab company written in gold braid across the front. As the company had not yet installed meters in the cabs, Tully's main duty was to take down the drivers' reports and turn them in to the night manager. While waiting for a cab, those clients seeking to conclude the evening with romance often consulted the starter. The madams who ran the brothels expressed their gratitude for being sent big spenders by kicking back 10 percent to the starter. His predecessor in the job, a young man promoted to driver, observed Tully's work for a few nights and took him aside. It was important for everyone's sake, Tully was told, that he be able to recognize the vice squad and not put down anything incriminating in writing. Tully disliked the job, but with a wife and child to support, he stayed on.

Late one night, a cab pulled up and several drunken men piled out—not by any means an unusual event, except that one of the men looked familiar. As the party disappeared into the nightclub, the driver motioned Tully over. The driver confirmed his suspicion. The familiar man was Jack

London and, the driver continued, as London was good for a five-dollar tip, he wanted Tully to send the group back to him when they were ready to leave. The driver promised Tully a dollar of the tip.

When London had not emerged by Tully's quitting time, six in the morning, Tully went in to ask London if his driver could be sent home. No, he should wait, London replied. Although Tully wanted to talk, extracting London from the noisy nightclub appeared impossible. Instead, he headed home, wondering if he hadn't just blown his big chance.

With the cab company about to install meters and put him out of a job, Tully realized that another chance meeting with London was unlikely. He was back at his room before seven and recalled that Nellie Dingley once predicted that he would someday write like Jack London. He sent a note to London's hotel, reintroducing himself as the road-kid who wanted to write. He asked for a meeting. Embarrassed by the cab job, Tully did not mention their brief encounter in the nightclub. London agreed by telegram to meet, but said that since he was leaving for San Francisco in the morning, Tully should stop by that night. They met in the Alexandria Hotel bar.[35]

The meeting proved not to be the literary epiphany Tully had anticipated. "He got me lit," Tully later recalled.[36] Tully began by saying how he had wanted to write from the moment years ago when he saw London's picture in a library magazine. London appeared bored.[37] Tully shifted gears. Referring to London's work, Tully helpfully pointed out that London was a "muddled" writer.[38] When London finally spoke, he seemed jaded on the subject of writing and cautioned Tully against pursuing such a career. Even London's parting handshake seemed lifeless and weary. On one point only could London offer encouragement.[39] With the words "Tully is a Mayo among Trees, a Man's Work" emblazoned across his business card, Tully assuredly became the only tree surgeon in the country to boast a testimonial from Jack London.[40]

While Tully would continue to cite London as a major influence, the meeting marked the beginning of Tully's disillusionment with his idol. So marked was the contrast between his image of London and reality that Tully felt compelled to reassess the famous author. He returned to London's stories of the road, looking for some clue, some insight. On second reading, they lacked an edge, the ring of truth that Tully recalled them having.[41] London's stories were unconvincing, Tully finally concluded, because London had spent only a short time on the road, eight months in all, and became more insulated from its harsh realities with the passage of time.⁴² Or as London biographer John Perry later pointed out, "Unlike Josiah Flynt, London romanticized his tramp sketches."⁴³ Since London could not or would not be honest, Tully resolved that he would be the first to write honestly about the road and the ring.⁴⁴

Whether to uremia, as his death certificate attests, or suicide, as his daughter Joan later told Tully, London died in November 1916, an old man at the age of forty.⁴⁵ Although Jim had outgrown London, he always kept a soft spot for his boyhood hero. Years later, for instance, Jim recalled sitting in a barroom with George Gershwin, thrilled by the composer's plan to set *Call of the Wild* to music.⁴⁶

While Tully honed his prose during the 1910s, he also honed another skill critical to the success of every aspiring writer: the knack for grabbing publicity. He pulled into Waukegan, Illinois, in 1916 to take a two-hundred-fifty-dollar job working on the trees at the courthouse.⁴⁷ As was his practice, he used the high-profile job to solicit more work. He was so successful at extending his stay that Florence and Alton joined him, the three of them rooming at the home of the sheriff's mother-in-law.⁴⁸

The Waukegan courthouse became the scene of one of greater Chicago's most sensational murder trials in 1916. E. O. Lambert of nearby Lake Forest was irritated one February afternoon when his daughter, Marion, missed her train home from school. He telephoned the high school. He was puzzled and concerned upon being informed that Marion had not reported to class that day. Lambert and his wife maintained a lonely all-night vigil, their anguish and dread growing with every tick of the clock. When he could wait no longer, he enlisted the aid of a neighbor and set out into the cold darkness to find his only child. His search finally led him to Helm's Woods, a lonely stand of oaks near the train station. There, in the snow, two sets of footprints led to his daughter's frozen body, her school books at her side. One set of prints led away from the body.

Police quickly determined that Marion died of cyanide poisoning. Suspicion immediately fell on her former boyfriend, a University of Wisconsin junior named William Orpet. Orpet's prearranged alibi putting him in Wisconsin on the fateful night unraveled when a witness placed him in the woods with Marion near the time of her death. Two weeks after Marion's poisoning, Orpet was charged with her murder. Public sentiment ran hot for Orpet's conviction, and 1,200 potential jurors were dismissed before an impartial jury of twelve could be seated in early June. At trial, Orpet admitted to meeting his former sweetheart in Helm's Woods, but only to break off their relationship once and for all, as he had become engaged to another. The defense argued that the heartbroken teenager had taken her own life and that Orpet's feeble alibi simply reflected his desire to conceal his absence from school from his stern father. And, they asked, what possible motive could the defendant have to commit murder?[49]

The press devoured every scrap, with as many as thirty reporters, including Ben Hecht, making the short trip from Chicago to cover the trial. After a day in the hot courtroom watching evidence and testimony bolster first one side, then the other, thirsty members of the press and other onlookers recessed to a local brewery to regard the brewer's art and discuss the trial. Tully, who had become something of a favorite at the courthouse (and the brewery), proved especially adept at supplying the gathered press with elaborate theories and colorful commentary—so much so that some reporters for the afternoon papers pleaded with Tully to save his best quotes of the day for them.[50]

The defense prevailed and a throng of revelers repaired to the brewery to celebrate Orpet's acquittal. Orpet, who obviously had the most at stake in the trial, joined the group but did not drink and participated little in the merrymaking. Tully, though, despite having no real stake in the trial other than being convinced of Orpet's innocence, celebrated mightily.

As for Marion Lambert, crime writer Otto Eisenschiml argues that she died of neither suicide nor murder.[51] In a desperate attempt to keep Orpet, she threatened to commit suicide on that night in Helm's Woods. To drive the point home, she'd shown Orpet a bottle of cyanide she'd brought along for the occasion. In a dramatic flourish meant to impress Orpet with the true depth of her feeling, she touched her tongue to the powder. Just a touch. She expected Orpet to be so moved that he would renounce his fiancée. She expected hot tears, a warm embrace, and a pledge of eternal fidelity. She did not expect the taste of bitter almonds and burning in her mouth, the salivation, or the waves of nausea.[52] Perhaps, despite the vertigo, confusion, and giddiness that followed, she felt the stiffness and convulsions, the crazy pounding of her heart, the arching of her back. Perhaps only then did she realize that she had given herself a lethal dose.

The Orpet-Lambert case was more than just a dramatic interlude for Tully. Watching the attorneys make their case to the public through the medium of the press was a lesson he would not forget. The press, he saw, could be very useful. Much later he would learn that the press was a double-edged sword.

Tully made the adventures of an itinerant tree surgeon the subject of his poem "Harlots," which was published in the *Kent Courier*. Another poem, "The Castle Built in Spain," was also published in the *Courier*, and these two poems seem to constitute his entire literary output for 1916.[53]

When World War I drove up demand for chain, Tully hired on as a government chain inspector.[54] It beat joining the doughboys overseas, he later claimed, as German Americans had treated him well during his years on the road and he had misgivings about shooting their relatives.[55] And, more than ever, Tully needed steady work. On November 13, 1917, Florence gave birth to a daughter named Jeanne.[56] As family lore has it, Jim was not present at the birth. When he returned to the family home in Pasadena, he so disliked the baby's name that he had her name changed to Trilby Jeanne. He commemorated her birth with the poem "When Trilby Came."[57]

Tully's focus, however, was no longer poetry but his prose. London and Wright aside, the idea of getting a boost from an established writer was sound, Tully reasoned, but who? Upton Sinclair, the author of *The Jungle*, a muckraking exposé of Chicago slaughterhouses, was then also living in Pasadena. His poor record with famous authors notwithstanding, Tully decided to approach his neighbor. If Tully had misgivings about Sinclair's socialist message, he believed Sinclair, a famous champion of the underdog, would be sympathetic to an underdog writer. Instead, Tully later wrote, Sinclair's stony gaze and cool academic manner made him feel unwelcome. While Tully departed with his respect for Sinclair's championing of the poor intact, he was struck by what he saw as Sinclair's naive view of human nature and a certain snobbishness.

His disappointment with Sinclair did not keep Tully from writing the author's patron, a wealthy socialist named Kate Crane Gartz, introducing himself as a struggling writer and seeking a loan of fifty dollars. She never replied. Nor did it keep Tully in 1919 from sending a draft of his novel to Sinclair for an opinion.[58] When he was unable to get Sinclair to read or return the manuscript, Tully sent Alton, not yet ten, the short distance to Sinclair's home to retrieve the manuscript. Dogs chased off the boy.[59]

Discouraged because Sinclair had been no more helpful than Wright or London, Tully brought to the business of writing the simple tactics of the ring: just keep punching.[60] He paused long enough from his prose in March 1920 to send a letter describing life in California to a Kent newspaper. Writing for an Ohio audience under the name Jimmy Tully, Tully let the folks back home know that "I would trade all of California (if the real estate people would let me have it) to live those days of my youth."[61] Tully returned to the pages of the *Cleveland Plain Dealer* on April 1, 1920, with "A Test," a sort of parody of Kipling's famous poem "If."

While Tully was always grateful to the newspapers back in Ohio for publishing his poetry, it was time to move on. Tully sent some poetry and an unpolished article about the road to Frank Harris, the flamboyant editor of *Pearson's*.[62] They came back without comment. The article was then sent to William Marion Reedy of the *Mirror,* a literary magazine. It was again rejected, but Reedy thanked Tully for the submission and suggested improvements and offered advice, most notably that preaching be avoided at all costs. While Tully had already outgrown the themes of his early poetry, casting off the sentimentality of Harold Bell Wright and the romanticism of Jack London's weaker material, he still clung to a hallmark of the worst work of Upton Sinclair: a tendency for thumping and propaganda. Reedy's clear-eyed advice freed Tully to pursue the hard-boiled realism that would distinguish his best work.

Seeking the literary approval and encouragement of Carl Sandburg in January 1921, Tully mailed the famous poet a poem he had written about a dead chain maker. Sandburg took the time to write back, politely praising the poem and promising to reread it several times.[63] A letter from Theodore Dreiser arrived in April, also confirming to Jim that he was on the right track.[64]

The librarian at the small library where Tully spent many of his evenings was a fan of the *Smart Set,* the most influential literary magazine in publishing.[65] Its list of contributors over the years reads like a who's who of twentieth-century literature, including F. Scott Fitzgerald, Ezra Pound, James Joyce, Dorothy Parker, Eugene O'Neill, William Butler Yeats, Dashiell Hammett, Joseph Conrad, Aldous Huxley, W. Somerset Maugham, and Tully favorite James Branch Cabell.[66] It was, as its cover boasted, "A Magazine of Cleverness" and its editors, George Jean Nathan and H. L. Mencken, were to become the most influential critics and editors of the 1920s.

Reading Henry Louis Mencken was a breathtaking experience. No one wielded "the American language" (as he titled his landmark study) with such mastery and humor, such fireworks, as Mencken. Tully and the librarian often discussed the sophisticated mix of essays, criticism, and literary bomb-throwing that Nathan and Mencken themselves contributed each month.[67] Nathan and Mencken didn't just jab at sacred cows. They skinned them, skewered them snout to tail, placed them over hot coals, and then gleefully turned the spit. Such assaults on the flanks of belles lettres delighted many readers but also left more than a few enraged. The librarian mentioned that Nathan and Mencken never failed to set one friend of hers, a writer named Eugene Manlove Rhodes, to fuming. Knowing of Tully's growing admiration for Nathan and Mencken, as well as his own interest in writing, she arranged a meeting for him with Rhodes. Although Tully cared little for Rhodes's work, he found himself impressed with the older writer's honesty. Here, at last, was a working writer who might advise Tully on his work and recommend sympathetic publishers.

The pair got together often to talk about various writers, including Rhodes's favorite, Robert Louis Stevenson, and the craft of writing. Their talk renewed Tully's enthusiasm and he began work on a short story. When it was completed, he handed the manuscript to Rhodes for his opinion. Rhodes judged it bad, populated by unbelievable characters whose language was stiff and academic. The criticism moved Tully to rip up not just that story but also, as he later claimed, drafts of all his stories, his articles, and even *Emmett Lawler,* his novel of more than 100,000 words. He would have to start over.

A few days later, Rhodes dropped by. He hadn't reconsidered his opinion—the story *was* bad—but he did regret causing Tully so much misery when he clearly was trying. Tully was silent, too moved by Rhodes's consideration for his feelings to respond. Tully finally revealed that he was still learning to write and expected criticism. He thanked Rhodes for stopping by. As Rhodes turned to leave, he paused. There was another writer Jim should know. Rhodes urged him to send a letter to a successful Hollywood writer named Rupert Hughes. Perhaps Hughes could help. Rhodes departed, becoming ill shortly after this meeting. He and Tully never saw each other again.[68]

Rupert Hughes, not nearly as well known today as his fabulously wealthy and eccentric nephew, Howard, had begun as a novelist and playwright on the East Coast. By the late 1910s, he was the hottest screenwriter in Hollywood.[69] His work for the silent movies was so highly esteemed that studios regularly engaged in bidding wars for his work.[70]

The letter Tully sent Hughes seeking his advice was, by Tully's own admission, full of bile, reflecting his growing frustration with writing. Hughes generously encouraged Jim, asking him to send a sample of his writing. Having just destroyed all his unpublished work, Tully had nothing prepared. And, as he was again broke, he had no time to write more. Instead, he borrowed money from Joe Bertucci and left for Omaha, where he planned to find work as a tree surgeon. It rained for a week. He was a stranger in town and killed time in his hotel room, reading the Gideon Bible.[71] He drifted off to the library and reread one of his favorite novels, Conrad's first book, *Almayer's Folly*.[72]

While out walking one evening, Tully came upon a road-kid begging for a handout in a doorway. Tully's usual response was to dig out a quarter, but he was so struck by the boy's loneliness that he forgot his own troubles and invited him to dinner. The youth was impressed that Tully had also been a road-kid and was awed at his relative success. Now in his mid-thirties, Tully realized that other than being able to buy dinner—with borrowed money—he really hadn't achieved any of his dreams. The unscrubbed boy sitting across from Jim aroused in him a flood of emotions, mostly reminding him that the years were slipping away. They paused outside to say good night. Jim handed the boy fifty cents. As he watched the road-kid disappear into the rainy night, Tully resolved to "write or starve."[73] It was a turning point and as important as his earlier decisions to hit, and then leave, the road.

The ever-loyal Joe Bertucci wired Tully return fare to California. Tully whiled away the trip in the day coach, thinking about his decision. It certainly simplified his life, giving him focus and forcing him to succeed. He had gotten by on little money before. He could do it again. The only flaw in the plan was that, unlike in years past, he now had a wife and two children to support. And, increasingly, his aging father was appealing for help.

His first stop after arriving home was a pawn shop, where he collected thirteen dollars in exchange for a gold watch and an ebony cane. It was enough to buy him a little time. Working under the pressure of his self-imposed decision to "write or starve," he began again on his novel, *Emmett Lawler*, and sent the opening chapter of 5,000 words to Rupert Hughes. When, after three weeks, he could wait no longer, he took a nickel from his meager savings and called Hughes from the library telephone. Doing his best to sound casual, he identified himself and asked for Hughes. The seconds it took for Hughes to speak seemed like minutes. And when the warm voice was heard, Tully could hardly believe his ears. Hughes was delighted to hear from him and just that day had mailed him a letter stating that, on the basis of what he had read, he believed that Tully was destined for greatness. Staggered, Tully thanked Hughes, left the library, walked home on a cloud, and waited for the morning mail.

Hughes had carefully read the manuscript, and his accompanying letter fully lived up to expectations. Hughes marveled at Tully's keen observation and use of language and exhorted him to let nothing stand in the way of his writing. He then asked to see the new chapters as they were completed, suggesting that Tully stop by one evening so they could discuss the project.⁷⁴ Just as he had suspected that his ears had deceived him the night before, he reread the letter several times to be certain his vision was not also faulty.⁷⁵

When, on the night of Tully's visit, Hughes realized that his guest hadn't eaten dinner, he instructed his cook to prepare a meal. Hughes was spellbound by Tully's tales of the road and again expressed his enthusiasm for the book, offering to help in any way he could.⁷⁶ That help took the form of patiently wading through chapter after chapter that Tully began sending in May 1921. Without fail, they were returned with extensive suggestions. Years later Tully could not say which had been more important, Hughes's advice or his encouragement.⁷⁷

While Tully's writing progressed, thanks in part to Hughes, at a fever pitch, the sticky problem of feeding a small family remained. But that small family no longer included Jim. Jim and Florence had been drifting apart for years and had regularly been apart while Jim was on the road. Their legal separation was a mere formality.⁷⁸ After his separation, Tully visited his friends Edwin Justus Mayer and Al Lewin, then sharing an apartment. They invited Jim to take his cap off and stay a while, which he did—for three months.⁷⁹ However, Jim remained a determined if not lavish provider. He again turned to old pal Joe Bertucci. The Alexandria Hotel, where Bertucci worked, laid out a small spread each evening in a back room for the porters. Jim could dine with the porters and carry back enough food for Florence and the children. It proved a workable plan.⁸⁰

Despite the upheaval in his personal life, the writing continued. By the end of June 1921, Jim was at the halfway point. Even the loss of a 15,000-word chunk of manuscript in the mail in July, for which Tully had no carbon copy, slowed him down but little.⁸¹ He rewrote the lost chapters from memory and sent them along to Hughes.⁸² One passage in the manuscript troubled Hughes: Emmett's horizontal encounter with a prostitute. Hughes counseled discretion. The dialogue could stand, but certain words were to be avoided. And to have the characters converse while in bed was to invite suppression. It was awful, Hughes allowed, that such silly rules need be observed, but worse still to have one's hard work go unpublished or banned.⁸³

By late September, *Emmett Lawler* was complete and ready to make the rounds of the four publishers Tully had in mind.⁸⁴ After several weeks of waiting, hope gave way to despair when Harper & Brothers and then George H. Doran turned it down. He sent it to Harcourt, Brace and Company and waited.

A telegram dated October 18, 1921, arrived at Tully's tiny residence on La Salle Avenue in Los Angeles, where he had moved from Pasadena the year before.[85] It was from Alfred Harcourt. *Emmett Lawler* was accepted. Details would follow by letter. At last, Jim could consider himself a writer. A letter from the post office arrived shortly after to notify him that the missing parcel containing his manuscript had been found. It would require twenty cents to forward it to Hughes. It was more than he could afford.[86]

Nothing could please a young writer more than to have his hometown paper trumpet the news of his first book on the front page, and the *Kent Tribune* did not disappoint: "Big New York Publishing House Accepts Jim Tully's Production, Former Kent Boy Writes Book Getting Praise from the Big Ones" (Nov. 17, 1921). Perhaps simply to show Upton Sinclair how he had improved the book since 1919, Tully sent him a chapter of the accepted novel in November 1921.[87] Sinclair, who hadn't responded or even returned the manuscript before, now wrote back suggesting the use of shorter sentences and more references to Emmett's age.[88] Tully's response to this late advice, now that the book was on its way to publication, was testy and defensive.[89] By December, Tully had cooled down enough to thank Sinclair with an autographed photo, but the question of Sinclair's contributions to *Emmett Lawler* would persist for years.[90]

9

Emmett Lawler

Autobiography shades every page of Jim Tully's first book, *Emmett Lawler*. As if to emphasize that the book would not stray too far from actual experience, Tully gave young Emmett, the title character, his mother's family name. It's a meaningful choice. On the basis of family lore (most of the details of which were later corroborated by his father),[1] Tully described the Lawlers as "physically brave. Their tempers were impetuous; their intelligence always superior to their environment. Open to every impression, they were extremely volatile.... Their simplicity was childlike.... There was in all of them, a holdover from ancient days—a deep mystical strain."[2] These were traits Tully believed he had inherited from his mother's family. And these were traits he passed along to the hero of his first book.

The writer also would have us believe that the character's first name is significant. Consider this intriguing passage in his opening chapter: "When Emmett was christened there was some hesitation about who should name him. His father, who had never before bothered about names for his children, now insisted that the boy be named after him. His mother reluctantly consented. But in her heart she called him her dream name. So he bears that name in this biography."[3]

The story might be fanciful, but its intention is clear. Given both Biddy's "dream" name and her family name, Emmett Lawler is more than just Jim Tully's literary stand-in. He is Tully's "dream self," a mirror image that allowed Tully to examine his life. The book is, in many ways, a young writer's attempt to put his life in perspective on the printed page. Tully wanted to understand how a life—*his* life—could withstand such malignant forces.

How did it happen? Why did it happen? *Emmett Lawler,* then, may be seen in part as an exercise in self-discovery.

Jim uses his life as a template for Emmett's. Like Jim, Emmett is one of six children born to an impoverished Irish American couple in St. Marys, Ohio. He is sent to an orphanage at the age of six. He becomes a road-kid after working for a brutish farmer (Boroff in real life, Soaroff in the book). And he learns the ways of hobo camps, chain factories, and boxing rings. Tully did not bother to change or disguise some of the most specific autobiographical details. For instance, Emmett's first poem, like Jim's, is "On Keats' Grave" and is published by *Cleveland Plain Dealer* columnist Ted Robinson. Still, *Emmett Lawler* is not autobiography. It is an autobiographical novel and the work of a first-time author still searching for his voice.

Tully was not satisfied with his first book and began taking elements of *Emmett Lawler* and thematically fleshing them out in the five individual books that would become his Underworld cycle: *Beggars of Life, Circus Parade, Shanty Irish, Shadows of Men,* and *Blood on the Moon.* All appearing within ten years of the 1922 publication of *Emmett Lawler,* these books would represent a powerful shift in the literary course taken by their predecessor. They are not, strictly speaking, novels and may be more accurately described as memoirs using the techniques of the novel. And it was in this approach that Tully found his true voice as an American writer. *Emmett* may not have blazed the trail, but it certainly cut the path.

Almost all the reviews for *Emmett Lawler* reflected this. They were, for the most part, encouraging but restrained. "It is worth reading," noted the *Bookman,* "but more as a psychological study of its author, than as a piece of writing."[4] Equally balanced were the reviews appearing in the *Saturday Review of Literature* ("The whole has a human and pleasant touch") and the *Freeman* ("In spite of its faults it is well worth reading; and as a piece of human expression, it is far superior to most of the literate novels that contrive to get themselves talked about").[5]

Tully's friend Rupert Hughes wrote the *New York Times* review. Given the role Hughes played as an adviser and mentor to the fledgling author, by current standards the paper's choice of critic would appear to be an obvious conflict of interest. It should be noted, however, that in the 1920s, literary logrolling was a generally accepted practice and Hughes was more than happy to get things rolling for his promising pal. "He makes the reader know what he knew," Hughes wrote. "Some of it is very impolite. Some of it would have been even impoliter if it had not been impolitic and unprintable. The acute reader will read much in that place where the best of all literature is stored—between the lines. He has much more to say, but he has already said a brave and priceless bookful."⁶

Even Upton Sinclair, who would prove to be petty and irksome on the subject of his contribution to *Emmett Lawler*, wrote a favorable review. "There is no preaching in this book," he asserted, "and if you have a couple of dollars to buy a novel, buy this one!"⁷ And back in Kent, the *Tribune* was characteristically enthusiastic, noting brisk sales down at Donaghy's drug store.⁸ The *Tribune* also reprinted Ralph Block's *Los Angeles Times* review: "*Emmett Lawler* is the record of a soul's searching for beauty, and still firmly believing in the fabled pot of gold at the foot of the rainbow."⁹ Elsewhere the *Los Angeles Times* proclaimed, "Jim Tully is the literary sensation of the year."¹⁰ Perhaps the most balanced judgment was handed down by Hulbert Footner in the *New York Evening Post Literary Review*. "It's an uneven book. There are many good things in it, things which would be good in any man's book. On the other hand, there is a bit of sentimentalizing here and there."¹¹

The publication of a first book might be expected to be a source of pride for an author's family. Given Jim's unflattering portrayal of his father in *Emmett Lawler*, Jim must have been apprehensive about facing his father. Jim recalled him saying simply, when they finally met—their first meeting in ten years—"It's the truth."¹² And while the road to *Emmett Lawler* was anything but certain, one person seemed never to doubt that Jim would produce a book. When he finished the rambling first draft of *Emmett Lawler*, his sister Virginia told him, "I just know you have a story, Jim." Sure, he replied, "but where is the damn thing?" With simple and unswerving belief, she solemnly encouraged him: "It's there." And when *Emmett Lawler* was published, she declared to him, "I'm somebody now—just think, my brother wrote a book." He was tickled when Virginia visited St. Marys with a copy, walking up and down Spring Street, "proud and swift as old."¹³

Yet Tully knew he could do better. He also wasn't unmindful of the sentimental aspects of his writing. In a 1923 letter to the caustic critic and author H. L. Mencken, soon to become a close friend, Tully wrote, "I often wonder why you did not slam *Emmett Lawler*. I know it was not wonderful—but I'm coming on—at least trying to write of the things I know without sentimentality—that curse of the Irish."¹⁴

Mysticism and sentimentality, though, would always be a part of his character. "I retain from Catholicism only a certain mysticism, common to the Irish," he wrote eight years after the publication of *Emmett Lawler*.[15] But traces of neither mysticism nor sentimentality proved to be the weaknesses Tully sometimes imagined them. Indeed, when properly channeled, they provided his writing with a lyrical quality that added poignancy and power to even the most brutally realistic passages. The inexperienced author imagined that he was struggling against sentiment in *Emmett Lawler*. In reality, he was, rather, learning how to accept and accommodate the romantic part of his nature while remaining true to the notion that all life should be depicted accurately.

By his own admission, he had left St. Marys expecting to find grand adventures waiting around every bend of the road. That romantic spirit certainly was dampened during this rugged period, but it was not altogether extinguished. As Tully himself suspected, environment could not completely obliterate the emotions bestowed by heredity. He was a romantic by birthright, a realist by experience, which was why Dickens could be as much of an influence on his writing as Gorky. So, not just a chronicle of Gorky's "lower depths," *Emmett Lawler* was as much a journey of self-discovery as *David Copperfield*. One side Tully correctly described as the Irish dreamer. The other might be called the boxcar pragmatist. What Tully discovered, consciously or by instinct, was that these two aspects of his writing did not have to be in conflict. Indeed, they could complement each other, giving the best passages in his books a stunning one-two literary punch.

The problem with the briskly paced yet ragged *Emmett Lawler* is that these writing weapons are not effectively deployed. Nor has Tully fully committed to the hard-boiled machine-gun style that would so energize his later books. It was an auspicious if not stunning literary debut. *Emmett Lawler*, therefore, is fascinating as Tully's literary point of origin. It is the book that points the way. The critics of 1922 saw the great promise in this novel. The reader of today can see in it the thematic road map for his later, better books. Perhaps the most remarkable thing about *Emmett Lawler* was that it was written at all. Here was a book completed by a former road-kid against the most improbable of odds. He could at last legitimately call himself a writer.

While Tully was aware of the novel's flaws, he was proud to finally have his name on the cover of a book brought out by a major New York publisher. This sense of accomplishment could, understandably, get the best of him. "I still feel that *Emmett Lawler* will eventually be the American *Oliver Twist*," he immodestly wrote to producer Jesse L. Lasky in 1927.[16] Was this the same book that had him apologizing to Mencken in 1923? As he was pitching

Lasky in 1927 on a film version of *Emmett Lawler*, Tully's high opinion of *Emmett* may simply reflect how well he'd come to appreciate the art of hype in Hollywood.

Tully dedicated *Emmett Lawler* to "all those with whom I have shared hunger and cold, and the loneliness that gnaws and gnaws."[17] Despite the heady success following the publication of his first book, the gnawing loneliness, Jim would learn, was a demon never to be slain.

10

Hollywood Writer

There was a brief moment of euphoria that followed the publication of *Emmett Lawler* in early 1922. The realization that he had achieved his goal of becoming a writer was overwhelming to Jim Tully. Considering his passage through fire, it is understandable that he described himself as "in the clouds."[1]

When the first-time author returned to earth, a rather sobering dose of reality was waiting for him. While his book had put him on the map as a writer, it had done nothing to fortify his anemic bank account. Taking stock of his literary and economic situation, Tully would quip that he "was still dazed and poverty-stricken from the experience" of seeing *Emmett Lawler* in print.[2] It had been a long road from flat-broke drifter to impecunious writer.

The glory of publication did not erase the question of how to support a wife and two young children. He had not thought to ask for an advance from Harcourt, Brace and Company. And the publisher, Tully sardonically observed, evidently had not thought to offer one. The amiable Rupert Hughes again rode to the rescue. Through his influence, Tully was given a job as a reader in the scenario department of the Culver City studio then known as the Samuel Goldwyn Producing Corporation. His salary was thirty-five dollars a week. Hughes was the first of many new friends whose wisdom, guidance, and beneficence saw Tully through the next two uncertain years.

Every day, Tully made the trip from Hollywood to Culver City, where, seven years earlier, pioneering filmmakers Thomas H. Ince, Mack Sennett, and D. W. Griffith had started building what would become "one of the largest and most modern" movie studios in the world.[3] The state-of-the-art facility was taken over by producer Samuel Goldwyn in 1918. He lost control during a 1921 contract dispute, but not before building up the studio's roster of talent. Two years after Tully's brief tenure as a reader in Culver City, Metro Pictures purchased the Goldwyn studio and put Louis B. Mayer in charge. The new Hollywood entity soon would be known as Metro-Goldwyn-Mayer, MGM for short, although the G in MGM, Samuel Goldwyn, had no direct involvement with this new Hollywood entity. Indeed, he had ceased being a presence at the Samuel Goldwyn Producing Corporation when Tully reported for work there shortly after *Emmett Lawler* saw print.

The job of the reader was to summarize and evaluate literary and stage works for producers. Although grateful for the weekly paycheck, the irony of his new position was not lost on Tully. Eager to capitalize on his status as a writer, he was making his living as a reader. And most of what he was given to read could be charitably categorized as drivel. Still, the job was not without benefits. There was a dependable income, and his duties were not overly taxing, allowing him to start work on a second manuscript, a novel about migrant laborers to be called "Passing Strangers."[4] And the Goldwyn studio paid him to read Joseph Conrad's *Lord Jim* and Stendhal's *The Red and the Black*. Although he advised against a film adaptation of *Lord Jim,* Conrad remained one of his favorite authors.

As unrewarding as the work proved to be, he had turned an important corner at Goldwyn. Never again would Tully have to support himself and his family through manual labor. Sitting at his desk in a tiny pine-board studio office, he could not, of course, in 1922 be certain of this. To be sure, the former chain maker and roving tree surgeon required little prodding to summon memories of the grueling jobs he hoped were forever behind him. He was sitting at a desk. He was working with words, and this change would be permanent.

Tully soon realized, however, that the mundane work of a studio reader did not suit him. By his own admission, he never quite mastered the studio lingo necessary to translate a story into a Hollywoodese synopsis. And he couldn't hide his disdain for the bilge tossed on his desk every day. So when a research position opened up at the studio, he put in a strong bid for it. He was surprised and frustrated when the job was given to a young electrician's assistant with no literary experience.[5]

More bad news followed. A week after moving to Culver City, Tully was laid off. The courtly Goldwyn executive in charge of the scenario department, his friend Paul Bern, told him that the dismissal had nothing to do with the quality of his work. A cutback had been ordered, and being the last hired, Tully had to be the first to go. Already an experienced director, screenwriter, and film cutter, the round-faced, soft-spoken Bern insisted that Tully keep in touch. After the formation of MGM in 1924, Bern rose rapidly in the studio ranks, eventually becoming the top assistant to Mayer's brilliant young head of production, Irving Thalberg. This would make Bern one of the most powerful men in Hollywood.

Moving back to Hollywood, Tully completed "Passing Strangers," his novel about migratory labor, and in April 1922 he left for New York with the manuscript. Although Alfred Harcourt had not asked for an option on Tully's sophomore book, he agreed to look at what the author of *Emmett Lawler* was bringing east.

Stopping in Chicago, Jim visited Virginia and described his plans for a book about the tramps he had known as a boy. Virginia exclaimed, "That's right, Jim, stick to the poor, whipped beggars of life."[6] The work that would become Jim's breakthrough book had its title.

While in Chicago, he wrote author-editor H. L. Mencken, thanking him for his support of *Emmett Lawler*. It was the beginning of a warm friendship that would last the rest of Tully's life. Not yet forty-two, the Sage of Baltimore was the country's most celebrated journalist and most powerful literary critic. Mencken delighted in shocking the species he defined as "boobus Americanus." Chomping on his favorite cigars, a local brand known as Uncle Willies, he reserved his choicest and most comic invective for politicians and other peddlers of moral uplift. A proud iconoclast, Mencken believed that "the liberation of the human mind has been best furthered by gay fellows who heaved dead cats into sanctuaries and then went roistering down the highways of the world. . . . One horse-laugh is worth ten thousand syllogisms. It is not only more effective; it is also vastly more intelligent."[7]

Nowhere were his thundering insights and critical acumen more needed than in the world of literature. It was into this dusty sanctuary that he would heave one dead cat after another. Since being recruited with George Jean Nathan as a *Smart Set* reviewer in 1908, Mencken had, in the words of biographer William Manchester, "fired away at every accepted literary standard and a few that were not literary at all."[8] His mission as a critic was to dethrone the novel of manners and morals. Out with the wafer-thin romanticism of Harold Bell Wright, Kate Douglas Wiggin, and Gene Stratton-Porter. Make way for the liberating likes of Theodore Dreiser, Willa Cather, and James Branch Cabell. "Utterly unafraid," wrote Mencken scholar Charles A. Fecher, "he heaped ridicule on established figures who had long been revered, and eagerly hailed new writers who were bringing a fresh and more realistic voice to the novel and short story."[9] He was the American champion of such writers as Conrad, George Bernard Shaw, Friedrich Nietzsche, and Henrik Ibsen. He generously aided such promising native talents as Sinclair Lewis, Ring Lardner, Edgar Lee Masters, F. Scott Fitzgerald, and Jim Tully.

His call for realism was not meant for a select few. "If Mencken had certain set ideas concerning the novel," William H. Nolte wrote in *H. L. Mencken: Literary Critic*, "it is nonetheless clear that those ideas leave room for the artist to move freely about, to experiment, to blaze new paths."[10] His definition of realistic literature, therefore, covered a multitude of styles, philosophies, and approaches. Or, as writer James T. Farrell explained, Mencken preferred "books in which you could find truth, a sense of reality, a feeling for the complexities and inexplicableness of men and of their varied destinies."[11] This encompassed everything from the war stories of John Dos Passos to the fantasy of Lord Dunsany.

In Tully, Mencken found one of those fresh and realistic voices—one that talked bluntly about people traditionally held to be unfit subjects for literature. And like Tully, Mencken was fond of good beer and good talk. While their backgrounds were vastly different, they were in many ways kindred spirits. Tully was more sentimental and Mencken was more cynical, but each mistrusted any man quick to boast about how moral and honest he was. Acerbic in print, Mencken was genial and charming in person. Always touched by kindness, Tully responded enthusiastically to the leading literary critic's unselfish and unflagging interest in his career.

Writing from Chicago in April 1922, Tully informed Mencken that he was having "happy talks" with Sherwood Anderson, Ben Hecht, Carl Sandburg, *Chicago Daily News* literary editor Harry Hansen, and "others of the Chicago crowd."[12] Mencken must have been pleased, having aided both Hecht and Anderson.

Leaving Illinois, Tully paused in Ohio. In Kent, Tully caught up with old friends and enjoyed the recognition of having become a published author. Following an interview, a local reporter wrote that "It is Jim's ambition to be the novelist of Ohio and picture the state with the same truth to life and detail that Thomas Hardy pictured his section of England."[13] As Tully greatly admired Sherwood Anderson's *Winesburg, Ohio*, the idea of being associated with his native state had enormous appeal.[14]

While in Kent, he also met with President John E. McGilvrey of the Kent Normal School (later Kent State University) and toured the campus to gather material for a novel to be based on a Kent coed who moves to Hollywood to work in the movies.[15] The idea for such a book may have come from a letter Tully received in July 1921 from a Kent high school student seeking advice on getting into the movies. Tully's response, a long letter to "Dream Girl," was published in the *Kent Tribune*.[16]

His joy was tempered by the knowledge that Nellie Dingley had not lived to see his first book. Nellie had resigned her position at the Kent library in 1910 to study nursing, eventually volunteering for the Red Cross during World War I and sailing to Europe in 1918. Less than a week after landing in France, she came down with pneumonia. She died on August 28 and was buried near Paris.[17]

Finally moving on to New York on May 13, Tully delivered "Passing Strangers" to Harcourt and awaited a verdict. It was not long in coming. The publisher turned it down, suggesting the writer instead tackle a story about "a Hollywood woman."[18] While he had been thinking about a Hollywood novel, it was not the book he wanted to write in 1922. He returned to California determined to write a book about his years as a road-kid. To cut down on expenses, he moved into the Hollywood home of Joe Bertucci, who was now deriving the bulk of his income from bootlegging. Tully stayed for two months, completing the first draft of *Beggars of Life*.

Much work had been done in the roller-coaster year of 1922, but the need for money was becoming overwhelming. Putting aside his attempts to work on *Beggars of Life*, Tully thought he could successfully ape the formula used for stories printed in publisher Billy Fawcett's *True Confessions*. Under the influence of novelist and travel writer Lafcadio Hearn (1850–1904), he pounded out a 5,000-word composition titled "Confession of a Japanese Geisha Girl."[19] The magazine purchased it for a hundred fifty dollars. A few days later, a short story was accepted for publication, bringing in another ten dollars. And in June, he converted his Chicago "talks" with Anderson, Hecht, and Sandburg into an article that *Los Angeles Times* editor Harry Carr purchased for eleven dollars.

"Ben Hecht is a Byronic type," Tully wrote of the legendary Chicago reporter whose acclaimed novel *Erik Dorn* had been published in 1921. "But he is entirely Ben Hecht. . . . Hecht said, 'No writer ever sells out. He writes at all times the best that is in him. If that best is drivel, it is all he has to sell.'"[20] Recalling that he had met Hecht six years before, during the

William Orpet trial, when "I was slowly and ponderously getting away from my tramping and prize-fighting days," Tully noted that the journalist, novelist, and playwright was "generous in praise of other writers, and tolerant of critics who abuse him."[21]

After his experience at the Goldwyn studio and Harcourt's rejection of the second book, this quick succession of acceptances was as important to his morale as it was to his wallet. Perhaps it *would* be possible to support himself as a writer. Stunned by the size of the *True Confessions* check and the ease with which the story had been pieced together, Tully immediately set out to concoct more articles for the magazine. There was no guarantee that these "confessions" would be accepted, however, so Tully was pleased when Carr asked him to write Sunday features for the *Times*. His assignments included interviews with notable California convicts and a piece on the Chinese lottery.[22] Carr "also wants me to give Dreiser a big story," Tully wrote to Mencken, "but Dreiser, the big churl, refuses to answer my letters."[23]

He ended up writing eighteen features for the *Times*, earning between ten and thirty-five dollars for each. That got him through the summer of 1922, when he was renting a furnished room in Hollywood for five dollars a week. His income from the *Times* just covered his own meager expenses, but not those of Florence and their two children. Another stay from steady employment arrived when his interview from San Quentin with convicted murderer "Blue Beard" Watson was published.[24] And Fawcett purchased Tully's profile of a beauty parlor operator who had once been the madam at a house of prostitution.[25]

In the fall, he started selling boxing stories for a hundred dollars each to Robert H. Davis, chief editor of the Munsey magazines (a group that included *Cavalier, Ocean, All-Story,* and, of course, *Munsey's*). One of these, "The Circus Flea," appeared in July 1923, featuring a young middleweight contender named Eddie Adair and the two women who love and beguile him, named, not coincidentally, Nellie (Dener, not Dingley) and Mary (Boyle, not Lygo). Unlike real life, in the story the young boxer manages to get one of the girls (Nellie).[26]

By the end of the year, though, things were again looking desperate. It was at this low point that Rupert Hughes offered to finance another trip to New York. Hughes argued that Tully could use this Manhattan sojourn to meet with magazine editors and to circulate the manuscript of *Beggars of Life*. Hughes insisted. He paid for Tully's room at New York's Algonquin Hotel and, on January 5, 1923, loaned him three hundred dollars. "Never mind about the note," Tully's benefactor told him. "Pay it when it's convenient and don't worry."[27] This was hardly uncharacteristic behavior for the witty author and screenwriter. Hughes once listed a "futile eagerness to help everybody" among his most notable attributes.[28]

The trip paid off in several ways. Some publishers did express interest in *Beggars of Life*, and Tully started selling more pieces to an increasingly wide variety of magazines in 1923. There was, for instance, the start of a three-year association with the *Literary Digest International Book Review*, which ultimately published more than a dozen pieces by Tully—features and book reviews that carried such titles as "My Literary Fight, Round by Round" (1923), "Jack London's Baffled Greatness" (June 1923), "Famous Battles of the Prize-Ring" (Aug. 1923), and "The Real Truth about the Hobo" (May 1924).

And before 1923 was out, he sold a boxing story, "Brothers in Battle," to a California-based magazine, *Overland Monthly Outwest Magazine* (Oct. 1923), and an essay titled "Writing the Novel" to *Writer's Digest* (Oct. 1923). But his most significant sale of the year was to Mencken, who published Tully's "A Declaration" in the December issue of the *Smart Set*. It was a particularly satisfying achievement for Tully—another signal to the world and to himself that he had arrived as a writer.

Ten punchy paragraphs summarizing his beliefs and philosophies, "A Declaration" starts with an amusing yet sardonic observation certain to appeal to Mencken: "Life, to me, is a mirror, moved three times by a transfer company. Every time a fellow tries to adjust it, he cracks it a little." His sympathies were strong, he said, and his heart went out to the "head-battered and bloody" union organizers, even though "I do not like the mob. I had contempt for them when I was a tramp. I am still a snob. And yet, I'm considered a whale of a mixer."[29]

"A Declaration" had the distinction of appearing in the last issue of the *Smart Set* edited by Mencken and Nathan. They had run the magazine since 1914, "as we have written our books," Mencken explained, "primarily to please ourselves, and secondarily to entertain those Americans who happen, in general, to be of our minds. We differ radically in many ways. For example, Nathan is greatly amused by the theatre, even when it is bad, whereas I regard it as a bore, even when it is good. Contrawise, I am much interested in politics, whereas Nathan scarcely knows who is vice-president."[30] Nathan too would become a trusted friend. "No man I have ever known has greater power of attention," Tully would say of the country's leading drama critic. "It is respectful, intense. . . . Not a lover of people in the mass, he has a horror of those who pretend. This keeps his circle small. Those in the enclosure remain for years."³¹ Mencken had never liked the title of the *Smart Set*. He also thought the magazine cheaply printed. He yearned for a magazine with a more prestigious title and design. He got his wish when the first issue of the *American Mercury* appeared just before Christmas in 1923. Edited by Mencken and Nathan, it became a regular outlet for Tully's best magazine work.

Whatever Jim's future held, it would not include Florence and the children. They had been formally separated for two years, and on October 25, Florence Bushnell Tully was granted a final divorce decree in Las Vegas. "Cruelty and desertion" were listed as the grounds, and Jim agreed to pay twenty-four dollars a week in child support.³² Alton was twelve years old. Trilby was just about to turn six. The marriage had lasted thirteen years.

Regular child support payments meant returning to a steady job. Now it was Paul Bern's turn to do Tully a favor. The producer secured his friend a job as a studio press agent at Goldwyn. The writer was offered a weekly salary of fifty dollars a week, but he asked for twenty-five and the freedom to work only three days a week. In one sense, the necessity of taking another studio job must have been frustrating. Yet, Tully realized this time that he would not be returning to Culver City as a reader. He would be writing. His first assignment was to ghostwrite an article summarizing Hollywood trends as identified by one of the town's leading screenwriters, former Metro power player June Mathis. The story appeared in the newspapers under her byline, followed by Jim's profile of Mathis for *Story World*.³³

Mathis and Irving Thalberg would both be working at the new MGM in a few months, with Thalberg editing director Erich von Stroheim's *Greed*. Thalberg's stock went up with the signing of silent-screen legend Lon Chaney, with whom he'd worked at Universal. The "Man of a Thousand Faces" starred in MGM's very first film, *He Who Gets Slapped*, a box-office and critical success that hit theaters in November 1924. About seven years earlier, Tully had become friendly with both von Stroheim and Chaney when the three of them were regular commuters on a small black bus that made the four-mile trip from the corner of Cahuenga and Hollywood Boulevard to Universal City. One-way fare was ten cents. Each member of this odd trio was unknown at the time but would become a national celebrity within ten years.³⁴

After finishing the Mathis story, Tully asked for permission to interview Elinor Glyn, the outspoken English novelist just signed to a studio contract.³⁵ Tully asked her ten questions and wrote an article that was immediately shelved by the publicity department.³⁶ The enterprising writer did, however, get another hundred and fifty dollars from *True Confessions* when he arranged for a story to appear in the magazine under Glyn's byline. In the meantime, he tried selling his Glyn interview to *Vanity Fair*. After initially declining the piece, *Vanity Fair* reconsidered and purchased it for $300.[37] "My Interview with Elinor Glyn"[38] came to be regarded as a classic interview for, as one critic wrote, "allowing Elinor Glyn to make a fool of herself."[39]

Another studio reorganization occurred at about the same time "A Declaration" was printed in the *Smart Set*. When the new head of the publicity department finally saw Tully's pronouncements, he was far from overjoyed with some of the "philosophies" put forward. And Tully was far from overjoyed with the head of the publicity department. It was probably this combination that put Tully's name at the top of the list for dismissal. Tully immediately found another job at twenty-five dollars a week. He wrote publicity material—small newspaper items—for a hospital being built in Hollywood.[40] But 1924 started with few prospects and even fewer dollars in his pockets. Over the past several years, though, Tully had become rich in friends—Hughes, Bern, Chaney, Nathan, Mencken. One of them always seemed to step forward whenever he required a boost.

At this low point in Tully's life, the role of benefactor was again played by Bern. Born Paul Levy, Bern was "the only man I have ever known who practiced the teachings of Christ."[41] Bern's assistant, Ralph Block, was giving a party, and Tully just had to be there. Block also had faith in the writer's talent, certain that Tully was more than a "one book man."[42] So Bern and Block wanted their friend to meet the biggest star invited to the party. The celebrated guest's name was Charlie Chaplin.

11
The Road-Kid and the Little Tramp

Jim Tully felt out of place among the well-dressed guests at the opulent Hollywood dinner given by studio insider Ralph Block. He was surrounded by women in elegant gowns and men in fashionable evening attire. The former road-kid was quickly overwhelmed by the sheer excess on display. Everywhere he turned, something resplendent caught his eye—shining silver, glimmering glassware, highly polished woodwork. Mountains of food sat on tables covered in the finest linen. He was shy, unsure of himself, and silent. It was at this awkward moment that he was introduced to Charlie Chaplin, the planet's reigning comic genius.[1]

The suave and gracious fellow shaking Tully's hand seemed like a wealthy, cultured, and therefore distant relation to his ragged screen character, the beloved Little Tramp. But it was in this guise that Chaplin "conquered the world with his comic and eloquent silence."[2] Wherever flickering images were shown in darkened theaters, audiences immediately recognized the wistful wanderer with his trademark derby, bamboo cane, and twitching mustache. Waddling through life in oversized shoes and baggy pants, this ever-hopeful dreamer could evoke laughter and tears with either artistic grace or outrageous slapstick. "Out of uniform," Chaplin cut quite a handsome figure. "Having learned to observe men during seven years as a road-kid, and later as a wandering bruiser," Tully would later recall, "I was soon aware that success had put a polish on the screen vagabond. If manners were a cloak to hide feelings, he wore a gorgeous garment."[3]

With the cultivated Block and the courteous Bern smoothing the way, Tully warmed to the conversation and impressed Chaplin with his insights on everything from authors to directors. When the party broke up, the

Little Tramp offered the road-kid a ride home—in a limousine. "Go ahead, Jim," Bern pushed, "Everything will be all right." The next day, Chaplin sent a picture of himself with an inscription: "From your fellow comrade, Charlie Chaplin."[4]

Tully was unsure about following up on this meeting with the master comedian. Even with his economic situation growing more desperate, he was reluctant to be seen as manipulating his way into a job. Nor was he comfortable with Hollywood money. Just a few years earlier, Tully had written disparagingly of the Little Tramp in the *Kent Tribune*: "When Charlie Chaplin, a clown, can earn a million a year—did I mention the taste of the public—there is room for improvement."[5] Hungry families have little regard for such critiques.

"The wolf was under the bed," Tully related. "Paul Bern drove him a few hundred feet away. By a ruse and a telegram he convinced Chaplin that I could be useful to him. It was not an important matter to the comedian. My salary of fifty dollars a week would make no dent in his million a year." When Tully balked, asking what he could possibly do for Chaplin, Bern said, "Take a pension from a king when you can."[6] Bern bolstered his argument by informing Tully that their mutual friend, "the major," considered this a wonderful idea. "The major" was their affectionate nickname for Rupert Hughes.

In February of 1924, Tully reported for work at the Hollywood studio Chaplin had built six years earlier on a lot bordered by La Brea Avenue and Sunset Boulevard. He was walking into a magical realm built by a king. Bern had not been wrong in using that term. Chaplin's ascension to Hollywood royalty was meteoric after his film debut in *Making a Living*, a 1914 Keystone Company comedy short. A gruff but fun-loving Irishman, Keystone founder Mack Sennett was then the infant film industry's unquestioned "king of comedy." As a director, producer, studio boss, and sometimes-actor, he had hit America over the head with slapstick—and America screamed for more. His ability to recognize talent was almost as true as his aim with a custard pie. "The secret of Mack Sennett's success was his enthusiasm," Chaplin wrote in his autobiography. "He was a great audience and laughed genuinely at what he thought funny."[7] Keystone's king, however, entertained some early moments of doubt about the English performer he had started at a hundred fifty dollars a week. Sennett did not yet realize that life had made his young employee both resourceful and ambitious.

Born Charles Spencer Chaplin in the Walworth section of London on April 16, 1889, the agile performer had survived a childhood of poverty and privation. He had received his earliest training in the English music halls, moving into the legitimate theater as a juvenile. At the age of seventeen, he was hired by impresario Fred Karno for one of his many touring companies. During his seven years with Karno troupes, Chaplin learned hundreds of vaudeville routines and music-hall sketches. While Tully was receiving body blows in boxing rings, Chaplin was receiving advanced degrees in mirth-making, miming, monkey-shining, and mugging. Sennett first spotted him in New York playing the drunk in the Karno comedy *A Night in an English Music Hall*.[8] Three years later, Chaplin was on his second Karno tour of America and Sennett asked him to join Keystone. The Sennett offer caught up with Chaplin in May 1913. It was for three times what the twenty-four-year-old Chaplin was making with the Karno company.

Groucho Marx remembered crossing paths with Chaplin on the vaudeville circuit. The one and only Groucho had already determined that the soft-spoken Englishman was a brilliant comic, so he was astonished when Chaplin said he was thinking about turning down Sennett's offer. No comedian, Chaplin reasoned, was worth that much money. And what would happen, he asked Groucho, if he took the money and failed to make good? "Then where will I be?" Chaplin asked.[9] Just three years later, he would sign his third studio contract, this one for ten thousand dollars a week.

After his Karno contract ran out, Chaplin showed up at Keystone in December 1913. In this rough-and-tumble atmosphere, Chaplin developed his screen persona, the Little Tramp. Chaplin described the character: "You know this fellow is many-sided, a tramp, a gentleman, a poet, a dreamer, a lonely fellow, always hopeful of romance and adventure."[10] Signing increasingly lucrative contracts with other production companies, Chaplin eventually set up shop in his own studio. When Tully joined Chaplin in 1924, the Little Tramp had formed United Artists (in partnership with D. W. Griffith, Mary Pickford, and Douglas Fairbanks) and was getting ready to start work on the film many believe stands as his masterpiece, *The Gold Rush*. After ten years in Hollywood, he had assumed Sennett's throne as the king of comedy.

What were Tully's duties at the Chaplin Studios? He was to be a ghostwriter, turning out articles that would appear under the comedian's name. He was to attend story conferences, responding to questions about casting and plot points. He was to be a sympathetic ear whenever his boss was in a talkative mood. And he was to be part of the king's court—a court that included jesters, counselors, ministers, and royal flatterers.

The inner circle was not wide. It included former Karno manager Alf Reeves, an affable Cockney who handled all financial matters for Chaplin. A former bruiser named Chuck Riesner was Chaplin's easy-going assistant director (also spelling his name Reisner, he later directed films starring Buster Keaton, the Marx Brothers, W. C. Fields, and Abbott & Costello). H. d'Abbadie d'Arrast, a horse-faced nobleman known as Harry, also served as an assistant director. Kindly Henry Bergman was a hulking former weight lifter. There was R. H. "Rollie" Totheroh, the comedian's cameraman. Charles D. Hall, a former Karno employee, was the studio's art director. And there was Eddie Sutherland, the able assistant director who would later direct comedies with Fields, Laurel & Hardy, Abbott & Costello, and Eddie Cantor.

Bern believed that Chaplin and Tully would discover they had a great deal in common. Each had overcome Dickensian childhoods. Each had a sardonic sense of humor. "Though deference was a mask we both wore," Tully observed, "it did not always conceal fierce ego and indomitable pride. . . . Both entirely self-taught, and seeing the worst of life early, we were equally cynical and well trained for the roles assigned to us in life." But while Chaplin played a tramp on the screen, Tully had been the genuine article. "I was a curiosity to him," Tully would say of the great clown, "a vagabond, like himself, who had bulged his way upward. And there the resemblance ceased. The same winds of environment had shaped us differently."[11] As if examining his own creative soul through such comparisons, Tully started cataloging the differences between them. "My equal in apprehension," Tully concluded, "he was my superior in the social graces. Reading deeply from childhood, I had absorbed the great minds of the ages. . . . With the exception of stage and screen, his knowledge of all other subjects was superficial."[12]

Charlie Chaplin for years would cultivate the image of an intellectual comfortable trading philosophical points with the likes of George Bernard Shaw, Albert Einstein, Winston Churchill, and Mahatma Gandhi. Tully challenged this view of the Little Tramp, realizing that it was the adoring intelligentsia who saw in Chaplin what they wanted to see. "His reputation brought with it a certain awe," Tully said. "As a result, people listened politely who knew more about the subject of which he was talking than himself."[13] It was enough to Tully that the comedian was a great artist. Was it necessary to go along with the fiction that he was also a deep thinker?

Chaplin was given to making sweeping statements about art and artists, but unlike most members of the inner circle, Tully would not always let them go unchallenged. "A great artist must have a great audience," the comedian told Tully during his first week at the studio. "How about Whitman and Nietzsche?" the new employee countered. Chaplin looked at him, puzzled by the question. "They might have been members of a vaudeville team" to Chaplin, Tully later remarked. "He made no comment."[14]

There was another obvious difference that Tully realized would make friendship difficult. Chaplin already was hailed as a genius. With only one published book, Tully was "striving to be an artist."[15] Even if they had managed to navigate their differences, a close bond would have been difficult to forge. Tully was incapable of fawning—a survival skill in Hollywood—and both men were subject to dark moods. It was a doomed relationship from the start.

Still, in February of 1924, Tully was unaware of this. He was willing to take that pension from a king. Reporting to work at Chaplin's studio, he was assigned an office with a worn red rug, two ancient swivel chairs, and a yellow rolltop desk. Pictures from such Chaplin comedies as *The Kid* and *Shoulder Arms* decorated the walls. A dust-covered typewriter sat on the desk. Eighty feet away was Chaplin's office. For two weeks, Tully never even saw the famous comedian. Then, with filming about to begin on *The Gold Rush*, Chaplin walked into Tully's office, snapping his fingers. "Well, Jim," he asked, "how do you like it?" Warned by Riesner to always be restrained in "the presence of the master," Tully kept his reply to two words: "All right." "It's a job," Chaplin observed. "Yes," Tully agreed, "it's a job." Head down and hands behind his back, Chaplin paced the red rug as if burning off an excess of nervous energy. He finally asked Tully about being a writer. But seeing Reeves go by the office, Chaplin did not wait for an answer. He simply turned and walked out the door.[16]

What to make of such an exchange? Chaplin had seemed so earnest and intensely interested when he posed the question, yet this interest had disappeared as quickly as the Little Tramp himself after spotting a police officer. Tully soon realized that Chaplin had the type of restless mind that raced and sometimes became "submerged with ideas."[17] He eventually reached the conclusion that Chaplin's interest was miles wide but not very deep.

He also learned not to pay attention to the comedian's moods. Over the next two decades, Tully frequently tried to summarize the many contradictions that made up Chaplin's personality. It was a fascinating inventory fashioned from vivid memories, but not colored by either blind idolatry or hatred. "If at times I make of Chaplin a toy Hamlet in a tinsel town," Tully wrote,

> I hope it will be remembered that my compassion and understanding cover much.
>
> His early years wrote with heavy and terrible hand upon him. Though he became their master, and in so doing acquired the manners of a Chesterfield, a remembered sorrow had early turned to gall with him. For what was left of an accidental battle with environment, I had something like respect.[18]

And something like sympathy. Tully could relate to accidental battles with nature. The more he looked at Chaplin, the more complex the great clown seemed to become. But it was not the easy assumption of complexity casually expressed by Chaplin's more ardent admirers. "Often childish in quarreling, he was above vengeance," Tully wrote years later, refusing to either romanticize or disparage the Little Tramp.

> Imperious and scornful and often attacked with acute melancholia, he would hide such qualities in public. . . . Volatile, turbulent and petulant, his malice died with his anger. . . . His charm, his ease of manner, his graciousness, were undeniable. He never made comment on those who had wrongfully used him. Neither did he ever speak of a kindness he had done for another. . . . Inept upon the screen, the helpless foil of invidious circumstance, in private life, he was forceful, domineering, arrogant. . . . He had no antagonism toward any race or creed. . . . He had no vanity about personal appearance. . . . A superb ironist, he knew when to laugh at himself. . . . He could be amazingly kind and understanding in those rare moments when the cynical curtains of his soul were parted. . . . Restless as a storm, his mind was always active.[19]

Indeed, Chaplin's mind was always active to the point that he might not wait for an answer to his question. And Tully would spend years trying to take the measure of this restless mind.

After this initial encounter at the studio, conversations between Chaplin and Tully grew more frequent. Reeves would tell the writer, "The boss wants you, Jim," and Tully would be on his way to Chaplin's office, limousine, or mansion. Sometimes they would walk to one of the Hollywood Boulevard restaurants that Chaplin liked to frequent, say, the Armstrong Carlton Café or the Musso & Frank Grill. Sometimes it was just the two vagabonds, sharing some thoughts and a meal. Sometimes they would just walk. It all depended on "the mood of the master," Tully observed.[20] And that mood could change over lunch. Chaplin might suddenly forget that Tully existed and not talk to him for weeks. During these periods, Tully would be kept informed of studio doings by Riesner, the king's favorite jester.

While Tully remained unsure of where he stood with the king, he was on surer footing with members of the royal court. Riesner, Sutherland, and Reeves proved to be sources of both sound advice and companionship. Sutherland later recalled Tully as "an awfully nice man" who "wrote powerfully." But he also thought the former road-kid's years of wandering and poverty had given him something of an inferiority complex. And Sutherland praised Chaplin for giving Tully a weekly paycheck and an office where he could write. For someone who was "supposed to be very tough with a buck," Sutherland concluded, this was uncharacteristically generous.[21]

Tully was grateful for the help, but gratitude did not stop him from wondering about an employer who was a genial genius one minute and a temperamental tyrant the next. Did Chaplin like him? There certainly were times when Tully felt they'd had heartfelt conversations. And there were times when other studio employees would repeat words of "sly ridicule" that Chaplin had hurled at Tully.[22] Tully determined not to take any of it personally. Life at the studio, after all, was far from dull. Chaplin, dark moods and all, was never less than fascinating. And besides, "the check was regular."[23]

The writer wasted no time enhancing that income with a profile of Chaplin, almost certainly authorized, for the March 1924 issue of *Motion Picture Classic*. "The Loneliest Man in Hollywood" was a largely flattering and romanticized portrait of the man who was supplying the regular check. The title was drawn from a conversation Chaplin had with Tully about Thomas Hardy, the English novelist then in his eighties. Tully asked Chaplin if he would be satisfied with the type of solitary existence the author of *Jude the Obscure* and *Tess of the D'Urbervilles* was living. "Yes, indeed," the comedian replied. "I would welcome it. For even now, I am the loneliest man in Hollywood."

Two more assignments followed. Both were to be ghostwritten by Tully and would appear in the June issue of *True Confessions* under Chaplin's byline. The first of these, "My Impressions of Folk, Movies, and Edna Purviance," is, in one sense, a failure: it sounds considerably more like Tully than Chaplin. "Justice may be blind at times," the article tells us, "but public opinion is becoming more alert each year. . . . The heart of the man in the street beats true."[24]

The daughter of a miner, Edna Purviance had been Chaplin's leading lady since 1915. She was a stenographer with no acting experience when the comedian recruited her for his films, but the beautiful blonde from Nevada was a quick and able student. She was also intensely loyal to Chaplin, turning down offers for many times the weekly salary of one hundred dollars. By the time Tully was tackling this *True Confessions* article, she had appeared in thirty-four of the comedian's thirty-seven films, including *The Tramp, The Immigrant, Shoulder Arms,* and *The Kid.*

When Chaplin attempted a "serious" feature-length movie in 1923, he gave Purviance the lead role. He directed and kept his screen time to a cameo appearance. She responded to his direction, proving a capable dramatic actress in *A Woman of Paris,* which costarred Adolphe Menjou. But, except for extra work in *Monsieur Verdoux* (1947) and *Limelight* (1952), this would be the last film she'd make for Chaplin. He would choose a new leading lady for *The Gold Rush*. Still, Tully would remain impressed by Chaplin's devotion to Purviance. Long after she stopped appearing in movies, Chaplin continued to send her two hundred fifty dollars a week. "Her wage with him was never more than that amount," Tully observed in 1943, "while women of the same ability were earning several thousand weekly. But Edna had not worked in many years."[25]

It was another Chaplin contradiction that fascinated Tully. The fabulously wealthy Hollywood king was notoriously thrifty (particularly where salaries were concerned), yet, as Sutherland was quick to point out, he also could be generous and repay loyalty. When comedian Mack Swain was blacklisted by a studio mogul, Chaplin hired him at two hundred fifty dollars a week for *The Gold Rush*. And when the king convened his court at a restaurant, no one "was allowed to pick up a dinner check at Chaplin's table."[26]

Much of the ghostwritten "My Impressions" article for *True Confessions* was a Chaplin-ordered defense of Edna Purviance, who had recently been touched by scandal. She had seen her chauffeur gun down an acquaintance. The American public quickly agreed that she was guilty of nothing more than having poor judgment in her choice of chauffeurs. Although the affair passed quickly from the headlines, the specter of trial by sensationalism was a genuine source of terror in Hollywood. In 1921, the career of Roscoe "Fatty" Arbuckle, whom Chaplin had known at Keystone, was destroyed when San Francisco prosecutors charged him with manslaughter. A young starlet, Virginia Rappe, had died of a ruptured bladder after attending a hotel party thrown by the comedian. With the 320-pound star accused of having sexually assaulted Rappe, the newspapers whipped outrage to a fever pitch. Acquitted by a jury, Arbuckle had already been convicted in the court of public opinion. "There were two hung juries," critic Walter Kerr wrote. "A third jury cleared him in six minutes, issuing a remarkably strong statement in his defense. A week after his *acquittal* the Hays Office, newly formed watchdog of Hollywood morals, barred him from ever working on the screen again."[27]

The Hays office had become something to fear, so Tully had to choose his words carefully for Chaplin: "While I deplore the occasional scandal that comes to light among moving picture folk, the same as among all other classes of people, I do not forget for a moment that there is always another side of the shield."[28] Those words would take on increasing irony as Chaplin himself became embroiled in several scandals over the next two decades.

The second *True Confessions* article appearing under Chaplin's byline in the June 1924 issue, "Charlie Chaplin Builds a House," was something of a guided tour—complete with illustrations—through the comedian's home. It was innocuous and guaranteed to please the boss.

The major focus for everyone at Chaplin's studio during this period was preparation for *The Gold Rush*. Neither casting nor the script had been finalized, but the comedian had more than a general idea of the story he wanted to tell. Set in Alaska, *The Gold Rush* opens with the Little Tramp as a lone prospector seeking refuge from a raging snowstorm in the cabin of feared outlaw Black Larson. The Little Tramp eventually falls in with another prospector, Big Jim McKay (played by Mack Swain), and falls in love with a Klondike dance-hall girl. Although the story doesn't sound like much, the resulting masterwork would contain some of the funniest and most moving moments Chaplin ever put on film. While many critics believed he surpassed this triumph with *City Lights* (1931), Chaplin himself singled out *The Gold Rush* as the movie for which he wanted to be remembered.

In what is perhaps the film's most memorable scene, a starving Little Tramp boils one of his oversized shoes, devouring the shoelaces as if they were spaghetti and picking clean the nails as if they were turkey bones. Stranded with the Little Tramp in an isolated cabin, a ravenous Big Jim is driven mad by hunger. Hallucinating, he sees his diminutive companion as a rooster ready for the oven.

The inspiration for this hilarious sequence couldn't have been more grim. Chaplin had read a book about the infamous Donner Party, a group of settlers heading for California in 1846. Snowbound in the Sierra Nevada Mountains, the Donner Party endured a brutal winter of cold and hunger. Most perished. A few cooked their moccasins as a source of sustenance. Some, it was discovered, had resorted to cannibalism.

Filming on *The Gold Rush* started at about the same time Tully began working at the studio. On February 8, 1924, Chaplin started shooting the scene where the Little Tramp happens on Black Larson's cabin. With vaudevillian Tom Murray cast as the villain, these early moments were captured on a studio set. Wind machines provided the necessary blizzard.

Late in February, with this early footage in the can, Chaplin traveled about four hundred miles north with Riesner, Hall, and Totheroh to scout locations around Truckee, California, near Donner Pass. Since filming in the Klondike was impossible, the comedian needed a snowy spot that could pass for gold-rush Alaska. He found it in this wintry area about thirty miles from Reno. It was here that a studio crew built a replica of Alaska's Chilkoot Pass.

The Chaplin team braved the cold of Truckee for five days, leaving February 24. Back at the Hollywood studio, Chaplin immediately began wrestling with a key question. Whom to cast as his leading lady in *The Gold Rush*? Edna Purviance had been his only female costar since 1915, but the filmmaker believed that *A Woman of Paris* would establish her as a dramatic actress, and he didn't want to endanger this new standing with another comedy role.

Chaplin soon made it known that his choice for *The Gold Rush* was Lillita McMurray, a sixteen-year-old who lived near the studio in a small bungalow with her mother and grandparents. At the age of twelve, she had appeared in a dream sequence for *The Kid* and as a maid (with her mother, Lillian McMurray) in *The Idle Class*. Four years later, Chaplin was smitten. He let the teenager test several times for the role. She had little experience, but then Purviance had had no experience when signed by Chaplin.

The tests were run for the inner circle, and the yes-men dutifully agreed that the boss couldn't be more right about this young newcomer. Only Tully and Rollie Totheroh "were bold enough to express their dismay," film critic and historian David Robinson wrote in his exhaustive biography of Chaplin.[29] "Foregoing lunch, we waited to see it upon the screen," Tully said of the test. "Though she had less acting ability than any girl who had applied, Chaplin began to say, 'Marvelous! Marvelous!'" When the comedian later asked him his opinion of Lillita, Tully was brutally frank. Yet Tully knew that Chaplin would disregard his opinion. When told that the role was hers, Lillita McMurray clapped her hands and hopped up and down, shouting, "Goody, goody." The puerile display amused Chaplin. Tully was sickened.[30]

When she stopped hopping, Lillita McMurray agreed to change her name to Lita Grey. She was "bold as a pirate and carefree as the wind," Tully said. "Black eyes, black hair and a round face, she had neither sensibility, poise nor thought."[31] A signing ceremony was held March 2, 1924, and Tully suggested photographs be taken to document the event.[32] Watching Lita sign her contract were Chaplin, Tully, Reeves, Sutherland, Riesner, Bergman, publicist Eddie Manson, and Lillian McMurray. "Don't look at your salary," the Little Tramp said with a laugh. Why was this man laughing? "He had engaged a leading lady at $75.00 a week," Tully explained.[33]

Work proceeded on *The Gold Rush*, with Jim Tully in charge of publicity. After shooting several cabin scenes with Swain, Chaplin readied his team for location shooting at Truckee. Not long after the train with the cast and crew departed Hollywood in mid-April for Truckee, Tully knocked on the door of the drawing room Lita Grey shared with her mother. Notepad and pencil in hand, Tully announced that it was time to crank up publicity for *The Gold Rush*. "We can't start too soon getting the public to know you," he added. Ready to hear the teenager's life story, he sat down, crossed his legs, and yawned. Lita Grey later recalled that it was as if Tully wanted "to convey to us that he was here merely to earn a living, that he was full of disdain over this chore that had befallen him."[34]

"Whatever his misgivings about her talent," Robinson wrote in his biography of Chaplin, "Tully did a valiant job on the press. During the succeeding weeks American newspaper readers were constantly regaled with Lita's slightly squinting portrait and fulsome stories of her beauty, talent, charm, innocence and aristocratic lineage."[35] The copy Tully churned out in praise of Lita Grey ran from flowery to mawkish. "My economic law," the writer reasoned, "it had to be obeyed."[36]

But one passage in Tully's press release would soon take on haunting significance. It was meant to quell any unfortunate gossip: "No love affairs have ever brought a quick beating to her heart, a flush to her cheeks. She idolizes Chaplin, but much as a child feels for some much older man who has shown her a great kindness."[37] Her cheeks would not remain unflushed for long. She and Chaplin were soon seen together in public. He was infatuated, though clearly realizing there were danger signs. When everyone at the studio had become aware of the romance, the boss asked Tully what he thought of Lita Grey. Again risking a rift with his employer, Tully replied, "A young animal—nothing more." To his surprise, Chaplin agreed. "I know," the comedian said, "I was teasing her last night. She admitted she might like me better because I'm Charlie Chaplin."[38]

Trying to make a teenager's prattle interesting was excruciating, but Tully did find something interesting to write about. He wrote movingly of the six hundred derelicts hired as extras for the movie. Rounded up by special agents of the Southern Pacific railroad, these vagabonds were brought in on a special train bound for Truckee and a scene set at Chilkoot Pass. "They came with their own blanket packs on their backs, the frayed wanderers of the western nation," Tully wrote in a press release. "It was beggardom on holiday. . . . A more rugged and picturesque gathering of men could hardly be imagined. . . . They trudged through the heavy snows of the narrow pass as if gold were actually to be their reward, instead of a day's pay."[39] What mattered to them, Tully observed, was that they would "be seen in a picture with Chaplin, the mightiest vagrant of them all. It would be a red-letter day in their lives, the day they went over Chilkoot Pass with Charlie Chaplin."

When the frozen vagabonds yelled out a warm greeting to Chaplin, Tully said, "They're cheering for you, Charlie." "I know," the comedian answered. "How'd you like to be back among them?" "It could be worse," the former road-kid told him. "I'd rather be me than them," Chaplin concluded.[40]

Leaving Truckee in late April, Tully returned to Hollywood with Chaplin. Filming on *The Gold Rush* resumed in early July.

How much Tully contributed to *The Gold Rush* is unknown. It must have been illuminating for Chaplin, the world's most famous vagabond, to have input from a writer with intimate knowledge of the road. Robinson's Chaplin biography maintains that Tully was "engaged to work on the script and on publicity copywriting," and he places the writer at script sessions with Bergman and d'Arrast.[41] Tully would never claim having made significant contributions to the film, but he did recall attending script sessions with Chaplin. "When I slumbered in a story conference of *The Gold Rush*," he remembered, "he awakened me with, 'Jim, you're a snob.' It was one of the few compliments he ever paid me."[42]

By the fall of 1924, Lita was pregnant and the McMurray clan, led by mother Lillian and an Uncle Edwin, who was a lawyer, was demanding that Chaplin do the honorable thing and marry Lita. The Little Tramp was marched to the altar on November 24, and it was announced to the press that the new Mrs. Chaplin was retiring from the screen.

Chaplin proceeded with *The Gold Rush*, replacing Lita with Georgia Hale (a move privately cheered by most of his employees). Tully was amused when the Los Angeles school system demanded that Lita, only sixteen, continue her education. Tutors were sent to the Chaplins' Beverly Hills mansion, where Lita and her mother now ruled the regal roost. But "she could not be forced to study," Tully observed. "The Board of Education pursued her with its truant officers and teachers until she was eighteen, and then retreated."[43]

Still, after the wedding in Mexico, Lita remained friendly with Tully. She was amiable by nature, and he found it impossible to dislike her. Chaplin, however, perhaps remembering Tully's brutally honest assessments, would begin to avoid his employee. A son, Charles Spencer Chaplin Jr., was born seven months after the wedding. A second son, Sydney Earle Chaplin, followed on March 30, 1926. A decree of divorce followed on August 22, 1927.

Whatever Tully's contribution to the script of *The Gold Rush*, his name did not appear on the film when it was released on August 16, 1925. Nor did his name appear in Chaplin's 1964 autobiography, but, then, no mention was made of Sutherland, Riesner, d'Arrast, or Totheroh (each of whom spent more years with Chaplin). Lita Grey is not mentioned by name, and her presence in his life is reduced to three sentences: "During the filming of *The Gold Rush* I married for the second time. Because we have two grown sons of whom I am very fond, I will not go into any details. For two years we were married and tried to make a go of it, but it was hopeless and ended in a great deal of bitterness."[44]

Tully certainly believed the marriage to be hopeless, given the differences in their ages and temperament. "Except for a love of play," he noted, "his child wife had nothing in common with him. There were chords in the great comedian that echoed to grander music."[45] Ironically, Tully soon would be in the middle of his own roller-coaster relationship with a much younger woman.

12

Beggars of Life

While work was proceeding on *The Gold Rush* in the spring of 1924, Tully was busy putting the finishing touches on what would be his second book. He'd been calling it "Tramp Days" before settling on the title suggested by Virginia, "Beggars of Life."[1]

With the publication of *Beggars of Life* in late August of 1924, Jim Tully found his voice as a writer. It was a voice that carried the echoes of many sounds: the hum of the railroad lines, the rumble of a boxcar, the roar of the chain factories. Pounding out the first draft over a six-week span in 1922, Tully poured what he had learned about the road and about life into the book's thirty-one lean chapters. The white heat of creation had taken his writing to a dynamic new level. Something stronger, harder, and tougher had been forged. Seared away were the weaker elements of his writing so evident in *Emmett Lawler*. Discarded too was Harold Bell Wright's foolish advice never to write in the first person. Accordingly, Tully had written *Emmett* in the third person, but *Beggars* was Jim Tully's story, written in his own crisp voice. So the descriptions are less sentimental, even though, as the writer himself observed, there are moments of high sentiment.

For *Beggars of Life*, subtitled *A Hobo Autobiography* by the publisher, Tully learned how to bring his hard-boiled form of writing to the boiling point. Indeed, it's the book that defines his style, setting the pattern for the twelve books that would follow over the next two decades. Tully never liked the subtitle, considering it inaccurate and misleading. He would take pains in print and in conversation to point out that the book largely detailed his years as a road-kid, not a hobo. Few bothered to make the distinction. Nor did it help that his publisher noted in its press release for the book that "Jim Tully was a hobo, not a poet or writer on a holiday."[2]

Jim Tully just wanted to be known as a writer. The success of his second published book put him on a road to fame as "hobo writer" Jim Tully. Wherever he went for the remaining twenty-three years of his life, this two-word title would follow him. It was the sort of typecasting that haunted so many who found their way to Hollywood.

Still, at least there was finally a measure of celebrity to be enjoyed, and Tully had *Beggars of Life* to thank for it. There had been too many years of struggle not to savor this delightful turn of literary events. He might write better books, but none would become better known or open more doors for him than *Beggars of Life*. Before the decade was out, there would be a Broadway version of *Beggars of Life* (adapted by no less than playwright Maxwell Anderson) and a film version (directed by William Wellman). The book would enjoy several printings, editions, and translations.

Published by Albert & Charles Boni and sold at the price of three dollars, *Beggars of Life* established the writer as a gritty Gorky-like chronicler of America's so-called underclass. At the same time that the Princeton-educated F. Scott Fitzgerald was turning out finely polished tales of Jazz Age wealth, the road-wise Tully was using his raw prose to tell readers about those at the other end of the spectrum.

From the opening conversation on a railroad trestle, *Beggars of Life* rattles along like the *Fast Flyer Virginia,* which Jim boards midway through the book. Chapter after chapter in *Beggars of Life,* one finds Tully sharpening the skills that would carry him through the rest of his writing life. And perhaps the most significant advance over *Emmett Lawler* is his ability to vividly describe an individual or scene with a few tersely worded sentences.

His devotion to such authors as Twain and London had taught him the importance of giving the reader a sense of place, and this he does brilliantly, again and again, throughout *Beggars of Life*. When we meet a hobo or railway detective in *Beggars of Life,* we are convinced that he is the genuine article, not some romanticized refugee from a cheap melodrama. Tully makes us feel the cold and hunger of a bleak winter ride. He makes us hear the train whistle and the sound of a skull cracking under the snap of a blackjack. He makes us see the tramps and the wanderers with a tenuous grip on the lowest rungs of the social ladder.

Beginning with *Beggars of Life,* when Tully wishes to transport the reader back to a different time and place, he accomplishes the trick with ease. What was it like waiting in the dark for a train? "Great clouds of steam and smoke fell all around us," he tells us. "A faded yellow moon would now and then shine through the vapor."[3] This is typical of the visual sense Tully displays in *Beggars of Life.* A Hollywood cinematographer could do no better.

In two finely crafted paragraphs, he gives us the sights, sounds, and smells of waking up on a flatboat near a hobo jungle:

> The sun climbed early over a wood nearby and threw its rays upon our faces. We sat erect and sleepily watched the peaceful scene around us. Some geese were swimming in circles in the middle of the river. A passenger train thundered over the railroad bridge on its way to Chicago. The frogs still croaked along the bank as we left the boat.
>
> We walked away from the railroad tracks for several hundred feet. Smoke curled through the air at the edge of a wood. As we drew near, we smelt the odour of frying meat and boiling coffee.[4]

Tully moves effortlessly from such straightforward detail to scenes that are evocative, even poetic. His recollections of a spring sunset are reminiscent of Twain's deft handling of hues and colors when describing a river sunrise in *Life on the Mississippi.* Tully is standing near a viaduct after being rousted out of a boxcar by an armed train crew:

> The sun soon sank, and the sky faded to a dull grey. Then a blood red cloud line appeared along the horizon, and grey clouds, resembling cement castles with turrets, rested upon it. Yellow clouds rolled above the castles, like immense butterflies unable to find a bush upon which to light.
>
> In a short time all turned scarlet, then purple black, then mauve. At last dark shadows crept over the earth, and all colours merged into blue, through which the stars shone.[5]

The influences of Tully's traveling companions, borrowed or pilfered from libraries across the country, are evident throughout *Beggars of Life.* The wryly matter-of-fact humorous observation, a Dickens specialty, for instance, becomes a Tully weapon of choice in *Beggars of Life.* "She had either been born tired, or become tired soon after birth," he says of a farm woman. "No woman could have become so tired without years of experience."[6]

It is Tully's depiction of sudden violence, however, that brings him into his own as a writer. Here he surpasses his literary heroes, and this would be a hallmark of his best books. Nowhere is this more evident than in his account of the hobo-jungle battle between Oklahoma Red and another vagabond:

> Red, a foot shorter than the negro, shot upward with each fist, and the thud of his hands on the giant's jaws could be heard across the jungle. . . . Oklahoma Red circled about until he had his back to the sun. His ponderous arms were in front of him, pugilist fashion. His jaws clamped as he moved his immense shoulders.
>
> The negro charged, holding the razor even with Red's throat. Red kept his eye on the blade, the set look never leaving his face. The black man drew nearer and swished the razor through the air within six inches of Red's throat.
>
> The latter's left hand drove like an iron weight a few inches below the blade. The razor turned in the negro's hand, and, driven backward by the blow, it slashed his cheek wide open. Red's right hand circled like a man throwing a ball. It covered the bleeding face of the now pain-mad negro, and the blood spurted several feet.[7]

Like the other aspects of hobo life, the violence is not romanticized. It's treated as a natural part of an overall pattern. Tully's approach is sometimes so casual that it drifts into the grimly humorous. Earlier in the book, a detective is knocked unconscious by a "husky hobo." The others wonder if the detective's jaw might be broken: "The husky hobo leaned down and worked the man's jaws sideways with his hands. 'Nope, they ain't broke. They just sag a little,' said he."[8]

Before 1925 was a month old, Tully's sophomore book had collected more than its share of rave reviews. The *New York Times* set the tone:

> Jim Tully's book is autobiography naked and unashamed. His story is pitiful and brave, too—the story of a boy who at 15 knew more of evil and the black pits of human nature than most men know when they die. Nobody can read it and question its truth. . . .
>
> The men and women that Tully knew in his impressionable years must have brutalized him beyond recovery. But there was something too strong and too fine in him for that to happen. . . .

Tully can make moments of action live again on the page. His style has crudities and suffers most when he indulges in literary fine feathers, but it has vitality, too, and the selection of detail makes for vividness.[9]

"How this man can write!" *Literary Digest International Book Review* critic R. A. Parker exclaimed. "Words that are like mountain breezes fresh from wild-flower fields. Words that leap, sing, crawl, explode. Always there is a beautiful rhythm."[10] "If all men wrote as honestly as Jim Tully," critic S. Martin wrote in the *Saturday Review of Literature*, "setting forth their goodness and their nastiness equally, with no attempt at exaggerating either, books would be better and fewer."[11] And from Mencken's *American Mercury*: "The best book of its kind I have ever encountered. Thirty-one strange chapters, and all of them good."[12]

O. D. Russell was more restrained, but enthusiastic, in the *New York Evening Post Literary Review*. "Tully's portraits of the persons he meets vividly acquaint the reader with his characters; he writes keenly of what he has observed keenly and his descriptions of long night rides on mail trains and the death of 'Oklahoma Red' are little short of fascinating. The flow of his narration moves easily and rapidly."[13] In much the same spirit, the *Springfield (Mass.) Republican* reviewer concluded that while *Beggars of Life* had "some rough passages," it was a "revealing and thought-provoking work of sociology as well as an interesting narrative."[14]

Two reviews must have been particularly pleasing. The first appeared courtesy of Nels Anderson, a sociologist whose pioneering work on vagabondage, *The Hobo*, had appeared the previous year.[15]

> In his effort to portray hobo life Tully has torn away the veil of mystery and convention thrown about the hobo by Yankee cartoonists and fiction artists.... The hobo is brought before us with all his faults and virtues....
>
> Besides being a faithful picture of the road, *Beggars of Life* is an excellent display of hobo slang, morals, ethics, and above all, the philosophy of the underworld. In this respect Tully has not been excelled.[16]

Tully must also have been thrilled with the wildly enthusiastic review that *Beggars* received back in Kent, where the local paper boosted the book as "the most lively and entertaining autobiography written by an American in many years." Indeed, "if this book is not awarded the Pulitzer Prize for being the best autobiography of the year, then the judges who award this prize are incapable of recognizing good stuff when they see it."[17] Those in the Ohio town who had known Tully as a chain maker, boxer, and Davey Tree employee must have been amused or amazed. The ex-vagabond was making good on his dream of becoming a writer.

Not that all the reviews were favorable. Glen Mullin, the critic for the *New York Tribune*, led the attack against *Beggars of Life*. "In craftsmanship the book is crude," he wrote. "The style is marred by mannered processions of short sentences thrown loosely together and constructed on the same plan. This style is particularly irritating in the expository passages. Possessed as he is of power, intelligence and excellent materials, Mr. Tully should have written a better book."[18]

Across the Atlantic, the *Manchester Guardian* was equally hostile to *Beggars of Life*. The review caught the attention of *Los Angeles Times* writer Harry Carr, who told his readers that the "highly respectable" English newspaper had been shocked by Tully's book, dismissing it "in cold and cutting words." Carr quoted those words in his regular column, "The Lancer," which the *Times* ran on page 1: "The life of an American hobo appears to consist mainly of stealing rides on goods trains, with a little fisticuffs and area-sneaking to vary it." Goods trains? Fisticuffs? Area-sneaking? It was all too good for the columnist to resist. "Doubtless Mr. Tully's grief and dismay will be tempered," Carr suggested, "by his scorn for any reviewer who could call an overland fast freight a 'goods train.'"[19]

Tully may have been even more amused by the critic for *Outlook* magazine. "The 'raw stuff,' both in incident and conversation," this reviewer noted, "is presented absolutely raw; which certainly makes for vividness. But is the life, even of the hobo, quite so consistently hideous as we have it here?"[20] Life had given him the experiences to fill many more books. He'd known for a while what he wanted to write about; now, at last, he knew how to write about it.

One of the more informed reviews arrived from San Quentin. Johnny Backus, a hobo known as the Flying Tramp, was temporarily grounded in the famous prison. The mighty vagabond wrote Tully to say how much he enjoyed *Beggars of Life* but added that he had once clung to a mail train farther and longer than the "world's record" described in the book.[21] Jim later showed his gratitude by helping Backus get paroled.[22]

Tully dedicated *Beggars of Life* to two men who had helped him in times of need: Rupert Hughes, "A Friend," and Charlie Chaplin, "A Mighty Vagabond."[23] The author, of course, gave a copy to Chaplin. Tully often spotted it on a large table in the center of Chaplin's office. It rested there with an odd assortment of books, including John Flinn's *History of the Chicago Police* and John Reed's *Ten Days That Shook the World*.[24] Chaplin never mentioned the book dedicated to him.

13

One More Illusion

For the first time in Tully's life, the spotlight that he had so welcomed in the buildup to *Beggars of Life* now followed him offstage. The attention was not, at least yet, unwelcome. The January 25, 1925, *Los Angeles Times* trumpeted the happy news: "Jim Tully Marries Co-ed." The coed in question was Margaret Rider Myers, Marna to friends and family. She was a slim brunette with a flapper-style haircut, a healthy bank account, and dreams of becoming a writer.

The differences between the groom and his young bride were dramatic. Indeed, at first glance, the differences appeared to be at least as great as those that had existed between Jim and Florence in 1910. Marna was twenty-one; Jim was thirty-eight. She was, in the words of one feature writer, "exquisite ... fragile and dainty."[1] She had grown up in a well-to-do Los Angeles home and attended college. She was the daughter of R. Holtby Myers, secretary of the Los Angeles Mutual Building Loan Association and an Episcopal rector.[2] Some newspapers even went so far as to describe her as an heiress. While Jim was a successful young writer working for Charlie Chaplin, he was also the son of an Ohio ditchdigger and the divorced father of two children. Even a sympathetic friend who thought them a good match readily conceded that they made "a strange pair."[3] But they shared a love of books and a passion for writing. And like Jim, Marna could feel empathy for a wide range of people. Those who met her, from H. L. Mencken to George Bernard Shaw, were invariably charmed.

The 2 P.M. wedding took place on January 24 at the Myers home in the Mount Washington area of Los Angeles. Edwin Carewe, the former hobo and actor who had established himself as a prolific Hollywood director, was Tully's best man. One of Carewe's best-known films was *The Girl of the Golden West* (1923). To Tully, the poor boy from Ohio, the title must have seemed a good description of his bride.

They had met six months before when Tully was invited to deliver a lecture at the Pen Point Club of the University of Southern California, where Marna was a student. She was captivated by the colorful writer regaling his audience with tales of life on the road. While hardly a matinee idol, Tully must have struck the Pen Point members as a dashing, even dangerous, figure. Years later, for example, novelist Dawn Powell jotted in her diary that Jim Tully looked like a "thug."[4] While she was far from alone in her opinion, many Hollywood women found Tully's brand of masculinity bracing and irresistible—a point not lost on the gossip columnists. One columnist described a famous but unnamed actress vying for Tully's attention at a party. She stroked his arm, whispered in his ear, and finally leaned in close enough for Tully to "glimpse her breasts." Tully was bored, finally dismissing her by saying, "Listen, kid, I'm not interested. You would be all right if gushing interviewers hadn't called you intellectual. You're just another example of a gorgeous body ruined by an illusion of intelligence."[5]

Jim was definitely *not* bored by Marna Myers. She introduced herself after the lecture, and Jim was smitten. If her parents initially objected to their swift courtship and engagement, as many believed, they soon reversed themselves. To all appearances, it was a love story made for the silver screen. Yet in a draft of Tully's unpublished autobiography, he hints at something less romantic. Tully recalls being overwhelmed by events and pressured by Marna's father, who talked about honor and maintaining the good name of the Myers family.[6] Feeling trapped but seeing no other way, Tully relented and announcements were issued.[7] The marriage, it might be noted, would produce no children.

The couple set up temporary housekeeping in Hollywood at 6404 Sunset Boulevard, not far from the Chaplin Studios at the corner of Sunset and La Brea. They moved later in the year to a comfortable house at 818 Kings Road. Marna dubbed their new home "One More Illusion." The name appealed to Tully's sardonic sense of humor.

Whatever misgivings he had about his marriage, 1925 couldn't have started better. Tully had an acclaimed new book and a burgeoning freelance career. Still, not so far removed from poverty as to ignore his finances, he dutifully started recording income and expenses in a blue "House-hold Money Saver" book. His total income for January was $483, with $250 of that coming from

Chaplin, the rest from magazines. One hundred twenty-five went to Florence. After everything and everyone was paid, there was money left over for his father in Ohio and the hoboes who regularly showed up at his door. Recalling his own years of hunger, he invariably greeted these vagabonds with the surest of welcomes: "Did you eat yet?"[8]

What impressed Tully was how quickly Marna opened her heart to these unfortunates. "The beautiful thing as I see it," he said, "is Marna's fine love for these rovers and her loyalty to them. I've watched eight or ten of them around her—and every one of them is in love with her. They would do anything in this damn sad world for her."[9] Tully's compassion was no less evident. Old friend Frank Scully recalled: "Nobody has ever been quite so willing to go in doghouses as Tully, feeling certain he'd bark his way out before dawn. And his bark, more's the pity, is far worse than his bite. He has a compassion for men which hobbles him at every turn, and that compassion, of course, takes him out of the running in the Superman Sweepstakes, the Nietzschean dope sheet which drove its author crazy, Mencken to beer, and Shaw to clowning."[10]

Sharing the wealth was indeed becoming easier. In February, he happily recorded in the blue "House-hold Money Saver" that his monthly income had climbed to $560, and for the first time, the majority was not Chaplin money. In March, his income jumped to $928. In April, it was up to $1,137, more than double the January figure. The magazine checks were making the difference. Getting the monthly check to Florence and the children was no longer a worry.

In addition to his skyrocketing career, 1925 began with more good news, this time concerning Gabriel Sullivan, his childhood friend from the orphanage. Four days before the wedding, Tully learned that Sullivan, then serving a life sentence in Columbus for murder, had finally been granted a pardon by the governor of Ohio. Tully believed that Sullivan had been made a scapegoat when a non-union printer ("a scab," in Tully's words) was killed during a December 1915 labor dispute at Cincinnati's Christ Hospital. When Tully learned of Sullivan's case in the early 1920s, he'd begun lobbying the governor, the chairman of the Ohio Clemency Board, and other state officials.

Upon his release, Sullivan could offer no fresh details of the slaying, saying only that his mind was "still in a daze as to just what happened on the night." On one point he was certain: "Jim [Tully] helped me a lot to get the pardon. . . . We were kids together . . . and we went out of the orphanage together. I got kind of tired of hoboing and picked the trade of painting.... Jim wrote to me all the time, when he found out where I was."[11] Three years later, Tully could proudly tell a friend that "Gabe is swinging a paint brush now, as useful as a citizen can be in Cincinnati."[12] It would not be the last time Tully interceded on the behalf of a prisoner.

Warmed by Mencken's praise for *Beggars of Life*, Tully was determined in January 1925 to make a sale to the *American Mercury*. He pitched Mencken a story about another old pal, the road-kid he'd known as Bright Eyes.[13] Mencken responded with enthusiasm and advice.

"Your letter is mightily fair," Tully wrote back on January 26, just two days after his marriage to Marna. "I'll do you a yarn devoid of all magazine tricks.... I'll not have to invent a single line—as life wrote the tale first. I will merely handle it with all the sincerity and respect possible.... You have my word as a yegg that I'll write 'Bright Eyes' to please myself—with the hope that it will please you."[14] Technically, he'd never been a yegg, but Tully kept his word anyway. Over the next eight years, he would be a regular contributor to the *American Mercury*. Other magazine sales earned him fatter checks by far, but Mencken's stamp of approval was validation that he'd become an important American writer.

A place at the grown-ups' table of American literature did not, however, prevent Tully from taking all that Hollywood had to offer. Hard experience had impressed upon Tully the importance of money—or lack thereof—and he made sure to divide his time between serious periodicals and more lucrative popular magazines. It was a heady time for Tully, with dozens of magazine editors eager to throw money at the hot new talent on the publishing scene.

In January of 1925, he continued the association with *Story World* that had begun the previous year by writing the cover story on suspense novelist Mary Roberts Rinehart. His lead story the following month was much more revealing.

> Jack London was one of the greatest literary successes in America, and one of the saddest failures.
>
> He had known hardship as few young writers have known it ... I rather choose to believe that the artist in him was killed by too much popularity.... An Eastern book reviewer once called Jack London a "titanic weakling." That in itself was a magnificent compliment. Napoleon was just such a weakling....

One of the two great writers California has produced, Jack London will take a lower rank than Frank Norris, for the reason that he was caught up in the swirl of money and lacked the patience to mold the great things that throbbed in his mind into artistic wholes.[15]

There were also sales to *Photoplay,* the *Literary Digest International Book Review, Liberty, College Humor,* and the *Saturday Review of Literature*. And befitting his status as an important author, he began giving lectures, as he did on February 19 when he encouraged a group of "clubwomen" to join the fight against "forced prison labor."[16]

For most of 1924, he had reminded himself that catering to Chaplin's every whim was an economic law that "had to be obeyed."[17] But with so much to occupy Tully's attention away from the studio, he was now finding it increasingly difficult to suffer the comedian's moods. Years later, Tully recalled one such episode. After weeks of getting the silent treatment from Chaplin, he received an order: "You are to see the prize fights with the boss tonight."[18]

Sitting in a Los Angeles arena for a charity event at which Jack Dempsey, the reigning heavyweight champ, was to take on three comers, Chaplin peppered Tully with questions about the fight game. As the third opponent was pounded to the canvas, the Little Tramp closed his eyes and muttered, "Terrible! Terrible!" Chaplin, obviously distressed, hurried to his limousine and instructed his chauffeur to drive along the Pacific coast. The spectacle had left the boss in a garrulous mood and Tully did his best to appear attentive, but as dawn approached, it was all he could do to keep his eyes open. Such sessions left Tully physically and emotionally spent. Some weeks later, he was at the mansion with Harry d'Arrast when Chaplin suddenly decided the three of them should go to the beach. Knowing this would turn into another all-night jaunt, Tully exploded when Chaplin went upstairs to change. "I'm going to tell him I'm through," he yelled at d'Arrast. "I've had enough of this—I'd rather starve." The affable d'Arrast put his arm around the writer and told him to "brace up." They were, after all, "both prostitutes."[19] Tully's anger passed, but the strain of working for Chaplin was becoming unbearable and, with Tully's growing outside income, unnecessary. A break was imminent.

May brought an economic windfall that made a break with Chaplin possible. Tully signed a work-for-hire contract to write a biography of the late Thomas Harper Ince, the innovative director, producer, and screenwriter.

Today Ince is remembered more for how he died than how he helped bring the infant film industry to life. In 1925, though, he was being justifiably mourned as the cinema's lost titan.

Ince, who had started as an actor, was a dynamic pioneer in the development of the studio system, establishing many of the production procedures that became standard for the movies. Ince was the first producer to demand complete shooting scripts, instead of mere outlines, and he all but invented the job of studio production chief. Many would talk of Hollywood's studio system. Few would realize how Ince had helped shape that system.

In November 1924, less than two weeks after celebrating his forty-second birthday, Ince died under mysterious circumstances. Six months later the movie industry was still abuzz with rumors concerning his last hours. Ince was aboard publishing czar William Randolph Hearst's 280-foot yacht, the *Oneida*, at the time he was stricken. It was a weekend party with a jazz band and several other notable guests invited by Hearst. The revelers included Hearst's mistress, actress Marion Davies; writer Elinor Glyn; and the Hearst newspaper chain's New York movie columnist, Louella Parsons. It is likely that the cruise from Los Angeles to San Diego was planned in part to celebrate Ince's birthday.

When Ince became ill, the yacht docked at San Diego, and Ince was carried ashore. He died a short time later.[20] Almost no two accounts of his death agree on anything else. Biographies, reference books, and film histories contain a maddening array of conflicting "facts." Ince died without regaining consciousness, or he was rushed to a hospital then taken to his home, where he was able to receive visitors before succumbing. Ince died the same day he was carried off the *Oneida* or he died two days or even weeks later. Even the cause of death was unclear, and as Ince's body was quickly cremated, an autopsy was not possible. Gossip shaped several theories—for example, Hearst, suspecting Davies of having an affair with Chaplin and overcome with jealousy, pulled a gun and shot at the Little Tramp, missed, and hit Ince. Chaplin claimed not to have even been present.[21] Others maintained that the cause of death was nothing more sinister than a heart attack or acute indigestion. "The absence of hard evidence made it easy to invent new rumors," David Nasaw wrote in his biography of Hearst. "In the years to come, Hearst would be accused of poisoning Ince, shooting him, hiring an assassin to shoot him, fatally wounding him while aiming at Chaplin—and, most recently and ridiculously, . . . accidentally stabbing him through the heart with Marion's hatpin."[22]

The rumor mill was still grinding when Tully was hired to write Ince's life story. Tully had heard the rumors, but there would be no airing of scandal in the Ince biography. Tully's contract was with the Thomas H. Ince Corporation, the president of which was Elinor Alice Kershaw Ince, the filmmaker's widow. This would be an authorized biography portraying her late husband as a genius and devoted family man.

Tully, though, did have intriguing views on the subject. While Ince's biographer hardly believed his subject was a faithful husband, he also didn't believe the rumors about a shooting onboard Hearst's yacht. "I'm writing this guy's life for the widow," Tully wrote Mencken on May 13. "Ince was an Irish Casanova—but the real yarn I can't tell—but a thousand a month helps me write what I like—at times. He died on Hearst's yacht—from twisted booze."[23]

Prohibition booze was notoriously untrustworthy, and while Hearst was by most accounts not a drinker, he always let Davies and their guests indulge. It has been suggested that the real reason Hearst wanted the San Diego district attorney's investigation quashed was the aroma of illegal hooch. The theory Tully put forth in private to Mencken is very close to the one publicly endorsed by Hearst biographers W. A. Swanberg and David Nasaw, writing about forty years apart. Hearst moved to hush up the story, Swanberg wrote, "anxious to avoid" harmful publicity and probably "thinking of what the newspapers could do with the story that Ince was taken ill after drinking aboard the *Oneida*."[24] Nasaw reached a similar conclusion: "While it was true that Hearst had done his best to keep Ince's presence on the *Oneida* a secret, he had done so not to cover up a murder, but because he did not want the press or the local police investigating his yachting party with champagne flowing in flagrant disregard of the Prohibition laws."[25] Neither Hearst biographer even suggested that bad booze might have brought on Ince's attack aboard the *Oneida*. But while Tully firmly believed this was the cause, he was going to keep the story to himself and a few trusted friends.

The book contract stipulated that Elinor Ince retained "exclusive rights of censorship" over the manuscript, yet Tully must have liked the other terms. He was to be paid $5,000 over twenty weeks for researching and writing the biography. The first $750 arrived in June.[26] He was to work "not less than 4 to 5 hours per day" on the book, and the Ince Corporation would make an office and stenographer available to him. In addition to the $5,000, he was to get 50 percent of the net sales.

There would be no net sales. Tully's "Life of Thomas H. Ince" was finished in October but never published, and no copy of the manuscript has surfaced. Tully, who was scrupulous about keeping everything he wrote, apparently did not keep a copy. One likely scenario is that Elinor Ince, unhappy with Tully's portrayal of her late husband, declined to publish the book and demanded all drafts be handed over before paying Tully for his work. Like Ince's death, the matter remains shrouded in mystery.

Tully couldn't be too disappointed. Unpublished, the biography made him more money than either *Emmett Lawler* or *Beggars of Life* through 1925. And the Ince biography did not keep him from other projects. He was looking forward to a New York stage version of *Beggars of Life*, adapted by playwright Maxwell Anderson. He had completed the second draft of *Jarnegan*, a novel about an ex-convict who becomes a Hollywood director. And he had been booked in June by the Leigh Lecture Bureau for a fall tour of speaking engagements. He would lecture "on Hoboland, on Charlie Chaplin and on picturesque literature."[27]

The anticipated break with Chaplin came in the summer. Flush with a $1,000 payment from the Ince Corporation, Tully's monthly income ballooned to $2,230 for July. The economic laws that ruled his universe had changed. The second draft of *Jarnegan* was at the New York offices of Albert & Charles Boni, where a friend of Chaplin's read a sardonic line in the manuscript that he considered derogatory to the comedian. He dutifully reported the supposed transgression to the Chaplin front office.

Alf Reeves, Chaplin's business manager, gave Tully the choice of removing the line or being discharged from the studio. It was just the right push at just the right time. Tully chose dismissal, explaining to anyone who cared to listen that he was leaving "through no fault of Chaplin's."[28] Eddie Sutherland had already left the fold to direct, and Tully missed him greatly. Of the remaining members of the inner circle, Tully was closest to Riesner. A week later when the king had dinner with the court, Riesner was the only one who didn't try to curry favor by denigrating Tully. When the last darts had been hurled, Chaplin gazed at his water glass and said, "Well, he deserves a lot of credit."[29]

Sutherland and Riesner would continue to speak well of Tully in the coming years. The other members of Chaplin's inner circle would not be so kind. Tully later recalled his time working for Chaplin with bitterness. He complained to William Saroyan, "I worked for him for a year, and he used my stuff, but he didn't pay me a dime. He really thinks it's enough for writers to be permitted to know him."[30] But if the June issue of *California Sports* was any indication, Tully had outgrown his job with Chaplin. The photo spread of America's reigning literary geniuses included Sinclair

Lewis, Eugene O'Neill, F. Scott Fitzgerald, Ben Hecht, John Dos Passos, and Jim Tully. A month after Tully left the studio, *The Gold Rush* opened in theaters. It was hailed as Chaplin's greatest film to date. With Chaplin, Ince, and Hollywood on his mind, Tully wrote Mencken in May of 1925 about contributing a profile of director Erich von Stroheim to the *American Mercury*.³¹ Mencken gently turned it down, decreeing that Hollywood stories were, for the most part, out of the magazine's line.

In July, Virginia Tully sent Jim and Marna a letter saying that, with any luck, she and their younger sister, Anna, would soon visit. Virginia also asked them not to send money to their father's boardinghouse, since James Dennis Tully, then about seventy-five, "works like a trooper there."³²

Then in early September, Tully left for New York City and the Greenwich Village opening of *Outside Looking In*, Maxwell Anderson's adaptation of *Beggars of Life*. Journeying to Manhattan "in a suit from the highest shelf in a second-hand store," he was eager to see how theatergoers would respond to the hoboes and yeggs from his book.³³

Outside Looking In was Anderson's third play produced in New York in less than three years. The second, the war drama *What Price Glory?* (written with Laurence Stallings), was one of the most acclaimed shows of 1924. And Anderson would eventually be awarded the Pulitzer Prize for drama. With Eugene O'Neill as one of its three producers, *Outside Looking In* debuted September 7, 1925, at the 299-seat Greenwich Village Playbill Theatre on Seventh Avenue. It received mostly favorable reviews, although *Daily Mirror* critic Robert Coleman found that "emotions and dialogues are consistently low and repulsive."³⁴

George Jean Nathan, the subject of a Tully profile published in the April 1925 issue of *College Humor*, wrote a positive review for the *New York Morning Telegraph*.³⁵ As a friend to Tully and a mentor to O'Neill, Nathan's praise might seem suspect, but glowing reviews also appeared in the *New York Times* and the *New York Herald-Tribune*. In fact, Nathan's review was a model of restraint compared to that of the celebrated *Herald-Tribune* drama critic Alexander Woollcott. The portly wit and Algonquin Round Table regular was most impressed with the actor chosen to play Oklahoma Red, a thirty-six-year-old former sailor and civil engineer. "It is a good play and the best bit of luck that befell it was the finding of a carrot-topped stalwart named Charles A. Bickford to play Oklahoma Red," Woollcott said of the actor, who later appeared in such films as *Of Mice and Men* and *Days of Wine and Roses*. "The hat of your correspondent has sat firmly on his head since the new season began. Now it goes back up into the air (where it belongs), once for 'Outside Looking In' and once for the welcome newcomer who plays Oklahoma Red."[36]

Proving he harbored no hard feelings toward his former employee, Charlie Chaplin happily endorsed the play with a letter to the drama editor of the *Herald-Tribune*. "'Outside Looking In,' by Maxwell Anderson is one of the most powerful plays I have ever seen," wrote the Little Tramp. "It is the primitive virility, the rough-and-ready humor and bravado of the hobo that appeals to me. I think it is on par with 'What Price Glory.' A strong and colorful drama. The acting is fine. I don't know when I've enjoyed anything more."[37]

When the curtain came down on the premiere performance, Tully was moved by the sight of his past brought to life on the stage. "The thunderous applause I did not hear," he recalled. The mood was broken, Tully said, when "George Jean Nathan touched my arm. We went to a little place in the Village, which sold milk, I think. And there sat [theater critics] Burns Mantle and Percy Hammond. They were not drinking milk."[38] The three critics gathered in the speakeasy and started discussing the play. Like Woollcott, they had been impressed by the tall Bickford's Oklahoma Red, but the veteran reviewers were equally impressed with the twenty-six-year-old Irish American actor chosen to play Little Red, the character based on Tully. "That kid who played Little Red is going places," Mantle observed. "He's already there," Nathan replied.[39]

The kid's name was James Cagney. A hoofer getting the chance to show what he could do as an actor, Cagney received a timely career boost playing the Jim Tully character. "One of the leading characters was 'Little Red,'" the future star of *Public Enemy* and *Yankee Doodle Dandy* wrote in his 1976 autobiography, "and because there were virtually only two actors in New York with red hair, Alan Bunce and myself, there wasn't much competition. I assume I got the part because my hair was redder than Alan's."[40] Jim Tully and Jim Cagney became friends and Tully hoped to craft a movie for the actor who had played him on the stage.

On the strength of the reviews, *Outside Looking In* moved uptown to the much bigger Thirty-ninth Street Theatre. Cagney, who had played all kinds of vaudeville houses, made the transition with ease. Anderson, though, was worried about the rest of the cast members, thinking they may have become accustomed to the far more intimate Greenwich Village Playbill Theatre. The playwright gathered the cast and shared his concern. He wanted everybody to speak twice as loud and twice as fast. "Everybody, that is," he added, looking at Cagney, "except you."[41]

One late notice of *Outside Looking In* rankled. Sinclair Lewis, the author of *Main Street* and *Babbitt*, took his nephew to see the play and wrote a letter to a New York drama editor. The boy, according to Lewis, liked the "joyous bums as Anderson has here brought to life, and with the unfooling perception of the youngster he found the play just as real as it is diverting." Miffed to see no mention of the author of *Beggars of Life*, Tully sent his own letter to the paper: "If some gentleman had taken Sinclair Lewis's 'Babbitt' and placed it on the stage he would possibly feel that he had something to do with the creation of Babbitt." Tully had nothing but praise for Maxwell Anderson, "the gentlest and finest of men," but . . .

> Did I not see the real Oklahoma Red's skull cracked open under an Arkansas moon? I can still hear him say, "Stick with me kid. . . ."
> I have been deloused in too many jails . . . and I gave the best of my adolescence—6 years, in fact—to the life of the hobo. I crawled out of it and banged my bloody hands on the iron gates of life, and not only survived it but became a top-notcher among the rough young pugilists of the Middle West. I would have gone to the top of that game, too, but I wanted to create characters for which Sinclair Lewis would credit another man.[42]

It would not be the last time Tully crossed swords with a critic.

A fringe benefit of Tully's time in New York was his assignment to cover the light heavyweight title bout between Paul Berlenbach and Jimmy Slattery with sportswriter Damon Runyon. While Berlenbach won the September 11 fight by a knockout in the eleventh round, Tully would remember the night as the start of a friendship with Runyon that would last the rest of his life.[43]

Riding the notoriety of *Beggars of Life* into the fall of 1925, Tully embarked on the Leigh Lecture Bureau tour. A highlight of the tour for the former road-kid was a November 22 stop in Chicago to lecture at Ben Reitman's Hobo College. Tully's subject, the *Chicago Post* reported, would be "Vagabonds in Literature"; the paper further noted that "all the literary hoboes will give Mr. Tully a jungle feast and smoker."[44]

Reitman was Al Capone's whorehouse physician, a social reformer, anarchist Emma Goldman's lover, and coauthor of a hobo memoir by Boxcar Bertha Thompson. His school offered hoboes classes in everything from economics to public speaking. "Night after night during the winter months," explained Reitman's biographer, Roger A. Bruns, "grizzled itinerants gathered at the college to hear Ben and other lecturers speak on such academic subjects as philosophy, literature, and religion and on such practical concerns as vagrancy laws and venereal disease."[45]

Described as a "sociological clinic" by the *Chicago Post*,[46] the Hobo College, Bruns noted, "held out the promise of fraternity and community" to a vagabond, "pledging to raise his intellectual sights and prepare him to confront a hostile society." Although the "most visible and prestigious" of several hobo schools around the country, Reitman's college frequently was forced to move, chased to new locations by impatient landlords and persistent fire marshals.[47] When Tully gave his first lecture there, the Hobo College was at 641 West Washington Street. Remembering the times when the city was his winter home, Tully told his Hobo College audience that "Chicago treats a bum better than any other place in the world."[48] Reitman responded by appointing Tully to the college "faculty," a "professor" of literature and road philosophy.[49]

The Chicago appearance also gave him the chance to catch up with his sisters, Virginia and Anna. Although she was only in her midforties, Virginia's reservoir of optimism was beginning to run dry after caring for so many others for so long. Her grateful brother wanted to do something special for her. "When money became more plentiful," Tully recalled in 1940, "I gave Virginia her choice of going anywhere in the world. She chose Mexico." The family's devoted "little mother" wanted to make "the long journey" to Tom's grave.[50] Jim, too, had been very close to Tom and was moved at Virginia's desire to see the spot where their brother had been buried nineteen years earlier.[51] Virginia "straightened the wooden cross and knelt for a long time," Tully related, "as one will whose heart lies buried in a strange and beautiful land."[52]

From Chicago, Tully lectured his way back to Ohio. In late November, he appeared before a Cleveland audience to talk about hobo life, literature, and Chaplin. The *Plain Dealer*, which had done much to launch Tully's career, heralded his appearance with the headline "Jim Tully, Tramp Poet, Won Notice Here."[53] And in early December, the "tramp poet" visited the town where he had once made chain. Kentites who had once listened to Tully for free in saloons and pool halls now had to march down to Thompson's Drug Store and plunk down fifty cents for a ticket. He spoke to the Kent Normal School audience about literature and Hollywood, noting that Ted Robinson of the *Plain Dealer* had changed his life.[54] The lecture tour then moved to the Northwest, where Tully spoke to a University of Washington audience at Meany Hall.[55]

Back in Hollywood, with 1925 drawing to a close, Tully could look back on a year that was very satisfying. Only a few years removed from his declaration to write or starve, Jim Tully was, by the second half of the 1920s, widely published, critically acclaimed, and financially secure. And to outside observers, there was no hint of the storm clouds that were gathering over his marriage.

14

Jarnegan

For the first time in his life, Jim Tully was free from financial worries. His income grew mainly as the result of a flood of magazine articles about Hollywood. The wide scope of magazine pieces that appeared between October 1925 and May 1926 shows how effectively Tully was taking advantage of his newfound celebrity. And he was writing about subjects, notably the circus and boxing, that interested him. Donald Freeman, the erudite managing editor of *Vanity Fair,* was so taken with Tully's writing that in February 1926 he offered the former Chaplin employee a contract for a series of twelve profiles of Hollywood luminaries. Tully was paid $250 or $300 for each of them.[1]

He had, of course, already written his share of Hollywood stories for several movie magazines, but the *Vanity Fair* pieces would be considerably more substantive than the typical fan fare. Tully might joke to George Jean Nathan that he lived "in Hollywood because as a kid I got used to carnivals," but he realized that the movie industry was growing up and deserved serious attention.[2] It was time, he reasoned, that a writer of national stature looked at Hollywood with a clear eye.

It was not the kind of attention Hollywood was accustomed to receiving. Entertainment coverage then fell into one of two categories: tabloid gossip or puff pieces generated and carefully controlled by the powerful studio publicity departments. The pieces for *Vanity Fair* would eschew both sensationalism and puffery. They would be tough, thorough, and thoughtful. And they would, along with *Jarnegan,* establish Tully's reputation as the most feared and hated man in Hollywood.³ Tully didn't care what pressure studio publicists might bring to bear. Nor, as a former bruiser, did he care if the subjects of these articles decided that his nose might make an inviting target.

The monthly *Vanity Fair* pieces, which began appearing in March 1926, included studies of such leading filmmakers as Erich von Stroheim, Cecil B. De Mille, Mack Sennett, Frank Borzage, D. W. Griffith, and Ernst Lubitsch. The success of these pieces led to a second series of twelve profiles that started with an article about producer Irving Thalberg in the October 1927 issue. It was followed by stories about directors James Cruze and Clarence Brown, producer B. F. Schulberg, and such stars as Greta Garbo, John Gilbert, Lon Chaney, Zasu Pitts, Adolphe Menjou, and Emil Jannings.

These articles seem tame by today's standards, but to Hollywood stars and executives spoiled by kid-glove treatment, Tully's pronouncements stung. One subject, matinee idol John Gilbert, was so incensed by Tully's profile of him that he began to nurse a grudge that would one day result in coast-to-coast headlines. Even when the profiles were largely favorable, Tully would get in his jabs at Hollywood and the studio system. He described director King Vidor as "the eighth wonder of the world—a director who reads books."[4] He wrote that De Mille "talks about his pictures as art no more than Barnum talked about the circus as art."[5]

The temperament in Hollywood was such that the merest criticism could spark indignation. Tully's largely favorable piece on Thalberg stopped short of declaring him an artistic genius, dwelling instead on his brilliance as a commercial producer: "Thalberg is boyish, kindly and intuitive. He has a quick mentality that runs in narrow grooves. If it were deeper and vaster and more profound, he would be a financial failure in the business of films. To Thalberg all life is a soda fountain. He knows how to mix ingredients that will please the herd on a picnic."[6] Thalberg, who had considered Tully a friend, felt betrayed. Donald Freeman counseled Tully not to let the tinniness of his Hollywood subjects bother him. They were, Freeman counseled, uninteresting people but still useful for sociological observation and comment.[7]

Tully's contention that Hollywood was more interested in commerce than art seemed like heresy in 1927. It was only a matter of time before the movie industry launched a counterattack. James Quirk, editor of *Photoplay*, blasted back in June 1928, labeling Tully the "ingrate of Hollywood . . . the hobo who was sheltered and petted by the motion picture people to whom he appealed for help.... Sponsored by Chaplin ... he repaid Chaplin by describing him as a child of the London gutter.... Utterly unlovable, he wanted to be loved by everyone. Failing, he turned bitter and has written more vicious stuff about motion picture people than any man."[8]

Tully was far from friendless in Hollywood, and his closest associates included Thalberg lieutenant Paul Bern, Rupert Hughes, Chaney, von Stroheim, and Cruze. Other publications rose to Tully's defense. Writing in *Screen Secrets,* Ralph Parker maintained that Tully was the "most hated man in Hollywood" because his "vitriolic pen has made him many enemies among those who fear exposure of their meager intelligence." Tully's reputation as "the bad boy of flickerdom," Parker continued, was the result of articles "written with a trip-hammer instead of the customary hack's teaspoon." To Parker, the industry's reaction to Tully was lamentably inevitable because it "is difficult for Hollywood to adjust itself to a writer who places loyalty to his innate sense of literature above pleasing some celebrity.... A writer who dared to insult the stars with the truth about themselves? Unthinkable!"[9]

When Parker spotted Tully with Emil Jannings, he wondered what the German actor thought about the profile of him in *Vanity Fair.* "You article—goot," the intellectual Jannings told Tully in broken English. "Many writers—Hollywood—write what you call fairy tales. You write truth—one international language. I like."[10] Jannings wasn't the only subject pleased with what Tully wrote in *Vanity Fair.* Clara Bow, the silent screen's "It girl," telegrammed to thank him for "the beautiful interview."[11]

Parker also observed Tully at Hollywood parties, puncturing inflated egos with a needle that could take the air out of a room. "You're lovely and admirable until you try to be an intellectual," he admonished Mary Pickford.[12] Sometimes he was more playful than provocative. "You're nothing but a dabbler in pink tea life," Tully teased F. Scott Fitzgerald.[13] He would later remember the author of *The Great Gatsby* as "a gentle and suavely humane fellow."[14] "The sad thing about you, Jimmy," he remarked to James Cruze, "is that a man of your genius calls producers 'mister.'"[15] The admiration for Cruze, though, was genuine and Tully used the director as one of his models for the central character in his next book, *Jarnegan.* A contract for *Jarnegan* was signed with Albert & Charles Boni on April 17, 1926, and the novel appeared a few months later. *Jarnegan* would do nothing to diminish the growing animosity toward Tully in some Hollywood circles.

Preparing for the climactic showdown in *Jarnegan*, Hollywood director Jack Jarnegan tosses back drink after drink. A storm is gathering. Jarnegan's fury is directed at the studio bosses and he vows to let loose "a cyclone out of a box."[16] The phrase also describes the author of *Jarnegan* from the spring of 1926 to the fall of 1928. During this especially productive period, Tully would write three books, coauthor two plays, and sell more than sixty magazine articles. The decade known as the Roaring Twenties was in full roar, and so was Jim Tully.

Jarnegan was not the first novel about Hollywood. It was preceded by, among others, Harry Leon Wilson's *Merton of the Movies*, a 1919 book turned into a 1922 Broadway comedy by George S. Kaufman and Marc Connelly, and later filmed by James Cruze. But *Jarnegan* was the first novel aimed directly at Hollywood's hollow heart, beginning a literary tradition that would grow to include Nathanael West's *The Day of the Locust* (1939), F. Scott Fitzgerald's posthumously published *The Last Tycoon* (1941), Budd Schulberg's *What Makes Sammy Run?* (1941), Michael Tolkin's *The Player* (1988), and Elmore Leonard's *Get Shorty* (1990). Years later Tully recalled the writing of *Jarnegan*: "I carried him in my mind for several years before the actual writing.... My method as an artist at the time was to write it HOT—I did not sit down to the typewriter while writing it unless I was in condition to fight six rounds at a pace."[17]

When Tully decided to write a novel about Hollywood, he quickly selected Cruze as the primary model for his title character. Tully and Cruze had known each other for years, hanging out on Hollywood Boulevard with a group of friends that included Lon Chaney, Paul Bern, Erich von Stroheim, Boris Karloff, Tom Mix, Harry Carey, Clarence Brown, and Al Lewin. All hoped to hit it big. "Each night we talked 'shop' after wearing ourselves out during the day with toil to escape conventional work," Tully remembered.[18] Mix and Chaney became leading stars before Brown, von Stroheim, and Cruze broke through as directors. "It's your turn next," Chaney told Cruze, then an aspiring actor. "Someday you'll hit—but never as an actor." Cruze wanted to know why. "That's easy," Chaney replied. "You're too self-conscious. If you hang around railroad stations long enough, though, you can always tell those that are going places by lookin' at their eyes—and you've got exactly what it takes to make it as a director."[19]

A Danish American born Jens Vera Cruz Bosen, the enigmatic actor turned director enjoyed keeping his past a mystery. Cruze amused himself by concocting different stories about his childhood for any interviewer foolish enough to try to get him into print. So when Tully informed Cruze that he was basing the character of Jack Jarnegan on him, the director said, "Don't make him like me."

Tully agreed, making Jarnegan a composite based on the personality of Cruze and the physical appearance of French revolutionary Georges Jacques Danton. As for Jarnegan's biography, Tully could keep that in the family, borrowing the idea of a criminal with a fresh start from uncle John Lawler. Jarnegan, then, is introduced as Jack Muldoon, who is sent to the Columbus prison for manslaughter. Muldoon spends two-and-a-half years behind bars and, upon his release, changes his name to Jarnegan and drifts to Hollywood. There he works on a construction crew and does a little acting before getting his chance as a director.

Paying tribute to his friend Cruze, Tully writes that Jarnegan "was the first director to realize the importance of pantomime. He did not know that he knew it—but life to him was a series of incidents and not a plot. He visualized his whole picture before a camera turned."[20] Cruze, Danton, Lawler—Jack Jarnegan was all of these, but he was also Jim Tully. Tully undoubtedly had himself in mind when he described Jarnegan. "A cynical realist," Tully wrote, "he fought against the sentimentality that was his Irish inheritance. At times, in his cups, he ended by being that most ironical of humans—a sentimental cynic."[21]

Even Tully's choice of Danton as a physical model suggests Jarnegan may in part have been a self-portrait of his creator. Eleven years after *Jarnegan* was published, journalist Frank Scully profiled Tully. "If you took the physical Danton . . . and cut him down a foot, and then gave him something of Longfellow's Village Blacksmith, and used Bunyan's Great Heart to set this massive and mighty machinery in motion, you'd get a good working blue print of Jim Tully."[22]

Cruze had his suspicions. "It was always the third act in a melodrama with him," he said of Jack Jarnegan, "and you pinned him on me." "He *was* you," Tully told his friend. "Are you kiddin'?" Cruze shot back, "Jarnegan was *you*—if you were a director like me." "A great director—like you," Tully added.[23]

Scully, too, saw more of Tully in Jarnegan than just the Danton resemblance. "He was the first Hollywood writer to release an unretouched portrait of a director," Scully observed. "That was Jarnegan who could be Jack Ford, Jim Cruze, Rex Ingraham or Jim Tully."[24] Tully never denied that he identified with his director hero. "I was the dark horse that won the race," he said when asked about his similarities to Jack Jarnegan, a character he often cited as his favorite.[25]

Although *Jarnegan* begins and ends powerfully, it is nevertheless an uneven novel, rambling uncertainly through the middle stretches. And for all his mighty blasts at the inanities of Hollywood, Tully fails to provide a cohesive vision and sturdy plot structure capable of supporting the ambitious mixture of satire, cynicism, and brawny realism. What does work in *Jarnegan* is Jarnegan. The only well-developed character in this early tale of Hollywood, Jarnegan emerges from Tully's novel as an irresistible force of nature—a cyclone out of a book, if you will. He overpowers what there is of a plot, just as he overpowers the other characters. Jarnegan is such a muscular presence in this early tale of Hollywood that the people he encounters seem to be objects placed in his whirlwind path as tackling dummies.

The novel's faults may simply reflect Tully's ambiguous feelings about Hollywood. Few attacked Hollywood as regularly as Jim Tully, but when Cruze criticized the town, Tully jumped to its defense. "I get tired of hearing the place abused—as though people were different here," the author of *Jarnegan* said.[26] That hypocrisy, greed, and corruption were part of the Hollywood landscape was not in dispute. Human nature, Tully believed, didn't change at the Los Angeles city limits. The scam artists working in the Dream Factories were just higher-paid versions of the scam artists he'd known in small carnivals.

The reviews for *Jarnegan* were mixed, as were the responses from the film industry. Tully characteristically shrugged off Hollywood outrage. "I can't help what Jarnegan says," he told a newspaper interviewer. "He's a character; he's alive. I'm not talking. It's him. If I want to make these people I create consistent, I must yield all control and let them run wild."[27] Some applauded Tully's blistering assault on the studio system. Among the actors wiring congratulations was matinee idol John Gilbert. "I hate to admit it, but the book is good," he announced by telegram.[28] Perhaps appreciating the attempt at a plot-driven novel, Mencken saw the book as an advance on *Beggars of Life*: "There is a great deal more than a picturesque past in Tully; he has begun to learn his trade."[29]

Tully, however, was hardly finished with his "picturesque past." Tales from his circus days that appeared in *Liberty, Vanity Fair,* and the *American Mercury* would soon become the basis for a much stronger book than *Jarnegan*.[30] Boxing also was as much on Tully's mind in 1926. He exchanged letters on the sweet science with a popular writer and a prominent fighter: Irish American humorist Finley Peter Dunne (Mr. Dooley) and "the Fighting Marine" about to challenge Jack Dempsey for the heavyweight championship, Gene Tunney.[31] And Tully wrote boxing articles that year for *Vanity Fair* and several newspapers.[32]

The ring still fascinated him, but Tully had no illusions. He wrote Mencken, "In Cleveland last winter a little featherweight as battle-worn as Chaplin's penis came up to me. He asked me if I remembered him. I did not. He told me of two fights I'd had with him fourteen years back. Patsy Brannigan . . . and other tough boys had pounded him so much later that I did not know him."[33] The disfigured featherweight was the once-handsome Johnny Sinclair.[34]

Tully's big project in the summer of 1926 was *Black Boy*, a three-act boxing play he was completing with prolific scenarist Frank Dazey. The collaborators described their story of an African American fighter as a comedy-drama.[35] Produced by the flamboyant Horace Liveright, then a year away from making Bela Lugosi a New York sensation in the title role of *Dracula*, *Black Boy* was set in the title character's training camp and Harlem apartment. The play went into rehearsals on August 23 in Mamaroneck, New York. It soon was clear that the script needed work, and Tully would regret not revising it. While aware of the play's drawbacks, Liveright believed the production would be carried by his formidable star, Paul Robeson, who had dazzled the critics the previous year in Eugene O'Neill's *The Emperor Jones*. Robeson himself was dazzled by Fredi Washington, the young black actress cast as the lead character's mistress, Irene, who is passing for white. Washington adopted the stage name Edith Warren for *Black Boy*, which began its out-of-town run on September 16 in Mamaroneck, but she'd be billed as Fredi Washington in later Broadway plays.

Making the trip from Hollywood to New York, Tully stopped off in Chicago for a visit with Virginia. He handed her the *Black Boy* script to read. She was upset that the boxer was robbed of everything "by his white-skinned brothers." "Why didn't you leave the poor fellow something?" Virginia asked him. After a long explanation, he made her a promise: "Some day, Sis, I'll write about you." The idea seemed to please her. She paused by the bronze gypsy statue in her apartment and said, "Wait until I'm pushing the clouds. And then you'd better be careful—and be nicer to me than you were to the poor prizefighter. I'll be peeking from behind a cloud."[36]

The production moved to Manhattan's Comedy Theatre for a week of preview performances on September 30. Staying at the Algonquin Hotel, preparing for the official premiere attended by the New York critics, Tully became acquainted with the play's cast. Robeson immediately impressed Tully as "sensitive, gentle, and highly intelligent." The pair dined at a restaurant "where colored people dined without too obvious discrimination."[37] At another dinner, this time at the home of Harlem Renaissance writer Walter White, Tully and Robeson discussed writing with their host. "You fellows should write about your own people," Tully suggested, "as Gorky writes about tramps." Robeson agreed, "We've got to develop our Gorky and we will."[38] White, whose recent novel *Fire in the Flint* (1924) dealt with racism and lynching in the South, politely declined comment. Tully's comments on black literature were not as ill informed as they might appear. Just a few months earlier he had contributed "The American Negro Enters Literature" (March 1926) to the *Literary Digest International Book Review*.

While in New York, Tully received devastating news from Chicago. Virginia had been stricken a few days after his visit. She had refused to let any word of her illness reach New York, as Jim "has trouble enough with the play."[39] When a telegram finally was sent on October 3, it was to tell him that Virginia was dying. He left immediately for Chicago.

Recognizing her brother's voice, Virginia rallied. "Hello, Jim, boy, I knew you'd come," Jim recalled her saying. "Why, I'm all right—I'm not going to die now—my kid brother all famous and everything." She had spent countless hours alone in the dark with only her bronze gypsy for company. Her face lit by its red glow, "she would sip black coffee and wonder about life."[40] Now unable to see the bronze gypsy, she had Jim move the three-foot statue near her bed. Not yet fifty, Virginia Tully died having seen her dream for her youngest brother come true.

15

Circus Parade

Black Boy had its official premiere on October 6, 1926. The opening-night crowd included such stage and screen stars as Judith Anderson, Louis Wolheim, Norma Talmadge, and Marion Davies. Most of the luminaries were invited to a lavish opening-night party thrown by Liveright.[1] Also in attendance was an aspiring poet, playwright, and novelist later befriended by Tully. "I remember well . . . my first party after a Broadway opening, the one Horace Liveright gave for Paul Robeson and Fredi Washington, following the premiere of Jim Tully's *Black Boy*," Langston Hughes later wrote.[2]

The reviews in the next day's major New York dailies were unenthusiastic but not unkind. "Although Jim Tully's and Frank Dazey's play, 'Black Boy,' mounted at the Comedy last evening, dissipates a picturesque theme in tawdry theatrical effects and in countless dramatic irrelevancies, a certain freshness of viewpoint now and again brings this odyssey of pugilism to life," wrote *New York Times* critic Brooks Atkinson.[3] Reviewing for the *New York World*, Alexander Woollcott thought *Black Boy* was a "raucous, vehement, cheap, yet not unentertaining piece."[4]

The play didn't make it out of October, closing after twenty-seven performances. If the failure to establish himself as a Broadway playwright troubled him, Tully gave no indication of it. What *did* bother him was that critics and reporters assumed his model for *Black Boy* was Jack Johnson, the first black heavyweight champion. Tully tried in vain to set the record straight by pointing out to interviewers that his true inspiration was Joe Gans, the brilliant lightweight who began a six-year reign as champion in

1902. Gans was "a sorrowful devil," Tully explained. Felled by tuberculosis in 1910, "he died out there on a peak in Arizona, forgotten by everybody but God."[5] Joe Gans was thirty-five.

Tully remained far too busy to dwell on either the loss of Virginia or the quick collapse of a play. He was preparing for the publication of an ambitious four-part *Pictorial Review* series about his former boss, Charlie Chaplin. The articles would be the basis of a full-scale biography he had agreed to write for Albert & Charles Boni as the follow-up book to *Jarnegan*.[6] Hoping to secure an interview, Tully wrote Chaplin in October, assuring him that the articles would be written with "the utmost sympathy and with all the understanding I possess."[7] Chaplin would have none of it. Nervous about the inside information Tully possessed from his time at the studio, he moved to quash the series that the *Pictorial Review* was billing as "Charlie Chaplin: His *Real* Life Story."

Chaplin had good reason to fear Tully. Chaplin biographer Joyce Milton describes a lunch at the Hollywood Writers' Club at which Tully claimed to be writing a profile of Chaplin that would depict the Little Tramp as a miser and fraud. Seated across the table, Hollywood gossip writer Rob Wagner was so alarmed that he took the news right to Chaplin. Wagner claimed that when John Wheeler at *Liberty* magazine later contacted him about publishing the article, he replied that it was based on Tully's personal animus. The piece was killed.[8]

Certain that Tully was nursing a grudge, Chaplin went to federal court in Manhattan on January 7, 1927.[9] He filed a $500,000 suit against *Pictorial Review*, claiming his right to privacy had been infringed. His lawyer, Nathan Burkan, asked for a temporary injunction to halt publication, arguing that the articles would subject his client to scorn and contempt. It was not granted, and a judge weighed the evidence as the first two monthly installments appeared in January and February of 1927. The third was published in March, the same month the federal court ruled that, as a public figure, Chaplin could not sue for invasion of privacy. Round 1 went to Tully by decision.

With all this unfolding, their meeting at a Hollywood party given by Frank Dazey's wife was not as awkward as might be expected. Another guest, actress Marion Davies, the third point of the rumored triangle with William Randolph Hearst and Charlie Chaplin during the Thomas Ince affair, was escorted to the party by Chaplin. He seemed genuinely glad to see his unauthorized biographer. "Why, hello, Jim," Chaplin greeted the writer. "I've wanted so much to talk to you."[10] Perhaps he meant it. While Tully was preparing a book he'd call *Circus Parade* for print, Chaplin was working on his follow-up to *The Gold Rush*, *The Circus*.

When a charades tournament was organized, Chaplin picked Tully as his partner. When it was suggested that the goal was to guess words with four syllables, Chaplin laughed and said, "Lord, I don't know any."[11] Chaplin was at ease, and the appearance of Tully's *Pictorial Review* profile should not have changed his mood. Tully was as good as his word and wrote about his former boss with sympathy, understanding, and insight. "To deal fairly with Charlie Chaplin while he is at the zenith of his career is a difficult task," Tully conceded in the first *Pictorial Review* story. "His laughter is often that of a man who would keep his heart from breaking. His humor, on the screen and in real life, is the twin brother of sadness."[12] Tully's goal was to present the comedic genius and intriguing personality behind the Little Tramp image— a complex "human riddle." This wasn't about settling scores or tarnishing a Hollywood star. Chaplin, as it turned out, had nothing to fear from the most feared man in Hollywood. When Rob Wagner saw the profile, he was surprised at its tepid tone. He later met the *Pictorial Review* editor in New York, who claimed to have defanged the piece.[13] Doubts about Tully's veracity seem not to have deterred either Wagner or John Wheeler, as both provided regular outlets for Tully's Hollywood writing.

But privacy increasingly was an issue for the control-minded Chaplin. He undoubtedly resented Tully delving into his sad childhood; his mother's mental illness; his divorce from his first wife, Mildred Harris; his mood swings; and his disastrous marriage to Lita Grey. Although Tully was restrained in his treatment of these sensitive subjects, they were not, after all, topics Chaplin was accustomed to seeing discussed in print. Seething over his inability to block the *Pictorial Review* series, Chaplin cast Tully in the role of disgruntled and ungrateful ex-employee. Many in Hollywood were all too eager to approve of this casting.

In April 1927, Tully traveled to New York to find a publisher for *Circus Parade*, his recollections of his roving days with a small-time circus. He met with Maxwell Perkins, the legendary editor at Charles Scribner's Sons, before again signing a contract with Boni.[14] In addition to *Circus Parade* and the Chaplin biography, Tully promised Boni "Denis Darel," a novel, as well as a work about his childhood, *Shanty Irish*. He was less successful in having Perkins arrange an interview with another of his literary heroes, Ring Lardner.[15] Still, for years after, he would continue to pitch book ideas to Perkins.

That August, Tully visited his aging father in Dayton, Ohio.[16] It led to a warm correspondence between the two Jim Tullys. Determined to render the Tullys and Lawlers as faithfully as possible in *Shanty Irish*, Jim probed his father for tales and details. The letters, charming and sad, shed light on the two families' fortunes in America.

If all went well, Tully would have four more books in stores by the end of 1928. All did not go well. As publication for Jim Tully's "Life of Charlie Chaplin" drew near, Chaplin's legal team turned up the heat. Boni, more or less resolute to this point, buckled under the pressure and withdrew the biography.[17] Round 2 went to Chaplin. Tully never gave up hope for his Chaplin biography, continuing to reshape and revise the manuscript through the 1930s and into the 1940s. His tone remained evenhanded despite Chaplin's efforts to suppress the book.

Having written so much about Hollywood since the 1924 publication of *Beggars of Life*, Tully returned to the relative comfort of the gritty world of the drifter for his next book, the autobiographical *Circus Parade*. Completed in March of 1927 and hitting print that summer, Tully's fourth published book may be viewed as a sequel to *Beggars of Life*.[18] Indeed, they became the first two volumes of what he would later call his Underworld books.

Introductory blurbs on the dust jacket were provided by Harry Hansen ("the small town circus as it was, in straight-hitting fashion") and William Allen White ("hard, terrible realism that will shock the life out of unsophisticated readers"), as well as early Tully booster George Jean Nathan, who was especially enthusiastic: "Tully has got the rawness of life as few American writers have been able to get it, and, with it, a share of poetry and of very shrewd perception ... a view of mortals and of their sawdust hearts that will not soon vanish from the memory."

Tully dedicated *Circus Parade* to Nathan and Mencken, *Vanity Fair* managing editor Donald Freeman, and Hollywood pals James Cruze and Frederick Palmer. Mencken's editorial contributions went beyond friendship, and Tully inscribed his copy: "To H. L. Mencken with high appreciation to one who made the book possible."[19] If Tully appreciated Mencken's assistance, Mencken certainly appreciated Tully's hard-edged, straightforward style.

Some writers, like musicians, seem to write to an internal metronome. Tully wrote to the click-clack-click-clack of the rails, which became the unadorned, crisp, staccato rhythm of his prose. And like the view from an open boxcar, his best works, *Circus Parade* among them, consist of a series of vignettes, each flashing by without reflection or rumination before the next scene is in front of the reader.

Tully's narration in *Circus Parade* is as memorable as it was in *Beggars of Life*, but while *Beggars of Life* is a panorama of great memories, *Circus Parade* is a panorama of great characters. And those characters populate the tents and wagons of an outfit grandly billed as Cameron's World's Greatest Combined Shows. Despite the name, no one would confuse Cameron's ten-car collection of carnies, freaks, and other sawdust celebrities with the Greatest Show on Earth. The characters populating *Circus Parade* range from the sympathetic and innocent through the merely distasteful and cold hearted to the cruel and black hearted.

The boyhood dream to run away with the circus ran deep in the American psyche. "When a circus came and went," wrote Mark Twain in *Life on the Mississippi*, "it left us all burning to become clowns."[20] As Tully describes the lions in their cages, he is struck by his own sense of freedom. His gaze shifts to the crawlers—legless men strapped to small, wheeled platforms and, to boost their take from the crowd, moaning in pain. It is a clear message. Tully has not set out to write a romantic story of a boy joining the circus. He knows too well its seamier side. *Circus Parade* is as far removed from *Toby Tyler* as *The Maltese Falcon* is from *The Hardy Boys*. Instead, over the course of the book, Tully paints a picture of life at the edges—earthy, wolfish, and brutal. "A circus is, or was," Tully writes, "generally a canvas nest of petty thieves and criminals among the lower gentry."[21] The lambs among them repeatedly fall to the predators.

With *Circus Parade*, Tully's dreams of popular and critical acceptance were met. Sales were strong,[22] the Literary Guild quickly contracted for a 16,000-copy reprint,[23] Hollywood sought the film rights,[24] and the comments from friends and formal reviews were laudatory, even ecstatic. One reviewer noted that the book was not for those "easily shocked. . . . But," he continued, "there is something other than bare naturalism in this book, a glowing overtone of humanity, comprehension, and pity that cannot be too highly prized."[25] *New York Times* writer Edwin Clark wrote of *Circus Parade*, "Jim Tully is a novelist who writes of hard facts—as distinguished from the expression of sentiment and sentimentality. He has been the novelist of the hard-boiled."[26]

A teenage James Agee wrote that *Circus Parade* was "remarkable chiefly for its nakedness of style, and for uncovering the most abysmal brutality I've even imagined could exist."[27] Harlem Renaissance poet Countee Cullen took note of the book's several black characters. "This book," he wrote, "will destroy some illusions, but that is the natural function of truth."[28] And years later Langston Hughes would write Tully that he was on his third reading of the book.[29]

There were, predictably, naysayers. Father Francis Finn, SJ, who recalled Jim as a scullery boy at St. Xavier's College in Cincinnati, recognized Tully's literary talents but decried what he saw as Tully's paganism and gloom. He further found Tully's work "offensive to Christian modesty," for which he blamed the bad company of hoboes in general and Chaplin in particular.[30] Critics found the chapter in which a young black girl is mercilessly degraded especially outrageous. Tully later noted that he recalled the incident from his circus days and put it to paper with little embellishment.[31]

With equal parts glee and urgency, Charles Boni telegrammed in late July: "*Circus Parade* banned in Boston." Boni promised to fight the censors and urged Tully to fly to New York to begin the public relations counterattack.[32] The Boston ban was being pressed by the Watch and Ward Society, which placed *Circus Parade* on a list of banned books that included Sherwood Anderson's *Dark Laughter*, William Faulkner's *Mosquitoes*, Theodore Dreiser's *An American Tragedy*, Sinclair Lewis's *Elmer Gantry*, and Hemingway's *The Sun Also Rises*.[33] Adding to the furor, the Brooklyn Public Library prohibited its copy from circulating.[34] A library in Idaho, according to one Tully correspondent, circulated the novel, but with the offending chapter ripped from the book.[35] In a letter to Mencken, whose *American Mercury* had run afoul of Boston's Watch and Ward Society the previous year, Tully joked that he planned to go there and pass out copies of the book to the hoboes, as they were "the only cultivated men I could find in the city."[36]

While Tully could laugh off criticism from Boston, a bad review from St. Marys stung. Tully's hometown newspaper, the *Evening Leader*, in an editorial titled "Filth in Books," claimed to be "unpleasantly surprised that so much dirt could be packed between the covers of a book." In the view of the *Evening Leader*, "*Circus Parade* was written without excuse, except perhaps of making money." While acknowledging that Tully was a "clever writer" and "knows of what he writes," the newspaper could see no justification for exposing the public to such sordid subject matter. Tully's hometown paper widened its condemnation to include *Beggars of Life* and *Jarnegan*, advocating that the publication of all such books be prohibited.[37]

Hurt and angry by criticism from home, Tully responded in a letter to the editor published in October 1927. Tully cited Mencken's comparison of him to Gorky and noted that he and the great Russian writer of the underclass had something else in common: both came from hometowns ashamed of them. Clearly old wounds had been opened. "When I was a hungry boy in St. Marys," he continued, "I got no understanding. I am getting none now." If his goal was getting rich, he argued, then he might adopt the maudlin style of the then-popular novelist Harold Bell Wright. Instead, "I write the truth." Things might have turned out differently had he stopped there, but some bridges were made to be burned. In words that soured relations with many in his hometown for the rest of his life, Tully noted that "St. Marys is still in the same mental rut that it was in when I had the sadness of living there." And, for good measure, Tully insisted that he refused to deal in the "childish terms of small Ohio towns."[38] The sarcasm of the paper's response dripped off the page. "Jim, you are great. Wonderful! You and Gorky!"[39] Not content to get the last word but once, the *Evening Leader* returned to the subject of its famous native son in November by noting and reprinting the poor review of *Circus Parade* that appeared in a South Bend paper.[40]

The central criticism of the Indiana review, that *Circus Parade* presented an inaccurate picture of circus life, echoed the view of Eugene Whitmore in the *Bookman*. While acknowledging that *Circus Parade* had been "hailed by dozens of critics as a masterpiece of realistic writing," Whitmore charged that the book was "no more than old fashioned melodrama, minus the lily-white hero and heroine." And, Whitmore continued, "Tully paints in dark colors, with no lightening contrasts."[41] On the first point, Whitmore was half right. There are no heroes in *Circus Parade,* but a hero's struggle is an essential element of melodrama. Whatever *Circus Parade* was, it wasn't "old fashioned melodrama." On the second point, there can be no argument. Tully did paint in "dark colors." If Whitmore had opened the book looking for simple morality, he had come to the wrong place and the wrong writer.

In building his case that *Circus Parade* was not realistic, Whitmore relied on what he saw as factual errors about circus life. He chided Tully for faulty geography, quoting Tully for writing, "We traveled as far inland as Beaumont, Texas," when, in fact, Beaumont is a port city on the Gulf of Mexico. Tully's meaning of westward travel is clear, however, when he is correctly quoted: "We had journeyed along the Gulf of Mexico and as far inland as Beaumont, Texas."[42] Whitmore, who claimed "a lifetime of contact with circuses," also objected to "Tully's ignorance of the nomenclature of circus tents," his description of loading and unloading the circus train, the troupe's travel in the South before the "cotton has been picked and marketed," and, in his view, other implausibilities and misstatements of fact.[43] Clearly, *Circus Parade* was not to the liking of old circus men.

James Stevens, whose acclaimed novel about Paul Bunyan and lumber camps had appeared in 1925, wrote Burton Rascoe, the editor of the *Bookman*, to defend *Circus Parade* against Whitmore's attack. Twain's nonfiction *Life on the Mississippi*, he noted, was roundly denounced by "old steamboat men," and lawyers quibbled with Dreiser's *An American Tragedy*. A writer, Stevens argued, is certainly allowed to sacrifice "fact for effect."[44]

For his part, Tully dismissed Whitmore as a circus press agent.[45] And if some of the book seemed implausible, he had in fact excluded some memories that readers might have found too far-fetched. Tully wrote H. L. Mencken that he had omitted as unbelievable the tale of a drunk emerging unhurt from a lion's cage after flopping there for the night, even though he had witnessed it.[46]

Circus fans and apologists would not yield. The Literary Guild received many cancellations over its selection of the book,[47] and when it appeared in 1929 that a film version of *Circus Parade* would be produced, the Circus Fans Association mounted a vigorous publicity campaign opposing the movie.[48] It was never made. A gritty portrayal of the big top would finally reach the big screen in 1932. It was *Dracula* director Tod Browning's *Freaks*, and it too was roundly condemned, even banned, before being recognized as a horror classic.

The uproar over *Circus Parade* would not be the last time that Tully ended up in the gun sights of censors and other self-appointed guardians of public taste and morality. In an odd footnote to *Circus Parade* and its censorship, John O'Hara evoked the book in defending his use of the word "nookey" in a story he submitted to the *New Yorker* in 1960. If Jim Tully could use "goosey" in *Circus Parade*, O'Hara argued to editor William Maxwell, then "nookey" should be allowed to stand.[49]

In *Beggars of Life* Jim Tully found his voice: raw, powerful, savage, yet lyrical. In *Circus Parade* that voice reached full-throated maturity: still savage, yet more confident in its ability to guide the reader down dark roads.

16

Shanty Irish

Little more than a year after the release of *Circus Parade* came news of the death of one Harry Price of Columbus, Ohio. He was found penniless and alone on the third floor of the back room of an East Town Street boardinghouse. His few personal effects included racing sheets, turf magazines, and a few yellowing newspaper clippings about Jim Tully. He'd acquired the nickname Blackie from his habit of wearing black shirts. Jim had met Price while both were employed at a chain works in Columbus in 1907 and the pair had hoboed out of town together.

When word reached Jim that his brother of the road and one of the central characters in *Circus Parade* had died, Jim responded with a letter to a Columbus paper: "It was 'Blackie' who told me that an excellent hobo and a poor chainmaker was lost when I became a worse writer. Peace to his red hot soul, may the winds of eternity never make it cool."[1] Jim's brother Charles, then living in Columbus, was tracked down for comment and shared that Jim had recently sent the old hobo $100 to travel to Hollywood. When the money was lost at the track, Blackie wrote his old pal, explaining that Hollywood was just too far from High Street.[2]

In September 1927, Tully began what would be a long and warm correspondence with Vincent Donovan, a Catholic priest who greatly admired his writing. The good Dominican father was the brother of William Joseph "Wild Bill" Donovan, the World War I Fighting Sixty-ninth commander who would become known as the father of the CIA. Vincent Donovan's attempt to lure Jim away from agnosticism failed. The friendship did not.[3]

That same month, Tully was in Baltimore, visiting Mencken. On September 30, Mencken wrote Tully with a special request. His close friend and *American Mercury* contributor Sara Haardt was about to visit Hollywood. Could Jim recommend a quiet, conservative hotel? Would Jim act as her unofficial guide, chaperon, and protector? This was more than just a favor. It was in the nature of a chevalier's commission. Mencken, a sworn bachelor, was, as biographer William Manchester pointed out, "drifting into marriage in 1927."[4] It was a leisurely drift, to be sure, but Henry and Sara did stun the nation in 1930 by getting married.

"Sara Haardt and Jim Tully were an oddly assorted pair for Mencken to have thrown together, even in Hollywood," observed friend and writer Sara Mayfield. "Mencken's attachment to the Irishman derived in part, I think, from transference of his youthful admiration of Mark Twain's Huck Finn to Tully, who shared so many of Huck's foibles and virtues."[5] It was fitting, therefore, that Tully selected the Mark Twain Hotel for Haardt's lodging, a modest establishment on the stretch of Wilcox Avenue between Hollywood and Sunset boulevards. "Mencken not only had a deep affection for him but trusted him as he did few men," Mayfield wrote of Tully. "Therefore, convinced that Sara would be safer in the care of the stocky Irishman . . . Mencken selected Tully to act as her cicerone amid 'the levantine debaucheries' of Hollywood."[6]

Tully met Sara Haardt in the lobby of the Mark Twain. The tall, gracious lady from Alabama was immediately charmed by the short, rugged fellow from Ohio. She recalled her first glimpse of him for a profile published in the May 1928 *American Mercury*:

> His head was tilted to one side, and as he raised it, it seemed to me that it was literally on fire. His hair is a tangled wiry mop of flaming red curls, so thick and unruly that, with his muscular shoulders, it gives him the appearance of being top-heavy and possessed of an enormous strength. And like most red hair it creates a strange, almost startling impression of youth. I had the feeling, as I looked at him, that I was seeing him as he looked that day, years ago, when he sat by the high trestle spanning the St. Marys river in Ohio. . . . He got to his feet, and I saw that he was short and powerfully built; that he was heavy-jowled; that his chest was thrust out, that the muscles of his arms bulged his sleeves. Yet, for all his bulk, I sensed a quickness, a kind of shrewdness in his movements. I could imagine his muscles springing into action so quickly that they almost thought for him.

Haardt also offered a detailed description of Tully's office at the Kings Road home he shared with Marna: "Tully works in a big oblong room on the second floor . . . a room lined with books from ceiling to floor, and containing a flat square desk with a swivel-chair, a great dictionary on an old-fashioned brass tripod, an old beer-table—a real one with a hole in the center where the press-button used to be—and two huge armchairs. Back of the desk is a tiny window with iron gratings."[7] She took particular note of several small framed pictures of writers, including Mark Twain and Joseph Conrad. This was no ordinary pantheon of writers. All had spent some part of their lives as drifters.

One paragraph in Haardt's profile of Tully would create months of headaches for Mencken. Tully had told Haardt about sending the manuscript of *Emmett Lawler* to the Pasadena home of Upton Sinclair, who had promised to look at it. Weeks later, he sent his son, Alton, to retrieve it, only to have Sinclair's dogs chase off the young boy. Enraged by Tully's account, Sinclair wrote to Mencken in late April of 1928, calling Haardt's *American Mercury* article libelous and demanding an apology. Mencken tried to jolly the indignant Sinclair, saying it would be foolish to allow a difference in recollection to reach open warfare. Sinclair would not be jollied. Letters continued to be exchanged throughout May, with Mencken wearying of Sinclair's fuming and fussing. Mencken tried to broker a peace by suggesting a meeting between Tully and Sinclair. Tully was willing. Sinclair refused, continuing to bombard Mencken with documents and arguments.

Distressed that Sinclair was being a nuisance to Mencken, Tully said he would go along with anything "that will keep him from pestering you."[8] Mencken, hearing that Sinclair had recently been attacked and bitten by a dog in Long Beach, expressed the frail hope that this might help Sinclair see Tully's side of things. It did not. Tully then wrote directly to Sinclair, suggesting that he stop badgering Mencken. Sinclair continued to badger. Finally, on June 8 Sinclair went too far. In a telegram to Mencken, he tendered his usual demand that the *American Mercury* reveal Tully for the ingrate he was. Sinclair then made veiled threats against the magazine and, worse, Sara Haardt.[9]

Mencken, exasperated and hoping to put an end to the whole business, again wrote Sinclair, summarizing both sides of "the great feud."[10] He detailed the inconsistencies in Sinclair's version of events and insisted that the whole mess could have been settled had he agreed to meet with Tully. He further suggested that it would be unwise to make threats against the

American Mercury and Sara Haardt. Tully thought Mencken's letter was fair and that Sinclair should appreciate the effort but predicted he wouldn't. It was an accurate prediction. Sinclair's wife wrote on June 11 to say they believed the summary was slanted to Tully's side.[11] Sinclair had to content himself with officially accusing Tully of being ungrateful in the August issue of *Haldeman-Julius Monthly*.[12]

If F. Scott Fitzgerald had had his way, Tully would have tangled with another American writer in the summer of 1928. Hoping to goad his blustering friend into the ring with a real fighter, Fitzgerald sent a letter to Ernest Hemingway, suggesting he take on Jim Tully in a boxing match. Papa didn't take the bait.[13]

Tully, meanwhile, was putting the finishing touches on his fifth book, *Shanty Irish*, an autobiographical novel set in and around the St. Marys of his youth. Published by Boni that fall, *Shanty Irish* is both an exploration and a celebration of his Irish American family. It is also Jim Tully's most personal, lyrical, and humorous book. The crisp phrasing and cold-eyed brutality of *Beggars of Life* and *Circus Parade* are again evident in *Shanty Irish*, yet it is in *Shanty Irish* that Tully gives freest rein to the sentimental, poetic side of his nature. These two disparate sides of the writer's personality are in dynamic balance, the sardonic Irish rover's rough instincts tempered by those of the Irish poet.

Although Irish immigrants were hired as manual laborers on canals and railroads well before the Great Potato Famine of the 1840s, their story had not yet been widely told. The Irish American experience was first explored from the humorist's perspective in Chicagoan Finley Peter Dunne's Mr. Dooley books, published between 1898 and 1919. And Irish American writers had made towering literary contributions before *Shanty Irish*. One need only mention Eugene O'Neill and Fitzgerald. But neither Irish American writer had yet set his sights on the Irish American experience.

Blending humor and heartbreak, realism and lyricism, Tully's *Shanty Irish* anticipates the 1930s work of another Chicagoan, James T. Farrell. But where Farrell was interested in the experience of the Irish American in the city, Tully's people are country and small-town folk. Unlike Fitzgerald, who wrote so brilliantly about the riches and glamor of the Jazz Age, Tully was drawn to Gorky's lower depths—the underclass, the disadvantaged, the disenfranchised. Even though a proud Irish American, Al Smith, ran for president the same year that *Shanty Irish* was published, America was not that far removed from the days of signs that declared, "No Irish need apply." Tully's parents toiled at the only jobs open to them: work as ditchers and domestics.

A book soaked in mud and whiskey, *Shanty Irish* charts the Tully-Lawler journey from the horrors of the potato famine through the author's own childhood. His hard-drinking grandfather, Old Hughie Tully, emerges as the book's most vividly drawn character, and his life and death frame the narrative. A constant presence in *Shanty Irish*, Old Hughie spins yarns of Ireland, of his emigration, of his days traveling through the antebellum South as a lace "piddler," of "throwing dirt" for a living, of friends, and of enemies. Old Hughie is "capable of turning death into an Irish wake and pouring liquor down the throat of the corpse."[14] *Shanty Irish*, though, is far from a one-grandfather show. It is, indeed, a book loaded with unforgettable characters.

Just as William Faulkner would soon create a fictional world in his Yoknapatawpha County, Tully would do the same with the Auglaize County of his boyhood. Within the covers of this work, we meet the author's father, whose stooped shoulders carry "the inherited burdens of a thousand dead Irish peasants."[15] We meet his mother, Biddy, a "woman of imagination" who "had all the moods of April."[16] We meet his ruthless uncle John Lawler. We meet Aunt Moll and hear how she shocked the family and the community by attempting to join the Walnut Grove Methodist Church. And we meet Virginia, who inherited her mother's faith and mysticism.

These are not the Irish American stereotypes that flourished on the vaudeville stage during the first twenty years of the twentieth century or would populate so many Hollywood films in the 1930s. The author of *Shanty Irish* makes them distinctly Tully and distinctly Lawler. Yet through the prism of his family, he captures the shanty Irish American experience. For all his rough-hewn sensibilities, *Shanty Irish* is dappled with warm and affectionate childhood memories.

Tully's use of irony is particularly sharp throughout, but never more so than when he describes the roistering Lawlers as "all devout Catholics during mass on Sundays."[17] It's the type of terse turn of phrase that was a Mark Twain specialty. Perhaps there's an echo here of Twain's infamous line about "the serene confidence which a Christian feels in four aces."[18] With few words Tully tells so much about his relatives. "At heart my father was an agnostic without knowing it," he writes. "His wife relied much on God. He did not interfere."[19] He has, in three short sentences, defined their marriage, their beliefs, their understanding.

Tully inherited his father's love of reading and his agnosticism, but he also inherited a reluctance to judge friends and foes. Tully again echoes Twain when he discusses Virginia's devotion to Catholicism. "It rests me, and I feel better when I go to church," she says. "Even if in the end I find out I'm wrong I'd still think it was wiser to kid myself."[20] Somewhere in there is Twain declaring that faith is believing what you know "ain't so."[21]

Given the Irish love of storytelling, it is not surprising that Tully spent his childhood immersed in family lore. For stories set in Ireland, there was no shortage of accounts of the famine. And in a small 1854 volume titled *Sketches of the Irish Bar* by Richard Lalor Sheil, Tully found the story of John Walsh (changed by Tully to Tim Walsh) that appears in the second chapter of *Shanty Irish*. The story about the 1827 murder of a rent collector and its bloody aftermath is drawn by Tully with little embellishment from Sheil's account.[22]

The question one always faces when reading Tully is: How much is true? Responding to a query from an encyclopedia editor, Tully wrote, "Both my father's and mother's people are described quite truthfully in *Shanty Irish*."[23] But what of the rest? Tully opens *Shanty Irish* with a clue. Hugh Tully is certainly the most memorable character in all of Tully's books, yet Jim was only fourteen when his grandfather died in 1900. And young Jim had spent six of his fourteen years in an orphanage, separated from his grandfather. When Tully sat down at his desk to write about Hugh Tully, he could recall his grandfather's "sardonic attitude" but had to concede that "I had no samples of his wit in my memory."[24] While family members could add a few stories to Jim's memories, much of what Jim wrote about his grandfather came about through the hard business of writing. When Jim prefaced *Shanty Irish* with a quote from Irish physicist John Tyndall (a move applauded by Mencken), he no doubt had the creation of Old Hughie in mind: "There is in the human intellect a power of expansion—I might almost call it a power of creation—which is brought into play by the simple brooding upon facts."[25]

Jim later recalled writing and rewriting the scene that opens chapter 8. He originally wrote the scene with Hughie and a "group of hospitable yokels" sitting around a roaring fire one rainy night. When Jim was unable to loosen his grandfather's tongue, he tried a change of venue. Instead of a campfire, Jim placed Hughie in a saloon. His writer's block was broken with the introduction of a one-legged stranger who walked through the swinging doors and pushed the scene in a new direction.[26] The barroom stories that followed, Jim later wrote, came not from any particular memory but from "the simple brooding upon facts"—and the imagination, one might add, of a gifted and unique writer.

For all his hard-boiled grittiness, Tully could also be a fabulist. Nowhere was that more evident than in the *Shanty Irish* chapters about the One-Legged Stranger, who claims to have been in the Battle of Bull Run. He soon is in a drinking battle with Old Hughie. "The one [story] I had the most fun in writing," he wrote Mencken, "was the *One Legged Stranger* and the drinking contest."[27] As was his custom, Tully offered the chapters of *Shanty Irish* to the trusted Mencken for inclusion in the *American Mercury*. Mencken, who could be gentle but firm in declining work not up to his high standards, snapped them up.

In the foreword to a later book, *Blood on the Moon*, Tully described *Shanty Irish*: "In 'Shanty Irish' was depicted the background of a road-kid who became articulate. Down the avenue of years my grandfather, who dominates the book, has been very real to me. I can still hear, on quiet nights, the whisky rattling down his bony throat. That he talked a great deal was natural, of course, being Irish. He was a sad old man with a broken dream in his head and a fear of death in his heart."[28]

Broken dreams fill *Shanty Irish*, but Jim inherited neither his grandfather's sadness nor his fear. In an early chapter of *Shanty Irish*, Jim wrote of his father. "A most amazing Irishman was my father—one devoid of sentimentality. A man without tears, he often seemed without pity."[29] Like his father, Jim was a man without tears. What made him different from both his father and grandfather—and from lesser writers—was his great capacity for empathy.

Mencken was the first to recognize the book's excellence and contributed a blurb that appeared opposite the title page. "If Tully were a Russian, read in translation, all the Professors would be hymning him. He has all of Gorky's capacity for making vivid the miseries of poor and helpless men, and in addition he has a humor that no Russian could conceivably have. In 'Shanty Irish,' it seems to me, he has gone far beyond any of his work of the past. The book is not only brilliantly realistic; it also has fine poetic quality."[30]

Reviews of *Shanty Irish* were mostly positive. James M. Cain's was so enthusiastic that Boni included part of it on the book's dust jacket: "A yarn that soars up into the vaulted blue. It is, we submit, literature. In it, for a moment, the national letters have a glorious reversion to the roaring vigor of yore." Mencken believed that such praise, given Cain's "bilious" nature, would boost the book immensely.³¹ The *New York Post* concluded that *Shanty Irish* was "Jim Tully's greatest contribution to literature. In our opinion it will become a definite part of our national belles lettres."³²

The *New Republic* objected to the book's sentimentality, which took the form of Tully's sweetening his hard-boiled dialogue with "locutions." Still, "it must be added that some of the bar-room yarns his people tell are both grand and glorious."³³ Percy Hutchison at the *New York Times* concluded that Tully was "like no other writer." He doesn't write so much as he "spits forth images, words, sentences, as a machine gun spits forth bullets." This has the effect that, while Tully is "aiming at his individuals," Hutchison wrote, he "hits mankind."³⁴

The *Chicago Daily Tribune* was both amused and shocked, citing the book's "blasphemy" and "words that aren't pretty," but was forced to conclude that "there is something sturdy and lusty about it."³⁵ Perhaps not quite so lusty as Tully intended. In the One-Legged Stranger's story, Tully originally had the old man saying, "Gigantic copulations shook the sky." Tully would later complain bitterly to Mencken that *Shanty Irish* was "the most horribly proof-read book in America."³⁶ Whether out of timidity, as Tully suspected, or sloppiness, "copulations" became "osculations" in the published book.³⁷

A review that must have particularly pleased the author washed up from Dublin. The *Irish Times* concluded that *Shanty Irish* was "far in advance of anything he has previously done." It praised the book's "clear-cut economy of phrase and stark precision of characterisation, a book wherein tragedy is splashed with humour and comedy steeped in sadness."³⁸

Even Upton Sinclair put their feud aside to declare that *Shanty Irish* was a "chunk of real life. It made me feel human and humble, which is good for anybody."³⁹ The two never became friendly, but the peace held and Tully agreed to serve on a committee of writers supporting Sinclair's 1934 bid to become governor of California.⁴⁰

Not everyone approved, and some of the dissent was predictable. The leftist writer and founder of the *New Masses*, Michael Gold, who had praised Tully's earlier work, panned *Shanty Irish*, blaming the pernicious influence of H. L. Mencken.⁴¹ And another Dublin paper, the *Irish Independent*, under the heading "A Slobbering Idiot," considered Hughie just another drunken Irishman.⁴² And in Tully's hometown of St. Marys, Ohio, his cousin Gertrude Lawler wrote that the book was widely read, but never openly discussed.⁴³

Perhaps the most thoughtful criticism of *Shanty Irish*, intended as a complaint, was registered by a young James T. Farrell. Writing in the student newspaper at the University of Chicago, Farrell concluded that "Tully is at best a surface realist." Tully can, Farrell allowed, "depict action with a brusque clarity, and he has a formula for building up plausible saloon and jungle dialogue. Against this must be weighed his sentimentality, his melodrama, and his antisocial attitudinization, which is masked by a savage and staccatoed crudeness of style, and a barbarity of subject." Farrell continued, "Tully lacks the power, the intensity of vision, the subtlety of feeling to transform this raw, crude stuff into something on a higher artistic level."[44] There is more than an element of truth in all this, although it must be pointed out that there is no evidence that Tully ever aspired to create art, high or low, that conformed to any particular definition.

Shanty Irish sold well in both the United States and England, and as late as 1945, Tully could tell friends that the book was still selling.[45] The book's success certainly had much to do with the comic and roguish Old Hughie, whom Jim immediately tried to make the main character of a stage version titled "God Loves the Irish." He finished a three-act first draft in late 1928, with most of the emphasis on Hughie and John Lawler.[46] Again turning to a collaborator for the theater, he finished a second draft with Charles Beahan in early 1929. All efforts to get "God Loves the Irish" staged or turned into a movie ended in failure.

What made *Shanty Irish* different was that Tully was the first to write in something other than strictly comic tones. Scholar Emory Elliott concluded "that by its focus on a poor Irish family [*Shanty Irish*] set the theme and by its title's ugly epithet set the tone for the breakthrough of Irish Americans into the fiction of cultural mediation."[47] "I developed early a capacity for remembered sorrow," Tully wrote in *Shanty Irish*. "It is possible that I remembered too much."[48] It is from this well of remembered sorrow—and empathy—that Jim Tully fills *Shanty Irish*.

Jarnegan, Circus Parade, and *Shanty Irish* emerged as the tent poles during this three-ring period of Tully's writing life. In addition to working on the books and many magazine articles, he was spending a considerable amount of time advising a couple of aspiring writers behind bars, as well as attempting to save a third prisoner from execution. Nor did the failure of *Black Boy* sour him on playwrighting. In late 1927, Robert Holden & Company of London published *Twenty Below*, a three-act hobo drama by Tully and Robert Nichols. One of England's acclaimed poets of the Great War, Nichols had been the subject of Robert Graves's poem "To Robert Nichols." Following the war, Nichols wrote, taught, befriended the likes of Aldous Huxley and Nancy Cunard, and, for a year, lived in Hollywood. During that year, the *New York Times* noted, he "castigated the film community more effectively than any other writer."[49] This, combined with his interest in boxing as well as the tramps, drifters, and yeggs of England, made his meeting and partnership with Tully seem foreordained.[50] The second in Holden's "Plays for the Theatre of Tomorrow" series, *Twenty Below* is an odd collision of American and British road sensibilities. Set in America in a small-town jail, *Twenty Below* began a three-week London run in May 1928.[51] Attempts to mount a New York or Los Angeles production of the play failed.

In February of 1928, Paramount purchased the film rights to *Beggars of Life* and the play based on it, *Outside Looking In*.[52] The movie quickly went into production under the tutelage of William "Wild Bill" Wellman, the director who had been at the helm of *Wings* (1927), the first film to win the Academy Award for Best Picture. In June, Paramount signed Tully to collaborate with Harry Behn on "Passing Strangers," an epic tale about hobo life borrowing the title of Tully's unpublished 1922 book.[53] The project never got off the ground.

Then in late September of 1928, Tully made it to both the silver screen and the Great White Way. Reviews of Wellman's *Beggars of Life* appeared in the New York newspapers on September 24, the same day that Beahan and Garrett Fort's dramatization of *Jarnegan* opened at the Longacre Theatre. Fort, who died at forty-five in 1945, is best known for his work on the screenplays for such Universal horror films as *Dracula* (1931), *Frankenstein* (1931), and *Dracula's Daughter* (1936). He also worked on the screenplay of the film noir classic *The Letter* (1940), directed by William Wyler and starring Bette Davis.[54]

Aging matinee idol Richard Bennett had the title role in *Jarnegan*, which was labeled a "vulgar, raucous and extremely profane play" by the *New York Times*.[55] The *Herald-Tribune* critic said it was "considerably less than a good play" but found the story "fairly exciting," and Bennett's youngest daughter, cast as the Hollywood ingenue, "unbelievably beautiful."[56] Near the end of her life, Joan Bennett recalled that she was underage when her mother signed her to play Daisy Carol in *Jarnegan*, which allowed her to break the standard run-of-the-play contract and accept a film offer from United Artists.[57] Two other future stars, Lionel Stander and Sam Levene, had small roles as guests at a party.

Despite the poor reviews, *Jarnegan* became a surprise hit, running 136 performances, then moving to Chicago for another round of negative notices and another lucrative engagement. A national tour followed. The secret of the show's success might have been that Bennett made no secret of his disdain for Hollywood, motion pictures, and critics. He loved playing Jack Jarnegan, frequently carrying the spirit of Tully's hero into fiery curtain speeches.

Critic and theater historian Burns Mantle felt that the curtain speeches "built a good box office" for the "mud-slinging play." Audiences "hastened to hear Mr. Bennett chastise the critics, and came away ruminating on his voluminous (and very vocal) arguments for Truth in drama," Mantle wrote. "Bennett's expert showmanship, equaling his ability as an actor, was responsible for one of the season's most profitable engagements."[58]

At fifty-eight, Bennett was older than the dynamic director in Tully's novel. But the actor felt a spiritual connection to both the character and the author. Like Tully, Bennett was a midwesterner who had tried his hand at boxing and traveling with small-time carny shows. He often singled out Jarnegan as his favorite role, and when the theater veteran died in October 1944, Tully was an honorary pallbearer (with Lionel Barrymore, Burgess Meredith, and Orson Welles).[59]

A transitional sound film (with music and sound effects), Wellman's *Beggars of Life* starred Wallace Beery as Oklahoma Red, *Wings* star Richard Arlen as Jim, and Louise Brooks as Nancy, a farm girl who has killed the foster father trying to rape her. She goes on the road with Arlen's character, disguising herself as a road-kid. Three years earlier, none other than Charlie Chaplin had taken Brooks to see *Outside Looking In*, the stage version of *Beggars of Life*. Chaplin, with whom she was having an affair that summer, told her he'd already seen it twice.[60]

In late May 1928, prior to location shooting, Tully wrote Mencken that he knew Brooks was "going around on the set calling me after Quilp—'unloved and unlovable.'"[61] Years later, she repeated her reference to the hunchbacked villain of the Dickens novel *The Old Curiosity Shop*. She wrote film historian Kevin Brownlow that Tully "was the most repulsive little Quilp I ever knew," with "his belly hanging over his belt, yellow teeth to match his face and hair, full of the vanity of *Vanity Fair* and H. L. Mencken."[62] Tully was accustomed to being in bad odor in Hollywood, but Brooks's hatred puzzled him.

The cast and crew of *Beggars of Life* moved to Jacumba, California, near the Mexican border, at the end of the month for location filming. In early June, Tully visited Jacumba to watch the filming of his autobiography. Brooks wrote Brownlow that "we were sitting on a rock posing for still pictures and he reached over and touched my breast, under my grey flannel shirt."[63] The truth behind the incident may never be known, but her account is suspect, in part because of her description in the same letter of Tully's "yellow" hair, but more significantly because the many photographs taken that day show Brooks in a white shirt and pullover sweater, not the gray flannel shirt she later described.

Nor did Brooks have fond memories of others on the set. She disliked Arlen, who became surly when she laughed at his claim to having flown with the RAF during the war (he had), and Wellman, whom she considered a cowardly misogynist. Yet they come off as saintly compared to her stunt double, Harvey Parry. Impressed by Parry's physical courage, Brooks invited him into her bedroom. The next day, he humiliated the actress in front of several hobo extras and crew members, telling her that his girl was about to arrive and he wanted to know if Brooks had syphilis.[64] Disgusted with Hollywood, the independent Brooks packed up her naturalistic style and moved to Germany, where she made two highly acclaimed 1929 films with director G. W. Pabst, *Pandora's Box* and *Diary of a Lost Girl*. Today film scholars and Brooks devotees rightly view *Beggars of Life* as one of her defining roles.

Reviews of the *Beggars of Life* film were mixed. Perhaps the most informed (and least public) review came by letter from hobo scholar Nels Anderson, who had lavished praise on the book. Anderson had previewed the film for Paramount and wrote Tully that Hollywood's disdain for reality had marred the film. Sharp-eyed viewers, Anderson wrote, would quickly spot sagebrush and California road signs in scenes supposed to be set in Minnesota. And perhaps most embarrassing of all, one scene showed "an oil burner engine from the southwest pull up to a water tank." Still, Anderson continued, the film was historically significant in capturing the rural hobo before city life and the automobile moved him from the tracks back to the highway, where he had been before the railroads. The hobo, Anderson further observed, "is being crowded out of existence by the hitch-hikers."[65]

The arrivals of *Beggars of Life* as a movie, *Jarnegan* as a play, and *Shanty Irish* as a book propelled Tully to a new height of notoriety, yet fame did not bring happiness. Instead, he suffered bouts of depression—"moods" so severe that Marna too felt overwhelmed.[66] Their three-year marriage began to unravel.

17

Shadows of Men

With his career rocketing to new heights, Tully took stock of his goals. "I'd like to devote my life to real writing if I could," he wrote Mencken. "It's only been five years since I got started but in another year I'll be worth around a hundred thousand dollars."[1] After so many years of privation and hard work, the money was finally rolling in. With it came the freedom to write about the people who most interested him: road-kids, yeggs, hoboes, drifters, and other denizens of the American underclass.

Yet he would later acknowledge to a reporter that he was still haunted by old fears. "I've stood on the bread line so much . . . I'm afraid of being broke again. And I don't believe I could stand it. I wouldn't have the nerve to go through it again. Yes, people like my stories, but I'm afraid they'll change their minds. . . . But, damn it, I can't get over being afraid. Maybe it's a flash in the pan and my luck will change. . . . I wonder from force of habit how I'll eat tomorrow."[2]

Beside the obvious financial relief, the past five years had brought other changes as well. H. L. Mencken had gone from being a name on a masthead to a confidant and trusted editor. As was Tully's pattern, he reserved his best work for the pages of the *American Mercury*. Under Mencken's sympathetic and watchful eye, he could try out material that he could later incorporate into his books.

The idea of men in jail had interested Tully for years, going back to his own time behind bars but also to his youthful reading of Dostoyevsky's *The House of the Dead*.[3] The possibility of writing about prison first surfaced in 1922 when Fremont Older, the editor of the *San Francisco Call and Post*, hired the author of *Emmett Lawler* to cover a hanging at San Quentin.[4] Years later, in March 1927, Tully traveled to San Quentin to visit several prisoners, including Kid McCoy, a former hobo and light heavyweight champion serving time for manslaughter;[5] Tom Mooney, imprisoned for the 1916 San Francisco Preparedness Day bombing;[6] and J. B. McNamara, who was serving a life sentence for the 1910 bombing of the Los Angeles Times Building.

The March visit planted the seed of an idea. He would write an in-depth piece on an execution. Tully floated the idea by *Scribner's*, but editor Alfred Dashiell hedged.[7] When Tully turned to Mencken, who had been pressing for an article about San Quentin's most famous prisoners, the execution idea was quickly accepted.[8] The resulting article, "A California Holiday," became one of Tully's most famous short pieces.[9]

Earl Clark, the condemned man, had been convicted of killing a sailor who had been wooing Clark's girlfriend with roses. Clark escaped from the Los Angeles county jail and settled in a small South Dakota town, where he married a woman who was unaware of his past. He began a painting business. Clark's undoing was the stuff of film noir: a young man who'd taken a mail-order detective course picked up his trail and turned him in.[10]

Mencken penciled in Tully's account of Clark's hanging for the January 1928 *American Mercury*, an issue that Mencken expected to be the finest ever published.[11] Columnist Frank Scully later wrote that Tully "stood by the scaffold and watched the lad's neck pop, then sat down without a quaver of emotion or a break in a line and wrote his most hard-boiled report. Without even one aside, 'A California Holiday' remains the most terrible indictment against capital punishment as yet written in America."[12] The piece has drifted in and out of print ever since its publication and been praised by figures as disparate as Ruby Darrow, wife of Clarence; Walter Winchell; and hobo scholar Nels Anderson.[13]

While "A California Holiday" focused on the plight of one prisoner on death row, a follow-up piece in the *American Mercury*, "Two-Time Losers," looked at the California prison system as a whole.[14] It included a brief history, as well as an account of three of its most famous writers in residence: Ed Morrell, Ernest Booth, and Robert Tasker. Morrell had been a member of the notorious Sontag gang that preyed on the Southern Pacific Railroad in the 1890s. Once apprehended, Morrell was sentenced to solitary confinement for life and, for good measure, spent days at a time in a straightjacket, or "the one-eyed pirate's coat." He came to the attention of Jack London, who collected Morrell's chilling stories in *The Star Rover* (1915). Unhappy with both his compensation and London's work, Morrell dictated his autobiography, which was published in 1924 as *The Twenty-fifth Man*. Robert Tasker had been getting advice from both Tully and Mencken on the writing of his autobiography, *Grimhaven,* which would be published in 1928. The book's publisher, Knopf, described it as the first book written and issued while its author remained behind bars. Ernest Booth, a lifer at Folsom, had been recruited by Mencken and Tully to write "We Rob a Bank" for the *American Mercury*.[15]

In addition to these nonfiction prison pieces, Tully was also writing autobiographical stories for the *American Mercury*. "Jungle Justice" recalled the brutal murder of a railroad detective.[16] In a letter that demonstrated why he commanded such fierce loyalty from Tully and other writers, Mencken cautioned that we "can't go on asking you to accept our low rates indefinitely when your stuff is in such demand everywhere else."[17] Tully stuck with the *Mercury* for "Jungle Justice" and took Mencken's advice to rewrite the last few pages and use the story's real-life ending.[18] These and other stories that passed across H. L. Mencken's desk from 1927 through 1929 became the chapters of a book that Tully planned to call "Jailbirds."[19] Marna, however, hated the title and Tully considered "Taken from Thieves" before settling on a title suggested by Mencken, "Shadows of Men."[20]

Published by Doubleday, Doran and Company in January 1930 and illustrated by *Circus Parade* artist William Gropper, *Shadows of Men* was dedicated to Tully's Hollywood pals Al Lewin and Paul Bern. An ungrammatical introductory note reading, "None of the characters in this book are completely imaginary," gave Tully's critics an immediate toehold. Tully later claimed that the line appeared as intended and, he further noted, was later employed by Ernest Hemingway without complaint.[21]

While *Shadows of Men* is autobiographical, it is not, strictly speaking, autobiography. The book opens with Jim and his buddy Blink drifting into a "scrawny town in a Western state."[22] Over the next sixteen chapters, Tully describes the lives of men in the shadows, lives caught in an endless cycle of road and jail, freedom and confinement. Tully interrupts his narration to let this assortment of hoboes, forgers, hustlers, con men, yeggs, pyromaniacs, murderers, drug addicts, and prisoners tell their stories.

Their narratives are dark, gritty, and decidedly lacking in the romance of the road or class struggle. Gone too is the sentimentality of *Shanty Irish*. In

Tully's view, there is often little moral distinction between the "knights of the road" and those charged with protecting society from their predations. The chapter titled "Jungle Justice" is illustrative. It depicts the hobo camp trial of notorious railroad detective One-Lung Riley. Charged with killing hoboes, he is dragged into the Willow Creek jungle along the Mississippi River to face his accusers. He is summarily found guilty and shot. Riley's body is stripped naked, mutilated with knives, lashed to a log, and consigned to the dark currents of the Mississippi. The hoboes disperse along the paths, and "In a short time the jungle was silent."[23]

The power of the story derives not so much from the characters as from the place—dark, isolated, foreboding, dangerous, evil. In Tully's hands the hobo jungle was a land of nightmares. As critic Gerald Green noted:

> Even a Neanderthaler like Jim Tully can induce a rare and believable terror, open our eyes to a kind of world that surely exists—one that we might never know about if it were not for Tully. Go back and read "Jungle Justice." . . . Genet's pederasts, Burroughs' junkies, and all the minor scarecrows—Selby, Rechy, Schneck, LeRoi Jones—are all schoolboys alongside old Tully. And at least he has the virtue of absolute honesty, of innocence. He is not at all concerned with promoting himself; he wants to tell you a story. He is concerned with other people.[24]

The setting made a strong impression after the story first appeared in the *American Mercury*. When the Associated Press reported on the 1929 destruction of the hobo jungle known as the Willows, located near Memphis, it noted the camp was "the scene of Jim Tully's famous story, 'Jungle Justice.'"[25]

Midway through *Shadows of Men*, Tully briefly pauses to describe prison life. It is a grim and crowded world of vermin, human odor and filth, solitary confinement, cigarettes, furtive conversations, glimpses of female prisoners, and misery. Mostly, Tully describes hope swirling down the drain: "We stood in a half circle, watching the door. It had become an obsession with me. For nearly four months I had watched men pass through it, with hands locked and heads bowed, to the most dismal of destinies."[26]

While Tully's description of life on the road in *Beggars of Life* and other works anticipated Jack Kerouac's *On the Road* by nearly three decades, in *Shadows of Men*, Tully tried his hand at subject matter later made famous by Kerouac's fellow beat writer William Burroughs. A chapter titled "Bull

Horrors," which first appeared in the October 1927 *American Mercury*, explores the world of the junkie. It was not the first time Tully had written about narcotics. Five years earlier, he had alarmed *Los Angeles Times* readers with a detailed story on widespread drug use ranging from the use of opium in Chinatown to cocaine in Los Angeles.[27]

In "Bull Horrors," Tully describes a train rattling through the Texas night. In a dark boxcar, Jim watches an older hobo fitfully smoke a cigarette. The older man fidgets, takes his coat off, and begins to shake. Jim notices his bruised and needle-scarred arms. "He fumbled in his coat pocket and took from it the small tin lid of a typewriter ribbon box. He filled it with a powder which looked yellow in the moonlight."[28] He added water to the powder, struck a match, and warmed the mixture. He drew it into a syringe made from a glass dropper, had Jim tie off his arm, and "shot the dreams into his arm."[29]

Nightmares too are let loose, and the man's ravings swirl through the dark boxcar: "I just got outta Shreveport three months ago. I done twenty years straight. It sure was a tough break. An' kid, the night o' the big trouble you should 'a' seen me. I plugged her perty, I did. I says, 'Listen, listen little girl, I'm goin' to let your soul out,' an' I spit the bullets through her double-crossin' heart."[30] The junkie spent the next week in a morphine and cocaine haze, haunted by the ghost of a blond girl with a "body like white velvet" and with "blood splotched on her breast."[31] When the train slows at a crossing, seeing his chance, Jim decides to leave. The old man vows to "run this train to the moon."[32] Jim hops off and the ghostly train disappears into the night. Tully later concluded that "Bull Horrors" and another *Shadows* chapter, "The Graveyard that Moved," ranked as the best work he'd ever done.[33]

In the final two chapters of *Shadows of Men*, Tully returns to more familiar ground. Both chapters are nonfiction pieces that first appeared in the *American Mercury*. The first of these, "Bright Eyes," profiles Blink Thomas, Tully's pal from the Newsboys' Home in Chicago.[34] Tully recollects how Thomas, then nicknamed Bright Eyes, lost his eye in a print shop accident and received an eye patch and a new nickname, Blink. Years later, Jim found Blink in Southern California. The one-eyed road-kid was facing six months in jail unless he could find work. Despite his fear of going blind, he got a job at a Los Angeles newspaper as a printer's devil. His remaining eye, "long weakened," began to trouble him.[35] His friends persuaded him to go to the county hospital. "When the doctors had finished there were two empty red sockets in his head." Jim recalls one hospital visit. "He would lie on the bed, his raven-black hair rolling back from his forehead, and the tears welling out of the red holes in his head like water from a spring."[36]

It was decided that Blink would be transferred to the Institution for the Blind. When Jim visited, he found his friend profoundly depressed and preferring death to the years that awaited him in the institution. Jim was moved to write the publisher of the Los Angeles newspaper where Blink had worked, seeking a downtown street corner where his friend could sell papers. His letters were never answered. Jim persisted. He went to the publisher's office to make his case. Granted an audience with the publisher, a once physically imposing man slowed by age, referred to in *Shadows of Men* as "General," Jim interrupted his blustering about unions long enough to make his case for Blink. The General was unmoved.

In an attempt to buy time, Jim visited Blink and lied that the General was considering the matter. Three months passed. Collecting almost seventy dollars for Blink, Jim and his friends took it to him for Christmas. They assured him that he'd get his street corner yet, then changed the subject. After his visitors left, tired of waiting and tired of life, Blink escaped from the hospital on the outskirts of town and traveled the four miles into the city. There he visited a movie theater, "where there was music," found his way to a pawnshop, purchased a revolver, and checked into a cheap hotel.[37] Later, Jim's pal and sometimes-roommate Joe Bertucci received a package wrapped in brown paper, the scarcely legible address scrawled in pencil. It contained fifty-one dollars and a suicide note. The next morning, Blink found his way into the General's paper when the *Times* ran a brief story about the suicide of a printer named Frank Thomas.[38]

Jim Tully's story had one problem. It was true. After reading the chapter in manuscript, Harry Maule, Tully's editor at Doubleday, Doran, warned Tully in July 1929 that his description of the General, which was clearly based on the staunchly anti-union publisher of the *Los Angeles Times*, Harrison Gray Otis, would almost certainly invite a libel suit.[39] *Times* columnist Harry Carr, who had read the chapter in the *American Mercury*, also wrote to protest Tully's treatment of Otis.[40] The chance to poke a windy and powerful man in the eye proved irresistible to Tully. The chapter stood.

Tully concludes *Shadows of Men* with "A California Holiday," his account of the hanging at San Quentin reprinted from the *Mercury*. As the execution took place more than two decades after the events in the preceding chapters, this final chapter does not follow the narrative of the rest of the book. It is not, however, merely an afterthought. The piece ranks with Tully's most powerful work, owing to his restraint in describing the growing horror as the hour of death approaches. Tully and the other observers share an awful knowledge: they know the precise time and place of a man's imminent and intentional death—a knowledge that is only slightly less ghastly for the witnesses than for the condemned. It is not a static horror. As Tully notes the passing minutes, time becomes a palpable presence filling the chapter with tension and unspeakable dread. The men mark time by discussing the condemned man's case, gazing out the window at the sun-washed bay, or nervously laughing at gallows humor. Tully studies the room, the guards, and, finally, the condemned man. At the appointed hour, the prisoner is carried to the platform, a hood placed over his head, and the rope put around his neck. "The warden's hand raised. The trap sprang with an awful noise. The man's body dropped ten feet. It did not move."[41] Tully describes but does not react to the scene. Grown men faint; others weep.

Reviews of *Shadows of Men* were generally good. Bruce Catton, who would become the most popular Civil War historian of his generation, declared: "Jim Tully is a strange and compelling writer. His work may delight you or it may shock and disgust you; but it will never, never bore you.... There is more red blood in him than in a dozen run-of-mine novels."[42] The *New York Times* noted that Tully's writing gave the book "a lurid fascination" and that "Mr. Tully is a master of several underworld idioms."[43] Praise for Tully's talent for hard-boiled realism was echoed by the *New Yorker*: "Mr. Tully is a born story-teller. He writes because he is naturally articulate and dramatic, and for the decidedly Irish pleasure of amusing, shocking, and stimulating you.... He has none of the set sensationalism of your journalist making copy of desperate characters. He is not astonished or horrified that a man happens to be a murderer or a thief."[44] Writing for the *New York Herald-Tribune*, Donald Henderson Clarke raved: "When he is telling stories of the tough gents he knows so well he smokes along at a dizzying and sometimes a terrifying pace.... He never avoids using the right word when the right word might prove offensive. He couldn't paint these characters in pastel shades."[45] *Time* noted that "Jim Tully does not like to be called hard-boiled himself, but the people he writes about are not ladies' men. He continues to write about the hoboes he knew when he was one of them because he thinks it is good for men to know all their brothers and because not one writer in a hundred knows the idiom that he does."[46] The *Cleveland Plain Dealer* proclaimed simply: "He has arrived."[47]

The *St. Marys Evening Leader* headline blandly announced: "Jim Tully Writes Another Book." The review was more restrained than the paper's *Circus Parade* editorial, but hardly the sounding of trumpets an author might welcome from home. "If our suggestions would be solicited, we would drop the word to Jim to veer away from doting on the doings of the underworld, and give us something of a more constructive nature."[48] The *New Republic*, though, had its own views on what constituted uplifting literature. It unfavorably compared Tully to the more "progressive" Michael Gold, noting that for Tully, "the simple lives of yeggs and hoboes merely garnish his philosophy of weary misanthropy." By comparison, "the workers of Michael Gold are lighted by a passionate pity."[49]

While Doubleday professed to be disappointed by sales of *Shadows of Men*, Tully could take cold comfort in the fact that the book, like *Beggars of Life* before it, proved to be a best seller in Russia—where royalties could not be taken out of the country.[50] Looking back on his career, Tully would one day write Maxwell Perkins that *Shadows of Men* was his best book.[51] A film adaptation, written by Tully and Robert Nelson, was considered by one of the studios but was ultimately abandoned as maudlin and unworthy of the book.[52]

Wallace Beery played the mighty hobo Oklahoma Red and Richard Arlen took on the role of Jim in director William Wellman's 1928 film version of Tully's *Beggars of Life*. Authors' collection.

Jim Tully and *Beggars of Life* director William Wellman. Authors' collection.

Page left: Richard Arlen and Louise Brooks in a *Beggars of Life* (1928) publicity photo. Authors' collection.

"Let me enjoy the earth no less because the all-exacting might,
That fashioned forth its loveliness, had other aims than my delight."

The Hobo College
1118 West Madison Street

WILL RE-OPEN

Saturday, May 11, 1929

DR. BEN L. REITMAN,
Educational Director
PHONE DEARBORN 3837

Grand Opening Entertainment
AND
FREE LUNCH at 6 p. m.

The following will participate in the Program:

RICHARD BENNETT,
Noted Actor (and Company)

JIM TULLY, Author

JOHN LANDESCO,
Criminologist

DR. DAVID ROTMAN,
Psychiatrist

AL. DUNLOP
President Press Club

PROF. E. W. BURGESS,
Sociologist

PROF. F. O. BECK,
Social Pathologist

CHARLES BOYD,
Illinois Free Employment Bureau

The Hobo College is dedicated to the study of the OUTCASTS—"Unfriended, Melancholy, Slow"—the submerged and the seared.

LECTURES EVERY TUESD'Y, THURSD'Y, SATURD'Y SUND'Y NIGHTS

Dr. Ben Reitman appointed Tully as a professor of literature and road philosophy at his Hobo College in 1920s Chicago. "Unfriended, Melancholy, Slow" are from the opening line of Oliver Goldsmith's poem "The Traveller," a Tully favorite. Authors' collection.

Gossip columnists and cartoonists found the 1930 fight at the Hollywood Brown Derby between Jim Tully and John Gilbert irresistible. From "They Take it on The Chin," Screen Book, July 1935. Authors' collection.

Jim Tully, 1930. Authors' collection.

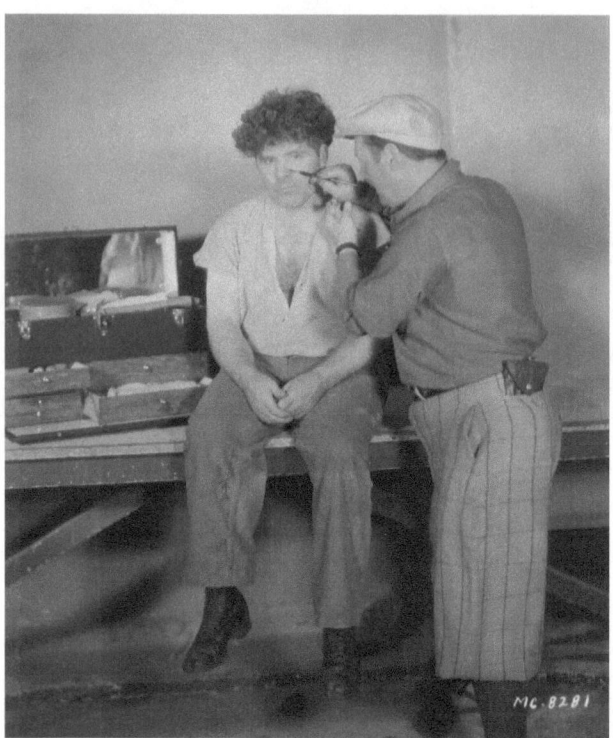

A make-up artist prepares Tully for a scene in *Way for a Sailor* (1930). Tully's hair was, as ever, untamed. Authors' collection.

Tully (second from left) and Wallace Beery (third from left) belly up to the bar in *Way for a Sailor* (1930). Authors' collection.

Tully sitting for an MGM publicity photo for *Way for a Sailor* in 1930. Authors' collection.

Way for a Sailor (1930) featured a fading John Gilbert (second from left). It was hoped that surrounding him with tough guys Wallace Beery (left) and Tully (behind Gilbert) might shore up his image. Authors' collection.

Above: W. C. Fields (second from left) dips into his bag of tricks at a Hollywood party with three close pals: writer Gene Fowler (left), editor Roscoe Fawcett, and Toluca Lake neighbor Jim Tully. Family of Trilby J. Tully Beamon; Jim Tully Papers (Collection 250). Dept. of Special Collections, Charles E. Young Research Library, UCLA. Below: Former lightweight boxer Jim Tully climbs into the ring for a gag shot with two heavyweight champions, Max Baer (left) and Jack Dempsey (right). Family of Trilby J. Tully Beamon; Jim Tully Papers (Collection 250). Dept. of Special Collections, Charles E. Young Research Library, UCLA.

Tully drops by during the filming of his book *Laughter in Hell* (1932), posing with the movie's director, Edward L. Cahn (left), Clarence Muse (second from left) and the film's star, Pat O'Brien (second from right). Family of Trilby J. Tully Beamon; Jim Tully Papers (Collection 250). Dept. of Special Collections, Charles E. Young Research Library, UCLA.

Tully and Pat O'Brien on the set of *Laughter in Hell* (1932). Authors' collection.

Tully and Walter Huston. Authors' collection.

Jack Dempsey met Tully in Salt Lake City in 1912. Friends for life, both men fought their way out of hobo camps. Authors' collection.

Featherweight champion and Tully's pal from their boxing days Johnny Kilbane with Wallace Beery (center) and Tully. HL Mencken Papers, New York Public Library.

Tully caught in conversation with Jimmy Cagney, who had portrayed him in the 1925 New York stage adaptation of *Beggars of Life*. Family of Trilby J. Tully Beamon; Jim Tully Papers (Collection 250). Dept. of Special Collections, Charles E. Young Research Library, UCLA.

Right: Working on a script at MGM. Family of Trilby J. Tully Beamon; Jim Tully Papers (Collection 250). Dept. of Special Collections, Charles E. Young Research Library, UCLA.

Below: Jim Tully poses with a group of friends and colleagues at a Hollywood party: left to right, boxer-turned-actor Frank Moran, director Frank Capra, attorney George Steadman, MGM executive and producer Albert Lewin, Tully, unidentified, W.C. Fields, writer Gene Fowler and editor Roscoe Fawcett (two men at right are unidentified). Authors' collection.

The writer at his desk, surrounded by pictures of favorite authors, including, in the upper left hand corner, Mark Twain. Family of Trilby J. Tully Beamon; Jim Tully Papers (Collection 250). Dept. of Special Collections, Charles E. Young Research Library, UCLA.

John Barrymore, a prince of the stage, meets a knight of the road. Authors' collection.

Jim Tully in Hollywood. Happiness would prove elusive. Authors' collection.

Tully wed his third wife, Myrtle Zwetow, in June 1933. This marriage survived Jim's growing health problems as well as family and financial troubles, lasting until his death in 1947. Family of Trilby J. Tully Beamon; Jim Tully Papers (Collection 250). Dept. of Special Collections, Charles E. Young Research Library, UCLA.

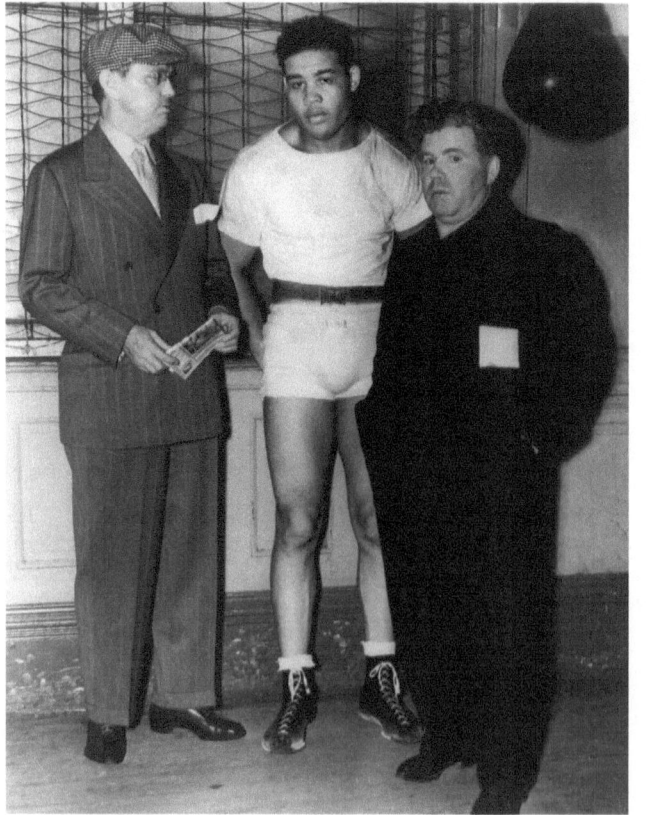

Above: Tully, Mary Brian, and Bing Crosby in a 1934 Paramount publicity photo. Tully and Crosby, along with W.C. Fields, Gene Fowler, and Mack Sennett, formed a short-lived production company in 1934. Authors' collection.

Left: Damon Runyon and his pal Jim Tully pay a visit to one of the greatest heavyweight boxers of all time, Joe Louis. Family of Trilby J. Tully Beamon; Jim Tully Papers (Collection 250). Dept. of Special Collections, Charles E. Young Research Library, UCLA.

Above: Jim Tully (left), boxer Henry Armstrong (third from left), and Langston Hughes (second from right). Family of Trilby J. Tully Beamon; Jim Tully Papers (Collection 250). Dept. of Special Collections, Charles E. Young Research Library, UCLA.

Right: Actor Jean Hersholt relaxes with a good book. Hersholt's impressive library included a large collection of Hans Christian Andersen whose work the Danish-born Hersholt translated into English. Authors' collection.

Alton Tully, affectionately dubbed "The King of Ireland" as an infant, became a constant source of trouble to his father and the law in the 1930s and '40s. Family of Trilby J. Tully Beamon; Jim Tully Papers (Collection 250). Dept. of Special Collections, Charles E. Young Research Library, UCLA.

Slowed down by heart ailments and arthritis, Tully poses with his daughter, Trilby. Family of Trilby J. Tully Beamon.

"Toward Los Angeles, California," a 1937 photograph by Dorothea Lange, shows two hoboes heading for the city former wanderer Jim Tully would call home. By the Depression, many hoboes had moved from the tracks to the highway. Dorothea Lange, Library of Congress, Prints and Photographs.

Jim Tully and beverage. Family of Trilby J. Tully Beamon; Jim Tully Papers (Collection 250). Dept. of Special Collections, Charles E. Young Research Library, UCLA.

18

Beggars Abroad

During this time, one of the most productive periods of his career, a family crisis erupted. On June 12, 1928, newpaper headlines proclaimed that Marna had filed for divorce.[1] The news quickly brought out the Dutch uncle in Mencken, who wrote: "You children must not indulge in any such nonsense."[2] The suit was withdrawn, and on June 15 Tully telegrammed Mencken that he and Marna were back "home together . . . we assure you that newspaper reports are quite exaggerated."[3] While Jim could downplay problems in his marriage, he could not escape them. His moodiness often yielded to "intense fits of melancholy."[4] The marriage might have survived his bouts of depression but there was a far greater obstacle. Marna had a rival—a rival whose memory had smoldered for years. Despite his misgivings about the marriage, Jim had tried to make things work with Marna, but he had been unsuccessful in pushing Mary Lygo from his thoughts.

It was Virginia's death in October of 1926 that had stirred the embers. Meeting Jim in Chicago, Mary proved a great comfort. No longer under the reproachful watch of his sister, Jim came to regard his marriage as the only obstacle to his happiness. It would not prove to be an insurmountable obstacle. And yet he had no desire to hurt his wife, for whom he still had great affection, if not wholehearted love.

Mary's move to Hollywood to work in film ignited a chain reaction. Jim invited her to his home. His intentions remained relatively pure, if unrealistic. He would honor the letter if not the spirit of his vows. Marna would be present, a friendship between his wife and the woman he secretly loved would blossom, and all three would live happily ever after. Instead, he found himself comparing the two women, to Marna's disadvantage. Marna was educated, the daughter of wealth and privilege, and, Jim concluded, a bit shallow. Mary was self-educated and stunningly beautiful and possessed a natural elegance. Without Virginia around to douse the flames, Jim and Mary again caught fire.[5]

After many happy weeks, Jim stopped by the Brown Derby to see his friend Wilson Mizner, part owner of the famous restaurant. If a job description ever needed to be written for raconteur, Mizner, an immense and witty fellow, would have proved an excellent model. In the past, Jim had found Mizner's ear sympathetic, but when Jim had sought his counsel on the question of leaving Marna for Mary, Mizner demurred on the grounds that affairs of the heart were beyond his considerable purview. This time Mizner had troubling news. Mary had just left the restaurant, where she had been drinking heavily with a famous director. Tully, hurt and jealous, went to her. He was alarmed by what he saw. The alcohol could mask neither her beauty nor her pain. Both knew that things could not continue as they had. Jim asked about the director. Mary asked about Marna. If Jim really loved her, why couldn't he finally leave Marna? It was a conversation as old as married men and unmarried women. Knowing the situation would never resolve itself in her favor, she announced that she would work as "atmosphere" in the famous director's next film.[6] Furthermore, she intended to take up the director on his offer to set her up in an apartment. The director, Jim pointed out, was also married. The difference, Mary replied, was that she didn't love the director. Once again, Jim felt Mary—and happiness—slipping through his fingers. He returned to the Brown Derby, where he met Marna and tried to hide his broken heart. Mizner, aware of these recent developments, did his best to cheer him up.[7]

Later, Jim went to Mary's new apartment but was turned away when he tried to kiss her. It was a point of honor that she not kiss Jim in an apartment paid for by another man.[8] The only ray of hope for Jim was that, after resisting the director's advances, she had decided that she could not work in his movie.[9]

When Jim saw her next, she was planning to go to New York by way of the Panama Canal. Jim begged her to stay in California. She relented, and he gave her a small book of poetry by Ernest Dowson. The poet is largely forgotten, but Mary read aloud a few lines of one poem several times.

They are not long, the days of wine and roses:
Out of a misty dream
Our path emerges for a while, then closes
Within a dream.

The following morning she telephoned Jim. With desperation in her voice, she begged him to come at once. He replied that he was busy but would come as soon as possible. That, she warned, would be too late. She had threatened suicide before and Jim expected her depression to again lift. Instead, she was found dying the following day and was rushed to the hospital. Her suicide note read, "Please cremate my body. I don't want to go home."[10] Also nearby was a volume of poetry by Sara Teasdale given to her by Jim, and an open trunk. The trunk had contained letters, photos, and telegrams from Jim. Only ashes remained.[11] The unquenchable fire that had burned in Jim for so long had raged out of control and consumed the only woman who had ever made him happy.

In his anguish Jim turned to old friend Paul Bern. They rode for miles along the coast in Bern's big car. Just as Tully had consoled Bern over Barbara La Marr's death in early 1926, now Bern consoled Tully. Bern was typically sympathetic and gentle. Tully never forgot what he said: "You're slightly confused, Jim. All men are when they find that any sort of freedom is just another jail." Jim thought of La Marr. La Marr, who had been known as "the Girl Who Is Too Beautiful," had described Mary Lygo as the most beautiful girl in Hollywood. Now both women were gone. Paul finally pulled off at a roadside inn, and over brandy, he and Jim gazed out at the sea.[12]

By late June of 1928, Jim suspected Marna of having an affair. She was young, beautiful, immature, and vulnerable. He was older, famous, insecure, and vulnerable. Both were given to drink. The combination proved toxic. When Marna refiled for divorce in September, the alarming details quickly reached the newspapers. Marna accused Jim of associating with "women of the underworld," of being a law unto himself, and, most troubling, of having beaten her so severely that her nose was broken.[13] She further alleged that he raged at her desire for children and, in one instance, for having spent $4.98 for a hat. Tully blamed Hollywood gossips and his enemies, who "attacked him through his home," and denied all charges.[14]

By January 1929 the situation had moved from simple melodrama to the stuff of tabloid headlines. The press became overheated when Tully named the third part of the triangle: Hollywood director Marshall Neilan.[15] To make matters worse, Neilan accused Tully of trying to extort $25,000 to keep his name out of Tully's divorce cross-complaint, an accusation the author hotly refuted. For their part, Marna and Neilan denied the affair. She suffered a nervous breakdown while Neilan nearly died from carbon monoxide poisoning when he locked himself in his garage with the car running.[16] Things were spiraling out of control.

Old friends, notably Paul Bern and H. L. Mencken, effected a reconciliation in March 1929.[17] Roscoe Fawcett, the editor at *Screen Secrets*, wrote Jim that despite the pain she had caused Jim, it was apparent that Marna loved him and had gotten bad advice from her lawyer. Fawcett also recognized that Jim and Marna were "temperamental" and advised them "to lay off the liquid lacquer."[18] Friend and noted prison reform advocate Judge Ben Lindsey wrote of his delight at the Tullys' reconciliation. "And don't let IT happen again," he added.[19] Marna proclaimed to Mencken that she and Jim would be "very happy."[20] The crisis passed.

The title "King of the Hoboes" was an honorific that delighted the press. Silly as it was, there was no shortage of pretenders to the throne, and disputes, played out in the newspapers, inevitably arose. One dragged Tully into the fray in March 1929. A Cincinnati hobo turned "king" named Jeff Davis complained that a rival king, Al Kaufman, lacked the requisite job experience.[21] Hoboes like Kaufman and, Davis noted, Jim Tully had tarnished the good name of the hobo by spreading falsehoods that engendered needless hostility for the "knights of the road." Kaufman's motivation in such a scheme was left to the reader's imagination, but Tully's motive was clear to Davis. Jim Tully had cashed in.

Davis had founded the Hobos of America in 1908, becoming the hoboes' most visible spokesman for nearly five decades. He also became a minor irritant to Tully, popping up in the press every few years to question Tully's credentials on the subject of hobo life—a charge that ironically was later made against Davis.[22] Davis's 1929 jab brought a response from Tully that was, for him, subdued. In a letter to Mencken, Tully calmly pointed out that he had been one of the first to classify the various types of hobo in an old article for *Liberty*, and that his hobo bona fides remained intact.[23]

The past two years had taken a toll: the headline-making divorce charges and counter-charges; Marna's nervous breakdown; the feuds with Upton Sinclair, James Quirk, and Jeff Davis; and various Hollywood squabbles, along with the pressure of turning out new material while adapting old material for the stage. An old solution presented itself. Tully would return to the road, but this time, befitting a successful author, he would travel "on the cushion." To seal their reconciliation, Marna would join him.[24]

And it would be unlike any previous trip in another way. He would travel to Europe, and in a departure from his usual interviews with Hollywood celebrities, he would profile some of the most important figures of the day—all of it to be packaged in a book titled, with a nod to Mark Twain, *Beggars Abroad*. Tully sounded out possible interviews with Nathan and Mencken, suggesting Freud and asking Mencken to arrange meetings with Kaiser Wilhelm II and Hindenburg.[25] Claiming to be on bad terms with both German leaders, Mencken declined, further noting, "You will get nothing out of them save dull platitudes."[26]

With a book contract in hand from Doubleday, Doran, Jim and Marna made plans to sail from New York to London on May 25, 1929.[27] Tully left America, he maintained in the opening page of *Beggars Abroad*, to escape boredom: "I had wandered nearly all my life in its every far-away section. I had found it a land of fakers and fools; of those who grope for light and those content to live in darkness; of gentlemen who talk of chivalry toward the ladies and lynch black men at night; of reformers and informers, of all the variant kaleidoscopic peoples who have made of America the most gruesome and grotesque show on earth."[28]

His last minutes on American soil were, however, anything but boring. Marna, who had overseen their travel plans down to drawing a map of their cabin's location on the *Samaria* and charming the ship's head waiter, had become confused about the departure time. Following a leisurely last breakfast with Judge Lindsey, the Tullys arrived at the pier at eleven. To Marna's horror, the *Samaria* had sailed at ten. Reflecting a stoicism acquired over a lifetime of missed trains, Jim simply noted, "Sixty minutes are not of much importance in the aeons of time. They do count vastly when one is catching a boat."[29]

With the help of a shipping news reporter sent to cover their departure, they learned that the *Samaria*'s sister ship, the *California*, was about to sail for Glasgow. Jim and Marna, whom Jim had playfully taken to calling "Thomas Cook Jr." after the famous travel agent, exchanged tickets and boarded ship without further incident. As the *California* passed the Statue of Liberty and the New York skyline began to grow distant, Tully's thoughts turned to his native land.

> For the first time in my life America loomed large in perspective. Seventy years before, my grandfather, strong and lusty with Irish peasant blood, had arrived in America.

The United States had at least given him something priceless—the expansion of his life.

The wild Donegal primitive had moved into a larger neighborhood.[30]

Arriving in Boston the following afternoon, Jim and Marna found cause to again be grateful for the intercession of the shipping news reporter in New York. Sparing them some embarrassment, his story noted that heavy traffic had caused them to miss the *Samaria*.[31] As Jim observed, "Thomas Cook, Jr., smiled."[32]

As the *California* steamed across the chilly north Atlantic, the talk turned to icebergs and, inevitably, to the sinking of the *Titanic*. A retelling of the *Titanic* story would not seem to be particularly fertile ground for a travel memoir—especially one written nearly twenty years after the fact, but in Tully's hands the familiar story is stripped of bathos. There is heroism, to be sure, but with a sardonic twist. "It was proven later that men in the engine room, begrimed and worn with labor, kept the ship afloat a full hour longer than would have been possible without their heroism. They thus saved many lives. Before the end, they prayed to the God of all the water before He allowed it to swirl down their throats."[33]

After spending a week at sea, meeting other passengers (including a Scotsman who recognized him as the author of *Beggars of Life*), and gazing at the horizon, they spotted land. It was the moonlit, rocky coast of Ireland. The ship hove closer.

> Imperceptibly came the early morning light. Soon water and green verdure glowed under the first rays of the sun.
>
> Not far were green valleys and low hills. Yellow roads stretched over them. Peasants' homes, more charming than American mansions, dotted the beautiful landscape.[34]

Tully's reaction at first seeing the land of his ancestors was more American than Irish. It was a "dream country."[35] And while he recalled his grandparents' talk of "the Black Irish," the Orangemen of Belfast, and other groups, he writes, "Even in childhood, the quarrels of the Irish had never been my own."[36]

Arriving finally in Glasgow on June 3, 1929, Jim and Marna stayed at the Central Hotel before departing by train for London that evening.[37] His initial impressions of Scotland were not so romantic—"The first thing we noticed was the bad teeth of the citizens"[38]—and in a letter to Mencken he complained, "The beer's warm as hell."[39] Mencken, who considered himself "ombibulous," helpfully replied, "Beware of the English beer. It causes gallstones and worse. Get to Germany as soon as you can and immerse yourself in the genuine article."[40]

The craft of travel writing, Paul Theroux has observed, "involves rumination, mimicry, joke-telling."[41] Given the wanderlust of his youth, innate curiosity, keen eye, and well-honed ability to eavesdrop, Tully was well suited for the role of travel writer. What sets *Beggars Abroad* apart from so many other travel books is Tully's ability to observe the daily life of ordinary people. Orators (and their hecklers) in Hyde Park, street musicians on the Strand, a sidewalk artist in Trafalgar Square—Tully captures them all. And Tully had the fortune (at least for a writer) to be one of those magnetic people who attracts characters.

Tully was in the unusual position of having traveled extensively—indeed, it's hard to imagine anyone having logged more miles in the days before air travel—without having been a sailor or railroad porter. So once settled in London (for at least part of their stay in Alfred Knopf's London home), Jim and Marna set out to see the city and surrounding countryside. But Jim was no ordinary American tourist.[42] He wanted to see the England he'd read about in books—the England of Charles Dickens, William Blake, Samuel Johnson, and the many others who had kept a young boy company while he waited on a train or passed a winter's day in a warm library.[43]

Among its many other charms, England also provided Jim with a fresh audience, and Jim had confided to Alfred Knopf his disappointment with lagging book sales in Britain.[44] English newspapers quickly found Jim a source of good copy. In an interview with the *London Daily Chronicle*, Jim extolled the virtues of the rugged life. "Perhaps the greatest example of the virtue of roughing it in modern times was Theodore Roosevelt. As a youth he was puny and sickly." And what of American letters? "The only three men in American Literature of the first rank in point of force and originality were Mark Twain, Walt Whitman and Herman Melville." Each roughed it. "No man worth his salt is whipped by circumstances. He is whipped when he bows to circumstance."[45]

Looking around him, Jim observed no shortage of "circumstance." "Nearly two million people in London exist on the very edge of abject poverty. . . . About half the children die before they are five years old—most of them in their first year," he later wrote in *Beggars Abroad*. "These people are given the same lying platitudes handed the abject in all countries. Uncouth and wasted, with rotting teeth and dirty bodies, they cheer the king, bow in reverence to God, and go their dismal, ignorant way into the swamp of the final oblivion."[46] "In America," he concluded, "poverty is at least belligerent, defiant, hopeful."[47] Marna also found London gloomy. Near the Strand, she noticed dates carved in the sidewalk and realized they were standing on a grave. "To me . . . it is a city of the dead—a city of memories—most of them sad."[48] Like so many millions of tourists before and since, Jim and Marna crossed off sights from a mental checklist, pausing at each to remark on some point of history: the Tower of London, St. Paul's Cathedral, Westminster Abbey. At the last, he lingered at the Poets' Corner and again at the chapel named for Henry VII, where so many kings and queens are interred. And *unlike* so many tourists before and since, they paused at the grave of John Broughton, the eighteenth-century boxing pioneer and champion.[49]

Having paid homage to Britain's literary past, Jim and Marna visited three of Britain's current literary titans, two of them, much to Jim's delight, Irish. Making their way to Whitehall Court, he and Marna arrived at the apartment of George Bernard Shaw. They were met by Shaw's secretary, who ushered them into the study. Shaw, the 1925 recipient of the Nobel Prize for Literature and then in his early seventies, greeted them in a soft Irish brogue.[50] "I watched him for a moment—highly nervous, fingers long and slender, hands eternally moving. His face lined with wrinkles of laughter, his teeth large, his lips full, his mouth generous. His eyes are soft blue and quizzical. . . . He dresses carelessly and well."[51]

Tully, a veteran of countless Hollywood interviews, wanted to talk about Shaw and socialism and Ireland. The famous playwright politely responded to each subject, but at every turn quickly steered the conversation back to a favorite topic: boxing. Struck by his legendary wit and conversation, Tully later called Shaw "the most charming man alive."[52] At last, not wishing to overstay their welcome, Jim and Marna rose to leave. They declined with great regret Shaw's invitation to his country house.[53] Shaw bowed to Marna then smiled at Jim and said simply, "My love to Ireland."[54]

H. G. Wells had been propelled to fame on the basis of his three late nineteenth-century science-fiction novels: *The Time Machine*, *The Invisible Man*, and *The War of the Worlds*. But he had recently turned to writing nonfiction, including the best-selling *The Outline of History*, published in 1920. Jim and Marna found Wells at his London residence, the top floor of a hotel. He had, Jim noted, the same nervous energy as Shaw. Warned that he would not like Wells, Jim found him "direct and honest" with "an air of kindliness."[55] Overlooking the simple apartment was a bronze bust of Tolstoy, a gift from Maxim Gorky.[56]

Crossing the English Channel to France, Jim and Marna made their way to Paris, stopping by Père Lachaise and the graves of Molière, Corot, Chopin, and others.[57] They visited, of course, the Louvre and Versailles, and Jim even acquiesced to Marna's request that he join her in a shopping excursion to a shoe store.[58]

The final interview for *Beggars Abroad* occurred in James Joyce's Left Bank apartment. With the auburn fading from his hair, expressionless eyes (due to failing eyesight), and an "austere, ascetic" face elongated by a Vandyke, Joyce reminded Tully of a portrait of Christ.[59] Joyce was just four years older than Tully. But in the same year that Tully's rudimentary first novel, *Emmett Lawler,* was published, Joyce's inspired use of language resulted in his groundbreaking *Ulysses,* considered by many to be the most important book in modernist literature.

Joyce spoke little and, Tully wrote, "in a voice so crooning that one must listen closely to every word." He had "a liquid melody of speech similar to that of George Bernard Shaw. It is shot through with the poetry of the Celt."[60] They discussed Joyce's work, including his current manuscript. "His idea, in *Work in Progress* is to use all the languages familiar to English-speaking people or those which have been used previously to form the English speech of to-day."[61] *Finnegans Wake,* as it came to be titled, is considered by many to be Joyce's masterpiece. Tully's discussion with Joyce ranged from Joyce's fear of thunder and lightning to music (he prefered English, Purcell and earlier).[62] "No subject," Tully later wrote, "with the exception of politics, is uninteresting to him."[63]

Jim and Marna left the Continent for one last port of call, arriving in Ireland in early July 1929. Free of the obligatory tourist destinations of London and Paris, they contented themselves with seeing some of the countryside, including the interiors of pubs. As before, some of the best moments of the trip and of *Beggars Abroad* occurred when Jim encountered the working class. In Dublin, he shared a bottle of Jameson's with an old man returning to Ireland from America to see his sister for the first time in sixty-one years.[64] In Cork, he and a pub full of Irish patriots were entertained by a barroom orator's recitation of Robert Emmett's 1803 speech from the scaffold following his conviction for treason by British troops. The actor's voice raged, softened to a whisper, and rose again to a stirring finish. "Let no man write my epitaph," he thundered. "When my country takes her place among the nations of the earth, *then and not until then* let my epitaph be written." The rapt crowd broke into raucous applause and more rounds of drinks were ordered. Tully recalled the scene in *Beggars Abroad*.

> An old man, late in arriving, stepped close to the actor.
> "A great speech was Robert Emmett's—and you do it well—it would make the sad heart of him that made it glad to hear you say it."
> The actor turned to me.
> "Who the hell was Robert Emmett?"[65]

If Tully harbored any romantic notions about the land of his forbearers, he had shed them by the time he sailed home. Ireland needs more factories and fewer edifices, he told one reporter. "If Irish-Americans who are sentimental about the old country, went back there and built some factories," things would begin to improve.[66]

19

Blood on the Moon

Tully returned to California the summer of 1929 to find troubles large and small awaiting him. Mencken wrote that a "Chicago idiot" had charged Tully with the plagiarism of a song. Mencken dismissed that charge as "probably libelous."[1] And a deal to bring *Black Boy* to the London stage collapsed when English censors demanded significant changes to the script.[2] And most serious of all, now back on American soil, Tully's marriage began to unravel in earnest.

Judge Ben Lindsey again stepped into the breach. Writing to Marna's father, he noted that Jim and Marna seemed to genuinely love each other. And for his part, Jim had often spoken of Marna as the only one who could soothe the loneliness and depression that sometimes engulfed him.[3] By late September, the couple had again reconciled and Tully wrote George Jean Nathan in New York that they were considering a trip east in the fall.[4] Instead, they separated again in November and by Christmas were making plans for a divorce.[5] Tully wrote Mencken that the separation was giving him some peace. He had the eight-room house to himself, but with a maid, a cook, and Marna dropping by, he wasn't entirely alone.[6]

Nor was he inactive. He revised *Beggars Abroad*, as well as "God Loves the Irish." And he proceeded with plans to sell his property and make a fresh break from his life with Marna. "Marna will be free in six more weeks," he wrote Nathan, "and I'm not only content but glad. One hates to be a sap—and I'll be careful in the future." And perhaps betraying a short memory, he added, "I can't recall that I've ever loved a woman."[7]

Marna Tully's divorce decree was granted, on the grounds of extreme cruelty, on February 25, 1930. She asked for neither alimony nor court costs, remarking to the court that her husband's "temperament was too much to bear."[8] For all the headlines leading up to the end of their marriage, it was an amicable if not a clean break. Marna visited her ex-husband often,[9] and Jim would later admit to Mencken that he still loved her.[10]

There would be no calm after the storm. More than the divorce headlines, the banned books, the hard years with hoboes and boxers, the caustic and cynical articles on Hollywood, more than any of these, one incident would cement Tully's image with the general public as a genuine tough guy.

The greatest male star of 1920s Hollywood, the era of silent films, was the Italian-born actor Rudolph Valentino. In movies such as 1921's *The Sheik*, Valentino established a screen persona that fueled the romantic fantasies of millions of women. His death in 1926 shocked the world and his funeral in New York was a spectacle. Even H. L. Mencken, no fan of Hollywood, dined with Valentino shortly before he took ill and wrote a sympathetic article on his passing.[11]

The sudden death at age thirty-one of Hollywood's greatest matinee idol left a tremendous void. Hollywood looked to another star of the silent screen to fill it. He was John Gilbert, who had been paired with Greta Garbo, most notably in *Flesh and the Devil* (1926). The offscreen romance that ensued cast them as Hollywood's most glamorous couple. But despite his popularity with some fans, and his reputation as "the Great Lover," it was becoming apparent that Gilbert was, at best, a poor woman's Valentino.

By the midtwenties, much of Tully's freelance work on Hollywood had jumped from the fan magazines to the glossier pages of *Vanity Fair*. In May of 1928, John Gilbert got his turn. It was perhaps the most brutal of all of Tully's Hollywood work. Pulling no punches, the article began, "His emotion is on the surface. His nature is not deep. His enthusiasms are as transient as newspaper headlines. He has no sense of humour." And as to Gilbert being the next Valentino, Tully wrote: "But where Valentino had marched like a gallant Italian despoiler through the flower-bedecked portals of female hearts, Mr. Gilbert was only admitted with reservations. Even after the debonair ruler had forever retired from the conquests of love, Mr. Gilbert was only able to enthrall the weaker subjects in his kingdom."[12] The pummeling continued as Tully portrayed Gilbert as the worst kind of ham actor: vain, cowardly, preening, and pretentious. His sins included rudeness to the gracious Lon Chaney and hostility toward his own father, a minor actor much less successful than his famous son.

Gilbert was reportedly so unnerved by the piece that he threw up after reading it. He was, in his daughter's words, "shattered."[13] Even Tully would later admit that the piece was harsh.[14] Yet he seemed surprised that Gilbert and MGM might be upset over it.[15] Later, he even considered writing a more flattering article on Gilbert by way of apology.[16] If the *Vanity Fair* piece sounds a bit churlish by current standards, it was positively vicious by the standards of the twenties—which is not to say that it was untrue.

Tully's Gilbert profile may not have hit a man when he was down, but it did hit a man who was sinking. It had only been eighteen months since the release of *Flesh and the Devil*, and with Valentino's death, Gilbert was the reigning matinee idol. Yet Gilbert's career was already taking on water, and as he had made a powerful enemy in MGM boss Louis B. Mayer, his future was far from certain. While Tully's profile could not be blamed for the collapse of Gilbert's career, it did appear at a time when he could ill afford bad press. When audiences howled with laughter at his romantic scenes in his first talkie, *His Glorious Night* (1929), a career that was listing began to founder. Anita Loos, an acclaimed Hollywood screenwriter and novelist, expressed an opinion held by many (but not all) that Gilbert's high-pitched voice wasn't well suited for the talkies then replacing silent pictures. And, she added, while the studios could have deepened his screen voice, they were just as happy to be rid of him.[17]

It may not have been Gilbert's lack of a deep voice that did him in so much as changing audience tastes. After Valentino and Gilbert, audiences were moving away from effete leading men, preferring instead two-fisted actors like Clark Gable and Gary Cooper.

Gilbert saw the hand of Mayer in a concerted campaign to destroy him.[18] While there was much truth in Gilbert's suspicion of Mayer, Tully's Gilbert profile was solicited by Donald Freeman, managing editor of *Vanity Fair*. "He is a dreadful ham as you know," Freeman wrote Tully.[19] Nearly two years had passed since Tully's Gilbert profile in *Vanity Fair* when, in early February 1930, Gilbert walked into the Brown Derby in Hollywood. In that time, Gilbert had watched it all slip through his fingers. Roles had dried up, he was nearly broke, and he was spending more time with his Scotch bottle than with his Hollywood friends, who had mostly drifted away.[20]

The two main accounts of what transpired come from Tully, who wrote of it in the early 1930s, and Gilbert's daughter, Leatrice Gilbert Fountain, who was not present and described it in her biography of her father in

1985. While the two accounts vary in certain details (Tully claims he and Gilbert had already met[21] while Leatrice Fountain maintains that her father had never before met his antagonist), the main points are in agreement. In the early morning hours, Gilbert, seated at a table with his wife, Ina Claire, and impresario Sid Grauman, noticed Grauman return a wave to a casually dressed, short man with flaming red hair and ruddy skin. Gilbert looked across the restaurant and spied the odious little man who, two years before, had written the article that began his downward spiral. Gilbert rose and strode across the restaurant with Grauman, perhaps sensing trouble, right behind him. Approaching Tully's table, Gilbert called the author by an epithet. Someone, it's not clear who, suggested the unsuspecting author get on his feet.[22] Startled, Tully sprang to his full five feet, three inches, resembling a "large question mark ... ready to leap." He had what one interviewer called "the thighs of a burlesque queen."[23] His fists, small and pudgy, clenched as the taller man advanced. An almost certainly apocryphal variation of what transpired had the ubiquitous Wilson Mizner, one of the restaurant's owners and seated at Booth 50 with Tully, try to hand the author a ketchup bottle to bludgeon the actor and soak him with ketchup for maximum effect.[24] As it happened, no special effects were required. Tully wrote that Gilbert rushed him, throwing a right and a left, both of which missed. Tully stepped into the opening and snapped Gilbert's head back with an uppercut, bloodying his mouth, and knocking him out cold.[25] In a slightly different and playfully dramatized version, Tully told William Saroyan: "I hit him over the head with the beer bottle beside my glass—but lightly, otherwise I might have killed him."[26]

It was recorded as a one-punch knockout, and the matinee idol was carried out on his shield.[27] When asked about Gilbert's two wild punches, Tully cracked that he was afraid the Great Lover might hurt himself, "so I put him to sleep for his own protection."[28]

While some suspected the fight to be nothing more than a publicity stunt, it was in fact kept quiet for more than a week. And it was, at least for Gilbert, unwelcome publicity. Tully speculated that Mizner, who *did* stand to gain by having it known that his restaurant was the scene of the fight, finally alerted the press. "John Gilbert Is Failure at Use of Fists," "Jim Tully Drops John Gilbert," and other headlines blared in the news.[29]

Promoters dangled four-figure purses to get the pair in the ring.[30] One proposal was for a ten-round bout at Pittsburgh's Motor Square Garden, with Tully to receive 25 percent of the gross on an expected $6,000 gate.[31]

Gilbert, who had repaired to a Palm Springs resort, was forced to deny that he was in training for a rematch. He held no grudge but promised "trouble" should he meet the author again.[32] Finally, tiring of the fuss, the two met at a party given by Herman Mankiewicz and proclaimed an end to hostilities, although Gilbert wasn't entirely pleased that Mankiewicz had not let him know in advance that Tully would be present at the gathering.[33] An exchange of letters between the two combatants settled the matter.[34]

Not wishing to waste perfectly good publicity, MGM executives Eddie Mannix and Irving Thalberg quickly hit on the idea of casting Tully, then working with John Howard Lawson on dialogue for MGM's *Trader Horn*, in Gilbert's next film.[35] Tully and Gilbert would be joined by Wallace Beery in a film called *Way for a Sailor*. Based on a novel by Albert Wetjen, it would be Gilbert's third talkie. Gilbert had failed miserably in making the jump to talkies, and it was hoped that buddying up the limping lothario with a couple of old salts, played by Tully and the barrel-chested Beery, might put some swagger back in his career.[36] By July of 1930, shooting had moved from MGM to four chartered ships off the coast of Wilmington, California.[37] The *Washington Post*, perhaps at the instigation of a studio flack, even went so far as to report that Gilbert and Tully would re-create the Brown Derby fight on film.[38] Gilbert needed the work but, according to Leatrice Gilbert Fountain, he was not happy about having to work with either Tully or Beery. Worse, she writes, her father suffered the indignity of having to learn a Cockney accent from Tully, who was making his first and only screen appearance.[39] Tully, who spoke (and wrote) at a "breakneck pace," forced himself to speak his lines slowly.[40]

If there was tension on the set, Tully seems not to have noticed. He enjoyed both the money, $14,000, and the hours.[41] The crew benefited from Gilbert's contract, which stipulated his day end at 5 P.M., and dubbed him Five O'Clock Jack.[42] And Tully seems to have genuinely enjoyed his time with Gilbert and Beery, as well as actresses Leila Hyams, Polly Moran, and Doris Lloyd and director Sam Wood.[43] "Gilbert," Tully recalled, "was a grand sport. I played with him fourteen weeks, and there was never a time when he did not stand ready to help me appear to good advantage."[44] And Beery may well have saved the rookie actor's life. As they prepared to shoot a scene in which Beery was to heave Tully overboard, Beery asked Tully if he could swim. When Tully admitted that he could not, Beery replied, "You'd be a sap to try it. Where's Jim's double?"[45]

Between takes, Tully told anyone who would listen about an executed prisoner named Robert Blake and the play based on his life, *The Last Mile*.[46] Blake had asked Tully and Mencken to witness his execution, and both had worked to spare Blake's life. Tully thought the twenty-one-year-old showed literary promise and read Blake's last letter, which expressed sadness for his mother, who would lose her youngest of seven boys. Polly Moran wept while Gilbert and Beery were reduced to silence.

Way for a Sailor was released in October 1930, and the comedy about three boisterous sailors received tepid reviews. The *Washington Post* found Gilbert's voice acceptable but the script weak.[47] Edwin Schallert of the *Los Angeles Times* was unenthusiastic about the film but thought Gilbert was good even as the script strained to make him "he-mannish."[48] The *Chicago Daily Tribune* generously noted that Tully was more interesting than Beery.[49] And Hollywood historian and Thalberg biographer Samuel Marx thought Gilbert's performance inferior to Beery's and even weaker than Tully's.[50] As for the film itself, the *New York Times* noted that the glimpses of other vessels in the background were "infinitely more interesting than the actual doings of the characters."[51] Harshest of all critics was Jim Tully. He later claimed that *Way for a Sailor* was "the worst film ever made and I was the worst actor."[52] He couldn't resist adding, "I am such a bad actor in *Way For a Sailor* that I am afraid I will be flooded with offers."[53]

While Tully was not flooded with acting offers, his increasing fame made him a popular choice for various political groups seeking celebrity endorsements. He had as little use for organized politics as he did for organized religion, and given his expressed philosophy of "What the hell—the grave ends everything,"[54] he was deeply suspicious of what Mencken called "uplift." He did, however, have personal views that sometimes bled over into politics. He had no "Messiah complex," as he told one interviewer. "But there's a sort of ghastly futility about the idea of sitting still and doing nothing about it."[55] William Saroyan recalled that in the late thirties, when Hemingway and others were rushing to Spain to support the *republicanos* in the civil war, Tully was content to remain holed up at the Mark Twain Hotel, where he sometimes kept a room to write, think, or just snooze.[56] Still, groups dedicated to prison reform as well as ending red-baiting and Prohibition could depend on the use of Tully's name.[57] And a group from Moscow, the International Union of Revolutionary Writers, perhaps overestimating Tully's reach, sought his help in ending Japanese attacks against the USSR.[58] All this mixing of Tully's celebrity and politics was not without its headaches. Pulitzer Prize–winning novelist Edna Ferber wrote to complain that she was being pestered by a San Quentin ex-con who was claiming to be a friend of Tully's.[59] Worse still, Tully eventually attracted the attention of the FBI, which kept a dossier on his activity.[60]

Whatever his exact political and religious views were, he was, above all, not a true believer. He regarded atheism as equally absurd as religious belief. Proof was completely lacking for the existence or absence of a supreme being, although he did allow that appearances pointed to the former. His agnosticism was the product of clear and honest thought, and he was deeply critical of those opposed to reason. He viewed the religious indoctrination of children as the spreading of lies to those least capable of resistance. And he was unpersuaded by the argument that since the faithful took such comfort from religion, the nonreligious should avoid doing anything to cause them doubt. Such comfort, he maintained, was nothing more than the dope addict's plea for more heroin.[61] When pressed by interviewers, he would claim simply that his religion was "love of the land."[62]

While Tully was not inclined to plunge himself into matters of faith or politics, he did immerse himself in work. *New Movie Magazine* begged for a Chaplin piece, offering $400.[63] Tully's files were overstuffed with Chaplin material, so the work would be easy, the money good, and any objections by the subject would land on the desk of *New Movie Magazine* editor Frederick Smith. Tully accepted.[64] And he was busy in the spring of 1930 selling off the travel pieces he had written, some of which would find their way into *Beggars Abroad*.[65]

Although not interested in politics, Tully admired the Industrial Workers of the World and considered it "the bravest organization ever born."[66] He'd long ago consigned to his desk drawer a story about the deportation of Wobblies from Arizona during World War I.[67] He dusted it off and pitched it to Mencken. Mencken suggested a book rather than an article, and there the matter sat. Some months later, a letter from Upton Sinclair caused him to again consider the Wobblies manuscript. It introduced Fred Moore, an attorney who had defended many Wobblies and anarchists, including Sacco and Vanzetti.[68] Moore was now interested in producing realistic movies about the American working class.[69] In the end, Tully returned the manuscript to the desk drawer, but not before pocketing $18,000 from Paramount for film rights.[70]

Tully had been a popular speaker for several years and had come to regard the lucrative lecture circuit as a source of quick cash. And with an opinion on every conceivable subject, he did not lack for speaking engagements. In May of 1930, the Columbia Institute in New York City even booked him to speak in its series on foreign policy.[71]

His growing stature also attracted other writers seeking help. Despite his frenetic schedule, Tully was generous with his time, especially where young or unknown writers were concerned. He contributed a preface to *Easy Pickings*, an autobiographical novel of the underworld by Al Hill, and helped George Milburn locate songs for a revision of his seminal collection, *The Hobo's Hornbook*.[72]

Perhaps most gratifying was a correspondence between Jim and his elderly father that brought the two closer than they had been at any other time in their lives. The correspondence between father and son began back in 1927, when Jim was seeking family history that might be worked into *Shanty Irish*. The old man's reminiscences were tinged with sadness and often wistful. "Your mother was a good kind woman and mother. There was no better. She and I never had a real quarrel in our lives, and if she had lived things would have been a lot different for all of us."[73] Elsewhere he wrote, "I never drank or caroused until after my wife's death and you know the rest."[74] Jim routinely sent his father money and the elder Tully wrote back, mostly about family matters.[75] He also mentioned how much he enjoyed reading his son's work, singling out a *Vanity Fair* piece on Ireland.[76] "It sure made me feel like singing 'How Dry I Am,'" wrote the elder Tully. "I can just see them standing at the bar."[77]

Reviews on Tully's travel writing were mixed. The *New York Times* book critic praised *Beggars Abroad* upon its release in late 1930 and noted, "Perhaps the most curious feature of the book is the bitter feeling about his native land which he frequently expresses." While the places Tully visited were "hackneyed," the people, ranging from Joyce and Wells to a broken-down London boxer, were "entertaining" and "interesting." Overall, *Beggars Abroad* "should be taken as proof of his genuine flair for authorship."[78] Mencken, however, was sour. *Beggars Abroad*, he wrote, "seemed to me to be below your average. Well, every man is entitled to write a bad book now and then."[79] In the end, even Tully's opinion of *Beggars Abroad* curdled. "I am rather ashamed of *Beggars Abroad*," he wrote Mencken, "but then, I am ashamed of many things. I could not do better at the time. The miracle is that I wrote the book at all."[80]

With *Beggars Abroad* behind him, he paused to look back on his career in a November 1930 *Writer's Digest* article. "Writing an honest book should be as simple and elemental as blacking a bootlegger's eye. . . . I make my own compromises. But they are the shrewd compromises of a hobo gentleman."[81] It was also time to find a new publisher. He wrote Mencken of his disappointment with Doubleday, Doran, publisher of *Beggars Abroad*. "They made a greater failure with me than on any book since *Emmett Lawler*." He outlined a plan to Mencken. He'd come to see *Shanty Irish*, *Shadows of Men*, *Beggars of Life*, and *Circus Parade* as part of a cycle, "each a dramatic phase of a man's life or family, an Irish family, the small prison, the road and the circus. The next will deal with my adjustment in the social scheme, via the ring and the road."[82]

By mid-January of 1931, Tully had completed the first draft of this final book in his cycle, calling it *Blood on the Moon*, "signifying trouble to sailors and the Irish."[83] He retired to his sanctuary, the large, oblong, book-lined room on the second floor of his Hollywood home with a beer barrel next to the swivel chair that Sara Haardt had described in her 1928 *American Mercury* profile.[84] He spread the manuscript across his square desk, and two busy and anxious months later, it was done. His editor at Coward-McCann, his new publisher, assured him that it ranked with his best work and would be issued in late April.[85]

The two primary distractions during the writing of *Blood on the Moon* were of the sort to make many a family man nod in commiseration: an immature child and an aging parent. Support for his father had been provided solely by Jim for the past seven years. At brother Hugh's insistence, the elder Tully moved, temporarily, as it turned out, from Lima, Ohio, to California. Jim had hoped that the four surviving children would share their father's expenses.[86] But in early 1931, Anna Tully Durr notified her famous brother, by way of attorney, that she and her husband had separated and she would be unable to provide any support for their father. Hugh Tully, the attorney pointed out, worked seven days a week, making just $75 a month.[87] Clearly, Jim would be expected to contribute the lion's share.

Alton's troubles were more serious and had been brewing for years. While considerable skepticism must be directed at Alton's later claim that when he was five or six years old, his mother roped him to the clothesline and directed him to hoe every weed in reach, it is certainly true that Florence, a single mother, had her hands full with her oldest child.[88] As a student in the Los Angeles city school system, Alton was mostly indifferent and often truant.[89] When confronted by school officials in early 1927, fifteen-year-old Alton complained that things at home were "absolutely unbearable."[90] Florence wrote Jim, begging her ex-husband not to believe

Alton's lies about his home life. Florence even seemed afraid of her son and his relentless demands for money.[91]

While Jim was not a daily presence in his son's life, canceled checks attest to his steady financial support of his two children and their mother. And when Alton was nineteen, Jim secured him a job with one of the studios and loaned him money. Claiming medical bills and a traffic accident, Alton did not repay his father.[92]

On the night of September 12, 1930, Alton drove a seventeen-year-old girl to a secluded spot on Garvey Road. She later told police she had been raped. At minimum, police reasoned, Alton Tully could be charged with statutory rape. He claimed that the girl, Mrs. June Butler, went willingly and that he was unaware of her age.[93] Alone and depressed, Alton wrote his father from jail ("Dear Mr. Tully"). He maintained his innocence and thanked his father for sticking by him.[94]

Despite his son's troubles, Tully still had *Blood on the Moon* to promote, and in June of 1931 he traveled to New York. With the country almost two years into the Great Depression, a *New York World-Telegram* reporter caught Tully at the Algonquin and asked the former road-kid about the swelling numbers of homeless and destitute drifting around the country. If the reporter expected a lecture on class struggle and the suffering of the masses, he was disappointed. The man who had stood in New York bread lines cooly responded, "Take all the hungry men in this country and feed them a good square meal and they'll forget their complaints. Feed them a week and they'll be ready to take a gun and go out and shoot the tramps from another country in a slightly different uniform." Displaying a certain nostalgia for the bad old days, he continued, "Those kids [Dempsey, Ketchel, and others] went out and battled society. They fought for every mile they traveled and every bite they ate. Nowadays, they get rides in automobiles. If they are clean and neat and well-mannered, they have a much better chance of being picked up. The old road will be entirely gone in a few years more."[95]

While giving another interview at the Algonquin, Tully demonstrated that he could still take a punch. He was handed a telegram, which he silently read without expression and tucked in his pocket, and continued talking about the large number of fan letters he received from prisoners. Someone suggested dinner, and as the interview concluded, Tully calmly read the telegram to the small group. It was from his secretary regarding one of his bank accounts. "Does it interest you Bank of West Hollywood

CLOSED DOORS TODAY?"[96] The account contained all his available cash and forced him to rearrange his plans for several weeks, in addition to canceling a trip to Baltimore to see Mencken.[97] Unlike many Americans, Tully was fortunate. He eventually got one hundred cents on the dollar when the bank reopened.[98]

Jim also stopped in Cincinnati to be honored at a dinner at the Greater Hotel Gibson, where he had worked as a busboy in the bar twenty-seven years earlier. A small pamphlet of Jim's reminiscences, *Man of the New School*, was given to each of the guests. Few copies seem to have survived.[99]

By July, Alton's situation had deteriorated. His teeth were turning black and he was broke. He wrote his father for money to purchase toiletries at the commissary. While Alton could look to his father for support, he could not expect sympathy. Jim had received few breaks in life, but he'd managed to stay out of serious trouble. His son, who'd never been forced to sleep without a roof over his head or wonder where he'd find his next meal, was charged with a serious crime. Jim was furious, as was Alton's sister, Trilby.[100] Alton said his father was calling him "an ungrateful brat, a liar, and a damn fool."[101]

An ungrateful brat Alton may have been, but, by early October, he was an ungrateful brat with clean teeth and toiletries. And he faced a decision—plead guilty or go to trial. What, he wrote his father, would people think of him should he plead guilty to rape? What would his girlfriend think?[102]

Help came from an unlikely source that November. Ben Axley, Alton's attorney, received a letter from June Butler's stepfather that called into question the character and motivation of the victim and her mother.[103] Still, it was not enough, and on November 18, 1931, Alton pleaded guilty to statutory rape. He was granted time served plus one year probation, provided he maintain employment in a job Jim had lined up for him as a cadet aboard a cruise ship.[104] The cruise, set to sail in December from San Francisco, would give Alton a fresh start.[105] Jim chipped in the cost of a cadet's uniform, and despite more dental problems and complaints about the long hours and filth aboard ship, Alton seemed to be back on track.[106] Alton even recognized that two of every sailor's favorite subjects, women and liquor, were best avoided.[107]

While Alton finally had his father's full attention, Trilby, who had just turned fourteen, did not. When Jim failed to answer Trilby's letter in November thanking him for birthday gifts—a red leather coat, a scarf, and money—and when she did not see him on Christmas, she wrote him again.[108] She begged him for a letter, a visit, or just a phone call.[109] She might have taken some solace from her father's description of her to Mencken. Mencken wrote in his diary that Tully "says she is very beautiful, and also intelligent. He seems to be very proud of her. She has artistic tastes, and hopes to be a designer."[110]

As 1931 drew to a close, Jim couldn't help but be encouraged. He'd managed to get his son straightened out and, with *Blood on the Moon*, completed the cycle of five autobiographical books. He believed these five books would stand as his greatest triumph. "To those critics," he wrote in the foreword to *Blood on the Moon*,

> however kind, who contend that I am a novelist trying to find myself, I will here answer for the first and only time. If I have not been able to invent a new medium in my picaresque books, I have at least been strong enough not to conform to one that is outworn.
>
> I did not study the people in these books as an entomologist does a bug on a pin. I was of them. I am still of them. I can taste the bitterness of their lives in the bread I eat today.

Blood on the Moon opens with young Jim in St. Joseph's Orphan Asylum. It charts the long road from Cincinnati to the Boroff farm to Chicago and other road stops and to the chain works in Kent and the boxing ring. It chronicles his journey from a lonely childhood to the moment he fully resolved to become a writer. His grandfather Old Hughie makes a return appearance but does not dominate the book as he did *Shanty Irish*. He is but one of the many people Tully recalls from his wanderings, including boxer Joe Gans and Kent librarian Nellie Dingley.

Reviews of *Blood on the Moon* were largely positive. Virginia Peterson Ross at the *New York Herald-Tribune* raved: "The stuff of his experiences is sensational and pitched at a furious tension. Treachery and brotherhood, starvation and gluttony, murder and love run in streamer headlines across these dizzy reminiscences. Mr. Tully, rushing rampant down the days of his life, paints them a bloody red."[111] Not to be outdone, Frederic F. Van de Water at the *New York Post*, wrote:

> A person whose chief desire is to stretch out somewhere and yawn at a ceiling or sky shouldn't have anything to do with the works of Jim Tully.
>
> BLOOD ON THE MOON is excessively exhibitionistically vigorous. . . . Mr. Tully writes with a sledgehammer. . . . Mr. Tully has no smoothness of

style. His sentences bark. His paragraphs are clumsy, but, gosh, Mr. Tully has vigor![112]

The *Chicago Daily Tribune* was equally enthusiastic about his

> forthright, honest delineation of low characters. There is little loveableness, little sentiment, little of any of the finer sensibilities in it. But there is at the same time a certain terrific reality about it that makes it important as honest social observation. . . . He writes little of mental suffering, which readers are so wont to associate with records of hard living. But in that lack his power lies. . . . But if there is little mental suffering, there is profound physical suffering. Some paragraphs about everyday life in "Blood on the Moon" are as cruel as anything that has been written about war. And irony stalks on its pages. There are a hundred novels undeveloped in them.[113]

Percy Hutchison at the *New York Times*, in what must stand with the most perceptive of all of Tully's reviews, began by noting, "If ever there was a drifter it was Jim Tully." The fundamental riddle of Tully, Hutchison noted, is knowing just how much of Jim's life is poured into his books.

> To be sure, the reader is never quite certain whether Tully is relating bona fide experience or whether he is drawing out the bow a trifle more than experience justifies. But whatever may be between the covers of *Blood on the Moon* is essentially true. . . .
> In other words, Tully may be a very tall teller of tales; but he is intimately aware of the fundamentals of those tales. . . .
> Again and again the reader will find himself exclaiming, "Can such things be?" And the next chapter not only proves that they can, but others much worse.[114]

Having seen the essential truth of Tully's writing, Hutchison also recognized the dramatic effect of Tully's staccato style, his rugged but honest use of language, and the absence of self-pity in his work. "We should not like a library of Tullys," Hutchison concluded. "But one lends something of zest for those not too queasy."

Fred Marsh at the *Nation* went so far as to proclaim *Blood on the Moon* the best book of Tully's Underworld series.[115] Tully even heard from Jack

Bracken, his old boss from the Kent chain works who had pitched for the Cleveland Blues in 1901. After decades of obscurity, the old ballplayer was thrilled to see his name mentioned in *Blood on the Moon*.[116]

A film version of *Blood on the Moon* was considered by one of the studios but, like *Circus Parade* and *Shadows of Men*, was never made.[117]

20

Laughter in Hell

With *Blood on the Moon* successfully concluding his five-book cycle of autobiographical works and his divorce more or less behind him, Tully seemed to be in good spirits in early 1932. A guest at one of Tully's parties recalled:

> I felt at home from the moment I crossed Mr. Tully's threshold. . . . His books leave the impression that he is pretty hard-boiled. It may be that he does have a hard-boiled side. But he does not reveal it in his home. There he is gently and kindly with a certain salty sweetness. . . . He retains a boy's joy in life. . . . He had more fun at his party than anybody else who was there. . . . The Tully house is not one of the swankier places. . . . It is just a comfortable good-looking Spanish-type house, attractively furnished and with good rugs, excellent pictures, and many books.[1]

While Tully had been comfortable, if not happy, in the home he'd shared with Marna at 818 Kings Road in Hollywood, what he really wanted—and could finally afford—was land.

So in May of 1932, he paid $30,000 cash for three-and-a-half acres on a peninsula point on Toluca Lake. The site was heavily wooded with hundred-foot eucalyptus trees and oaks. Although a mere five miles from Hollywood, rustic Toluca Lake seemed much more distant. Plans were drawn, a few trees were cleared, and construction commenced. A local reporter stopped by the job site and was surprised to find, amid the carpenters, masons, and other contractors, "a stocky fellow, with a mop of red hair," who seemed to be the crew's foreman.[2] Construction of the stone and red-brick home, Tully would later explain, had been a spiritual experience, with the blueprints serving only as a starting point.[3] Building the house had "been a democratic, almost a communistic venture. Every man on the job was free to offer any suggestions. They did, and many of them were good."[4] And by supervising construction, Tully cut the construction costs by half. The new house, which he named "Tall Timbers," had nine rooms and a basement gymnasium. The ground floor had a large living room with a beamed ceiling and handmade doors and was warmed by a large fireplace. Tully was especially proud of his upstairs study and library, with its carved panels and view of the lake.[5]

In addition to giving him elbow room, he wrote Mencken, the move in late 1932 helped him put his painful and costly divorce from Marna in the past.[6] His feelings about his ex-wife had hardened in the years since their divorce. Marna, he wrote one friend, was "one of those women who try to bungle up strong men's lives and only succeed in hurting their own. She is now like some parrot-faced wench I saw in a long ago dream. What a magnificent and sad and bewildering thing life is."[7]

Still, Marna's remarriage in 1933 must have stung. That her new husband was an aspiring writer and that they were living in Jim and Marna's old house, which she had acquired in the settlement, couldn't have helped.[8] Jim could therefore be forgiven for taking some pleasure in one story that reached him. Her new husband, finding Marna in a drunken rage, tried to calm her. "No one can touch me but Jim Tully," she snapped.[9]

Mencken was delighted by photos of the Toluca Lake house. "Your new place looks almost perfect," he wrote. "I am sorely tempted to come out to California and drink you out of house and home. Unfortunately, I fear the movie people would drive me crazy with offers to play heroic parts."[10] While it all sounded "lovely" to Mencken, in private he was less sanguine. It was a large and isolated house, and a fellow as gregarious as Tully was sure to be lonely there. "He'll probably fall for a movie girl next time," he wrote in his diary, "and she will make off with what remains of his money."[11]

While the vicissitudes of the heart *did* appear to be a mystery to Jim, there was at least one unsuitable woman he did not fall for. Over the years, Jim had maintained a correspondence with a cousin from Ohio, Gertrude Lawler, the daughter of Jim's uncle James Lawler. She welcomed—and misinterpreted—the attention of her famous first cousin, finally professing her deep and unashamed love for him. Jim, and the passage of time, finally discouraged her.[12]

Jim's attention to Gertrude Lawler was not unique. Where family and old friends were concerned, Tully was a faithful correspondent and a loyal friend. He was, for example, still exchanging letters with "Uncle Dan," the janitor he had befriended at St. Xavier's College in Cincinnati two-and-a-half decades before.[13]

What next? Casting about ideas for a new book, Tully considered writing about boxing or perhaps a novel about prostitutes. Instead, he returned to an idea from the previous summer. Tully's secretary had mentioned a friend's childhood memory of the nineteenth-century yellow fever epidemic in Memphis. Intrigued, Tully had her research the outbreak. They learned that chain gangs had been used to bury the dead. The idea of a book about one such unfortunate began to take hold. This research joined some earlier research on coal mining, and together they became the basis for *Laughter in Hell*, which was published in autumn 1932. The line "The shadow of a good woman lingers long in the land and a bad one makes laughter in hell" had been written for Old Hughie in *Blood on the Moon*.[14] Slightly altered, it found its way into the new book, providing the title. It was, in Tully's words, simply a story "about a mick who kills two people, and goes to the chain gang."[15]

The idea of a railroad man who kills his unfaithful wife in a drunken rage was not unique. Indeed, engineers and brakemen, often away from home for days at a time, were given to drink excessively on their return. It was a perfect recipe for domestic violence and, in the most extreme cases, murder, as any railroad town newspaper of the period may attest. Honorable and hardworking Barney Slaney, the main character in *Laughter in Hell*, is such a man. His world crashes when, drunk on brandy, he finds his wife with another man and murderers them both. In an unusual act of mercy, the judge spares his life and sentences him to work on a chain gang.

Laughter in Hell is an exploration of how much a man can endure in exchange for his freedom, and Barney Slaney's escape from the chain gang is rich in the sort of detail acquired by Tully in his road years. While on the run, Slaney stumbles into an abandoned hobo camp. Starving, he finds sustenance in a handful of old coffee grounds that he scoops up and chews. And he is hellishly tormented when a screw fly begins buzzing around an open wound on his upper back. He knows the eggs it will lay will produce larvae, larvae that will feed on his flesh.[16]

After the *Beggars of Life* movie, Hollywood had been lukewarm to proposals to film Tully's books. With *Laughter in Hell* in press, Tully found himself in the happy position of owning just what the studios wanted. Word got out that Warner Brothers was working on *I Am a Fugitive from a Chain Gang*, starring Paul Muni. The other studios, then as now, were eager to get in on the next big thing. Rights to *Laughter in Hell* suddenly became a hot property and Universal quickly locked up the story for $11,500.[17] Initial plans were to have John Ford, fresh off the Oscar-nominated *Arrowsmith*, direct. Charles Bickford, who had starred in the stage version of *Beggars of Life*, was considered for the lead, as was boxer turned actor Victor McLaglen. In the end, Edward L. Cahn (later a director of cult favorites *Girls in Prison* [1956], *Invasion of the Saucer Men* [1957], and other B movies) was chosen to direct *Laughter in Hell*, and Tully recommended Pat O'Brien to the Selznick office for the role of Barney Slaney.[18] It was perhaps inevitable that two of Hollywood's most famous sons of Ireland would meet. Tully often visited O'Brien on movie sets and had promised to one day write a story with a part for him. O'Brien would later recall: "A hard Irish potato of a little man, with a rough carved weather-beaten face, curly uncut red hair, he knew he was a kind of folk hero. He drank everything, he read everything. . . . Some writers, like some actors for no known reason fade too quickly and are forgotten. Jim was one of them—the hobo who went a little mad with love of words."[19] Joining O'Brien in the film was Gloria Stuart, more than six decades before her role in *Titanic*, for which she would be nominated for an Oscar.[20]

Almost immediately there was trouble. Will Hays, charged with discouraging the studios from making films that might offend public morality, took a dim view of chain-gang films. As the *New York Times* noted, plots ran along two lines: either the prisoner was wrongly convicted, which cast doubt on the justice system, or the prisoner was rightly convicted but the crime was somehow justified.[21] Either way, brutality and an escape into the waiting arms of an attractive young woman ensued. Sex and violence never failed to raise eyebrows at the Hays office. Hollywood's morality police were spurred to action by the possibility of a full-frontal assault on public virtue by a veritable army of men in chains clanking across the silver screen. Under pressure, the studios either shelved their planned movies or tried to appease Hays with script changes. Plans for *Laughter in Hell* were suspended in June of 1932, and Patrick Kearney, who had written the script for *An American Tragedy*, was brought in to smooth out the rough edges.[22] Tully could afford to take the news in stride, writing his cousin, "Universal bought it—and now they don't know what to do with it. But they paid!"[23]

The news on the *Laughter in Hell* book was more troubling. Mencken's initial enthusiasm cooled when the manuscript finally came to rest on his desk and he could find nothing to use in the *American Mercury*.[24] Shaken by the rejection, Tully immediately began to doubt his ability as a novelist.[25] Mencken, Tully reassured himself, had also not liked "A Boy from the South," which had appeared in *Shadows of Men*. So perhaps Mencken was simply wrong about *Laughter in Hell*.[26] *Laughter in Hell* wasn't bad, Mencken responded, just different from the character sketches and autobiographical work that preceded it. "The influence of the movies upon it is apparent."[27] This was not the barb that it might appear. The chapters in Tully's earlier books were essentially set pieces and could easily stand alone. The longer continuous narrative of *Laughter in Hell*, Mencken wrote, made its chapters much less suitable for magazines. What Mencken understood about Tully's autobiographical work was that its strength was the very short distance between life and art. In writing a novel in the third person, Tully was taking a risk by moving away from this strength.

When Universal finally did begin production of *Laughter in Hell* in September 1932, they appealed to Tully to "give them the music for the Negro songs in the book."[28] He wrote George Jean Nathan that he would probably recommend "Lead Kindly Light."[29] It was a sardonic choice. The nineteenth-century hymn was sung aboard the *Titanic* as it sank.[30]

While the book and film reviews of *Laughter in Hell* were not quite catastrophic, they were not good. The *New York Times* found the book a "slight amateurish story" belonging to the "pulp magazine school of fiction." It bore the "marks of haste and indifference" and managed to be both "padded" and "sketchy and incomplete." The *Times* reviewer felt that *Laughter in Hell* was simply not up to the high standard set by Tully's earlier work. In the Underworld books, Tully had created "five passionate volumes, often attaining to a high level of power in literary expression." The old Jim Tully "created living figures and portrayed, as no one else has, a now disappearing element of American life." *Laughter in Hell*, the *Times* concluded, was a letdown, and a writer of Tully's stature and following deserved "no quarter."[31]

In its review, *Time* compared Tully to Sherwood Anderson and Theodore Dreiser, but whereas "Dreiser and Anderson have won life memberships in the U.S. literary Senate[,] Jim Tully's persistent clamor in the lobby has not yet gained him admission. Crudely violent writer of crudely violent melodramatics. Author Tully has done better books than *Laughter in Hell*."[32] The *Saturday Review of Literature* was more encouraging. While the book was "naïve" and lacked any "pretense of subtlety," the novel "is so honestly felt that it holds the reader's interest and sympathy. The emotion of the author is a driving force that makes the story well worth while."[33]

As for the film, opinion was divided—even in the same paper. When *Laughter in Hell* opened, an entertainment writer for the *Washington Post* proclaimed: "Seldom does the screen reflect such bold, passionate, vivid drama of a purely elemental nature as it does at the Rialto Theater this week, where a truly great and startling picture is being shown to Washington audiences for the first time."[34] The formal review, however, appearing in the same edition, soberly noted that "there is not the slightest ripple of mirth—a sordid, gruesome in spots, stark story of a chain-gang convict." Worse still, *Laughter in Hell* didn't even measure up to other chain-gang movies. The Paul Muni film, which was nominated for three Academy Awards, "was a scathing indictment" of the U.S. criminal justice system, while *Laughter in Hell* used the chain gang for nothing more than story material.[35]

The *New York Times* found the film to be "a lugubrious tale," and the direction "heavy-handed and amateurish."[36] The harshest review came from the book's author. Tully wrote Mencken, "Tell Sara [Mencken's wife] that I saw *Laughter in Hell* and, she may not believe it, but it is far worse than the book."[37]

The road, as always, proved a tonic. But when the road tugged in 1932, Tully took to it in the manner befitting a successful writer, riding in a private coach en route to William Randolph Hearst's San Simeon castle or driving his 1930 Packard to Lake Tahoe.[38] He told one interviewer that his days of travel by rail were over. "There was some adventure and glamor to riding freight trains," he said. "But traveling as a passenger in a Pullman is dead monotony."[39] It was a long way from the days of catching an open boxcar in St. Marys.

The invitation from Hearst, the notorious and ruthless newspaper magnate, came at the end of 1931. As Tully had been contemplating writing about Hearst since his name surfaced in the 1924 death of Thomas Ince, the summons proved irresistible. Roughly midway between Los Angeles and San Francisco, Hearst's enormous, mountainside estate was often the site of dinners and parties of Gatsbyesque proportions. Tully later recalled his February 1932 visit. His mysterious and usually invisible host demanded that certain rules be observed: there was to be no swearing, and guests were expected to be abstemious and prompt for meals (although Hearst was usually either absent or late) and properly comport themselves (one actor was summarily dismissed for bringing a woman not his wife to the festivities—this despite the fact that Hearst openly kept a mistress). Most guests, especially movie people, feared Hearst and went to great lengths to stay in his good graces. Many suspected that not only did his servants spy for him but the rooms were bugged.[40] Mencken was so delighted by Tully's description of life at San Simeon that he recorded it in his diary.

> Tully, who is a very innocent fellow, was in great fear that he might do something that would induce Hearst to kick him out. . . . It is considered disgraceful in Hollywood to suffer that experience. . . . Tully says that a short while before his visit there had been an enormous fight one evening among drunken actors. As a result, Hearst forbade the circulation of jugs after dinner. This bore harshly on Tully. He was relieved by Marion Davies [screen star and Hearst's mistress], who produced a couple bottles of Scotch. They were drunk in Tully's room by Davies, Tully himself, Constance Talmadge [an actress] and Hearst's son, George.[41]

As for the mansion itself, Tully found it hideous but was forced to admit that a few of the rooms were lovely and reserved special praise for Hearst's fine library.[42]

By late spring, he was off again on the first of two trips in 1932 to the East Coast. The first was to New York City to visit George Jean Nathan.[43] On his second trip, Tully drove to Lake Tahoe on the Fourth of July weekend with old friends Jack Dempsey and cowboy actor Tom Mix. Tully detected a certain coolness upon being introduced to Mix's recent bride. He learned that she was an an ex–circus performer and had read—and strongly disapproved of—*Circus Parade*.[44] The group moved on to Reno, where they watched heavyweight Max Baer defeat King Levinsky in what turned out to be the last twenty-round fight to go the distance.[45] And at the end of the month, when the summer Olympics opened in Los Angeles, Tully covered the games for Fremont Older's *San Francisco Call-Bulletin* (previously the *San Francisco Call and Post*).[46]

In addition to his occasional reportage, Tully's Hollywood pieces flowed unabated in the early 1930s (1932 alone saw pieces on Barbara Stanwyck, Mary Lygo, William Powell, Leland Curtis, Janet Gaynor, Victor McLaglen, Charles Bickford, Boris Karloff, Paul Bern, and Clara Bow).[47] His influence on the Hollywood magazine, and the way celebrities are covered by the press, is inestimable.

Tully's interview method was, by his own admission, unorthodox. He never, for example, looked his subject in the eye. From so many nights spent in so many barrooms, he had learned that people are most revealing when observed indirectly, watched in the mirror behind the bar. He put his subjects at ease by seldom asking a direct question and never taking notes. He had acquired the latter skill back at the orphanage, where he learned to listen to the priest on Sunday and repeat the sermon back to the nuns on Monday. The interviewer's art, Tully understood, was to catch people off guard.[48]

In addition to his Hollywood work, Tully was also influencing a far different sort of magazine. Pulp magazines, so-named for their inferior paper stock, were at their peak in the early 1930s, and the king of pulp writers was a young Texan named Robert E. Howard. Howard was a frequent and important contributor to the legendary pulp *Weird Tales* and is perhaps best remembered as the creator of Conan the Barbarian. A voluminous correspondence exists between Howard and his friend H. P. Lovecraft, Edgar Allan Poe's heir as the American master of the horror story. In late 1932, the king of the pulps wrote the master of horror: "As for American writers, I think yourself and Jim Tully are the only ones whose work will endure; among the writers now living, I mean."[49]

If life is the experience of having loved ones taken away one by one, then Tully was to learn that life really begins in middle age. Paul Bern was Tully's oldest and closest friend in Hollywood. Bern's big heart never failed to affect Tully. He never forgot, for example, Bern's kindness in the days following Mary Lygo's suicide. Nor could he forget the dampness in Bern's eyes on the day Sacco and Vanzetti were executed.[50]

Bern was seemingly on top of the world. He had just produced with Thalberg that year's Academy Award winner for best picture, *Grand Hotel*, with an all-star cast including Greta Garbo, John Barrymore, Joan Crawford, Wallace Beery, and Lionel Barrymore. (In an odd footnote to the film, Garbo had requested that her former fiancé, John Gilbert, be cast as the male lead, but Gilbert's stock had fallen so low by 1932 that the part went to John Barrymore.) The MGM publicity team's efforts on behalf of the film were without precedent, and a short promotional film was shot of the many celebrities arriving at the film's premiere at Grauman's Chinese Theatre. As the celebrities walked from their limousines to the front of the theater, they found a hotel desk meant to reflect the setting of the film. At the desk they were introduced to the crowd and asked to sign a guest book. Jean Harlow is seen walking to the desk in this short publicity newsreel and being introduced to the master of ceremonies, Conrad Nagel. Accompanying her is a small man in a gray fedora. Harlow is radiant, while her escort seems stuck in her orbit like a small and distant moon. The slight man in the fedora is not mentioned or acknowledged by Nagel. It is Bern.

When Bern stopped by to see Tully in mid-June of 1932, he had a major announcement. He was going to marry Harlow, or, as she came to be known, "blonde bombshell" Jean Harlow. Tully was puzzled. Wasn't, Tully asked, Bern already married to Dorothy Millette, a struggling actress? Bern simply shrugged his shoulders.[51] By the Fourth of July, Bern and Harlow were married. By Labor Day, Bern was dead. The shocking news of Paul Bern's death on the morning of September 5 was quickly followed by speculation and rumor, which persist to the present. Full accounts of Bern's death (with opposing conclusions) can be found in *Bombshell: The Life and Death of Jean Harlow*, David Stenn's biography of Bern's wife, and *Deadly Illusions: Jean Harlow and the Murder of Paul Bern* by Samuel Marx and Joyce Vanderveen.[52] The facts of the case are that Bern was found nude and curled up on the floor with a .38 revolver in his hand and a bullet hole in his head. MGM's attempt to cover up the death (they were on the scene before the police) and protect Harlow, who was under contract to them, only fueled the conspiracy theories. Was it suicide or murder? If the former, why? If the latter, by whom? Murder suspects included Harlow as well as Dorothy Millette, whose deteriorating mental state led her to commit suicide two days after Bern's death. Suicide motives ranged from the one promulgated by MGM—that Bern was impotent and unable to consummate his marriage to his much younger wife—to Tully's own position, which he outlined a week later in a three-page letter to Mencken. "I don't think Bern died because he was impotent. I think I have reasons to know; at any rate I will send off this confidential slant to you and you can feel that it is nearer right than anything that has been said. Bern despised the step-father, a pompous ass and a one time chauffeur. I think he had reason to feel that there was an intimacy between his wife and her step-father, still being continued."[53]

Tully then painted a portrait of a gold-digging wife and her parasitic family. They'd quarreled over the $65,000 house Bern had given her. Harlow wanted it deeded to her mother and stepfather. "Even a professional Christ could not stand such humiliation," Tully concluded.[54] Later, Tully recalled his friend's funeral and the eulogy delivered by the actor who played master of ceremonies in the *Grand Hotel* newsreel, Conrad Nagel.

> An actor talked over all that was mortal of the brilliant Bern, while leaders of the film industry allowed their greatest man to be patronized.
> "Paul was just a naive child," the actor said.
> I did not agree. Paul was a thousand years old at birth. Into his soul had seeped the frustrations of generations forever silent.[55]

A few months after Bern's death another blow fell. Tully had hoped that the addition of "convicted rapist" to his son's uncrowded resume was the result of youth, a spineless lack of direction, and alcohol. Any hope that all could be put right by salt air quickly evaporated. Word had come in April of 1932 that Alton had violated his probation by going AWOL in San Francisco from the Dollar Steamship Line.[56] When Alton next surfaced in October, he wanted to borrow money[57] and was, as Mencken noted in his diary, "studying the art and mystery of a filling station manager at a school maintained by the Standard Oil Company in Los Angeles." "The boy," Mencken dryly noted, "is apparently not much."[58]

By the start of the new year, the news was much worse. Alton was again facing rape charges. After initially pleading guilty to the charge of attacking twenty-one-year-old Frances Charbonneaux, Alton was permitted to change his plea and was scheduled for trial.[59] As was becoming his pattern, Alton said all the right things. He wrote his father, first to apologize to his family for embarrassing them again and then to plead his case.[60]

Getting at the truth where Alton was concerned was never easy. Jim was left in the position of suspecting the worst while hoping for the best. He could, as always, rely on Mencken to bolster his spirits. It was, in Mencken's view, more a financial problem than a criminal one. Most libel and plagiarism suits were, in Mencken's experience, settled for a fraction of the initial demand. "You are bearing the burden of all fathers. It hits one in one way and another in some other way, but all of them take their turns on the block." He continued, "Every youngster goes through his crazy, goatish period, and while he is in full blast he is an easy mark for any wench."[61] Tully was reassured and even planned for his son's acquittal by securing Alton a job in a Mexican mine.[62]

By mid-February of 1933 it was all over. Following two days of testimony, which included a witness who had overheard the victim brag that she expected to be coming into money, the jury took twenty-eight minutes and a single ballot to acquit, having concluded that whatever happened had been consensual.[63]

Jim's sense of relief was palpable and he decided to get away for a while. And what better way to unwind than in Baltimore drinking beer with H. L. Mencken at his famous Saturday Night Club? The club, then nearly three decades old, consisted of musicians, newspapermen, and scientists and stood on the three pillars of gemütlichkeit: beer, cigars, and music. The club's most notable feat had been its assault on Beethoven, an audacious but failed attempt to play the first eight Beethoven symphonies in order.[64]

Musical ability was not a prerequisite for membership. A love for beer was. And by those standards, Tully was eminently qualified. Tully was in fact the reigning beer-drinking champion of the club, having wrested the title from Mencken a few years earlier. His time of four seconds on a sixteen-ounce beer proved good enough to retain the title.[65] A sportswriter who had once witnessed Tully in a San Francisco contest could only marvel: "Tully simply held his mouth open and poured, the amber fluid rolling in a steady stream down his gullet. It was just like pouring it into a sink."[66]

Drinking with Tully required a stout heart and a thick hide. After the first round, Tully's "Let's have another drink" was more command than request. Hollywood writer and longtime pal Frank Scully lived to tell the tale: "If you don't let him have another drink, you'll find his wrath swerving from the generality to the particular, and you'll soon be writhing under the lash of his incredible candor. It is a curious mixture of Billingsgate and Shakespeare, a poet pelting you with manure. If you do let him have another drink, his voice goes more basso profundo, and deeper truths come out, all of them about you and all of them destined to make others grin and you squirm."[67]

Jim's most recent piece of real writing, a fine nonfiction account titled "Yeggs," described the princes of the underworld: safecrackers. It had been completed at the end of 1932 and accepted by Mencken for the *American Mercury*.[68] Now, with Alton's latest crisis behind him and not having worked for three months, Jim began considering new projects.[69] Over dinner with popular historian Will Durant, he hit upon the idea of traveling to Russia to interview Joseph Stalin and Maxim Gorky.[70] Mencken discouraged the idea, as there was then a glut of Russian articles, most of them reflecting Soviet propaganda foisted on writers dependent on Russian translators.[71]

Instead, Tully returned to more familiar ground. Boxing, specifically Jack Dempsey, was sure to sell.[72] A Dempsey profile was quickly accepted by Mencken in March 1933 for what would be Tully's final appearance in the pages of the *Mercury*, albeit at a slightly reduced payment owing to the Depression.[73] Tully had remained close to the former champ and the two planned to attend the June 8 fight between Max Baer and German heavyweight Max Schmeling at Yankee Stadium.[74] Tully visited sportswriter Damon Runyon's home a few days before the fight, took the measure of Baer and Schmeling, and predicted victory for the American boxer. Baer, in what is considered the best fight of his career, demolished the German in the tenth.

While heavy doses of beer and sports may be the perennial hallmarks of a happy bachelorhood, they are less often associated with wedded bliss. And having been KO'ed by two marriages, Jim must have been given pause by the prospect of a third trip to the altar.

It had begun more than two years before, when Jim was working for Al Lewin at MGM. Waiting for Lewin to emerge from a meeting, Jim had struck up a conversation with Lewin's secretary, Myrtle Zwetow. She entertained him with stories about her college friends and he found himself looking forward to killing time in Lewin's outer office.[75] Her dark hair and Russian Spanish ancestry gave her an exotic appeal.[76] Beneath that, Jim saw, was a woman possessed of an inner serenity, a calm that he found even more enchanting than her appearance. Originally from Illinois, she was, like Jim, a midwesterner who had landed in California. Kid McCoy's line about being "a sucker for a right" came to mind. "It was hardly that," he recalled. "I was hit from all angles."[77]

By late spring of 1933, Jim and Myrtle were planning to wed. Unlike the girls Jim had married before, Myrtle Zwetow was a woman. At thirty-five, Myrtle was more mature than Jim or either of his ex-wives had been at the time of their marriages. And with her work at the studio, neither her livelihood nor identity would be wholly dependent on her famous husband. When Myrtle invited Trilby to meet her for lunch at the studio, an invitation Jim's fifteen-year-old daughter was thrilled to accept, things seemed particularly auspicious.[78] With Jim twice divorced and Catholic, and Myrtle Jewish, a justice of the peace in Ventura was found and the pair wed on June 26, 1933.[79]

Later that summer, more than a quarter of a century removed from the road, Tully contemplated one last cross-country trip as a hobo. The plan, he confided by letter to William Randolph Hearst, was to begin in Washington with an interview of President Franklin Roosevelt, after which, concealing his identity, he would hitchhike across the country, interviewing people from all walks of life. He especially wanted to interview road-kids, guessing that there must be three or four hundred thousand scattered across the country. Not forgetting how unfriendly law enforcement could be to a drifter, he proposed bribing his way out of trouble or, if necessary, revealing that he was a journalist working a story. The trip never came off.[80]

A September piece on director and friend Rowland V. Lee for a film magazine brought an unexpected response. Tully had lavished praise on two films, both foreign:

> Two really great pictures have been made since the tinsel business was invented. I might say one-and-a-half.
>
> "Maedchen in Uniform" was complete. It was made, I think, in that hated Germany, whose art we wished to destroy during one of our recent wars.
>
> The next picture was "The Cruiser Potemkin." Had Eisenstein been able to forget the torn places in his great Soviet heart, that, too, would have ranked with "Maedchen in Uniform." The march of those soldiers up the steps! Mother of God—what an artist![81]

Tully could not have been surprised that someone in Hollywood would object to his inability to find a single American film worthy of his admiration. Nor could he have been surprised that the objection was raised by Charlie Chaplin, an old and familiar adversary. Jim had been called many things in life, but Chaplin's charge that Tully had "gone highbrow" was a first. While Tully might have rolled his eyes at the accusation, he did not find amusing the rest of Chaplin's letter, which had been syndicated and had run in newspapers across the country. After quoting one of Tully's articles, in which Jim describes his father and grandfather as ditchdiggers, Chaplin sarcastically added, "The above, I believe, explains much about Tully's scribblings. What his forebears did with a shovel, Jim strives to do with a pen."[82]

Tully detected a ghostwriter's touch in the letter. Still, coming from Chaplin, the criticism was especially hard to stomach. In response, Jim wrote a letter to Chaplin in which he quoted his father, then in his eighties, as recommending Jim take the high road and ignore the comedian's jibes. While the advice from his father was surely Jim's invention, it was good counsel and Jim made no public response.[83] Privately, Jim vented to Hollywood publisher Rob Wagner that he'd *always* been highbrow. He pointed out that he was still boxing when he wrote the poem "On Keats' Grave," and his literary self-education, begun when he was a road-kid, gave him every right to an opinion, whether highbrow or not.[84]

21

Ladies in the Parlor

Tully's family life had been tumultuous since early childhood, but by late 1933, at age forty-seven, Jim's personal life was finally stable and seemingly happy. He was newly married to Myrtle. His teenage daughter, Trilby, was busy with school. And since his acquittal, Alton, by his own account, was sober, employed at a garage, and going steady with an El Monte woman.[1] Jim was even getting along with Florence, the pair having been reunited over Alton's troubles.[2] It could not last.

On the night of December 4, 1933, a twenty-four-year-old housewife named Violet Robey spent the evening drinking at home with her husband. When the wine ran out, the couple drove to a speakeasy, where she began downing whiskey. On the way home, the couple argued. It was a classic car fight—two drunk people confined in a small space. And in classic car-fight fashion, the passenger, Violet Robey, jumped out and declared her intention to walk the remaining five miles home. Since it was early in the morning and the stretch of highway known as Coyote Pass was deserted, Mrs. Robey must have been relieved to see a passing car. She flagged it down. As it slowed, she was further relieved to see a couple and, by one account, even recognized the driver as an old schoolmate. Did she need a lift? She cursed her husband and climbed in. The male Good Samaritan dropped off his companion at her house before taking Mrs. Robey home. What happened next isn't completely clear, but Mrs. Robey claimed the driver tried to force himself on her, tore her dress, and struck her in the face some two-dozen times when she resisted. The Good Samaritan later maintained that Robey wanted more booze and money for a room, and that he only resorted to violence to resist her drunken demands. Later that morning, Violet Robey went to the police and Alton Tully was charged with attempted rape.³

As this was the fourth such incident (charges on one earlier case were dismissed when the complaining witness failed to appear in court),⁴ it was no longer possible to dismiss Alton's behavior as simply "goatish." The depth of Alton's problems shocked and saddened his father. "I don't know what to say," he told a reporter. "He's my son. I'm sorry for him. I'm sorry for his mother and sister. I've always done all I could for him. I want to help him now, but I don't know what I can do."⁵ Torn between defending his son and his own sense of justice, Jim found middle ground. He would, as before, help his son, but with the more limited goal of keeping him out of the penitentiary.

Tully, who had been working on a profile of director Frank Capra for both *Rob Wagner's Script* and *Esquire,* turned to his friend and neighbor for help.⁶ Capra phoned Mendel Silberberg, Louis B. Mayer's personal attorney, hoping Silberberg would take the case and arrange a plea resulting in a year or two in the county jail but keeping Alton from hard time. Silberberg declined Capra's request and the case moved to trial.⁷ On February 7, 1934, Jim sent a brief note to Alton at the county jail: "Either way I am standing by you. Jim Tully."⁸ At trial, Alton denied attacking the woman. He maintained that she was intoxicated and that he simply dropped her off at her home.⁹ Unable to reach a verdict, the jury was sequestered.¹⁰

Two days later, Jim was finally able to write his son at length. The wisdom of Jim's letter could not hide the anger, sorrow, and old wounds bubbling just beneath the surface. They had made the best case they could, he wrote, and now all they could do was wait.

> You must think quite seriously of the years ahead. While your conduct has been more idiotic than criminal, you must nevertheless try to realize that after four such episodes . . . people may be half right in considering you a social menace. You have given pain right and left, and you must now bear pain with all the poise you can muster. Try to feel that society has not been your enemy. It was quite willing to let you alone. If its method of punishing you is more primitive than is necessary for an enlightened age, the better part of prudence would have been to have avoided such episodes after the first time.
>
> It is too late to blame, and I have never been one to try to hurt when another is down. There is still a great chance for you to become a real man.

Your strength of character will be best tested by how you endure. So much is accidental in life, and so much ironical. I suffered enough long before you were born, for most men. I cannot now allow you to wreck what is left of my life. I dragged the name of Tully out of the mud, and you still have a chance to do something with it. Try not to be influenced by the weaklings and whiners against fate around you. Try to read and improve your mind. Even if you get the final sentence, you will not be much worse off than I was at your age. There is some quirk in your brain that must be ironed out. You should get out of California when this is over, and stay out.

But of this you can be certain. I will not desert you in your time of stress. This letter is written to keep you out of the bog of self pity. While it is harder for you, it is not easy for your mother, Trilby, and myself.[11]

Later that day, Alton Tully was convicted of attempted criminal assault.[12] With Alton's attorneys considering an appeal, Alton tried to rally his father.[13] "You probably think I am a damned liar but I did not commit this crime."[14] While he was resigned to his mother's willingness to believe the worst of him, he was particularly hurt that Trilby and his father now shared her low opinion of him.[15] It worked. Jim, finally convinced of Alton's innocence, wrote Capra that the appeal would include three witnesses who would testify that Mrs. Robey told them that her beating came at the hands of her husband.[16] Tully also mentioned to Capra that he'd heard that writer Jo Swerling, part of Capra's inner circle, had suggested that Alton be castrated. Tully responded, "That might be all right, if there weren't too many scenario writers in Hollywood already."[17]

The court showed no leniency. Probation was denied because of his past record, and on March 16, 1934, Alton Tully was sentenced to one to twenty-five years at San Quentin.[18] Jim, who was not present at the courthouse, took the news hard.[19] Over the next few weeks, while awaiting transfer to San Quentin, Alton wrote his father from jail that he'd already been visited by his uncle Hugh Tully and expected to see his mother soon.[20] Florence, Alton continued, was under the impression that those convicted of sex crimes were subject to castration. Perhaps, he asked, Jim could convince her otherwise. Characteristically, Alton veered from self-recrimination to self-pity. He added that he hoped that his ordeal might bring them closer together, suggesting that now more than ever he needed his father's wisdom. Then, he deftly shifted gears. "I can't tell you how many times I used to want to talk to you. I was lonely and wanted to tell you some of my troubles. Some one who would be interested, and have brains enough to give advice. You were always so busy and in a hurry that it seemed impossible."[21]

If Alton hoped to make his father feel guilty, he succeeded. By early April, expecting Alton to be moved to San Quentin any day, Jim wrote from Mexico City to a friend that he was "terribly unhappy." His pride was lacerated. His accomplishments seemed "hollow." He was powerless to help his son, and even though Myrtle was "a grand woman," his marriage meant nothing.[22] Alton's transfer to prison was delayed on April 7, 1934, pending appeal. He could, at least for a while, remain in the county jail.[23]

Jim was in Mexico City to interview Diego Rivera for *Esquire*.[24] Having written profiles of countless Hollywood celebrities and more than a few boxers, writing about the famous painter was a departure. Rivera was particularly newsworthy following the 1933 controversy surrounding his inclusion of Vladimir Lenin in the Rockefeller Center mural, *Man at the Crossroads*. A Rivera profile would pay well and was bound to be interesting.

On his return in late April, Tully wrote George Jean Nathan about his trip to Mexico City. He'd met Ed "Strangler" Lewis, a then-famous professional wrestler now remembered, if it all, as the inventor of the sleeper hold. The old bruiser and the Strangler decided to sample the city's nightlife, finally washing up at a brothel. Lewis, a believer in the bracing powers of cognac, got so drunk that he propositioned the madam. The following day, Jim accompanied the wrestler to work. Lewis politely bowed to the Mexican president seated at ringside then, as scheduled, threw two matches.[25]

As for Rivera, he was polite, diffident, "a charming fellow with whole continents of fantasy in his head."[26] They talked about politics and art before Rivera took Tully on a tour of his studio and home, where Tully was introduced to Rivera's wife. Tully seemed unsure what to make of Frida Kahlo, concluding that she was "unassuming" and "natural" and that a few of her paintings "reveal talent."[27] He found the footing surer in Rivera's small library. Rivera mentioned that three of his favorite American writers were John Dos Passos, Mike Gold, and Tully's old friend James Stevens, whose novel *Paul Bunyan* sat on a shelf near a copy of Tully's *Shadows of Men*.[28]

Two months later, Tully was back on the road, this time returning to Ohio to see a friend from his St. Marys days. It had been over thirty years since Jim met Charley Makley at the chain works in St. Marys, and both had achieved a certain notoriety. Makley's work as a small-time bank robber and hustler finally landed him in the Indiana State Prison, where he befriended several other bank robbers on sabbatical, most notably John Dillinger.

When Dillinger was released in May 1933, he made good on his promise to spring the others by smuggling guns into the prison. Ten armed convicts, including Makley, broke out that September and the Dillinger gang became an American legend. When Dillinger was arrested in Lima, Ohio, Makley, Harry Pierpont, and other gang members hatched a plan to free him. After robbing a St. Marys bank to finance the plan, on October 12, 1933, the gang launched their assault on the Allen County Jail. They freed Dillinger, killing the sheriff, Jess Saber, in the process. Makley was apprehended in Arizona, brought back to Lima for trial, and sentenced to death in March 1934.[29]

When Tully visited death row at the Ohio penitentiary on June 19, 1934, Makley failed to recognize his boyhood friend. The ten-minute interview, which Tully planned to turn into a story for a newspaper wire service after Makley's death, began with an awkward pause. While Makley was still hopeful that he might "beat the death rap," Tully left knowing that Makley's electrocution was a foregone conclusion.[30] As luck would have it, Tully ran into Harry Pierpont's parents at the prison and found them more than willing to speak about Dillinger and his gang. Hoping to round out the piece in a *big* way—and score a $100,000 payday—Tully had his pal Walter Winchell, the newspaper and radio commentator, report that Tully was seeking an interview with Dillinger, then on the lam.[31] The job of dumping ice water on the scheme fell to Tully's attorney, who informed his client that Jim's $100,000 interview would leave him open to the charge of harboring a fugitive.[32]

Any hope Makley had that Dillinger would again come to his rescue was dashed when Dillinger was gunned down by police and federal agents in Chicago on July 22. On September 22, Makley made his move. He and Pierpont fashioned fake guns from bars of soap, got out of their cells, and might have made their escape but for the penitentiary's new steel doors. Instead, Makley died in a hail of gunfire, while Pierpont survived to make his appointment with Ohio's electric chair.[33]

With his plans for a Dillinger piece shelved, Tully moved on. A boxing piece, "The Manly Art," appeared in the July 1934 *Esquire*. Two other *Esquire* articles would appear later that year under the bylines of W. C. Fields and Paul Muni but "as told to Jim Tully."[34] The summer of 1934 brought another intriguing assignment. John Wheeler, founder of the North American Newspaper Alliance (NANA) and the man who would send Hemingway to Spain to cover the civil war, proposed sending Tully to San Francisco to report on the longshoremen's strike.[35]

NANA had just pitched Tully on interviewing Al Capone and Tully was eager to get started when the longshoremen's strike went hot.[36] On July 5, 1934, San Francisco police responded to an angry mob of striking workers with bullets and tear gas, killing two and wounding many more. The day came to be known as Bloody Thursday. NANA wanted Jim's impressions of the violence and fear gripping the city.[37]

Despite his old card from the Chainmakers' National Union and his knee-jerk sympathy for the underdog, Tully's intention as he arrived in San Francisco was to write an unbiased account. Only moments after getting off the train, he realized just how badly the city was paralyzed when he tried to get to his hotel, the Clift on Geary Street. Nothing was rolling. Unable to find any transportation, he finally hired a private car. Nor was the luxurious Clift Hotel immune from labor strife. Tully found the dining room closed, the waiters having gone out in sympathy with the longshoremen. He wired Wheeler, suggesting an interview with Harry Bridges, who was leading the strike. Wheeler quickly signed off and Tully went to see Bridges.

He found Bridges surrounded by reporters and pushed his way in. A union official informed Bridges that the newcomer was a hobo turned writer. In a voice betraying his native Australia, Bridges looked in Tully's direction and needled that he'd just heard that "you never worked a day in your life." Tully shot back, "I was a longshoreman twelve years."[38] The ice was broken and Tully began asking direct questions. And Bridges, warming to the new guy, began providing direct answers. When Tully ran out of questions, he invited Bridges and his bodyguards to dinner at the Clift, where the dining room was scheduled to reopen that evening. Later that afternoon, Tully was surprised to see Bridges's answers to *his* questions in the afternoon newspapers. It was his first lesson in journalistic ethics. His second came at dinner with Bridges and his men (who were indignant that the waiters were back at work) when an acquaintance stopped by the table with *San Diego Sun* reporter Max Miller. Miller's reporting on the docks up and down the California coast had culminated in a best-selling book, *I Cover the Waterfront* (1932). As Tully's friend James Cruze had directed the film version of Miller's book the previous year, Miller and Tully should have hit it off. Instead, Miller saw Tully as an interloper and oozed condescension. Tully was furious at Miller's story the next day. Miller mentioned spotting Bridges and his men dining at the Clift, which seemed to suggest that the labor leader was accustomed to fine dining even as the rank and file were sacrificing blood and money for the union cause. He became angrier still when he noted that he wasn't even mentioned in Miller's story. It was left to Wheeler to pour salt in the wound. He praised (and paid for) Tully's Harry Bridges interview, calling it the best interview Tully had ever conducted, then killed it, opting instead to pick up the Miller piece.

Dillinger, Capone, a crippling strike, and the bloody attempt to quash it—all terrific subjects, all with the promise of a good, even a great, payday. And money, or the lack of it, had become a concern. The lingering Depression and Alton's mounting legal fees were taking a toll. Jim also had long supported his aging father. But when Mercer County, Ohio, officials requested more money for the elder Tully's expenses, Jim demurred. His finances were so bad, he wrote, that he'd paid no income taxes for 1933 and didn't expect to pay any in 1934. Although Jim had long ago come to terms with his father, he had neither forgotten nor forgiven the state of Ohio. "I am trying to write without bitterness, but I do feel I have done my duty toward him, inasmuch as the State of Ohio allowed him to desert me."[39] Nor was Jim's father, then in his mideighties, finding it easy to let go of the past. He later wrote from Celina, Ohio, thanking Jim for his financial support over the past decade and asking Jim to forgive him before he died for "acts of mine that have seemed out of place."[40]

Yet the money he was shoveling at Alton's attorneys was not wasted. In mid-August 1934, Alton's claim that he should have been allowed to present evidence suggesting that Violet Robey's wounds came at the hands of her husband was reviewed by the District Court of Appeals and he was granted a new trial.[41] With his father doing the heavy financial lifting, and with Florence both unwilling and unable to help, Alton turned to his new stepmother for money to buy sundries. Myrtle, who had every right to be unsympathetic and was by no means wealthy, borrowed money to send to her stepson.[42]

Alton's retrial, which had been scheduled for October 12, 1934, was moved to November 16 when Mrs. Robey became ill and was unable to appear in court.[43] As the case dragged on through the fall of 1934, all Jim could do was wait and visit his son in jail. On one visit he couldn't resist delivering fatherly advice on the dangers of a bad temper: "For god's sake develop a sense of humor, kid."[44] Humor and perspective had seen Jim through the worst of times and he'd gotten through the trial without animus for either the sheriff or prosecutors, even writing district attorney Buron Fitts that all involved had been "damned decent and understanding."[45]

It was impossible to write under the circumstances, so Tully puttered around the house and killed time. He tried and failed to sell a newspaper syndicate on a comic strip to be called "Road Kids."[46] He wrote astronomer Edwin Hubble, asking to visit the Mount Wilson Observatory, which overlooked Los Angeles in the nearby San Gabriel Mountains.[47] He tried and failed to get radio crooner Rudy Vallee to appear in "God Loves the Irish," the long-planned stage version of *Shanty Irish*.[48] Mostly, he just brooded. Finally, on November 15, having spent nearly a year in the county jail, and with Mrs. Robey unwilling to testify, Alton pleaded to simple assault and was handed a six-month sentence and sent to a work camp near Susanville, California.[49] After Alton settled in, Jim and Myrtle made the six-hundred-mile trip north to visit, bringing a pipe as a gift.[50] They returned home reassured that Alton had turned a corner and that better days were ahead.

By the fall of 1934, it had been nearly two years since the publication of Tully's last book, *Laughter in Hell*, and he increasingly felt himself pulled in the direction of a new novel. He had been considering a work about prostitutes for years, floating the idea to Mencken prior to his trip to Great Britain in 1929.[51] With Mencken's promise in August 1932 to run chapters in the *American Mercury*, the project took on life.[52] A draft of the book, titled *Ladies in the Parlor*, was completed in the summer of 1934.[53] Rising at four most mornings, Tully revised the manuscript until nine, when he began working on other projects, including "bastardizing," as he described it, a script of Poe's *The Raven* for Boris Karloff and Bela Lugosi, for which he was paid slightly more than $5,000.[54]

Both Simon & Schuster and Farrar passed on *Ladies in the Parlor*, but a small publisher, Greenberg, despite misgivings about the title, offered a contract in February 1935.[55] Tully considered changing the title but, on Mencken's advice, let it stand.[56] With the manuscript finally in the hands of a publisher, Tully began thinking about dramatizing *Ladies in the Parlor* for Broadway.[57] Tully wrote George Nathan that Sydney Sanders, Tully's agent, suspected that the book would be "quite strong for publication in a depression."[58] Still, Tully was optimistic about an adaption of *Ladies in the Parlor* for the stage. *Ladies in the Parlor* was many things, but 1930s Broadway fare it was not.

The book borrowed characters from *Jarnegan* and "Children of Thieves," a manuscript gathering dust in a desk drawer.[59] While not autobiographical like *Beggars of Life* or the other Underworld books, the family at the center of *Ladies in the Parlor*, the Blairs, does share certain similarities with the Tullys of Jim's childhood. The father is a railroad laborer, "a shambling man" overwhelmed by the financial demands of providing for his wife and nine children. His wife, a saintly but doomed woman of "flat breasts and a tired expression," struggles mightily to keep her large brood together.[60] After a fight with his father, one of the boys takes to the road.

And it is here that *Ladies in the Parlor* parts company with Tully's autobiographical books. This time Tully follows not the boy who runs away but the sister he leaves behind. Leora Blair's fate is not that of frigid boxcars and a railroad bull's truncheon but that of something Tully seems to suggest is worse: life on the wrong side of the tracks in a small Ohio river town.

Stephen Crane biographer R. W. Stallman notes that Crane's *Maggie* owed much to Zola's *Nana*. Both novels about streetwalkers, they share the "philosophical outlook that we are all the victims of our environments."[61] In that sense, *Ladies in the Parlor* is their direct descendant. While the sex in *Ladies in the Parlor* is more alluded to than described, the very idea was sufficient to inflame the censors. And a conversation about abortion, as well as the suggestion of lesbianism and sadism, was sure to be condemned. In describing the women of *Ladies in the Parlor*, Tully avoids the sentimentality of hooker-with-a-heart-of-gold stories. He is more interested in the road that led these women to prostitution and their daily existence. He writes of them with sympathy but not romanticism. Mother Rosenbloom, the madam and one of Tully's most memorable characters, is both vulnerable and cunning. "Sex was an eternal war to her, covered by smiles and deceits—but a war in which a truce was always dangerous."[62] And it seems clear that as Tully describes the plight of these women, he's thinking of his own youth and the course his life might have taken had he been born female and not had the option of escaping in a boxcar. When one of the working girls is told, "So get out of the racket, kid," Tully is recalling the admonition he received from Josiah Flynt decades before.[63]

Mencken liked *Ladies in the Parlor* very much. "In fact," he wrote, "it seems to hang together better than any of your previous books." The story moved along, the characters were "plausible," and Tully's commentary was "shrewd and sound." "If I had to frame an objection it would be that you don't show enough of the daily life of the house—the squalor and imbecility behind the scenes. Leora is really almost a Socrates, for a whore. Their general mental level is hardly above that of so many policemen."[64] Those reservations aside, Mencken concluded that *Ladies in the Parlor* is "your best book. It shows a clearer design than any of the others, there is smoother writing, and it seems to me that the characters are more vivid. I can't recall a spot in the whole volume that is thin."[65] Mencken did not, however, like the dust-jacket illustration, which, with all its bric-a-brac and china, looked like a tearoom. "Doesn't the artist know that the gentlemen who frequented such places often fell into their cups, and that when they began to stagger around the parlor anything breakable was doomed?"[66] And, Mencken wondered, what sort of brothel didn't have an upright piano?

The first sign of real trouble came when, just two weeks before its June 1935 release, a large bookstore in Los Angeles, where Tully had a large following, had not ordered a single copy.[67] The situation, as it turned out, worked to the book's advantage. When high demand bumped up against zero supply in Hollywood, the result was buzz.[68] And Hollywood buzz was the best kind of buzz. *Ladies in the Parlor* would need all the buzz it could get, because this time reviews were not going to help sales.

Ted Robinson, Tully's champion at the *Cleveland Plain Dealer*, led the charge. "*Ladies in the Parlor* is the novel which I long suspected Jim Tully would be unable to resist the temptation to write."[69] Reviews from the East Coast papers were uniformly bad, with the *New York Times* even refusing to accept advertising for the book. The hypocrisy angered Tully, who wrote Mencken that "few newspapermen will admit they know anything of such houses."[70] The charge was not without merit, as many of the reviews stood not on the quality of the writing but on the subject. The *New York Herald-Tribune* was typical: "Mr. Tully . . . has now turned out something that will only hold your attention as long as you are inclined to hold your nose."[71]

Reviewers wringing their hands about sex might even boost sales, but in Canada the situation was hopeless. *Ladies in the Parlor* was simply banned outright.[72] And in New York City, not a place normally thought of as squeamish about sex, the New York Society for the Suppression of Vice made a formal complaint, citing "27 instances of obscenity, filth and lewdness."[73] "Christ," Tully joked to Mencken, "I thought I did better than that."[74] Just three weeks after the book's publication, Tully received word from his publisher, Jae Greenberg, that with the firm's legal fees growing, the balance of the book's advance was being withheld.[75] The damage rippled. Tully's magazine agent wrote that the *Saturday Evening Post* and the women's magazines would no longer even consider publishing Tully's work.[76] While these were never regular outlets for Tully's freelance work, the news was hardly welcome, coming on the heels of Mencken's decision in late 1933 to retire from the *American Mercury*.

No *American Mercury* contributor was more hurt by the loss of Mencken than Jim Tully. Other Mencken favorites, writers James Branch Cabell and

Joseph Hergesheimer, for example, were already well in decline. Tully's literary standing was past its peak, but a comeback would now prove especially difficult without Mencken's unique roar on the pages of the *Mercury*. Even Tully wondered what had become of Mencken's stable of writers. "I'm the only one of the gang," he wrote Mencken, "who has never conformed, and who might yet come through with a slashing book before I die."[77]

While Tully was accustomed to calls for censorship of his work, never before had such calls been entertained by the government. On August 17, 1935, a Manhattan magistrate, Jonah Goldstein, decided in Yorkville court that *Ladies in the Parlor* was indecent and that Greenberg Publishers would be put on trial in Special Sessions. Goldstein may not have been able to define pornography, but he knew it when he saw it. "The manner in which the subject is treated, in my opinion constitutes a violation of the law. You can call a spade a spade, but you don't have to give it a name that savors of the sewer. Throughout the book there are many evidences of emphasizing dirt in the raw, and the book is barren of any effort to treat the subject in a literary way."[78]

Watching his literary reputation and all he had worked for start to slip away, Tully defended himself to anyone who would listen. In *Rob Wagner's Script*, he made a declaration: "George Jean Nathan said to me in New York this spring, 'Jim, you really started the hard-boiled school.' The synthetic Hemingway, and even Dorothy Parker, get the uncertain credit."[79] Elsewhere, Tully defended his legacy to William Saroyan. "The short staccato sentence," he protested, "was my discovery. I used it in my articles in *Vanity Fair* and in three novels before Hemingway was published, even." Fueling his anger and frustration was an artist's resentment at having to defend his work. Tully was used to being dismissed as a mere primitive, but having his work branded pornography was more than he could bear. Jae Greenberg, for his part, tried to reassure Tully that everything possible was being done to prepare for trial. Rushing a new book into print, he added, would at least take advantage of the publicity surrounding *Ladies in the Parlor*.[80]

The indignities of summer would give way to heartbreak by autumn.

22

Return to the Ring

"It takes courage to meet an insignificant black female journalist," Emma Lou Sayers wrote of Jim Tully in 1927. "He likes colored people," she noted. "We are human beings and Jim Tulley [sic] impresses one as liking all things human." And "colored people are no strangers to him. He has hoboed with them, slept, eaten, worked, and begged with them."[1] Sayers was further impressed that Tully had not only read the famous W. E. B. DuBois but also praised Eric Walrond, whose *Tropic Death*, a collection of short stories set in the Caribbean, had been published the previous year.

In light of all this, Tully's use of the word "nigger" in the presence of Langston Hughes must rank near the top of the long list of most embarrassing things any drunk has ever slurred. That it happened at a party in Hughes's honor puts it at the cringe-inducing pinnacle of social error. Hughes had been interested in Tully's work as far back as 1926, when he attended the New York premiere of *Black Boy*.[2] And with Hughes having spent part of his adolescence at sea as a mess boy, they had in common a youth of wanderlust and books. The occasion was a small dinner party for Hughes thrown by Lillian Mae Ehrman. Ehrman, whose brother was an important talent scout, was well connected to Hollywood's elite and phoned Hughes to ask whom he would like to invite. If she was surprised that the first person Hughes requested was Jim Tully, she didn't show it. And perhaps, Hughes continued, Katharine Hepburn could be invited.[3] And with that, the seeds of trouble were sown. Ehrman misunderstood Hughes and invited Theresa Helburn of the Theatre Guild. The party was set for Saturday, August 10, 1935, at Ehrman's Beverly Hills home.[4]

Jim Tully first stopped by a cocktail party, so that when he arrived at the dinner party with Myrtle, he was late, angry, and drunk. The attacks on *Ladies in the Parlor*, heaped upon his smoldering anger at Alton, and doused with whiskey, had left him in a combustible mood. Introductions were made, with Tully scarcely acknowledging two other members of the party, a European choreographer and an Earl Carroll showgirl. The group was seated in the dining room and had barely tasted their soup when Hughes innocently mentioned to Helburn that the Theatre Guild had once turned down one of his plays. As Helburn politely explained the play's shortcomings, Tully cut her off, saying he didn't see why Helburn had a right to express *any* opinion on the theater. There was a momentary silence before Helburn, ignoring the remark, continued her explanation.

Tully was not so easily ignored. Hughes recalled Tully's heated response. "But what is the Theatre Guild? Nothing but a great louse on the tree of the American theater!"[5] Helburn stared daggers in Tully's direction and icily launched a defense of the guild. She could scarcely be heard over Tully, who had reached full roar. Hughes, feeling he had somehow initiated hostilities, tried to defuse the situation. It was too late. Tully was volcanic and, turning on Hughes, erupted, "You don't need to be kind by trying to change the subject, Langston Hughes. . . . You look like a decent man. But you don't need to protect the Theatre Guild—that blood-sucking Broadway combine! You keep quiet."[6]

Cooler heads did not prevail. Helburn needled that she must have rejected one of Tully's plays. "You're not big enough to turn down a play of mine," Tully shot back. Ehrman, sensing that an evening of convivial literary palaver was teetering on the brink of epic social disaster, pleaded for calm. Tully again turned to Hughes, who recalled the evening in his autobiography *I Wonder as I Wander*.

> "Langston Hughes," said Jim Tully solemnly, "you have no business out here in Beverly Hills. These people will ruin you. And for God's sake, Langston, stay away from Hollywood! Look at me! As a writer, they've ruined me. Hollywood will buy you, and ruin you! They ignore you until they find out you've got something they can use. Then they buy you—and lynch you with money. Stay away from Hollywood! Stay away from Beverly Hills! Stay down on Central Avenue with your poor hurt niggers!"
>
> At the word *nigger* everyone gasped, except myself. The hostess reddened.

"Langston Hughes knows what I mean," said Jim Tully. "He's got their souls in his hands. He writes about them. He knows what I mean when I say niggers—as you people say it."[7]

Tully's version varied slightly. According to him, turning to Hughes, he said, "Keep still. You're a nigger, and I'm a bum, and we're here because we can string words together"—the implication being that the world of wealth and privilege would not otherwise have any use for them.[8] Tully's caution to "stay away from Hollywood" was more than friendly advice from one writer to another. It was a biblical warning not unlike Josiah Flynt's warning to Jim thirty years earlier that the road was crawling with serpents.

The exchange, which left Ehrman mortified, Myrtle Tully embarrassed, and Helburn in tears, would even find its way into the *Los Angeles Times*.[9] Least affected were Hughes and Tully, who stayed long after Helburn fled the party. Tully further explained himself and insisted Hughes come to lunch at his home the following week.[10] Hughes recalled Tully's parting words: "We've got things in common, you and I. We're both beaten up by life—but we fight back. That's what I like about you—you fight back, Langston! Call me up and tell me what day you can chow with me."[11]

The following day, Myrtle insisted Jim call and apologize. Myrtle was, as usual, full of good intentions but perhaps should have realized that her husband took direction, even sound direction, badly. Jim phoned Ehrman and scolded her for inviting Helburn in the first place.[12]

When Hughes called a couple of days later, he asked if he might bring Harry Armstrong, a boxer turned trainer who wanted to write. Tully quickly agreed and a date was set. Hughes and Armstrong planned on taking the interurban from downtown Los Angeles to Tully's home, an hour-and-a-half ride. Harry's protégé, Henry Jackson, who had taken his mentor's name and boxed as Henry Armstrong, was free that morning and offered to drive the men and wait in the car.[13] When they arrived, Hughes mentioned that the young boxer was waiting outside in the car and Tully immediately went out to invite Henry to join them.[14]

Like Langston Hughes and Jim Tully, so too does it seem that Henry Armstrong and Tully were destined to meet. In his autobiography, *Gloves, Glory and God*, Armstrong remembered lying awake one night in St. Louis when he felt the irresistible pull of California. It was the depth of the Depression, and neither Henry nor his trainer and running buddy, Harry, had anything like train fare to California. Writing in the third person, Armstrong recalled, "Well, if there wasn't money for the trip, maybe it could be made without money. He had read somewhere of an author named Jim Tully, who had been a fighter and a hobo. If Tully could make it all over the country as a hobo, surely Henry could get to California that way."[15]

They caught a westbound freight train in Carondelet, Missouri, and a few years later washed up at Tully's Toluca Lake door. Tully liked Henry Armstrong immediately. "When he entered the room," Tully wrote, "I knew at once there was a man in the house."[16] As badly as dinner with Hughes had gone the previous week, lunch with Hughes and the boxers proved a great success. Armstrong was mostly silent but listened intently as his trainer and Hughes described how tough it was for a boxer to make a living. Tully could only nod in recognition. Armstrong had lost fixed matches with the Mexican fighter Alberto "Baby" Arizmendi that he'd clearly won and was as broke in Los Angeles as he'd been in St. Louis. "You might see a way out, Jim," Hughes said. "Henry's beaten him twice and lost two decisions—he's innocent and honest, and it isn't right."[17] To make matters worse, Wirt Ross, who bought Armstrong's contract when the boxer was a minor, had scheduled him to again fight Arizmendi. Moved by the hobo turned boxer's plight, one he knew firsthand, Tully impulsively raised the possibility of buying Armstrong's contract from Ross. Armstrong was very enthusiastic, leaving Tully to mull it over. Watching his guests leave, Tully regretted not hearing more from the young boxer. "My God," he later commented, "a great man has been here. Armstrong was the wisest of us all. He saved his breath for the pork chops."[18]

The prospect of a return to boxing, albeit outside the ropes, was tempting. "For days the idea burned in my head. I would again enter the wild world of the bruiser. The thought made the bubbles burst in my blood. It would be a return to the care-free days I'd loved. I had fought hard for freedom and found it another jail."[19] It is a measure of how miserable Tully had become that he considered boxing a way out of writing, rather than the reverse. In the end, he came to the conclusion he'd reached more than two decades before and chose writing over boxing. Tully instead promised to speak to Al Jolson, who had both the interest and means to promote a young boxer.[20] Tully's decision not to buy Armstrong's contract seems not to have hurt the young boxer in the least. Armstrong fought another ten years and, for a few months in late 1938, simultaneously held the world's featherweight, welterweight, and lightweight championships. Armstrong was elected to the Boxing Hall of Fame in 1954.[21]

Boxing was one thing; *writing* about boxing was another. In his 1934 *Esquire* essay "The Manly Art," Tully wrote, "The great book of the prize ring is yet to be written. The man who will write it will be one who has been smeared with its blood."[22] While litterateurs as different as George Bernard Shaw and Ernest Hemingway had tried, none had boxed professionally and couldn't hope to really convey what it was like inside the ropes. Two years later, tired of waiting for an honest novel of the ring, Tully decided to write it himself.

Defending his son and *Ladies in the Parlor* in the first half of 1935 had been necessary but had cost him valuable writing time. To pay the bills, he dashed off a few Hollywood profiles (Joe E. Brown, Ginger Rogers, William Powell, W. C. Fields, James Cagney, Clark Gable, Gary Cooper, Barbara Stanwyck, Norma Shearer, Roscoe "Fatty" Arbuckle, Robert Montgomery, Wallace Beery).[23] He also collected rejections on a Clarence Darrow profile and a Chaplin piece that was considered potentially libelous.[24] And with radio commentator and columnist Walter Winchell and old friend Judge Ben Lindsey, Tully worked hard to save the life of Clyde Holford. A twenty-five-year-old orphan and former road-kid, Holford was slated for execution in Oklahoma for killing another inmate during a fight. Tully's public campaign to spare Holford added "sob sister" to the long list of names he'd been called.[25] And Jim received a letter about another former road-kid from an official in Arizona. Billy Ross, his friend from the orphanage and later his traveling companion, had died broke and alone. What should be done? Jim replied that Bill had "served time with me for being an orphan and that he had no kin." They should bury him where they bury all poor people. "He'd slept in harder beds than any in the Potter's field."[26]

Jim was anxious to return to real writing, and when Jae Greenberg, hoping to take advantage of the publicity surrounding *Ladies in the Parlor,* asked in mid-July of 1935 for the first 20,000 words of Tully's next novel, Jim had his chance.[27] By early September, he had a first draft and had built up a head of steam in the writing of a novel about a young boxer named Shane Rory.[28] His confidence in the work soared. The boxing novel was going to be good, *very* good. This one would restore his good name and get him the respect that he felt was his due. The past year had been one of survival, but now there was hope and he could finally feel his long depression beginning to lift. Two weeks later, he was knocked off the tracks.

Early on the morning of Sunday, September 15, 1935, sixteen-year-old Juanita Shepard of Westwood, California, was beaten and left unconscious at her parents' doorstep. Found and revived by her father, a local restaurant owner, she told a shocking story. She had gone to a dance in Susanville with a local lumberjack. On the twenty-two-mile drive home through the mountains, he attacked and beat her when she resisted his sexual advances. The girl's father called police. The suspect was arrested at his dormitory at the lumber camp and brought back to Westwood. When word of the attack spread throughout the small mountain community, a group of vigilantes formed outside the town jail bent on lynching the suspect. For his own safety, the suspect was returned to Susanville and held in the Lassen County Jail.[29] The news hit the papers when the suspect finally admitted to being the son of Jim Tully, the famed "hobo novelist."[30] The *Sacramento Bee,* whose coverage Jim would find objectionable, noted that Alton was defiant and quoted him as boasting, "My father will get me out of this."[31]

By the time reporters reached Jim Tully at home, the suspect's father was still stunned.

> I understood my son was making good progress in the lumber camp. If he is guilty as reported then I do not condone his action in any way, nor do I expect him to have any special treatment. I only want him to have a fair trial and justice be done.
>
> In view of the record of his case I am seriously considering asking the court to question his mentality, and if he be found mentally ill that he be placed in an institution where they take care of such sick people.[32]

With that, Tully, emotionally devastated, went into seclusion to await developments while Myrtle and a friend made the long drive north to cooperate with the authorities, see Alton, and visit the victim and her family.[33] Several months later, Jim recalled his devastation to Frank Scully, "I broke once in my life. You saw that—for a few minutes—but I took five raps and a thousand headlines before I did."[34] Friends, wanting to help, struggled to find the right words. Jack Dempsey phoned with an offer of ten thousand dollars.[35]

When Jim finally learned the details of the case, he issued a statement in what must certainly be the five most difficult paragraphs he'd ever written.

> I had an agreement with the boy that if trouble came again he would take it standing up. He is. His denials that he is my son were but pathetic attempts to shield me.
>
> While I have tried to protect him in every way possible, I now feel that something else should be done, not only to protect others, but himself. My deep sympathy goes to the girl and her parents.

So much sympathy has been extended to me across the nation that I can only hope that more will be reserved for the boy. He is suffering from a terrifying disease, for which he must wear the stripes of a felon.

I have been a more or less useful citizen. I now put my trust in the State. Will it cure or wreck him? It is seldom successful in curing, but then, in fairness, it must be said that most of the major ills of humanity are practically insoluble.

I ask nothing now but the cooperation of the State to cure the boy, and of the public, the charity of its silence.[36]

The statement reflects a view shared by Mencken in a letter six months earlier: "My belief is that all of the really salient human problems are intrinsically insoluble."[37] Against the advice of counsel, who saw the possibility of an acquittal, Alton kept his word to his father and insisted on pleading guilty. He was sentenced to San Quentin for one to fifty years. The choice of San Quentin could hardly have been more embarrassing to Jim. Seven years before he had visited the prison and described it as a "breeding place of crime" and called the California prison board "a bunch of illiterates with the psychology of babbitts."[38] Warden Holohan refused to discuss the insult with the press and promised that Alton Tully would be humanely treated. A ban on visits to San Quentin by Jim Tully would, however, remain in place.

Tully's views on prison reform made him an easy target. When one editorial writer attacked Jim, blaming him for abetting the attack, he wrote a letter to the editor:

I do feel that you should investigate the facts, both in Los Angles and Susanville as to my connection with the boy's escapades, and write a public apology. I may be "a so-called hobo novelist" but I have made myself an honorable citizen with the friendship of honorable men who are my friends in this trouble. . . .

. . . If the boy is a social menace we should make an attempt to cure him. It is true that a lynching would solve his problem, and slightly muddle mine. A sick youth is hardly a felon, though we are not advanced far enough as a social state to do anything else but put such a brand upon him. . . .

. . . If my letter has too much heat, I am sorry. I do not write it so. Many worse men than myself have not lived to see the day their son enters San Quentin.[39]

Sending Alton to prison rather than a mental hospital, Frank Scully cautioned Jim, not only would ruin any chance of Alton getting help but would irrevocably stain Jim's reputation. Alton must, Scully wrote, be sent to an asylum. "You see such a course is not only sensible; it blocks the stampede to kill you. 'Of course he rapes girls. Why wouldn't he? He reads his father's books.' That's the sort of attack on you which must be stopped."[40]

Alton wrote his father, asking for direction. Jim's two-page letter reflected his deeply held belief in the power of good books to transform broken lives. Hardy, Dostoyevsky, Tolstoy, early Gorky, Turgenev, and Sinclair Lewis are all recommended. Jim also suggested Durant's *Story of Philosophy*, with special attention to Schopenhauer, as well as Boswell's *Life of Samuel Johnson*, Pepys's *Diary*, and St. Augustine's *Confessions*. Jack London was recommended for light reading, and Dreiser for serious reading. Hemingway, he also noted, was "well worth your attention." Drama, Jim acknowledged, was not easy reading, but Shakespeare was essential. Finally, Jim urged Alton to avoid bitterness and self-pity, to treat his prison term as an extended college course, and to use his time for growth and development.[41]

Shakespeare could wait. Alton wrote back and mentioned without a trace of irony that he was currently reading *Memoirs of a Casanova*.[42] An unintended consequence of encouraging Alton to read was Alton's decision to write. Although Jim normally encouraged young writers, especially those incarcerated, he bristled at the idea of Alton becoming a writer. Alton tried in vain to reassure his father that publicity over his own writing would not attach itself to his father.[43]

Just a couple of days after he wrote to Alton, the subject of Hemingway surfaced again. Tully was always more than a little annoyed to find himself compared to the younger writer, but there was no denying Hemingway's talent. While their styles were similar, there was, in Tully's view, a significant difference between the two. Jim read that Hemingway had called some of his New York friends "angleworms in bottles." Jim wrote a friend, "He figures, I guess, that life isn't important in New York. I'm different—a stenographer's tears on Tenth Avenue mean more to me than all the lions in Africa."[44] Nor was Tully impressed with Hemingway's bravado. When Hemingway jabbed at F. Scott Fitzgerald by name in *The Snows of Kilimanjaro*, Tully saw it as the low blow of a typewriter tough guy.[45] And when Hemingway famously came to blows with progressive writer Max Eastman in Maxwell Perkins's office, Tully commented, "Neither could fight his way out of a paper bag." Eastman, at least, would laugh off the incident, "but Hemingway would still be mad."[46]

Perhaps the only good news to be found in watching his son enter San Quentin was that it may have slightly numbed Jim to the news in November of 1935 that the Special Sessions Court in New York City declared *Ladies in the Parlor* objectionable. The 2–1 decision banned the book and fined the book's publisher fifty dollars. Jim could take some comfort in the dissenting opinion, which noted that "The function of literary effort reaches beyond a bedtime story with an obligatory happy ending."[47]

Mencken suspected that an established publisher along the lines of Scribner's or Macmillan would not have faced such legal scrutiny, nor would a more respectable author. "The book, as a matter of fact, is extraordinarily clean. I marveled, reading it, at your skill in keeping it so. Certainly it is not one-tenth as dirty as some of the books of Hemingway and Faulkner, and yet they have not been molested."[48]

The decision was the end of *Ladies in the Parlor*. Greenberg notified Tully's agent that they were abandoning the book and were stuck with a thousand copies.[49] Jim complained to Greenberg, who responded, "You gave us a book which all the critics practically to a man agree is your worst book. The reviews were 100% unfavorable and they were reviewed by the same people who have praised your other books. Then the book is one which we were prohibited from selling in many quarters. . . . Finally, we fought the thing through the courts to the last ditch employing the best counsel and we took a financial licking on the book all around."[50]

For ever-vigilant New York City vice squads, *Ladies in the Parlor* was Public Enemy No. 1. Erotica was routinely confiscated and consigned to police bonfires, with full benefit of press coverage. At one such book burning officiated by a deputy police commissioner, *Ladies in the Parlor* enjoyed top honors, with 114 copies reduced to ashes.[51] "I worked three years on that book," Tully later recalled, "and as a result of the suppression found my whole income from that three years' effort amounted to five hundred dollars. The book at best never would have made its expenses, but at least it should have had a chance to prove Mencken's contention that it's the best of all my novels."[52]

Realizing that *Ladies in the Parlor* was beyond repair, Tully looked to crawl from the wreckage with a new book. He sounded out Maxwell Perkins, who had become a legend as the editor of Fitzgerald, Hemingway, and Thomas

Wolfe, on a book about boxing but was torn between fiction and nonfiction. He felt it necessary to convince the legendary editor that he was not a has-been. "I've played in bad luck the past few years, and have done considerable movie work, but I'm by no means out of the running as a writer."[53]

Tully was far from a has-been, but his year-end royalty statement punctuated a bad year. *Ladies in the Parlor* had earned him just two hundred dollars in the last six months of 1935.[54] Perkins declined a boxing history but asked to see the novel.[55] Tully returned to the Shane Rory manuscript he'd been working on before the tribulations of autumn, now titled *The Bruiser*. Perkins was not enthusiastic about the draft he received of *The Bruiser*, and for the time being, the two went their separate ways.

Capitalizing on the publicity from *Ladies in the Parlor* was paramount. To speed completion of *The Bruiser*, then nearly finished, Tully decided in March of 1936 that he could no longer freelance puff pieces like his recent *Los Angeles Times* story on Pete the dog from the *Little Rascals* series.[56] For the time being, he would forgo writing for the fan magazines.[57] He told one reporter that the pieces earned him two hundred dollars apiece, and "I do it to make a living and enable myself to write one honest piece a year, and anyway, what the hell, it's all honest writing, anyway. I write what I know... and believe me, they don't pay me what they pay Hemingway, although they should!"[58] It was becoming clear, however, that the "honest piece a year" might not be a novel. Jim wrote Frank Scully, "I'd like to find a new medium. I feel the novel is worn out. Even critics don't read novels."[59] Just what that "new medium" might look like remained to be seen.

Amid his various projects, Jim did find time to complete a small real estate deal, trading some bonds for a small ranch near Canoga Park in the San Fernando Valley.[60] The one-hundred-acre ranch, dubbed "Faraway Farm," was leased to an alfalfa farmer.[61] The deal appealed not only to Tully's love of land, but it would provide another source of income. And it was hoped that household finances might also be bolstered by the new firm of Newcom & Tully, which was Myrtle's entry into the world of Hollywood agentry.

With a solid draft of *The Bruiser* in hand, Tully began shopping the book around. Having immersed himself in boxing, he flew to New York in April to work with Jack Dempsey on a play based on the legendary champion's life.[62] Waiting for him on his return was a letter with the unwelcome news that his 1934 federal tax return was going to be audited.[63]

Tully first sent *The Bruiser* to Boni, the publisher of *Jarnegan* and *Laughter in Hell*, who wanted the manuscript so badly that he signed away the film rights.⁶⁴ By late June, Tully had misgivings about signing with Boni and his request to be released from his contract was granted.⁶⁵ Frustrated with what he saw as Jim's fussiness over publishers, Tully's agent, Sydney Sanders, temporarily quit, leaving Jim free to strike his own deal for *The Bruiser*.⁶⁶

Hoping that the *The Bruiser* would make a bigger splash with Simon & Schuster, which had rejected *Ladies in the Parlor,* Tully mailed the manuscript in July to Mencken, who hand-delivered it to Max Schuster.⁶⁷ With Tully now years away from having anything like a successful book, the rejection a few weeks later from Simon & Schuster rattled his confidence.⁶⁸ He wrote Mencken, "I am not hurt much, as I have such contempt for the novel, that I know I'm not much good at the writing of one."⁶⁹ While waiting to find a publisher for *The Bruiser,* Tully returned to the surer ground and better pay of Hollywood. Gossip columnists reported that Tully was regularly having lunch with Bette Davis, then in a contract dispute with Warner Brothers for agreeing to appear in two British films. The lunches proved to be business, not pleasure, when Tully's profile of Davis appeared in both British and U.S. publications.⁷⁰ And Tully picked up quick cash for an article on Jean Harlow for a British fan magazine.⁷¹

When Greenberg got back to Tully regarding *Ladies in the Parlor,* he managed to smooth things over with Tully by promising to "help me lift Ladies out of the mud."⁷² What exactly Greenberg or anyone could do to rescue the book is unclear, but it was what Jim wanted to hear, and he sent Greenberg a draft of *The Bruiser* in late July and signed a contract shortly after.⁷³ However, Greenberg's insistence that *The Bruiser* have a happy ending gave Tully pause.⁷⁴ Greenberg was not alone in finding problems with the book's conclusion. Mencken found the ending "abrupt."⁷⁵

Greenberg got right to work soliciting blurbs from Gene Fowler, Walter Winchell, H. L. Mencken, and Frank Scully.⁷⁶ He also contacted George Bellows's estate for permission to use his masterpiece, *Stag at Sharkey's,* for the dust jacket. The executor declined but wrote Greenberg, "If I could say yes to anyone it would be you for Mr. Tully's novel."⁷⁷

By early August, Tully had rewritten the conclusion.⁷⁸ As one reporter described it, "It was to end with the girl sending the discouraged fighter back to the ring with lusty admonitions about the old gutseroo and courage and try-try-again and I'll-be-waiting. So the guy goes back to the ring and finally he becomes champ but in the process he gets lobbed around until he's slug-nutty. Punch drunk. So he goes back to the Girl and marries her and she's got a slap-happy, drooling champ on her hands for the rest of her life."⁷⁹

This was not the happy ending Greenberg wanted and, with yet another ending, Tully delivered the completed manuscript that September.[80] *The Bruiser* was set for release later in the fall. Mencken wrote, "If I were still editor of *The American Mercury,* your description of that prize fight would already be in type."[81] Returning to the bout in another letter, he concluded, "It is one of the best things anybody has ever done."[82] Greenberg was equally optimistic and asked for a proposal for Tully's next book.[83] A month later, Greenberg's mood darkened. He complained that advanced sales for *The Bruiser* were poor, citing resistance from booksellers and women to boxing novels.[84] Tully, never known for patience with his publishers, could hardly be blamed for being irritated. Greenberg was well aware that he was publishing a boxing novel, and pronouncing a book a failure before a single review appeared was premature at best.

With his mood still soured by Greenberg's dire forecast about *The Bruiser,* Tully's career hit bottom when a letter from Bennett Cerf, the publisher of the Modern Library, landed on his desk with a thud. Cerf declined to reprint any of Tully's books in the Underworld series, noting, "I have done some quiet checking up on the sale of these books in the last few years . . . and am sorry to say that I find the demand, in New York at least, is practically nil."[85] All hope rested with *The Bruiser.*

23

The Bruiser

Novelists who choose sports as a central theme face a common pitfall. If, at the novel's conclusion, the protagonist proves the odds surmountable and knocks out his opponent or hits a home run with two outs in the ninth, most readers will leave thinking they've just finished a boilerplate boy's book. If the hero lands on the canvas or strikes out at the book's conclusion, readers will understandably feel let down. *Blue Ruin* by Brendan Boyd and *Shoeless Joe* by W. P. Kinsella, for example, wisely avoid this trap. And two of the finest sports films, John Sayles's *Eight Men Out* and Martin Scorsese's *Raging Bull*, perhaps the best of all movies about the ring, also succeed by not aligning their story with a particular contest.

The Bruiser follows Shane Rory from his days as a road-kid through his unsteady ascent up the boxing ranks and culminates in his title fight for the heavyweight championship. With the book so structured, Tully's problems with the book's ending were inevitable. His solution was to have Shane Rory win the title fight and hand over the crown to a black boxer and fellow road-kid whose route to the top would have otherwise been blocked by a color line. It was a happy ending, to be sure, but with a twist. If the conclusion of *The Bruiser* seems a bit pat, the thirty-one chapters that precede it are not. Shane Rory, like Jim Tully, was an accidental fighter. He tried boxing, won his fight, and "The course of his life changed. He was a combination road kid and wandering fighter."[1]

The description of road-kid and fighter could only have been written by one who knew both road and ring intimately. The action inside the ropes bristles with jabs, hooks, crosses, and uppercuts. And when Tully has a veteran boxer tell Shane, "I like you, that's all—you take it and lash it out—and you don't whimper," he is echoing Jim's parting words to Langston Hughes on the evening of that fateful dinner party just months earlier.[2] While Tully paints Shane in heroic colors, *The Bruiser* avoids sentimentality by taking an unflinching look at all the characters who encrust boxing, including broken-down punch-drunks, gamblers, cheats, and other denizens of the ring.

Like the book's author, Shane's life is transformed by books, or, in Shane's case, one book in particular: Helen Keller's *Story of My Life*. Reading the book in one sitting, Shane closes Keller's memoir and realizes that despite Keller's blindness and deafness, "She's seen more than I have." Shane "had never been aware of bees and flowers. The blind girl had. The world was a place he had never known."[3] It is one of Tully's favorite themes: a damaged life transformed by a book.

Reviews of *The Bruiser* were the best Tully had received in years and among the best he'd ever had. *New York Times* critic E. C. Beckwith acknowledged the novel followed the standard formula for boxing books but recognized that Tully had "manipulated [it] with so skillful an artistry that the resultant work acquires a freshness and vitality which one had long ago thought extinct in pugilistic fiction." There is a "touch of heart interest," Beckwith continued. "But it is in discourses expressed through his characters on ring science, in his descriptions of fistic events, in his firsthand knowledge of the game in every department, that Mr. Tully comes very close to writing, in *The Bruiser*, the best novel of its type this reviewer has read in late years."[4]

David Tilden, critic at *Books*, noted that *The Bruiser* is not "literary in any sense of the word, but the story is swiftly moving and, with just enough of disorder and emotion to make it a thoroughly human document."[5] Frank Scully picked up on Tully's accurate portrayal of a punch-drunk boxer, a subject that had received scant attention before *The Bruiser*. Tully's punch-drunk reminded Scully of Ad Wolgast, "a once prominent bruiser who ended his ring career throwing punches at shuffling phantoms in the cell of an insane asylum."[6] Wolgast was indeed the basis for Tully's punch-drunk boxer. Jim had kept tabs on his old boss who had been sent to the Camarillo State Hospital in 1927, where he remained for the rest of his life.[7] In addition to basing the character Adam Walsh on Wolgast, Tully used Joe Gans as the basis for Joe Crane, Jack Tierney for Chicago Jed Williams, and Johnny "Battling" Schultz for Battling Ryan.[8]

Jim was buoyed by the good reviews, writing Nathan, "The novel, 'Bruiser' is starting well—400 copies sold yesterday.... It's the starting of my second wind."[9] And to Mencken, Tully could crow that *The Bruiser* was proving to be his best book "critically and financially" since 1929.[10] And Stanley Rose did his part, filling the window of his famous Hollywood bookshop with copies of the new book.[11] With so much riding on *The Bruiser*, Jim was not above jousting with reviewers he felt gave the book less than its due. When his hometown paper, the *Los Angeles Times*, accorded the book the briefest of mentions, Jim complained, "Isn't a book that is the best of its kind on a subject worth more than two lines?"[12]

Praise for *The Bruiser* arrived from other quarters as well. Former heavyweight champion Gene Tunney, who had defeated Jack Dempsey twice, wrote to thank Jim for his inscribed copy. "It has great dramatic quality and from the pugilistic point of view is technically perfect."[13] Damon Runyon called it the greatest story of the ring ever told.[14] W. C. Fields thanked Jim for his copy, adding in typically Fieldsian fashion, "Not a spoonful of the vile stuff has passed underneath my nose these five months."[15] Nella Braddy, biographer of Anne Sullivan Macy, wrote on behalf of Helen Keller to say that "*The Bruiser* reached Miss Helen Keller's home in the midst of the greatest sorrow of her life—the death on Oct. 20 of the great Irishwoman, Anne Sullivan Macy, who had been her teacher and constant companion for forty-nine years." Braddy told Miss Keller about the book on the train returning from the funeral. "She was very much touched to know that you had thought of using her in the way you did and asked me to thank you."[16] Not all notices were so sublime. Alton wrote Myrtle from San Quentin:

> *The Bruiser* is going over with a bang here—everyone is asking to read it, some getting half sore when I let someone else read it before them. The average reader gets to the Cyclone fight on the 1st night before the lights go out—and comes to me the next marveling and talking of it, I think "Wait until you reach the Sully fight" sure enough they come out raving about it with a half dozen friends in tow asking to get on the line for it.... The old fighters rave about it more than the rest—all agree that dad is the master of his subject.[17]

Good reviews from inmates always pleased Jim, but he never knew quite what to make of his son. Alton would remain a mystery to his father for the rest of his life. When, in August 1936, Myrtle made the four-hundred-mile trip to visit him in prison, she was received with crude sexual comments. She left her stepson money and made the six-hour return trip in shock.[18] Despite his vulgarity, Myrtle continued to write Alton regularly, far more often than his parents or sister. Even the prison board commented on the "laxity of the Tullys in writing," Alton wrote his stepmother. "They don't miss a bet. One of them asked—Your father is a writer isn't he."[19] Jim's unwillingness to write his son fueled Alton's self-pity, resulting in a steady stream of woebegone letters to Myrtle.[20] Nor were Alton and Trilby close, having seen each other only twice in the past three years.[21] When in September 1936 Alton's prison term was finally set at twenty-five years by the State Board of Prison Sentences and Paroles, it would be Myrtle who served for years as Alton's only reliable correspondent.[22]

In fairness, Alton seemed just as puzzled by his distant father. He was fond of recalling the time the two of them were driving to San Francisco and Jim refused to yield the road to a hog "as big as an elephant," snuffling in the middle of the road. After missing the hog by inches, and going up on two wheels in one retelling, Jim turned to his ashen-faced son and said simply, "Everything alright kid?"[23]

While time crawled for Alton, it seemed only to accelerate with each passing year for his father. Two other events in 1936 served to remind Jim of his advancing years. Jim and Myrtle attended Trilby's high school graduation in June.[24] Upset about her brother, she came to her father in tears. Jim gently asked her to hold her head up. "You see, Trilby, he's ours—we've just got to stand by him."[25]

On December 27, Jim was notified by telegram that his father had died.[26] A visit from Jim's father two years before had gone so well that Jim had arranged for his father to travel by bus from Celina, Ohio, where he was living, to spend the winter, perhaps longer, with him in California.[27] Near Topeka, the old man had chest pains but refused to see a doctor and continued on to Las Vegas, New Mexico, where he was finally hospitalized. He spent a couple of days in the Catholic hospital before his heart gave out.[28] His last word was, simply, "Jim."[29] His eyes, Jim recalled, "were closed by Irish nuns."[30] Rather than have him transported to California or back to Ohio, Jim decided he would be buried in New Mexico. Myrtle made the arrangements, which included High Mass, by telephone.[31] "I smile in ironical sadness," Jim wrote a few years later. "A pagan all his life, and never inside a church, unless by force of circumstances, he now has the first grave at the entrance of a Catholic cemetery."[32]

Over the years, Jim had been as puzzled by his father as he would be by Alton. And as late as August of 1936, Jim learned he could still be dumbfounded by his elderly father. Mrs. Eva Mae (Rogers) Basch of Owasso, Michigan, wrote Jim that she was looking for the father who had abandoned her and her mother decades earlier. Mrs. Basch's mother told her that her father had once returned, but her mother, hurt by his desertion, had turned him away. When her mother named the father as Jim Tully, Mrs. Basch took a great interest in the famous writer and had followed Jim's career for years. Finally overcoming her hatred of him for his "seeming lack of decency," she now wanted to meet the man named as her father—all of which must have left Jim puzzled until he read that she was born in January 1895, when Jim was only eight. The relief that Mrs. Basch was not a long-lost daughter must have been supplanted by the creeping suspicion that she was a long-lost half-sister.[33]

Alton, typically self-absorbed, had never bothered to write his grandfather, as his father had repeatedly requested, but did show unusual insight in reflecting on his death. "Poor dad," he wrote Myrtle, "certainly has his hands full supporting the universe. No other Tully ever had the ability to make over 50¢hr; and the burden lands on him."[34]

The Bruiser would do little to lighten Jim's financial burden.[35] Through November of 1937, not many more than 2,300 copies sold, generating just a few hundred dollars for its disappointed author.[36] His experience with *The Bruiser* convinced Tully that books about boxing faced too many obstacles. Women simply wouldn't read them and fight fans might "pay $50 for a seat to a fight but not 5 cents to read about them."[37] Nor was an honest history of boxing likely to be successful, "because too many of its subjects have been outside the law. The early history of boxing is studded with men who ended in disgrace and on the gallows."[38] While slow out of the gate, demand for *The Bruiser* would remain steady and the book would be reprinted twice in the following decade.

Of all Jim's unpublished fiction, perhaps none is more tantalizing than "Half-Sister of the Lord." The idea of a book based on the life of Aimee Semple McPherson, the country's foremost evangelist, received a positive response from Mencken. "If you told the truth in it, of course, the old gal would bellow violently, but I don't think her bellowings would really incommode you."[39] Tully fiddled with the manuscript throughout early 1937 and, with sales of *The Bruiser* fading quickly, had high hopes of following *The Bruiser*'s critical success with a more marketable book. Undeterred by his experience with *Ladies in the Parlor*, he considered a scene with the evangelist engaged in sex until Mencken counseled, "Stick to her miracles, and keep off the fornication."[40] The book's premise of a love triangle with the evangelist, her boyfriend, and God was dangerous enough.[41]

Work on "Half-Sister of the Lord" aside, a follow-up to *The Bruiser* would not appear for another five years. Tully's output during the late 1930s and early 1940s was limited to magazine work. His fascination with boxing continued with a fine 1937 profile of Dempsey for the *Ring*.[42] And *Esquire* continued to be a reliable and, at $250 a pop, lucrative outlet.[43] *Esquire* ran an autobiographical hobo story, a prison story, and a Chaplin piece and even published Tully's version of "The Dying Hobo," an old hobo ballad that, by the 1930s, was heard more often in the classroom than in the hobo jungle.[44] Tully's original verses for "The Dying Hobo" marked his first published poetry since his Ohio days two decades earlier. And there was still a strong market for Tully's Hollywood profiles.

By midsummer of 1937 he had completed "Half-Sister of the Lord" but was having difficulty finding a publisher.[45] With no book forthcoming, everything in Tully's life was grist for a story. One newspaper syndicate passed on "Hollywood Marriage," Tully's account of his divorce from Marna. As Marna had fallen on hard financial times and her husband was an aspiring writer, the potential of a libel suit was too great.[46] And Tully looted his literary past as well, creating a series of stories about director Jack Jarnegan. He sold them to a major newspaper syndicate for $750 apiece. The money was so good for the Jarnegan short stories that Tully again stopped writing for the Hollywood fan magazines, although he was not above taking the fast cash the *Los Angeles Times* sent his way for short profiles on Carole Lombard, Marlene Dietrich, Tyrone Power, and others.[47]

Tully was himself the subject of a profile by old friend Frank Scully in 1937. Scully enjoyed throwing small parties at his home, and Tully, director John Ford, and producer Al Lewin were frequent guests.[48] No one, with the possible exceptions of Myrtle Tully and Mencken, knew Jim so well. The article in *Scribner's* (later reprinted in *Rogues' Gallery*, a collection of Scully's profiles) comes close to capturing the enigmatic writer in print, revealing what Scully called "the secret of what makes this *enfant terrible* of Hollywood a mighty oak of American letters": "The bigger you are the harder you fall. There isn't a mind in all Hollywood that can stand up to him in a finish fight. From picture producers down to stars, from script writers up to traffic cops, all of them have tried to kill him with logic, and the more foolhardy ones with their fists, and all of them have been dragged home, beaten men and women." None of which endeared him to Hollywood. Scully noted: "Producers rarely hire him. They'd pay a palooka as illiterate as a cow $2500 a week to do a circus picture before they'd pay Tully $600 to do a job ten times as well. The reason for this is they can impose their will only on inferior men." More significant, Scully recognized the link between Tully's life and his art. "His loneliness is a burden he can't shake off. With a fire roaring through a brain mixed up with the futility of all things human and divine, he is at heart an artist frustrated and contemptuous." Why write at all? Scully asked. Jim's answer underscored his fundamental nihilism: "I'm not exactly interested in writing—except there's little else to be interested in. Dying as I expect to die, out of the church, I can't go to heaven, and I'm too indiscreet to make limbo."[49]

While middle age had cooled Tully's fiery red hair with a frost of gray, it had also brought him a certain clarity about his profession. Writers who understand and interpret the conditions of the world and whose work reaches a large audience "*should* be a most important force in the world today," he told an interviewer. Tully's view of the growing irrelevance of writers in public discourse was prescient. "The spoken word due to the screen and radio, has grown more important than the printed word. The commentators, I believe, have more influence than the newspaper columnists." As to the craft of writing, a writer's style was "superficial" and meaningless if it didn't "clothe an idea that is of value to people. . . . The writer who forces people to think, who rouses them from their lethargy of 'I-want-only-to-be-amused' is worthwhile. He will last."[50]

Tully relished the company of other writers and enjoyed trading war stories with them as much as he did with old boxers. One of his favorite haunts was Stanley Rose's bookshop, where he frequently ran into William Saroyan and John Fante. Progressive journalist Carey McWilliams recalled Rose's legendary shops (there were two) as hangouts for writers and intellectuals. Over the years, a literary Who's Who passed through Rose's doors, including Dashiell Hammett, Erskine Caldwell, Horace McCoy, George Milburn, William Faulkner, W. R. Burnett, Budd Schulberg, F. Scott Fitzgerald, Louis Adamic, Nathanael West, Frank Fenton, Jo Pagano, and Owen Francis.[51]

John Fante, whose 1939 book *Ask the Dust* is considered one of the finest novels ever written about Los Angeles, and who was an enormous influence on both Jack Kerouac and Charles Bukowski, recalled the advice Tully gave him early in his career. "Save up your pennies and then go and get yourself a copy of this book," Tully advised. The book Tully waved at him was *The Oxford Book of English Verse*. Upon examining Tully's copy, Fante was amused to see that it bore the faded rubber stamp of a public library.[52]

While not as satisfying as writing, *talking* about writing, Tully learned, could be more lucrative. He'd first tasted the low-hanging fruit of the lecture circuit in the mid-1920s.[53] In June of 1938 he again signed with the Leigh Lecture Bureau and a tour was scheduled for 1939. The money was good, $300 a lecture, but not the $1,000 a week he'd requested.[54] Still, it was easy money for a man with no shortage of opinions and, when the mood suited him, a gift for gab. He could talk about writing but was just as happy to give the audiences what they wanted: Hollywood as seen by not exactly an insider but certainly a professional outsider. At a lecture at Hollins College in Roanoke, Virginia, for example, Tully held forth on his favorite actors, Ruth Chatterton and Ronald Colman, and a favorite movie, 1937's *Night Must Fall*, starring Robert Montgomery. Tully described it as "a weird story based on a psychological study of a man who just couldn't help murdering someone." In answer to a question, he correctly predicted that people would flock to a film version of Margaret Mitchell's 1936 novel, *Gone with the Wind*. And to the inevitable question about Chaplin, he replied, "Chaplin, in his scope, has greatness. He has sadness and a sardonic quality that gives him appeal. Though not brilliant mentally, his is a brilliant mimic. However, he is one of the most self-centered, selfish men I have known."[55]

A couple of weeks later, Tully caused a minor scandal at Columbia University by refusing to wear a required dinner jacket and tie. He instead "wore a blue suit with a gray, low-necked Hollywood sports shirt, with the flame-colored curls on his manly chest peeping shyly above the v-neckline of his bodice." If he was not exactly the stuff of a distinguished English department, nor was he a swaggering man of letters. He appeared "looking shy and sheepish" and "perspiring at every pore."[56]

In preparation for another Ivy League school lecture, Mencken counseled, "I only hope that you behave decently at the Harvard Club, and do not scandalize those delicate fellows. Please remember that chewing tobacco is forbidden on the premises."[57] There is a certain irony in Tully's trespass upon the hallowed groves of academe—places where his books might attract the attention of a few undergraduates but never, to use a Menckenism, the professori.

What writing Tully *was* doing in the late 1930s wasn't selling.[58] Greenberg, who felt he'd been burned by *Ladies in the Parlor* and *The Bruiser*, declined "Hollywood Decameron," a collection of short stories, several featuring Jack Jarnegan.[59] Tully's situation was not unique. Freelance work was drying up for everyone. The Depression was squeezing publishers, and those that had not succumbed, including *Esquire*, were forced to defer payments to authors.[60]

Since leaving the *American Mercury*, Mencken had tried to help in other ways and wrote his old friend Alfred Knopf in October 1938 to ask him to consider Tully's "Children of Thieves," a novel about the road.[61] The "Children of Thieves" manuscript got no farther than Mencken's desk. Rather than send it to Knopf, Mencken returned it to Tully with extensive notes for revision.[62] Tully continued to revise "Children of Thieves" in 1939 and even believed it could be a better book than Steinbeck's *Of Mice and Men*, which had been published two years earlier.[63] Publishers were not buying it. His agent, Sydney Sanders, wrote that part of the problem was that "You have written so much of hoboes and yeggs, etc., that I'm afraid you've rather milked this particular cow dry—so far as books are concerned, anyway."[64] Mencken also advised Jim to branch out. "Whoever tells you that you should have kept on doing tramp stories is simply idiotic. You were quite right to try to widen your field, and I see no reason why you shouldn't do it successfully."[65]

Accordingly, he spent less time on "Children of Thieves," and more reworking pieces of old books with new material into a manuscript titled "Out of My Heart," the autobiography he'd long wanted to write.[66] And for walking-around money, he began writing a column for the *Hollywood Tribune* called "Tully-Grams."[67] The $40 per week was insignificant, but the *Tribune* let Tully write as he pleased and it often pleased him to write about "old" Hollywood.[68]

In addition to savaging the publishing industry, the Depression by 1938 had spawned something far more pernicious. A special committee of the United States House chaired by Martin Dies Jr. was formed to investigate "Un-American Activities." The country was turning on itself, with hotly patriotic politicians eager to curry favor with an increasingly frightened electorate. Hollywood was a natural target, as were writers who had in any fashion criticized the government. The Dies Committee, as it came to be known, wielded the power of innuendo and routinely released the names of suspected Communists, including, in October of 1938, two of the country's best-known hard-boiled writers, Dashiell Hammett and Jim Tully.[69] Tully's foreword to a 1939 book on prison reform, *Parole Scandal* by Martin

Mooney, could hardly have endeared him to the Dies Committee.[70] Nor could wondering in a "Tully-Grams" column what J. Edgar Hoover "in his secret dick-heart must think... if he thinks at all."[71] A close reader of "Tully-Grams," however, would also have noticed Tully's general disdain for liberals.[72] For example, a letter to the editor from screenwriter Martin Berkeley, later a friendly House Un-American Activities Committee witness, called Tully "anti–New Deal."[73] Tully did indeed have reservations about Roosevelt and in 1940 supported Republican Wendell Wilkie's failed attempt to keep FDR from an unprecedented third term.[74] (Tully would have been greatly amused that accused spy Alger Hiss would one day describe his accuser, conservative hero Whittaker Chambers, as "a sort of deadbeat who purported to be a cross between Jim Tully and Jack London.")[75]

Liberals, anti-Communists, socialists, conservatives—Tully seemed to irritate them all. His luck with *real* Communists was hardly better. Jim had been hearing for years about the popularity of his books in Russia,[76] with both Ella Winter, Lincoln Steffens's widow, and historian Will Durant assuring him that he was "the most widely read American writer in Russia."[77] And Tully claimed in interviews that sales of *Beggars of Life* and *Shadows of Men* in the Soviet Union exceeded two million copies, a staggering record for any book.[78] Extracting royalties from the Communist state was another matter, however, and in June 1939 he was again rebuffed by the Soviet consulate.[79] With still-vivid memories of his impoverished childhood and men living in hobo jungles, Jim had never been an advocate of unfettered capitalism. But neither was he seduced by the blandishments of Marxism. A few days later, he addressed the subject in one of his "Tully-Grams" columns. "In my time, I have been accused of being a radical. That is wrong. I am merely one whose heart beats in unison with pain. Not a left winger, I am all wings.... When Irving Thalberg said, 'Jim, your attitude in Hollywood has cost you a quarter of a million dollars,' there was nothing I could say in reply."[80]

The unresolved tension of Jim's empathy for the downtrodden and his deep suspicion of "uplift" was not lost on Mencken, who wrote a week later, "Your difficulty, it seems to me, is a kind of confusion. You have a vast sympathy for the sufferings of the poor, and you apparently assume that any one who says he wants to help them is an honest man. The exact contrary is usually the case. I am convinced that Roosevelt, for example, is an unmitigated quack. If I thought he could really do anything to help the country I'd be with him completely. Unfortunately, my belief is that he is only making matters worse."[81] Tully conceded, "You are absolutely right about me being confused. All in all though I do not go for the sophistry of saving the world."[82]

Like so many who have reached middle age and watched their own children reach adulthood, Jim found his thoughts in the second half of 1939 returning to his own childhood. He betrayed a certain wistfulness in a letter to an old friend from home:

> It was thoughtful of you to send the photos of Ohio. I appreciate them a great deal. The one of the church and the village of silent Irish—my mother sleeps beside the tall stone—and Biddy no doubt sleeps well. I suppose I have disturbed her dreams now and then—but at least the most turbulent and sad of her children has written well about her. Many people think I took much from her—my father was quite a man—and I owe him an intelligent sardonic attitude toward life, which has undoubtedly cost me money, but is of no difference. My mother used to have moods that lasted for days. Many the horse of despair dashed through her brain. It is quite possible that without having inherited those moods I may never have been. At any rate, she was something more than a peasant girl, as were her wild Irish tribe, the Lawlers. Poor Aunt Sade must be very old now. I forgive her for being mad at me. I was always the young eagle she feared would fly over the barn-yard fence.[83]

The theme of family, the family of his childhood, was one that he would return to in the coming years. Of course, he had covered this ground more than ten years earlier in *Shanty Irish,* but he now wanted to write about two members of his family in particular: his enigmatic father and his beloved sister Virginia.

24

Biddy Brogan's Boy

Jim Tully spent his entire life trying to understand his father, and the old man's death in 1936 brought back a flood of memories. "Portrait of My Father," which appeared in the November 1939 *Esquire*, reveals a son who has reached an uneasy peace. The recurring question of the article, indeed the question that had tormented Jim since childhood, is this: How can a father who is in many respects a good man be so cruelly indifferent to his children? Jim wrote that his father was "A blending of the peasant and the philosopher, his eyes had never known tears. . . . Without deep affection, he was a somnolent, witty, irreligious man. He would desert but not whip a child." It is this distinction between active and passive cruelty that so perplexed his son. "The silent secret places in his heart were many," Jim recalled. "His compassion was a huge awning under which all could find shelter. He would give me his last dollar if I were with him. When gone, he paid no attention."[1]

After decades of thinking about his father, it wasn't likely that the mists surrounding James Dennis Tully would finally part. "Portrait of My Father" describes but fails to explain the elder Tully's impenetrable relationship with his children. Perhaps there was simply something missing in Jim's father, a void, an emptiness beyond understanding. "If he did nothing for me as a boy," Jim wrote, "he asked nothing of me as a man."

Jim imagined that his father would have been amused that even in death his son saw no money from his father. Jim was forced to use the proceeds of the *Esquire* profile to pay the old man's funeral expenses.[2] That the glossy pages of an upscale magazine became the final resting place of a man who had lived in shanties, log cabins, and boardinghouses his entire life appealed to Jim's sense of irony.

While Jim's father remained as enigmatic in print as he did in life, Jim's portrait of his sister Virginia was so revealing, so heartfelt, that *Reader's Digest* included it in its series "The Most Unforgettable Character I Ever Met." "My sister resembled a gypsy. She was dark, her nose aquiline. Her eyes, large, sad and gray, had an expression of surprise, as if they had opened too suddenly upon a world for which she was not yet ready. Always they remained the eyes of a little girl with the wonder of faraway places in them, a little girl who watched others go on journeys she could not take herself."[3]

When Biddy died in childbirth, it was Virginia, herself a child, who assumed her mother's role and tried to keep the family together. It was a role she fulfilled the rest of her life. "No matter how far I wandered," Jim wrote, "Virginia remained the fixed point of my compass, as she did for the other members of our family. I wrote long letters to her and when I felt the need too keenly would tramp hundreds of miles to see her." At the point in his life when it appeared he might follow his fellow road-kids into crime, it was Virginia who pulled him back and, by sheer force of will, pushed him into writing. Her faith in Jim not only changed his life; it may well have saved it. Jim recalled bringing a road-kid named Eddie Haney to Virginia's place in Chicago. When it appeared that Haney was trying to enlist Jim in a burglary, Virginia intervened. Haney went alone and received a bullet through the heart for his efforts.

Not a religious man himself, Jim readily admits that the source of Virginia's strength was her faith. "Her religion was simple. She was sure there was a God, that her mother was in heaven, and that the Church would eventually solve the woes of mankind."[4]

Jim's profile of his sister serves as a monument to Virginia's generosity of spirit. Her precarious financial position in no way dissuaded her from taking in the human driftwood that washed up at her door and giving away her few belongings with Franciscan abandon. She saved weeks for a new coat, Jim remembered, only to give it away a month later to an old woman who admired it.[5]

Why did Jim's father drift for decades in a sea of alcohol and misery? Why did Alton so irretrievably destroy his life that he spent much of it behind bars? And yet how did Jim, the link between so much human wreckage, himself the product of an adolescence that would make Dickens recoil, grow into a successful writer and manage to wring a fair measure of happiness out of life? Virginia. At every pivotal moment of his young life, Jim's sister refused to let him fail.

Virginia was less successful with her nephew. While in San Quentin, Alton read the profile and recalled his aunt's attempt to take him under her wing. He wrote his father, "I was young during my short time with her but she still stands out in my memory as the sweetest woman that ever lived. She was so patient with me while I was so home-sick in Chicago. I only wish that I could have had the guts to stick it out with her."[6] Maxwell Perkins, with whom Jim had been discussing a new novel,[7] wrote, calling the piece "unforgettable," and the profile of Virginia proved so popular, easily the most popular short piece Jim ever wrote, that years later it was retitled "Gypsy Sister" and included in a collection of the *Reader's Digest* series.[8]

Hoping to boost the piece, Tully turned to old friend Walter Winchell. Tully had once been a staple of Winchell's columns but had in recent years found himself frozen out. Surely, Tully thought, Winchell would mention the *Reader's Digest* profile of Virginia? When Winchell ignored it, as he had all of Tully's recent work, the friendship cooled.[9]

The years just before the war were spent on various projects that, with the exception of the pieces on his father and sister, never got off the ground. "Out of My Heart," his planned autobiography, stalled, as did a series on Al Capone he'd hoped to syndicate.[10] And, as always, he toyed with "The King of Laughter," the Chaplin manuscript based on his *Pictorial Review* series.[11] In its various guises, the biography had been dusted off and reshelved countless times.[12] After reading the manuscript for his boxing history, "Champions Inside the Ropes," his agent passed along some sobering news: "The sketchy, brief word pictures, which made Jim Tully famous, are no longer as acceptable as they were even a few years ago."[13]

Tully did manage to extract a $1,000 advance from Lippincott for a novel about female hoboes called "Road Girls." The project died on the vine when Jim refused to revise the manuscript to Lippincott's satisfaction.[14] Still, he had his "Tully-Grams" column, which gave him free rein to write about boxing, Hollywood, books, hoboes, and whatever else entertained or provoked him.[15] As he wrote gossip columnist Hedda Hopper, "I'm having a hell of a lot of fun, saying almost what I like."[16] Jim quickly realized that one of the perks of writing a newspaper column was enlisting someone else, a "guest columnist," to do the occasional heavy lifting. Jim didn't need to look far. Hugh Tully, who worked as a hostler for Spencer Tracy, wrote about his boss and recounted a few stories about his famous brother for the column.[17]

Despite nagging money woes, it was not an unpleasant time in his life.[18] Friends visited—as old boxing pal Johnny Kilbane did in August 1939, driving the distance from Cleveland. The pair hooked up with Wallace Beery and spent a pleasant evening recalling past glories.[19] And Tully, as always, traveled whenever his schedule and wallet allowed. On one trip to New York in 1940, he was invited to dinner at the home of Mack Kriendler, president of the elegant 21 Club. The *New Yorker* noted that following the evening of fine dining and sparkling conversation, Tully thanked his gracious host and departed. On the way home, he decided to drop by the 21 Club for a nightcap. He was stopped at the door for not wearing a tie, an article of clothing he abhorred. "T'hell with you," Tully was quoted as saying as he turned to leave, "if you think more of a tie than you do of people."[20]

While the newspapers might report Jim's exploits in the glamorous environs of Hollywood or at the 21 Club, the unhappy reality was that Jim and Myrtle's financial situation was becoming increasingly rocky. In addition to Jim's problems selling his work—and having to settle for less when he did find a publisher—Myrtle was having a hard time making a go of it as an agent. Newcom & Tully was consistently unable to attract new clients and retain old ones.[21] The firm generated a net income of just over $500 for 1939.[22]

By August 1940, it was clear that something needed to be done. That something was the painful decision to sell Tall Timbers, their house at Toluca Lake, and move to Faraway Farm, the hundred-acre ranch near Canoga Park.[23] Jim managed to keep his money troubles out of the press and cited the drone of airplanes and loss of seclusion as the reason for the sale of his beloved estate.[24] Alton wrote his stepmother, "It must tear your heart out at the very thought of losing it." Alton lamented that he held "a picture of a house and lake I will never see."[25]

Alton had long since become resigned to communicating with his father through his stepmother, but Trilby still hoped for something resembling a normal relationship with her famous father. Her phone calls and letters to her father went, for the most part, unanswered. Jim's anger and disappointment with Alton is understandable, but his apparent callousness toward his daughter is inexplicable. The man who had written so affectionately about his mother and sister seemed to have little to offer his daughter. By the spring of 1940, Florence had had enough. She wrote her ex-husband, "Why do you treat her as you do? She is your daughter and will be nearer to you than others long after they are gone." It all seemed to echo Jim's father's emotionally distant relationship with his children. Yet Alton and Trilby received considerable, even generous, financial support from their father and could never doubt that he would come to their rescue during a crisis. It was a shelter their father never had. Jim's relationship with the mother of his children was also strained. Florence continued, "I cannot see why you could have so much hatred for me; for I have do [sic] nothing to help you and be your friend."[26] The root of Jim's anger, not unique among divorced couples, was money. Jim complained bitterly to Mencken that nearly two decades after their divorce, he was still helping support Florence, long after his legal obligation ended.[27]

Trilby sent her father a postcard that October from Las Vegas, announcing her marriage to a young airplane mechanic, Raymond Beamon.[28] Trilby's wedding was a microcosm of her relationship with her father. He was absent from her wedding but later wrote Mencken of how proud he was of her and how impressed he was with Ray and included a photo of the happy couple standing in front of the small home he helped them obtain. Still, Jim sometimes felt manipulated. "She makes no pretense of knowing all the feathers in her wild Irish father," he wrote, "but she knows how to stroke them."[29]

A year later, however, things had not changed. Trilby was reduced to begging her father to visit her and Ray at their home in South Gate in Los Angeles County.[30] The realization that she stood a better chance of having her request granted by appealing through her stepmother must have been disappointing. "Myrtle," she wrote, "please don't let daddy try to get out of coming. I want him to come so bad."[31] Trilby believed part of the problem was that she had lost her father's trust and, with it, his love. Jim had loaned the couple money for the house with the understanding that he would be repaid before the house was fully furnished. Trilby bought furniture instead and missed a payment to her father when she became ill and incurred unexpected medical expenses. Knowing that she had disappointed her father, she wrote Myrtle to explain her situation and asked to borrow a painting owned by her father that was sitting in storage. "If he won't I can't blame him, maybe he would think it would be like the money we borrowed [and] 'hard to get back.' But I would enjoy taking care of it anyway. Maybe he would trust me once more. . . . Also tell Daddy I miss not hearing from him. What's the matter don't he love me anymore? When he does write it don't sound like it."[32] Myrtle moved quickly to patch things up and Trilby assured her that there were no hard feelings and that it had all been a misunderstanding.[33]

With the country drifting toward war in late 1940, Tully became increasingly vocal about staying out of what was up to that point a foreign war. He allowed his name to appear as a sponsor of the Committee to Defend America by Keeping Out of War. The committee in turn sponsored another group, American Peace Mobilization, which was thought to be dominated by Communists.[34] Tully's FBI file grew thicker. A few months later, Tully lent his name to the American Committee for Protection of Foreign Born. About 350 delegates and observers met in Atlantic City in March 1941. A "majority of persons attending were Jews and negroes," the FBI noted, many of them "known Communists." Speakers at the conference, the FBI reported in Tully's file, praised Sacco and Vanzetti and Harry Bridges. A "souvenir journal" available at the registration desk listed several-dozen sponsors, including Jim Tully.[35]

The one writing project in early 1941 that did find an enthusiastic publisher was a profile of Clark Gable for *Family Circle*.[36] Following his role as Rhett Butler in 1939's *Gone with the Wind*, Gable was the biggest male star in Hollywood and the subject of enormous interest. Gable and Tully had a particular affinity, as they were part of a small Hollywood fraternity—men who had spent part of their youth on the road. He was also an Ohioan who had, like Tully, briefly worked in Akron.

Anxious to get something a bit more substantial than the Gable piece off the ground, Tully traveled to New York in May 1941 and met Maxwell Perkins over lunch.[37] Tully had two books in mind for Scribner's. The first was "Hollywood Decameron," his collection of stories about Jack Jarnegan. The second book, an autobiographical novel, would be as "natural" as *Tom Sawyer* but "tougher."[38] Heeding the advice of Al Lewin to hew closer to Twain's humor than to Dreiser's realism, Tully envisioned a book more like *Shanty Irish* than *Beggars of Life*. As to money, a $500 advance with another $500 on delivery would be just fine.[39] A week later Perkins agreed to publish the second book, titled *Biddy Brogan's Boy*.[40]

To distinguish the new book from *Shanty Irish*, to which it would inevitably be compared, Jim informed Perkins that unless Perkins objected, he would write in the third person.[41] Jim promised to deliver the manuscript in six months.⁴² All of Jim's hopes to revive his flagging career now were pinned on *Biddy Brogan's Boy*.⁴³

As originally conceived, *Biddy Brogan's Boy* was to be "the story of a lad who became an artist."⁴⁴ It was Jim's initial desire to make his sister Virginia the basis for the central character—to the point of using the last few hundred words from the *Reader's Digest* profile to conclude the book.⁴⁵ He'd even considered the title *Biddy Brogan's Daughter*.⁴⁶

Early in his career, Tully had been most fortunate to find in H. L. Mencken a masterful editor for his short stories and essays. He'd fared less well with his books but finally, under Perkins's guidance, felt renewed. "I find Perkins a delightful and understanding man," he wrote Mencken. "My career, after nineteen years, is just beginning."⁴⁷

Perkins made extensive recommendations and marked several biographical passages for removal as having historical but not fictional value.⁴⁸ It was a unique problem. "The great trouble," he wrote Mencken, "has been to invent scenes better than those I have lived."⁴⁹ By the close of 1941, the completed manuscript was in Perkins's hands, and Tully returned to the subject of Hollywood for freelance work.⁵⁰

He was, however, increasingly drawn to the subject of "old" Hollywood. As one who had observed Hollywood since its early days, he loved to recall his favorite films and their directors. In one such piece, he singled out for praise John Ford's *The Informer, The Grapes of Wrath, Arrowsmith,* and *How Green Was My Valley;* Frank Capra's *It Happened One Night;* James Cruze's *The Covered Wagon;* and Lewis Milestone's *Two Arabian Nights*.⁵¹ Legendary films—and directors—all.

A reading of F. Scott Fitzgerald's unfinished and posthumously published novel about Hollywood, *The Last Tycoon*, sent by Perkins, also was cause for reflection.⁵² Jim had several Fitzgerald first editions in his library and remembered Fitzgerald, who had died of a heart attack the previous December, as "a sweet and gentle man—all the satin of him never turning into rayon."⁵³ In a letter to George Jean Nathan, Tully remembered Fitzgerald. "When I think of what the lad might have written and didn't I am sadder than usual."⁵⁴

With Alton coming up for parole in the autumn of 1941, Jim began in August to make preparations. He enlisted Mencken and others in a letter-writing campaign in support of Alton's case before the parole board.⁵⁵ And Jim began making plans to assist Alton in the writing of a prison memoir.⁵⁶

Jim's sudden interest in Alton's writing career was not just an attempt to give his son direction but was also designed to keep Alton from talking to the press at a time when an ill-chosen word could wreck his chance at parole.[57]

There was some cause for optimism. Alton, then thirty, had worked thirteen months at the prison jute mill and performed so well that he was given a job in San Quentin warden Clinton Duffy's office.[58] Jim had grown to respect Duffy and felt Alton would be given fair consideration.[59] Myrtle was typically understanding and offered Alton a room at their ranch, should he be released.[60] Alton thanked his father and stepmother and reassured them that he had been "cured" and would yet make something of his life.[61] Talk of being "cured" may well have been premature. The San Quentin psychiatrist had formed the opinion that Alton's psyche was a witch's brew of paranoia; an inferiority complex, especially about his small size (Alton had inherited his father's height but not his bulk); and a sense of entitlement stemming from his position as the son of a celebrity.[62]

On the morning of Saturday, November 22, 1941, Jim and Myrtle rose early and made the four-hundred-mile drive to San Quentin. Alton was surprised and delighted to see them. They made small talk for a quarter of an hour before Myrtle asked Alton when he was to appear before the parole board. It was Jim and Myrtle's turn to be surprised. They had departed that morning before the mail arrived with news that Alton had been granted parole.[63] Father and son shared a rare moment of genuine happiness. Jim's faith in Warden Duffy had not been misplaced. Duffy had accompanied Alton to his hearing and vouched for his rehabilitation.[64] With the promise to return in December to take Alton home, Jim and Myrtle departed.[65] Alton looked forward to what would be only the second trip he'd ever taken with his father.[66] With Alton's release and Perkins's enthusiasm for *Biddy Brogan's Boy*, the Christmas of 1941 was especially happy. Jim had every reason to look forward to the new year.

A few days after Christmas, however, with the corrected galleys of *Biddy Brogan's Boy* sitting on his desk, Jim suffered a heart attack and was taken to Van Nuys Hospital.[67] Unlike Fitzgerald, Tully would live to see his latest book appear in print. Tully convalesced at home, remaining fully engaged in the buildup to publication. From bed, he prodded Perkins to sell serialization and book club reprint rights and suggested possible reviewers.[68] He also managed to sell a couple of short travel pieces on the Great Salt Lake in Utah and Guadalupe Peak in Texas to Standard Oil of California at $100 a pop.[69] Mostly, though he waited and worried, both about the blood clot lodged in his artery and, following the recent bombing of Pearl Harbor, about a possible Japanese invasion of Southern California.[70] The man who had once jumped boxcars now used a cane.[71] By late February, the blood clot had shrunk and Jim was feeling well enough to sit at the typewriter and peck out letters to Perkins and Mencken.[72] Arteriosclerosis, however, had begun its insidious advance.

The coming release of *Biddy Brogan's Boy* was certainly on his mind, but so was his own mortality. "I seem to be getting stronger," he wrote Mencken, "but somehow I cannot get over the feeling that my little day of battle is mostly done, and strangely enough having been part of the show, I watch the curtain go down with almost no regret."[73] Jim's stoic front, however, hid a deepening gloom about his declining health.[74]

Biddy Brogan's Boy, Tully's final novel, is the story of his life, from his Ohio boyhood through his days as a road-kid, farmworker, and boxer and his maturation into a writer and concludes with the death of Virginia. While it covers some of the same ground as Tully's earlier books, especially *Shanty Irish*, the perspective is different. In *Shanty Irish*, Tully paid close attention to the Tully side of his family, particularly his grandfather, Hughie. With *Biddy Brogan's Boy*, Tully explores the wild Lawler side of his family, but especially his mother and, following her death, her surrogate, Virginia. In many respects, *Biddy Brogan's Boy* is a valentine across the decades to the two women Jim most loved and credited with his improbable success. Jim's bond with his mother was special. In his first book, *Emmett Lawler*, Jim had given his central character his mother's maiden name. In *Biddy Brogan's Boy*, his final novel, Jim nicknamed his central character after his mother. Tully seems to say that not only do mother and son share the same name; they are of the same spirit. The difference between *Biddy Brogan's Boy* and *Shanty Irish*, in addition to perspective, is one of tone. In *Shanty Irish*, Tully was amused by his wild Irish family. By the time Tully wrote *Biddy Brogan's Boy*, Tully was in his midfifties and had come to love and cherish their memory.

The presence of Virginia brings a spiritual quality to *Biddy Brogan's Boy* not found in any of Tully's other books. In a worldly sense, Virginia was an utter failure. "She spent all her years," Tully wrote, "making bad bargains with life."[75] To outsiders, she was just another struggling waitress, inconsequential and invisible, trying to survive in a big city. Yet some were fortunate enough to know her. Her rag-tag collection of friends, "incompetents, wastrels, degradants," in Tully's description, "all . . . found shelter in Virginia's house."[76] Virginia's bottomless well of compassion sustained all those around her. "When old Alvin Demarest Harvey, the street cleaner, whose job it was to spear stray pieces of paper with a nail, first came to her," Jim wrote, "she exalted him with the usefulness and dignity of his work."[77]

While *Biddy Brogan's Boy* may invite comparison with Joyce's *Portrait of the Artist as a Young Man*, it is a line from another Irish writer that Tully uses to define his sister. From the play *Heartbreak House*, Tully quotes Shaw: "When your heart is broken then comes the beginning of peace."[78]

The first copies reached Tully in late March of 1942 and, a couple of minor typos aside, he was initially delighted with the book's physical appearance.[79] With a few exceptions, he was also delighted with the reviews that started piling up in April. Thomas Quinn Curtiss of the *New York Times* was especially enthusiastic and took the occasion of the book's publication to reassess Jim's career.

> Jim Tully has always occupied a curious position in the American literary scene. He is conspicuous by his absence from Dr. Lewisohn's "Expression in America," and Edmund Wilson makes no mention of him in his study of Californian novelists, and yet there have been but a handful of artists since the turn of the century who have explored the American lower depths with sympathy and success. When Tully began to write during the early nineteen twenties many pedantic professors and academic critics were horrified. In their eyes he was illiterate, brutal, and blasphemous, and they sought to have done with him at once.

Curtiss further observed that Tully "has been deservedly compared to Maxim Gorky" and was writing about the American underclass "a decade before *Tobacco Road* and *The Grapes of Wrath* were ever heard of."[80] As for *Biddy Brogan's Boy*, Curtiss wrote, it "is an arresting and surprising book, and by long odds, the best thing that Tully has written to date." With its publication, Tully had finally written a book "approaching the fulfillment of his original promise. It is a strong and steady book," the review continued, "rich in both its tragedy and its humor, and the narrative flows along with a direct and natural simplicity unmarred by any of his early writing flaws." *Biddy Brogan's Boy* "is completely his story," Curtiss concluded, "and he is a master storyteller."[81]

The *Los Angeles Times* noted that *Biddy Brogan's Boy* "is rich in sentiment, in tall tales, in vigorous characters and dramatic action."[82] The *Phila-*

delphia Record wrote, "This is the first novel from Jim Tully's pen for quite a while but he hasn't lost the skill of blending the ingredients he knows best—the open road, the prize ring, and rough and tough men with hearts of gold."[83] From a corner of the fourth estate, always dear to his heart, the *San Quentin News* stated: "Here is Tully at his robust best. . . . For Jim Tully writes of a people who reflect a bright radiance of that most precious of all things—undying courage."[84] The *New York Herald-Tribune* was much more restrained, calling the book's narrative "haphazard" but allowing that "it is a robust yarn, suited to his free-swinging style."[85] The *New York Post* similarly complained that the book was "uneven and formless to a degree unusual even for Tully."[86]

By 1942, Tully was an old hand at reading reviews, good and bad, and still bristled at those he considered unfair.[87] Most upsetting was Ted Robinson's review in the *Cleveland Plain Dealer*. Robinson, who had been the first critic to champion Tully, assailed his lack of "inventiveness." It was a charge Tully had heard before and he dryly admitted to Mencken that his weakness as a writer was "not being able to invent situations like God did."[88] Sales of *Biddy* were also cause for concern. The early signs from Scribner's were good, but there was a dark cloud on the horizon. "I'm competing with a gal called Rawlings. . . . I guess she's good," he wrote Mencken. The parallels between *Cross Creek*, by Marjorie Kinnan Rawlings, and *Biddy* were striking. Both were autobiographical novels published by Scribner's, and both had been edited by Maxwell Perkins. As *Cross Creek* was the highly anticipated follow-up to Rawlings's Pulitzer Prize–winning novel, *The Yearling*, *Biddy* was in real danger of getting lost in the excitement. When the Book of the Month Club came calling, the book it wanted from Scribner's was *Cross Creek*. "How the hell was anyone to know we would come out together?" Tully moaned to Mencken. "Coming back," he continued, "is harder than getting anywhere in the first place."[89]

On April 23, Perkins delivered the bad news. "So far the sales are very discouraging for *Biddy Brogan's Boy* and I don't know how to account for it except that the Book Club does seem to overwhelm the whole market. Within a month they have taken 360,000 copies of our *Cross Creek*. How many more buyers are out there?"[90]

Tully, however, was not ready to throw in the towel. He requested additional advertising and publicity and was reassured by Perkins that Scribner's efforts would continue.[91] Tully did not stay reassured and, by the end of the month, had poured out his frustration to Perkins. "I am sorry to hear of the book's fate," he wrote. "My best imprint and my worst failure. Post mortems [sic] are foolish. They have never yet brought life. I was never consulted in regard to the book. The cover was hardly conducive to the buying by women . . . and it was that kind of yarn." While Tully had nothing but praise for Perkins, he believed Scribner's had not gotten fully behind the book. "I write out of a hurt heart," he concluded, "for only Steinbeck has the tales to tell that I have, and he has hit . . . and I will again."[92]

Perkins responded that *Biddy* had sold only a few more than 2,000 copies and that he was hearing that it was proving difficult to "sell a book by a writer who had been so celebrated at a period so far back."[93] He defended Scribner's by pointing out that twice as much had been spent on advertising as was justified, given the difficulties of wartime publishing, and that Scribner's had done no more for *Cross Creek* than for *Biddy*. Jim accepted the editor's defense, begged his continued moral support, and offered to forgo an advance on any future work for Scribner's.[94] By June, Tully had come to believe that the only mistake Perkins made with *Biddy Brogan's Boy* was timing. "Why did he put me up for the book of the month club with Marjorie Rawlings?" he wrote Mencken. "Sure I lost . . . so would Joe Louis with such a set up." The real blame, he had to admit, was with the book. "No reviewer remembers, or is too polite to say so, that *Biddy's Boy* is merely *Shanty Irish* in more popular garb."[95] Mencken disagreed with Tully's judgment of *Biddy*. "I read *Biddy Brogan's Boy* with the greatest pleasure," he wrote. "It is by no means a reworking of *Shanty Irish*. The approach is entirely different, and it seems to me that you have done a really excellent piece of work. Unhappily, it hit the market at the most unfavorable time imaginable."[96] A little more than five years after it was published, *Biddy Brogan's Boy* was remaindered and its plates melted. Scribner's never made back its $1,000 advance to Jim.[97]

Before the spring of 1942 was out, a year that had held such promise had turned to dust. Following Tully's heart attack at the start of the year and the commercial failure of *Biddy Brogan's Boy* came more awful news. The source, once again, was Alton.

25

The Last Division

It was all too familiar—a recurring nightmare. On the evening of April 28, 1942, Betty Baird, thirty-eight, met a man in a Hollywood bar and accepted a ride home from him. He drove her to a secluded spot in the Hollywood Hills and attacked her.[1] Baird told the police that her attacker threatened to kill her "if it's necessary."[2] Police had no doubt that Alton Tully was their man and quickly apprehended him at a Sunset Boulevard café as he tried to slip out the back door.

Florence and Trilby went immediately to see Alton in jail, but Alton refused to see his mother.[3] While the facts of the case were bad enough, the yellow press made it worse. Jim complained to Maxwell Perkins that a Hearst reporter portrayed Alton as "the hulking son of the hobo author" when he weighed but 138 pounds.[4] The bad press would pass, as would the averted glances of acquaintances. But the shame and embarrassment would linger. One well-meaning friend, real estate agent Bill McCann, had loaned Alton money and blamed himself for Alton's "break," which had been fueled by alcohol.[5] And as in the past, friends rallied to Jim's side. Father Vincent Donovan wrote the district attorney, seeking rehabilitation for Alton.[6] What Alton would not have this time was access to his father's checkbook. Jim's money was gone and Alton was assigned a public defender.[7]

At the trial on July 6, the defense presented testimony from a waitress that Alton had been a "perfect gentleman" and had received a beating by police when arrested.[8] The jury of seven women and five men took less than thirty minutes to acquit. The trial judge later wrote that the "unfortunate female only got what she was asking for." He also concluded that Alton was "a victim of circumstances."[9]

Any sense of relief Jim felt was tempered by more health troubles. He had fallen the week before and broken his shoulder in two places.[10] Alton's troubles, however, were not over. His consumption of alcohol on the evening of the incident constituted a parole violation, and he was returned to the jute mill at San Quentin on July 18.[11] Those few drinks cost Alton 117 months of good time credit.[12] In a disjointed letter to Mencken that reflected Jim's deteriorating condition, he wrote, "I don't give a damn about Alton."[13] A month later, he had cooled off sufficiently to make plans for Alton to join the Merchant Marine on his release.[14]

Having concluded that *Biddy* was a lost cause, Tully tried to get back to work. He was an old boxer and his instinct remained: keep punching, never stop punching. It was a sound strategy, but by the summer of 1942, Jim was fifty-six years old, had a failing heart, and had absorbed more physical and emotional punishment than most people experience in several lifetimes. Mounting yet another comeback would be almost impossible. He floated the idea of "A Broadway Doctor" (later titled "Rave Lafferty"[15]) past Mencken. It "is better than *Jarnegan* . . . about ny gangsters," but he worried that the timing was wrong. "Steinbeck knows when to strike," he continued. "His last [*The Moon Is Down*] is a peach."[16]

Although he still toyed with ambitious writing projects, the remaining years of Jim's life were spent on small jobs paying just enough to cover bills. When he sold a profile of director James Cruze to *Esquire*, he could joke about his late friend, "His ashes will keep the frost away this winter."[17] Jim was recognized in the 1940s as the nation's resident authority on vagabondage, and over the years, manuscripts by and about the subject washed up at his door. Among those seeking blurbs were Ben Reitman for *Sister of the Road*, the autobiography of Boxcar Bertha Thompson that he coauthored, as well as E. P. Dutton and Company for an autobiography by a young wanderer with a guitar.[18] In the latter book, Tully embraced a brother of the road.

> I have just read Woody Guthrie's *Bound for Glory* with a great deal of pleasure. It is the best book of its kind I have ever encountered. More engrossing than any novel, it points the way to the books of the future, when readers will be so busy living themselves that they will demand more life in their reading. When the GREAT AMERICAN BOOK, that myth of the second raters, is composed, it will be done in the abstract by the

academic, who will crib from this book. Guthrie's canvas is large, and his figures live upon it. He is a superb artist. Though he has been around enough, he accepts the thing as it is, and describes it, without the bitterness of which he should have the right.[19]

Jim also agreed to write the "hobo" entry for the *Encyclopaedia Britannica*, a job that paid all of $65.76.[20] "In a little while you will find yourself quoted gravely by learned men," Mencken joked.[21] And Tully turned out the occasional book review on subjects that interested him, such as a biography of legendary heavyweight champion John L. Sullivan.[22]

Other writers routinely turned to Tully for assistance. Hoping to sell his masterpiece, *Spoon River Anthology*, to Hollywood, Edgar Lee Masters asked for Tully's help.[23] And when Jack London's biographer, Irving Stone, began work on a biography of Clarence Darrow, he requested, and was given, Tully's notes on the legendary attorney.[24] In return, Stone unsuccessfully tried to interest the *Saturday Evening Post* in "Ringside," Tully's "personalized history of pugilism."[25]

The book that Tully finally did sell wasn't a boxing history or a novel but a collection of profiles titled *A Dozen and One*. It was published by Murray & Gee, a new Hollywood publisher willing to take a chance. *A Dozen and One* would be their first book. Murray & Gee was a long way from Scribner's, but when the small publisher dangled the possibility of reprinting *Ladies in the Parlor*, a book Tully believed had unfulfilled potential, a deal was struck.[26] After initially considering William Saroyan to write the foreword, Tully settled on a pal from ringside, Damon Runyon.[27] The thirteen profiles included Chaplin, Dempsey, Gable, Diego Rivera, Paul Bern, Henry Armstrong, and, of course, Mencken. The copy Jim mailed to Mencken was inscribed, "To the best editor this country ever had—Jim Tully."[28] Mencken replied, "I think the best thing in the book is the Dempsey chapter. I also like the Gable, despite what anyone else may say of it. The Chaplin, rather curiously, gives me a sense of incompleteness—that is to say, I gather the impression that you are telling only half of it."[29] More tantalizing was Irving Stone's suspicion that Tully knew more about Paul Bern's death than he committed to print.[30]

Released in early January 1943, *A Dozen and One* earned good reviews. The *New York Times* praised Tully's "penetrating skill" while noting that the Chaplin profile was a bit severe and the Gable too uncritical.[31] The *New Yorker* found the profiles "pithy and vigorous," while the *Saturday Review* of Literature noted, "It is difficult to pick out the best portrait. . . . All are entertaining and enlightening."[32] The *Los Angeles Times* noted that Tully was "Painfully honest toward his subjects, even when he dislikes them (and, personally, we don't think Jim dislikes anyone, he only sees them as they are)." One profile in particular merited special praise: "Charlie Chaplin could not ask for a finer biographer than he has in the 30-page portrait Tully does of the man for whom he worked, even if Jim does slip on that matter of whether Charlie is an artist or a gag man."[33]

Several of Tully's friends held a book party on April 7, 1943, at the Hollywood Roosevelt Hotel. Early Tully booster Rupert Hughes made opening remarks to a group of several hundred that included Frank Scully, Erich von Stroheim, Jean Hersholt, Al Lewin, and Rowland V. Lee.[34] *A Dozen and One* started strong, and, just a few weeks after its release, Tully claimed (incorrectly) that it had sold more copies than *Biddy Brogan's Boy* had in a year.[35] But *A Dozen and One,* Tully's final book, proved to be more of an interesting coda than grand finale to Tully's literary career. And Murray & Gee never did reprint *Ladies in the Parlor.*

Having lost Tall Timbers less than three years before, Jim and Myrtle left Faraway Farm in January 1943 and moved to a small Normandy house on South Carmelina Avenue in Westwood. To keep their monthly expenses down, the couple did not have a telephone installed in their new home.[36] And realizing that Jim's work was unlikely to command the prices it once had, Myrtle took a job as a stenographer in the War Department's Burbank office.[37]

Neither time nor diminished circumstances, according to a *Washinton Post* story, had cooled Tully's fire. At a party thrown in April 1943 by Sinclair Lewis to celebrate his latest novel, a guest admitted to Tully that he'd never read one of his books. "Then you haven't read the finest literature in America," Tully loudly proclaimed. "You must be an ignorant man, devoid of taste, not to have read my books," and he continued to heap abuse until Lewis intervened and insisted Tully leave. Tully and the target of his insults left together and, after a few drinks at a nearby bar, phoned Lewis to say they'd never speak to him again.[38] It was, alas, untrue. At a very small gathering at the Lewis home, Tully drank too much, grew maudlin, and along with the other equally intoxicated guests finally succumbed to boisterous laughter. Lewis, unamused, toddled off to bed, leaving his guests to see themselves out.[39]

Jim's drinking masked a gathering depression about his deteriorating health, and when house calls by his physician in early June 1943 proved ineffective, he was hospitalized.⁴⁰ He quickly chafed at hospital life and took an apartment with a hospital bed for the summer.⁴¹ Myrtle wrote Mencken that while she worked, Jim was left with "a competent nurse, who is neither very young nor glamorous."⁴² He remained bedridden for much of the summer and could only watch as medical bills piled up like jabs scored on an aging fighter.⁴³ Jim still sold the occasional piece—his profile of James Cruze ran in August's *Esquire*—but it was becoming increasingly apparent that he would never write himself out of his deepening financial hole.⁴⁴ He learned in August that *A Dozen and One* had faded quickly and sold a mere 555 copies. "Frankly, Jim, the book simply did not catch on," Ted DuBois of Murray & Gee wrote. "It should have sold ten times this much, had it touched the public pulse."⁴⁵

The strain of commuting to Burbank and caring for Jim grew to be too much, and in late August, Myrtle took a job closer to home at the RKO studios.⁴⁶ The only good news in the summer of 1943 was the birth of Bryan Tully Beamon to Trilby and Ray.⁴⁷ He was Jim's first grandchild. When the birth announcement reached San Quentin, Alton was delighted, both at becoming an uncle and at hearing from his sister for the first time since his arrest sixteen months earlier.⁴⁸

With all his usual literary avenues closed, and desperate to pay bills, Jim tried his hand at writing fantasy, hoping that a story titled "Winds of Wonder" would catch on with children.⁴⁹ It was mailed to Mencken but returned with a discouraging note reading, "I am simply unfit to judge fantasy."⁵⁰

By the end of summer, Jim was able to move back to the ranch, where he could at least rest outdoors, breathe fresh air, and enjoy the scenery. With Myrtle working days and work around the the ranch piling up, an old friend and retired sailor, Tom Murray, moved in to look after Jim and tackle odd jobs. Thinking a sun bath might help Jim's arthritis, Tom moved Jim outside, warned him to cover up if the sun became too intense, and disappeared to paint window sills. The combination of the California sun and Jim's fair Irish complexion resulted in a painful sunburn to add to his other miseries.⁵¹ As bad as his heart disease was, the arthritis proved more painful and debilitating, making it impossible to work.⁵² His left arm had become virtually unusable.⁵³ Typing was agony.⁵⁴

Throughout Jim's long illness, Mencken remained a faithful correspondent and true friend. Mencken summed up their long friendship: "Jim Tully is low Irish, and I'm low Dutch; we get along like brothers."⁵⁵ At Christmas, for instance, Mencken could write, "All the usual insincere and revolting holiday wishes," and know that Tully would chuckle in sympathy.[56] Tully put it differently. Mencken, he wrote, "is the only book man I ever knew . . . who is bar-room smart."[57] Their correspondence, which for decades had been a way for each of them to test ideas and make plans, now mostly looked to past glories. "Please tell him that the boys of the Saturday Night Club inquire about him every Saturday night," Mencken wrote Myrtle. "They still remember with lovely sentiments the memorable evening on which he drank their beer champion under the table, and then walked out perfectly sober. This feat they always think of as bordering on the miraculous."[58]

While the public had largely forgotten Tully by the 1940s, other writers did not forget. When author James M. Cain ran into Myrtle, a meeting between the two giants of hard-boiled fiction was arranged in May of 1944.[59] Cain, whose novel *Double Indemnity* was being adapted for the screen by Billy Wilder with a Raymond Chandler screenplay, later claimed that the Tullys "were the most interesting people he had met for years."[60]

Despite his crippling arthritis—work that once took half an hour now required a day's hard labor—Tully refused to give up.[61] In mid-1944 he was still trying to sell his gangster novel, "Rave Lafferty." He also was pitching a collection of profiles and shorter nonfiction pieces. These would include "Bright Eyes" and "Yeggs," as well as the acclaimed profiles of his father and sister. And as ever, he was angling to reprint some of his books, especially those to which Boni still owned the rights.[62] Elliott Macrae at Dutton, who had so loved his blurb for the Woody Guthrie autobiography, expressed interest in the Boni titles, as well as "Rave Lafferty."[63] He finally passed, citing the wartime paper shortage.[64] The death in September of Aimee Semple McPherson prompted Tully to dust off his "Half-Sister of the Lord" manuscript, which he offered to both Jae Greenberg and Maxwell Perkins.[65]

Much of this activity was simply the result of Jim's natural restlessness bumping up against his long confinement, but generating an income, any income, remained a concern. Hearing of their difficulties, Alton sent $100, but Jim insisted Myrtle write him that the money was not needed. Myrtle took the money and opened a savings account in her stepson's name.[66] As dire as Tully's finances had become, there were some jobs he declined. When Charles Angoff, Mencken's successor at the *American Mercury*, requested a profile of director Preston Sturges, Tully wouldn't be party to putting the director of screwball comedies in the pages of the *Mercury*. "He deserves a *Vanity Fair* article and that is all," he wrote Mencken.[67] And when a Nast editor solicited a thousand-word sketch on Humphrey Bogart for $125, well below his $300 minimum for Nast, Tully refused. "I thought then I must be going backward," he complained to Mencken, "so I did not write on Bogart—a decent fellow who does not believe his own publicity."[68]

Alton came up for parole in July of 1943 and was finally released in September 1944. While waiting for orders to ship out as a steward with the Merchant Marine, he stayed with Jim and Myrtle in Westwood.[69] Once again Alton showed promise. When arthritis afflicted Florence, her medical expenses fell on Trilby's husband, Ray, who was then stationed at the San Diego Naval Base.[70] Learning of his mother's troubles, Alton mailed a small amount of money to help his brother-in-law shoulder the load.[71] And from Luzon in June 1945, where he was delivering war supplies, Alton mailed a $50 money order to repay Myrtle for a loan. "Perhaps," he wrote, "some day we can live a normal life and see each other every day."[72]

Having already been largely robbed of his ability to write, Jim noticed in May of 1945 that his vision was deteriorating, slowly taking with it his ability to read, and the one sustained joy of his adult life.[73]

In October, Trilby gave birth to Jim's second grandchild, a girl, Dana Rae.[74] And Jim was also happy to hear from Clinton Sanders, an ex-con from Virginia who had married and become a "square john." Sanders had read of Jim's illness in one of Walter Winchell's columns. "Jim," he wrote:

> I want you to know that I shall always hold a tender spot in my heart for you for helping me when I was in the big house in Richmond. You wrote many letters for me, good ones too, full of Irish wit and dirty digs against this rotten penal system.
> Had it not been for you and Mencken . . . [75]

In his sixty years, Jim had found a roof over his head in places from St. Marys and Kent, Ohio, to Chicago, New York, Los Angeles, and untold places in between. And he'd spent many a night in hobo camps with nothing more than a canopy of stars overhead. Just before Christmas 1946, his travels effectively ended at the Las Encinas Sanitarium in Pasadena. Following a series of debilitating strokes that left him unable to walk, Myrtle made the difficult decision.[76] His stay, she told the press, would be temporary and she expected him home by February.[77]

Jim had interviewed, written about, and ghostwritten for W. C. Fields many times over the years.[78] He'd been delighted to learn that Fields had also passed through Kent around the turn of the century. On December 16, 1898, Fields, a young juggler with a traveling vaudeville troupe, rolled into town for a Friday performance at the Kent Opera House. The troupe, which had not been paid in weeks, long suspected that the allure of the evening's proceeds, when weighed against their unpaid bills, might prove too much for their manager. Fields and the others took turns keeping watch on his hotel room at night. Despite their vigilance, he slipped out, leaving behind the performers and an unpaid bill at Kent's Central Hotel. Fields, just a few dollars in his pocket, walked across the street to the Erie train depot to inquire about the cost of a ticket to New York. Eighteen dollars. A helpful young sport offered to pay four dollars for Field's overcoat plus an introduction to one of the chorus girls. The young lady agreed to help Fields, but negotiations broke down over the precise definition of "introduction." Fields punched the man in the face. Despite finding another customer for his coat in a saloon, Fields was still short six dollars. He put his twelve dollars on the ticket counter, looked forlornly at George Hinds, the Erie Railroad station master, and hoped for the best. The window slammed shut and Fields repaired to a nearby bench to consider his limited options. Hinds, who had witnessed Fields's juggling act, had a change of heart and approached him a few minutes later. With no serious expectation of being repaid, he handed Fields a ticket and two silver dollars.[79] According to Fields biographer James Curtis, Tully slightly irritated the comedian by later revealing that Fields eventually gave Hinds one hundred dollars for his kindness.[80]

While Tully and Fields had missed each other in Kent by only a few years, their paths had crossed and recrossed ever since. They had briefly even been in business together in 1934 when they formed a production company with Bing Crosby, Gene Fowler, and Mack Sennett. The plan called for Tully and Fowler to produce scripts, Fields and Crosby to be in front of the camera, and shooting to take place at Sennett's studios.[81]

Tully and Fields had also been neighbors at Toluca Lake, where Fields enjoyed hitting golf balls into the water to the manifest displeasure of the mute swans who lived there. The territorial swans retaliated and Tully, Bing Crosby, and other neighbors were treated to the sight of a man with a bulbous nose and unstable center of gravity flailing away at his attackers with a golf club, baseball bat, or whatever weapon was at hand. It got to the point where Fields was unsafe in his own backyard, so when his lease expired, he withdrew from the field of battle. After Fields had moved, Tully was sitting on his terrace one afternoon with Hollywood writer David "Spec" McClure, drinking Scotch. They watched as a flock of swans established a beachhead and warily padded toward Fields's former home. Tully observed this slice of military history for a few moments before remarking to McClure, "For Christ's sake, they must be looking for old Bill Fields!"[82]

Here they were in December of 1946, Tully and Fields, in a nursing home, neighbors again. Both were in very bad shape. In addition to his other ailments, Tully had by now developed Parkinson's disease, which reduced his speech to a whisper.[83] Hoping they might enjoy seeing each other, Tully's nurse wheeled him down the hall and deposited him at Fields's side. Fields's secretary, Magda Michael, recalled the scene in the biography by Curtis: "It was a pathetic sight to view these two formerly virile, strong, vivacious men sitting there in their respective wheelchairs while Tully's nurse and I carried on the conversation in their stead, recounting events and experiences they had shared in the past, and which we both knew about, while the two of them sat silently nodding their heads in acquiescence. I truly believe this was one of the saddest afternoons I ever lived through."[84]

On a rainy Christmas Day, just a few minutes after noon, Fields, who might have preferred Philadelphia, went to a place where he would no longer suffer the indignities of dogs and children.[85] (By a coincidence that Tully would have appreciated, nearly three decades later, Charlie Chaplin also died on Christmas Day.) Tully dictated the sad news to his nurse and had the letter mailed to Mencken. "W. C. Fields has passed on. His last gesture was a finger over his lips and a wink at his nurse." The details of these final moments might be dismissed as the sort of jocularity that Tully and Mencken routinely exchanged but for the following sentence: "That will not be for public print." It was the last letter Tully would write. "Fields had great brain power," Tully wrote of his friend. "He hated Will Rogers, but was very intelligent about his hate. Why are comedians smarter than other hams? Perhaps because they do not take themselves so seriously."[86]

Tully's nurse considered him a model patient.[87] When his course of physical therapy was completed, he returned home, stuck between wheelchair and bed. As always, Myrtle babied him, but this time it was different and Jim knew it.[88] There would be no comeback, and for the first time in his sixty-one years, Jim bowed to the inevitable and threw in the towel.

With bloodshot eyes—Frank Scully remembered them as *always* bloodshot—he stared for hours at the ceiling and waved off his nurse whenever she approached with a syringe. Tully's red hair, which had howled like some wildfire from deep within his core, now suggested a mere puff of smoke. He was "bleached white," desiccated, and spent.[89]

He remained at home but for a brief outing on March 5, 1947, to visit a friend in the hospital. The *Santa Monica Evening Outlook* got wind of the visit and sent a photographer.[90] Readers would have been hard pressed to recognize the frail seated man with gray hair and sunglasses but for the book clutched in his hand. It was a paperback edition of *The Bruiser*, which had been reissued the previous November by Bantam in a printing of 250,000 copies.[91] The accompanying story referred to Tully in the past tense.

The *Evening Outlook*'s use of tense was premature by three months. On June 17, two weeks after his sixty-first birthday, Jim's heart began to fail and he was moved to Cedars of Lebanon Hospital. Too weak to resist and not having received a sacrament in decades, he was given extreme unction.[92] At 4 A.M. the following Sunday, June, 22, 1947, Jim Tully's ride across the American landscape reached the end of the line.[93] As Scully later wrote, "All his life he had been a fighter, but an hour before he died . . . he finally decided to go quietly."[94]

The news had barely reached the papers when a telegram arrived from Baltimore. Myrtle read the simple note: "THE LONG FEARED IS NEVERTHELESS A GREAT SHOCK MY UTMOST SYMPATHY WHAT A GOOD WIFE YOU HAVE BEEN. H. L. Mencken."[95]

And with that, the reviews, this time on the man rather than his books, rolled in. Jim's hometown paper in St. Marys dispatched him in four short paragraphs, noting that of Jim's St. Marys family, only sister Anna Durr and brother Charles remained (missing Hugh, still alive in 1947 and living in the Los Angeles area).[96]

The *New York Times* remembered Tully as "a cocky, little fellow, with strong likes and dislikes, a flair for dispute that some thought almost exhibitionist, an uproarious sense of humor, and, most important, a knowledge of America and its people. . . . Mr. Tully ignored hostile appraisals. He was convinced that, better than Hemingway, he portrayed the vast majority of people. 'If I ever get to the stage where I am not interested in taxi drivers and waiters and cops and gangsters and all the miscellaneous run of human beings, I'll be lost.'"[97] One of the last to appear, in the *Providence Journal*, was also one of the most insightful.

> Jim Tully put his cue back in the rack the other day, and all he rated was a few paragraphs on the obituary pages. Time was when his death would have hit the literary world almost as hard as his iron-fisted prose once did. That was 20 years ago, when *Beggars of Life* and *Jarnegan* came out and *Circus Parade* and *Shanty Irish* were best-sellers.
>
> Those were really hard-boiled books, tough stories by a rough-storyteller. What made them catch on was not their sensationalism; it was that they opened up a whole new world, a world the reading public had never

entered because no man who really knew that world had the ability to tell about it until Jim Tully came along.[98]

The funeral was held at Forest Lawn Memorial Park's Church of the Recessional in Glendale, California, where the minister read Sam Walter Foss's sentimental poem "House by the Side of the Road."[99] Frank Scully, his mind wandering, thought of Jim's description of the Strong Woman's funeral in *Circus Parade:* "The audience looked bored with piety."[100] Burial, Scully noted, held one final irony.[101] Jim Tully was laid to rest on the same slope in the Whispering Pines section as John Gilbert.[102]

Later that summer, Scully wrote a retrospective piece on Tully for the *Screen Writer.* Much had been made in the obituaries of Tully's larger-than-life personality. This self-confidence, which had lifted him out of grinding poverty, many confused with an oversized ego. Scully knew better. "On the other hand," Scully wrote, "he could bury his talent for the glorification of others. I am not thinking particularly of his writings for Chaplin or other ghostings. I am thinking of a time ten or twelve years ago when it looked as if I would bow out myself. He offered to fulfill any of my writing commitments. I remember one he completed by stealing freely from his own files and putting my name on the finished product."[103]

What then is one to make of Jim Tully? "I am a blending of terrible humility and overwhelming pride," he wrote Frank Scully in 1936. He claimed that all his core beliefs were outlined in the final chapter of *Beggars of Life,* written a dozen years earlier. "It is not that I have not grown. I was made bitter early."[104] Scully summarized Tully's writing as well as anyone: "Tully raised the lowest form of writing, fan magazines, to its highest level and dragged the writing of novels from the lofty heights of *Lord Fauntleroy* down to the realism of *Shanty Irish.*"[105]

Why then has Tully's work been so utterly forgotten? A couple of reasons come to mind.

As Thomas Curtiss of the *New York Times* noted in his review of *Biddy Brogan's Boy,* the gatekeepers of American literature in university English departments dismissed Tully as a primitive—at best, a folk artist.[106] Consequently Tully's work was rarely taught or anthologized and, like mystery and science-fiction writers, Tully was simply ignored.

With the Depression's grip loosening, readers were ready to embrace a new generation of writers who had come of age during the war. Being the "tough guy" writer is a young man's game, and Norman Mailer and others were more than ready to assume the mantle. When Tully did attempt a comeback in the late 1930s, it was too late. H. L. Mencken, Tully's most vocal advocate, had seen his own stock fall. In 1948 he was silenced by a devastating stroke that left him unable to read or write. Mencken died in 1956.

Falling off the map was certainly not unique to Tully. Fitzgerald and Faulkner also vanished only to be rediscovered. Faulkner lived to see his revival, Fitzgerald did not. Indeed, the eclipse of once-famous writers is the norm and few reputations survive intact.

Ernest Hemingway is the writer to whom Tully, thirteen years his senior, is most often compared. Both wrote about and were regarded as tough guys. Both were uniquely American. Yet there was a key difference. Hemingway portrayed men as they wished to be seen: strong, virile, and courageous. Tully portrayed men as they are: sometimes tough, sometimes virile, sometimes courageous, but more often grasping, venal, and cowardly. It's not hard to understand why one has become an American icon while the other has been forgotten.

Tully, one suspects, would have little interest in any of this, preferring instead an epitaph of own creation:

> Hobo, writer, fool, now dead
> Forevermore to joy or pain,
> His life was like a book, well read
> With each page dotted by the rain,
> And if dear worms, he's a trifle late . . .
> He took his time on a local freight.[107]

Epilogue

Myrtle had Jim draw up a will in September 1946. The attorney's bill was addressed to her and there is no evidence that anything unusual took place, as Myrtle had been managing Jim's affairs since he'd become ill.[1] The will was filed with probate the month following Jim's death, and it was revealed that he had willed his entire estate, $25,000, to his widow.[2] Trilby, feeling that her legacy had been taken from her, filed suit two weeks later. Her suit alleged that her father was not of sound mind and had been "unduly influenced" by Myrtle.[3] A settlement was reached in September 1947, with Trilby and Alton receiving a cash payment and Myrtle agreeing to will them half of her estate.[4] Trilby and Ray had another child, Jim's last grandchild, Robin, in 1954.

The estate was hardly enough for Myrtle, age fifty-two, to live out her days in comfortable widowhood. She returned to work as a personal secretary to Judy Garland for five years, followed by three years with Greer Garson, before retiring after seven years with Deborah Kerr.[5] Her time with Garland was particularly memorable. Ten days after being suspended by MGM in June 1950 for repeated absenteeism, Judy Garland was calmly going over her options with her husband, director Vincente Minnelli, and Myrtle Tully. Neither Minnelli nor Tully noticed anything unusual when Garland withdrew to use the bathroom. Suddenly Garland screamed, "Leave me alone, I want to die!"[6] Her husband and secretary rushed to the door and found it locked. When Garland refused to unlock the door, Minnelli picked up a chair and smashed it open. They found Garland had cut her throat, not deeply, and was still clutching a broken water glass. Minnelli took the glass from her hand while Myrtle tearfully embraced the distraught star. Help was summoned while Myrtle pressed a towel to Garland's throat.[7]

Two years later, Tully, as Garland called her, served as Garland's matron of honor at her June 1952 wedding to Sid Luft.[8] Myrtle moved into the Motion Picture and Television retirement home in 1975 and died on August 31, 1982.[9] She was buried next to Jim in Forest Lawn.

From the misery of his later childhood to life on the road, and through his boxing years, Jim Tully had absorbed—and shaken off—many hard blows. "He could take a punch" could well have been his epitaph. But had he lived long enough for the hammer blow delivered by the April 20, 1950, *Los Angeles Times* headline, it would have loosened his teeth: "Author Jim Tully's Son Joins Wife in Suicide."

Following his stint as a yeoman with the Merchant Marine during the war, on October 16, 1946, Alton married Margaret Becker, an army nurse from York, Pennsylvania. He moved into her one-and-a-half-room apartment at 611 West 113th Street in New York City, just up Broadway from her job at Jewish Memorial Hospital. At five A.M. on April 10, Margaret noticed that Alton appeared agitated, and he told his wife he was wanted for rape. Depressed about the long prison term he knew would be coming, he walked out the door and disappeared into the early morning. An hour later the police arrived.[10] Alton was being sought in connection with burglary and the attempted rape of a fellow employee, a twenty-four-year-old Bellmore, Long Island, woman. When police didn't find him at home, they put out a thirteen-state alarm.[11]

His wife brooded the rest of the week before pouring out her soul to her neighbor, Mrs. Jean Garnier. Mrs. Garnier quoted Mrs. Tully as saying: "If I find him I'm going to talk him into ending our lives. There's no use in living on. He will get a long stretch. He would not have the nerve to do it alone. I love him so much I can't live with him or without him. It is better for both of us to die. The best way, the easiest way, will be by carbon monoxide in a car. All you do is put a hose in the exhaust pipe and we will both die together."[12]

The *Los Angeles Times* quoted Mrs. Tully as saying, "We can't go on living like this. If I find him, I'll try a suicide pact. He hasn't the guts to do it himself—and he's not fit to live in this world."[13] The following day, a Saturday, she received a letter from her husband. She again went to Mrs. Garnier and said, "Tomorrow I'm going to church. If I don't get back, notify my sister, Mrs. Eva Boyd, 471½ College Ave., York, PA. Tell her you think I have killed myself. I can't face this scandal in the hospital."[14] She then handed Mrs. Garnier an envelope containing her birth and marriage certificates and other personal papers and disappeared.

Three hundred miles away, on April 19, Pennsylvania state police near Bedford, tipped off by a woodcutter, located what appeared to be an abandoned black 1941 Oldsmobile with New York plates. A hose ran from the exhaust to one of the car's windows, the gap having been plugged with rags. Two badly decomposed bodies were found inside. The man's body had one foot on the pedal and his arm around the female's shoulders. Both wore wedding rings.[15] Identification was aided by a tattoo on the dead man's right upper arm. It was a dagger through a heart. And in bold letters the needle had left the words "Death Before Dishonor."[16]

Appendix

The Published Works of Jim Tully

BOOKS

Emmett Lawler (New York: Harcourt, Brace, 1922)
Beggars of Life (New York: Albert & Charles Boni, 1924)
Jarnegan (New York: Albert & Charles Boni, 1926)
Circus Parade (New York: Albert & Charles Boni, 1927)
Twenty Below (with Robert Nichols; London: Robert Holden, 1927)
Shanty Irish (New York: Albert & Charles Boni, 1928)
Shadows of Men (New York: Doubleday, Doran, 1930)
Beggars Abroad (New York: Doubleday, Doran, 1930)
Blood on the Moon (New York: Coward-McCann, 1931)
Laughter in Hell (New York: Albert & Charles Boni, 1932)
Ladies in the Parlor (New York: Greenberg, 1935)
The Bruiser (New York: Greenberg, 1936)
Biddy Brogan's Boy (New York: Charles Scribner's Sons, 1942)
A Dozen and One (Hollywood, Calif.: Murray & Gee, 1943)

PAMPHLET

A Man of the New School (a 1931 pamphlet by Tully published by the Greater Hotel Gibson in Cincinnati)

APPENDIX

The Unpublished Manuscripts of Jim Tully (most at UCLA)

"Passing Strangers" (novel about migratory laborers completed in 1922)
"The Life of Thomas H. Ince" (biography completed in 1925)
"Black Boy" (play, with Frank Dazey, produced in New York in 1926)
"Denis Darel" (novel worked on in 1927)
"The Life of Charlie Chaplin" (biography completed in 1927)
"God Loves the Irish" (play version of *Shanty Irish* completed in 1928; reworked in 1929 with Charles Beahan, and alone in 1936)
"Close-Ups" (series of profiles, probably *Vanity Fair* pieces, completed in 1929 and at one time slated for publication by A&C Boni)
"The Seventh Commandment" (play written in 1930 with E. M. Somlyo; never produced)
"Adventures in Interviewing" (book started in 1931, probably based on magazine interviews; title used for 1937 Cinema Arts column)
"Men in the Rough" (collection of profiles written in 1932 and 1933)
"Blood Money" (novel started in 1933)
"The Raven" (final draft of screenplay written with David Boehm for Universal, Nov. 23, 1934)
"All or Nothing" (draft of *The Bruiser*, Sept. 1935)
"Hollywood Decameron" (a collection of short stories about the movie industry, including some about director Jack Jarnegan—"A Hollywood Interlude" and "Enemies and Friends"—and "Puzzums," a satirical tale about a movie-star cat; begun in 1936, probably finished in 1938)
"The King of Laughter" (a new version of his Chaplin biography, started in 1936, revisited in late 1939 and 1940)
"Half-Sister of the Lord" (novel about evangelist Sally Slocum, based on Aimee Semple McPherson; started in 1936, first draft completed in 1937, revised in 1944 and 1945)
"A Stranger Appears" (twenty-six-chapter manuscript about the rambling visions of a wanderer and morphine addict; draft completed in 1937)
"Honor among Thieves" (undated manuscript submitted to Greenberg)
The Bruiser adaptation MS (with Walter Cohen; Motion Pictures of Tomorrow, Jan. 1938)
"Children of Thieves" (1938 manuscript about road-kids)
"Out of My Heart" (autobiography started in 1938 as "Not So Long Ago," changed to "Gone Are the Days," "I Passed by Here," and, finally, "Out of My Heart")
"Men I Remember" (collection of profiles, similar to *A Dozen and One*, started in 1939)
"The Winds of Wonder" (book of Irish fairy tales and folklore, started in 1939, worked on through 1942)

"Ringside: The Story of Pugilism" (1940 history of boxing based on his *Vanity Fair* series)

"Road Girl" (1940 novel)

"John the Great" (Sept. 26, 1942, draft of a review of Donald Barr Chidsey, *John the Great: The Biography of John L. Sullivan* [New York: Doubleday, Doran, 1942])

"Rave Lafferty" (novel started in 1942 as "A Broadway Doctor," later changed to the story of an Irish Jewish gangster who goes to war)

"New York Amusements" (undated reminiscence about St. Marys, Ohio)

"Road Kids" (undated manuscript)

"Champions Inside the Ropes" (undated boxing manuscript)

Undated manuscript about San Francisco

Major Adaptations of Books by Jim Tully

Outside Looking In, by Maxwell Anderson (play version of *Beggars of Life*, produced in New York in 1925)

Jarnegan, by Charles Beahan and Garrett Fort (play version of Tully's novel, produced in New York in 1928)

Beggars of Life, by Benjamin Glazer (film version of Tully's book, directed by William Wellman and released by Paramount Pictures in 1928)

Laughter in Hell (film version of Tully's novel, starring Pat O'Brien and released by Universal Pictures in 1932)

Notes

The following abbreviations are used throughout these notes:

B—Jim Tully, *The Bruiser* (New York: Greenberg, 1936)

BA—Jim Tully, *Beggars Abroad* (Garden City, N.Y.: Doubleday, Doran, 1930)

BBB—Jim Tully, *Biddy Brogan's Boy* (New York: Charles Scribner's Sons, 1942)

BL—Jim Tully, *Beggars of Life: A Hobo Autobiography* (New York: Albert & Charles Boni, 1924)

BM—Jim Tully, *Blood on the Moon* (New York: Coward-McCann, 1931)

CORN—George Jean Nathan Collection, Cornell University Library

CP—Jim Tully, *Circus Parade* (New York: Albert & Charles Boni, 1927)

DOZ—Jim Tully, *A Dozen and One* (Hollywood, Calif.: Murray & Gee, 1943)

EL—Jim Tully, *Emmett Lawler* (New York: Harcourt, Brace, 1922)

HLM—H. L. Mencken

HLMNY—Henry Louis Mencken Papers, Manuscripts and Archives Division, New York Public Library

HLMP—H. L. Mencken Collection, Princeton University Library

IPBH—Jim Tully, "I Passed by Here," unpublished MS, Jim Tully Papers (Collection 250), Dept. of Special Collections, Charles E. Young Research Library, University of California, Los Angeles

JARN—Jim Tully, *Jarnegan* (New York: Albert & Charles Boni, 1926)

JDT—James Dennis Tully

JT—Jim Tully

LAT—*Los Angeles Times*

LH—Jim Tully, *Laughter in Hell* (New York: Albert & Charles Boni, 1932)

LP—Jim Tully, *Ladies in the Parlor* (New York: Greenberg, 1935)

ML—Jim Tully, autobiographical notes about Mary Lygo, Jim Tully Papers (Collection 250), Dept. of Special Collections, Charles E. Young Research Library, University of California, Los Angeles

NYT—*New York Times*

OMH—Jim Tully, "Out of My Heart," unpublished MS, Jim Tully Papers (Collection 250), Dept. of Special Collections, Charles E. Young Research Library, University of California, Los Angeles

SCRIB—Archives of Charles Scribner's Sons, Dept. of Rare Books and Special Collections, Princeton University Library

SI—Jim Tully, *Shanty Irish* (New York: Albert & Charles Boni, 1928)

SM—Jim Tully, *Shadows of Men* (New York: Doubleday, Doran, 1930)

UCLA—Jim Tully Papers (Collection 250), Dept. of Special Collections, Charles E. Young Research Library, University of California, Los Angeles

UVA, H. L. Mencken Collection, Special Collections Dept., University of Virginia Library

Introduction

1. *BM*, 9; JT to HLM, July 25, 1942, HLMNY.
2. *BM*, 282; IPBH.
3. JT, "The Most Unforgettable Character I Ever Met," *Reader's Digest*, Jan. 1941, 12.
4. *BM*, 282–83.
5. JT, "Portrait of My Father," *Esquire*, Nov. 1939, 90–91.
6. *BBB*, 66; OMH.
7. JT, "Jim Tully by Himself," *LAT*, Nov. 20, 1921; also see *BM*, 330; IPBH.
8. *BL*, 327.
9. JT, "My Literary Fight, Round by Round," *Literary Digest International Book Review*, undated clipping (1923), UCLA.
10. JT to George Derby, Feb. 11, 1930, CORN.
11. *BM*, 349; JT to George Derby, Feb. 11, 1930, CORN.
12. *BM*, 12.
13. *BL*, 327.
14. JT to George Nathan, Aug. 19, 1931, CORN.
15. *SI*, Garden City, Garden City Pub., 1928, 251–52.
16. JT to George Derby, Feb. 11, 1930, CORN.
17. Edwin Clark, "Spielers, Shillabers, Fat Ladies and Clowns; Jim Tully's *Circus Parade* Is a Carnival of Low Life and Mixed Emotions," *NYT*, Aug. 7, 1927, BR5; Frank Scully, "Jim Tully," *Scribner's*, Aug. 1937, 51.
18. JT, "Are You Sitting in a Breeze?" *Rob Wagner's Script*, Aug. 24, 1935, 7.
19. Lee Server, *Robert Mitchum: "Baby, I Don't Care"* (New York: St. Martin's Press, 2002), 23–24.
20. Francis Davis, *The History of the Blues* (New York, Hyperion, 1995), 91.
21. Scully, "Jim Tully," 52.
22. Ibid., 51–52.
23. JT, "A Declaration," *Smart Set*, Dec. 1923, reprinted in *The Smart Set Anthology*, ed. Burton Rascoe and Geoff Conklin (New York: Reynal & Hitchcock, 1934), 460–62.
24. Jack London, *The Cruise of the Snark* (New York: Macmillan, 1911), 5.
25. Paul Chapman, "Tully, Jim," in *Ohio Authors and Their Books*, ed. William Coyle (Cleveland: World Publishing, 1962), 648; David D. Anderson, "A Portrait of Jim Tully: An Ohio Boyhood and Hollywood," *Society for the Study of Midwestern Literature Newsletter* 12 (Spring 1982); David D. Anderson, "An Ohio Boyhood in Jim Tully's Fiction," *Society for the Study of Midwestern Literature Newsletter* 24 (Fall 1994).
26. Ray Hinkle, *The Hobo from St. Marys: A Tribute to Jim Tully* (Blackwell, Okla.: Privately printed, 1986).
27. Maura McMillan, "Collecting Jim Tully," *Firsts: The Book Collector's Magazine*, Feb. 2001, 30–39; Charles Willeford, *Writing & Other Blood Sports* (Tucson, Ariz.: Dennis McMillan Pub., 2000), 89–105.
28. H. Bruce Franklin, *Prison Literature in America: The Victim as Criminal and Artist* (New York: Oxford University Press, 1989).
29. Charles Fanning, *The Irish Voice in America: 250 Years of Irish-American Fiction* (Lexington: University Press of Kentucky, 2000).
30. Ron Ebest, *Private Histories: The Writings of Irish Americans, 1900–1935* (Notre Dame, Ind.: University of Notre Dame Press, 2005).
31. Joseph Mitchell, *Old Mr. Flood* (New York: Duell, Sloan and Pearce, 1948), vii.
32. JT to George Derby, Feb. 11, 1930, CORN.
33. These manuscripts are located in the Jim Tully Papers (Collection 250), Dept. of Special Collections, Charles E. Young Research Library, University of California, Los Angeles.
34. JT to HLM, Oct. 27, 1939, HLMNY.
35. IPBH.
36. Tully was not consistent on this point and would sometimes refer to himself as a hobo. This was correct only in a generic sense. More often, he described himself as a road-kid.
37. Nels Anderson, "Raw Life," *Survey*, Dec. 1924, 289.
38. "Jim Tully, Hobo and Side-Door Pullman Passenger," *NYT*, Jan. 4, 1925.

39. JT to HLM, Aug. 25, 1927, HLMNY.
40. IPBH; also see JT to George Derby, Feb. 11, 1930, CORN.
41. "Death Takes Original of Tully's Character, 'Blackie' of 'The Circus Parade' Dies Friendless and Penniless in Columbus Lodging Home," *Kent Tribune*, Sept. 27, 1928.
42. *BM*, 11.
43. Scully, "Jim Tully," 52.

1. Coins for a Dead Woman's Eyes

1. *SI*, 1–3.
2. Cecil Woodham-Smith, *The Great Hunger: Ireland, 1845–1849* (London: Hamish Hamilton, 1962), 40.
3. Redcliffe N. Salaman, *The History and Social Influence of the Potato*, ed. J. G. Hawkes (1949; Cambridge: Cambridge University Press, 1985), 301.
4. Woodham-Smith, *The Great Hunger*, 411.
5. JDT to JT, March 13, 1929, UCLA.
6. JDT to JT, Oct. 5, 1927, UCLA.
7. Agnes Tully to JT, Nov. 20 [1927], UCLA.
8. JDT to JT, Oct. 13, 1927, UCLA.
9. Ibid.
10. JDT to JT, Oct. 3, 1927, UCLA; JDT to JT, Oct. 13, 1927, UCLA; JT to George Derby, Feb. 11, 1930, CORN.
11. JDT to JT, Oct. 3, 1927, UCLA.
12. Ibid.
13. JDT to JT, Oct. 5, 1927, UCLA.
14. JDT to JT, Oct. 13, 1927, UCLA; JDT to JT, Oct. 5, 1927, UCLA.
15. J. D. Simkins, *Early History of Auglaize County* (St. Marys, Ohio: Argus, 1901), 73, 78–82.
16. Ibid., 73.
17. C. W. Williamson, *History of Western Ohio and Auglaize County* (Columbus: Linn, 1905), 434–38.
18. JT, "Portrait of My Father," *Esquire*, Nov. 1939, 90–91.
19. JDT to JT, Oct. 13, 1927, UCLA.
20. Ibid.
21. Ibid.; James Dennis Tully and Bridget Lawler, marriage license, Feb. 8, 1875, Auglaize County, Ohio.
22. Agnes Tully to JT, Nov. 20 [1927], UCLA.
23. JDT to JT, Oct. 13, 1927, UCLA.
24. Bridget Tully, death certificate, Mercer County, Ohio, Probate Death No. 2, May 1, 1892.
25. JDT to JT, Oct. 13, 1927, UCLA.
26. JDT to JT, Oct. 3, 1927, UCLA.
27. Ibid.
28. OMH.
29. JDT to JT, Oct. 13, 1927, UCLA; OHM.
30. Order of Sale, Probate Court, Auglaize County, Ohio, July 6, 1892.
31. JDT to JT, Oct. 3, 1927, UCLA; JDT to JT, Oct. 13, 1927, UCLA.
32. JDT to JT, Oct. 13, 1927, UCLA.
33. Frank Cole to JT, March 7, 1941, UCLA.
34. JDT to JT, Oct. 13, 1927, UCLA.
35. James Tully, baptismal register, June 6, 1886, Holy Rosary Church, St. Marys, Ohio; Charles Tully, baptismal register, Feb. 10, 1884, Holy Rosary Church, St. Marys, Ohio.
36. JDT to JT, June 4, 1936, UCLA.
37. JDT to JT, Oct. 13, 1927, UCLA.
38. OMH.
39. JDT to JT, Oct. 13, 1927, UCLA.
40. JDT to JT, Sept. 31 [Oct. 1], 1927, UCLA.
41. JDT to JT, Oct. 13, 1927, UCLA.
42. *SI*, 34; OMH.
43. James Schultz to JT, Feb. 14, 1941, UCLA.
44. Ibid.
45. OMH.
46. JDT to JT, Oct. 3, 1927, UCLA.
47. James Schultz to JT, Feb. 14, 1941, UCLA.
48. Frank Cole to JT, March 7, 1941, UCLA.
49. *SI*, 51–52; OMH.
50. OMH.
51. Ibid.; *SI*, 52–53.
52. *SI*, 53–54; OMH.
53. OMH.

54. JDT to JT, Sept. 31, 1927, UCLA.
55. OMH; IPBH.
56. IPBH.
57. JDT to JT, Sept. 31, 1927, UCLA.
58. JDT to JT, Oct. 3, 1927, UCLA.
59. OMH.
60. Ibid.
61. *SI*, 38.
62. JT, "Portrait of My Father," 120.
63. *SI*, 36.
64. JDT to JT, Sept. 31, 1927, UCLA.
65. *SI*, 38.
66. JDT to JT, Oct. 13, 1927, UCLA.
67. JT, "Portrait of My Father," 91.
68. *SI*, 57.
69. Ibid., 58–59.
70. JT to George Derby, Feb. 11, 1930, CORN.
71. JDT to JT, Oct. 3, 1927, UCLA.
72. *SI*, 61.
73. Ibid., 70.
74. Ibid., 72.
75. JDT to JT, Oct. 3, 1927, UCLA.
76. OMH; IPBH.
77. IPBH.
78. Ibid.
79. *SI*, 33.
80. JDT to JT, Sept. 31, 1927, UCLA.
81. JT to George Derby, Feb. 11, 1930, CORN.
82. JDT to JT, Oct. 13, 1927, UCLA; JDT to JT, June 26, 1929, UCLA.
83. OMH.
84. *SI*, 240.
85. JDT to JT, June 26, 1929, UCLA. John Lawler's death is also given as 1894 in Tom Lawler to JT, Jan. 24 [1929], UCLA.
86. OMH.
87. JDT to JT, Oct. 13, 1927, UCLA; Margaret Lawler, death register, St. Patrick's Church, Glynnwood, Ohio, March 2, 1892.
88. *SI*, 97.
89. Bridget Tully, death certificate.
90. OMH.
91. IPBH.
92. JDT to JT, Sept. 31, 1927, UCLA.
93. Family lore gives the stillborn infant's name as Henry. Michael Hatherly, "Descendants of James Dennis Tully" (privately printed, 2003).
94. OMH.
95. Ibid.
96. Ibid.
97. Gertrude Lawler to JT, Aug. 17, 1931, UCLA; OMH.

2. Six Years of Imprisonment

1. IPBH.
2. Ibid.
3. Ibid.; OMH; Mary Ellen Brown, ed., *A History of St. Patrick Catholic Church and Glynnwood, Ohio* (n.p.: Privately printed, 2007), 19.
4. *BBB*, 61.
5. IPBH.
6. Ibid.; OMH.
7. IPBH.
8. Ibid.; OMH.
9. OMH.
10. JT, "Portrait of My Father," *Esquire*, Nov. 1939, 90–91.
11. IPBH.
12. OMH.
13. *BBB*, 65.
14. *SI*, 101.
15. Ibid., 102.
16. JT to HLM, Nov. 7, 1927, HLMNY.
17. IPBH.
18. JT to George Derby, Feb. 11, 1930, CORN.
19. *Chicago Daily News*, Nov. 11, 1936.
20. OMH; IPBH.
21. Ibid.; ibid.
22. IPBH.
23. H. F. Manchester, "Fear of Bread Line Still Dogs Jim Tully," *Boston Herald*, June 9, 1929.
24. Frank Scully, "Scully on Tully," *Screen Writer*, Aug. 1947, 8, UCLA.
25. IPBH; OMH.
26. JT to Frank Scully, July 9, 1936, carbon copy, authors' collection.
27. IPBH.
28. OMH.
29. Ibid.
30. IPBH.
31. Jim Tully, "A Declaration," *Smart Set*, Dec. 1923, reprinted in *The Smart Set Anthology*, ed. Burton Rascoe and Geoff Conklin (New York: Reynal & Hitchcock, 1934), 461.

32. *BM*, 25.
33. OMH.
34. IPBH.
35. Ibid.
36. Manchester, "Fear of Bread Line."
37. OMH.
38. IPBH.
39. OMH.
40. Ibid.

3. Hearts Ignorant of Homes

1. OMH; IPBH.
2. OMH.
3. Ibid.; IPBH.
4. W. T. Hoeken, "Jim Tully, Noted Hollywood Writer, Spent Early Years of His Youth in Van Wert County," Dec. 1, 1928, clipping from unknown newspaper, UCLA; OMH. Or to be precise, as Jim later wrote, it was "a mile or so from Biggett toward the Paulding County line, and is on the corner of the road that goes to Tully township." JT to Marie Kuhn, Feb. 26, 1939, Ohioana Library, Columbus.
5. Michael B. Lafferty, ed., *Ohio's Natural Heritage* (Columbus: Ohio Academy of Science, 1979), 238.
6. OMH.
7. *BM*, 32–33.
8. JT, "Portrait of My Father," *Esquire*, Nov. 1939, 90.
9. *BM*, 32–33.
10. OMH; JT, "Portrait of My Father," 90.
11. Thomas W. Schmidlin and Jeanne Appelhans Schmidlin, *Thunder in the Heartland: A Chronicle of Outstanding Weather Events in Ohio* (Kent, Ohio: Kent State University Press, 1996), 88–92.
12. OMH.
13. *BL*, 23.
14. Herbert Boroff to JT, Dec. 13, 1938, UCLA.
15. IPBH; JT, "Portrait of My Father," 90.
16. *EL*, 34–35; OMH; IPBH.
17. IPBH.
18. JT, "Portrait of My Father," 90.
19. *BM*, 33.
20. Hoeken, "Jim Tully, Noted Hollywood Writer."
21. *EL*, 51.
22. OMH.
23. *BL*, 23.
24. *EL*, 64.
25. Hoeken, "Jim Tully, Noted Hollywood Writer."
26. OMH.
27. *BM*, 51.
28. "Deaths," *St. Marys Argus and Democrat*, Aug. 16, 1900; Hugh Tully, death register, Holy Rosary Church, St. Marys, Ohio, Aug. 9, 1900, in Historical Archives of the Chancery of the Archdiocese of Cincinnati; gravestone, Hugh Tully, Old Catholic Cemetery, St. Marys, Ohio.
29. Gravestone, Catherine Tully, Old Catholic Cemetery, St. Marys, Ohio.
30. OMH.
31. JT, "Portrait of My Father," 90.
32. JDT to JT, Oct. 13, 1927, UCLA.
33. OMH; IPBH.
34. *EL*, 89.
35. Auglaize County Historical Society, ed., *A History of Auglaize County, Ohio* (St. Marys, Ohio: Auglaize County Historical Society, 1980), 1, 24.
36. *EL*, 90.
37. William McMurray, ed., *History of Auglaize County, Ohio*, vol. 1 (Indianapolis: Historical Publishing Co., 1923), 194.
38. St. Marys Spirit of '76 Bicentennial Committee, *Portrayal of St. Marys, Ohio: Past and Present* (St. Marys, Ohio: Allied Press, 1976).
39. JT, "New York Amusements," unpublished MS, UCLA.
40. McMurray, *History of Auglaize County, Ohio*, 28.
41. Ibid., 215–19.
42. St. Marys Spirit of '76 Bicentennial Committee, *Portrayal of St. Marys, Ohio*.
43. *EL*, 96.
44. OMH.
45. *EL*, 97.
46. Ibid., 96–97.
47. OMH.
48. JT to HLM, Dec. 12, 1938, UCLA.
49. OMH.
50. Ibid.
51. JT, "The Most Unforgettable Character I Ever Met," *Reader's Digest*, Jan. 1941, 10–11.

52. JT, "Portrait of My Father," 90.
53. *BL*, 11.
54. OMH.
55. Kenneth Allsop, *Hard Travelin': The Hobo and His History* (New York: New American Library, 1967), 159.
56. *BL*, 14.
57. Ibid., 13–14.
58. OMH.
59. Ibid.
60. Ibid.
61. *SI*, 249.
62. OMH.
63. *BL*, 12.
64. Ibid., 11–13.
65. Ibid., 14.
66. Ibid., 15.
67. Ibid., 19.
68. Allsop, *Hard Travelin'*, 105.
69. Cited in ibid., 110.
70. Ibid., 215.
71. *BL*, 20–21.
72. OMH.
73. Ibid.; St. Marys Spirit of '76 Bicentennial Committee, *Portrayal of St. Marys, Ohio*.
74. OMH.
75. Ibid.
76. *BL*, 21.
77. OMH.
78. Ibid.
79. Ibid.
80. Ibid.
81. Ibid.
82. Ibid.
83. JT, "Memorial to Charles W. Koch," *St. Marys Evening Leader*, March 18, 1939; JT to Marie Kuhn, Feb. 26, 1939, Ohioana Library, Columbus.
84. OMH.

4. Big Rock Candy Mountain

1. *BL*, 49.
2. JT, "The Most Unforgettable Character I Ever Met," *Reader's Digest*, Jan. 1941, 12.
3. *BL*, 334–35.
4. Kenneth Allsop, *Hard Travelin': The Hobo and His History* (New York: New American Library, 1967), 137.
5. *SM*, 7.
6. *CP*, 3–4.
7. Ibid., 4.
8. *BL*, 129; JT, "Sapping Day," *American Mercury*, April 1929.
9. JT, "Jim Tully, Author, Began Career with Pencil Stolen off Bum Here," letter to *Mobile Times*, undated clipping (Aug. 1933), UCLA.
10. Ibid.
11. JT, "Tully-Grams," *Hollywood Tribune*, Sept. 18, 1939.
12. Roger A. Bruns, *The Damndest Radical: The Life and World of Ben Reitman, Chicago's Celebrated Social Reformer, Hobo King, and Whorehouse Physician* (Urbana: University of Illinois Press, 1987), 37.
13. Quoted in Clark C. Spence, "Knights of the Fast Freight," *American Heritage*, Aug. 1976.
14. JT, "Jim Tully by Himself," *LAT*, Nov. 20, 1921.
15. *BM*, 9–10.
16. Roger A. Bruns, *Knights of the Road: A Hobo History* (New York: Methuen, 1980), 204.
17. Quoted in Bruns, *The Damndest Radical*, 44.
18. A glossary of hobo jargon may be found in Bruns, *Knights of the Road*, 200–204.
19. *BM*, 10.
20. *BL*, 41.
21. Ibid.
22. JT to HLM, July 2, 1940, HLMNY.
23. *BL*, 42.
24. Ibid., 45.
25. *Chicago Daily News*, Nov. 11, 1936.
26. Ibid.
27. JT to George Nathan, Aug. 19, 1931, CORN.
28. JT to Frank Scully, July 9, 1936, carbon copy, authors' collection; Frank Scully, "Jim Tully," *Scribner's*, Aug. 1937, 52; IPBH.
29. JT to Frank Scully, July 9, 1936, carbon copy, authors' collection.
30. *BL*, 50.
31. Ibid.
32. Ibid., 54.
33. JT to Frank Scully, July 9, 1936, carbon copy, authors' collection.
34. *BL*, 129.
35. Ibid., 153.
36. Ibid., 155.

37. Ibid., 158.
38. Ibid., 159.
39. Ibid., 163.
40. Ibid.
41. Ibid., 165.
42. Ibid.
43. Letter from St. Luke's Hospital, June 24, 1941, citing an interview with Tully in the *Chicago Daily News*, May 22, 1941, UCLA.
44. *SM*, 289.
45. *BL*, 166.
46. Ibid., 187.
47. Tully recalled it as the *Fast Flyer Virginia* in *Beggars of Life*.
48. Foster Egner, "Jim Tully's Tribute to Judge Lueders," *Western and Southern Life Insurance Company Field News*, Sept. 29, 1930, reprinted from the *Cincinnati Post*, UCLA.
49. *BL*, 197–98.
50. Ibid., 203.
51. Ibid., 207.
52. Ibid., 211.
53. JT, "An Ex-Hobo's Tribute to Olive Schreiner," *Literary Digest International Book Review*, Sept. 1925.
54. JT, "Women in Literature," *Story World*, May 1925.
55. *BL*, 268.
56. Ibid., 272.
57. Ibid., 273.
58. Ibid., 308–9.
59. J. Gordon Melton, *Biographical Dictionary of American Cult and Sect Leaders* (New York: Garland, 1986), 73–74; Philip L. Cook, *Zion City, Illinois: Twentieth-Century Utopia* (Syracuse, N.Y.: Syracuse University Press, 1996), 156; Rose A. Lie, "Career of a Former Barefoot St. Marys Boy," *St. Marys Evening Leader*, Nov. 9, 1914, reprinted from *Waukegan Daily Gazette*, Oct. 12, 1914.
60. Cook, *Zion City, Illinois*, 156.
61. JT to HLM, n.d., 1927, HLMNY.
62. Egner, "Jim Tully's Tribute."
63. *BM*, 152–53.
64. Ibid., 154.
65. *Adrian Telegram*, April 4, 1925, UCLA.
66. "Jim Tully Likes Boxing and Keats," *New York Post*, June 2, 1922.
67. Ibid.
68. Ibid.

69. JT, "Road Kids," unpublished MS, UCLA.
70. "Jim Tully Likes Boxing and Keats," *New York Post*, June 2, 1922.
71. JT quoted in "Radio Column," *Hollywood Citizen-News*, Oct. 4, 1937.
72. JT, letter to the drama editor, Sept. 15, 1925, clipping from unknown newspaper, UCLA; JT to HLM, Nov. 18, 1927, HLMNY.
73. *SM*, 134.
74. JT to HLM, Jan. 26, 1925, Enoch Pratt Free Library, Baltimore; *SM*, 287–91.
75. JT, "The Most Unforgettable Character," 11.
76. *CP*, 3.
77. Ibid., 31.
78. Interview with Eugene Rhodes in *Brentano's Book Chat*, June 1922, UCLA.
79. *CP*, 65.
80. Mark Twain, "Concerning the Jews," in *The Man That Corrupted Hadleyburg and Other Stories and Essays* (New York: Harper & Brothers, 1900), 254.
81. H. F. Manchester, "Fear of Bread Line Still Dogs Tully," *Boston Herald*, June 9, 1929.
82. *CP*, 50.
83. Ibid., 204.

5. The End of the Road

1. *BM*, 227–28.
2. Ibid., 230–31.
3. Foster Egner, "Jim Tully's Tribute to Judge Lueders," *Western and Southern Life Insurance Company Field News*, Sept. 29, 1930, reprinted from the *Cincinnati Post*, UCLA.
4. *BM*, 240.
5. Helen Detzel, *Cincinnati Times-Star*, Sept. 20, 1929.
6. Ibid.
7. *BM*, 268.
8. George Neargarder, *Auglaize County Postcard Images* (n.p.: Auglaize County Historical Society, 2008), 107; St. Marys Spirit of '76 Bicentennial Committee, *Portrayal of St. Marys, Ohio: Past and Present* (St. Marys, Ohio: Allied Press, 1976).
9. ML.
10. JT, "Romance Dead in Hoboland," *LAT*, June 18, 1922.

11. JT to Alfred Dashiell, Oct. 21, 1926, SCRIB.
12. Louis Filler, *Crusaders for American Liberalism* (Yellow Springs, Ohio: Antioch Press, 1964), 68–79, 398.
13. JT, "Romance Dead in Hoboland."
14. Ibid.
15. JT, "The Long Bulge Upwards," *Britannia & Eve*, Aug. 1929.
16. *BM*, 228–29.
17. JT, "Romance Dead in Hoboland."
18. "Josiah Flynt Willard Dead," *NYT*, Jan. 22, 1907.
19. JT, "The Most Unforgettable Character I Ever Met," *Reader's Digest*, Jan. 1941, 11.
20. JT, "Ex-Follies Girl," *Illustrated Love Magazine*, March 1932, 28.
21. Ibid., 28–29, 83.
22. JT, "The Most Unforgettable Character," 11–12.
23. Ibid., 12.
24. ML.
25. Ibid.
26. *BM*, 283.
27. IPBH.
28. ML.
29. IPBH.
30. Ibid.
31. ML.
32. Ibid.
33. *BM*, 282.
34. *BL*, 327.
35. Ibid., 198–99.
36. ML.
37. Ibid.
38. Ibid.
39. IPBH.
40. Ibid.
41. *BM*, 283.

6. The Fire and the Ring

1. James B. Holm, ed., *Portage Heritage* (n.p.: Portage County Historical Society, 1957), 337.
2. Ibid., 159.
3. *BM*, 263.
4. Karl Grismer, *The History of Kent* (Kent, Ohio: Courier-Tribune, 1932), 97–98.
5. Ibid.
6. "J. G. Evans, Sr., Started Business Here 44 Years Ago," *Kent Tribune*, Sept. 4, 1924.
7. Ibid.
8. Grismer, *The History of Kent*, 99.
9. Ibid., 91.
10. Ibid., 91, 138.
11. Ibid., 90, 200.
12. Ibid., 93.
13. IPBH.
14. Ibid.
15. Grismer, *The History of Kent*, 86.
16. *BM*, 283–84; Grismer, *The History of Kent*, 93.
17. *BM*, 274.
18. Ibid., 283–85; Russell Schneider, *The Cleveland Indians Encyclopedia* (Philadelphia: Temple University Press, 1996), 12.
19. *BM*, 284–85.
20. Ibid., 285.
21. Francis Kline, personal interview, Nov. 30, 1992; Grismer, *The History of Kent*, 106.
22. Ruth Greer, personal interview, Nov. 30, 1992.
23. Titus Jackman, personal interview, Jan. 25, 2000.
24. *BM*, 286.
25. Holm, *Portage Heritage*, 119–20.
26. G. R. Adams to JT, Feb. 8, 1933, UCLA.
27. IPBH.
28. "Radio Column," *Hollywood Citizen-News*, Oct. 4, 1937.
29. IPBH; Roger Di Paolo, "From Kent to the Battlefields of France," *Kent-Ravenna Record-Courier*, April 22, 1990; *BM*, 316–17; Roger Di Paolo, *Rooted in Kent: 101 Tales from the Tree City* (Kent, Ohio: Kent Historical Society, 2009), 171–72; Grismer, *The History of Kent*, 143–44.
30. IPBH.
31. Ibid.; *BM*, 316–17.
32. IPBH.
33. "Nellie Dingley's Last Letter Was Prophetic," *Kent Tribune*, April 14, 1918.
34. ML; IPBH.
35. Christine Caccamo, personal interview, July 8, 1993.
36. *BM*, 317.
37. IPBH.
38. ML.

39. IPBH.
40. JT, "Jim Tully by Himself," *LAT*, Nov. 20, 1921.
41. IPBH.
42. John Carson, personal interview, March 6, 2000; "J. G. Evans, Sr., Started Business."
43. Grismer, *The History of Kent*, 254–55.
44. IPBH.
45. Francis Kline, personal interview, Nov. 30, 1992.
46. IPBH.
47. Ibid.; JT, unpublished boxing MS, UCLA.
48. ML.
49. IPBH.
50. ML.
51. "Boxing: Jimmie Tully, of Kent, Is Matched . . . ," *Kent Courier*, Sept. 10, 1909; IPBH.
52. ML.
53. IPBH.
54. ML; IPBH.
55. IPBH.
56. *BM*, 324; See also JT, unpublished boxing MS.
57. IPBH.
58. JT, unpublished boxing MS; IPBH.
59. JT, unpublished boxing MS; IPBH.
60. *BM*, 327.
61. IPBH.
62. ML.
63. IPBH.
64. "Tully and Kelly in Carnival at Akron," *Kent Courier*, Jan. 29, 1909.
65. "Boxing: Jimmie Tully."
66. "Tully and Kelly Make Good," *Kent Courier*, Feb. 5, 1909.
67. "Tully to Meet Conway," *Kent Courier*, May 28, 1909.
68. William Rosenberg, *Toledo Times*, Jan. 27, 1939.
69. Bert Randolph Sugar, ed., *The Ring 1981 Record Book and Boxing Encyclopedia* (New York: Atheneum, 1981), 711–12, 837.
70. JT, "Portrait of My Father," *Esquire*, Nov. 1939, 91.
71. JT, "Handicaps Challenge Me," *Your Life: The Popular Guide to Desirable Living*, Nov. 1937, 14–17, UCLA.

72. Ibid.
73. "Tully to Meet Conway."
74. Sugar, *The Ring 1981*, 708–9.
75. JT, unpublished boxing MS.
76. Ibid.
77. IPBH; "Boxing: Jimmie Tully."
78. "Tully a Winner," *Kent Courier*, June 4, 1909; "Boxing: Jimmie Tully."
79. "Akron Story a Fake," *Kent Courier*, June 11, 1909.
80. "Tully Bests Gill," *Kent Courier*, July 2, 1909; "Boxing: Jimmie Tully."
81. JT, "Jim Tully by Himself," *LAT*, Nov. 20, 1921; also see *BM*, 330; IPBH.
82. "Boxing: Jimmie Tully."
83. ML.
84. *BM*, 32.
85. ML; JT, unpublished boxing MS.
86. ML.
87. Ibid.; JT, unpublished boxing MS.
88. JT, unpublished boxing MS.
89. Ibid.
90. Ibid. Stanley Ketchel's own fortunes were about to change. In his October 1909 fight with Jack Johnson, Ketchel put the champion down in the twelfth but Johnson recovered and knocked Ketchel out with the next punch. A year later, nearly to the day, Ketchel was dead—murdered by a jealous farmhand. Nat Fleischer and Sam Andre, *A Pictorial History of Boxing* (Secaucus, N.J.: Citadel Press, 1975), 214–15.
91. ML.
92. JT, "Tully-Grams," *Hollywood Tribune*, Sept. 18, 1939.
93. JT, unpublished boxing MS; IPBH.
94. OMH.
95. "Kilbane Busy Fighter," *Cleveland Plain Dealer*, Oct. 31, 1909.
96. "Tommy Kilbane and Kid White Will Fight . . . ," *Cleveland Plain Dealer*, Dec. 5, 1909; "T. Kilbane Draws with Kid White," *Cleveland Plain Dealer*, Dec. 7, 1909.
97. IPBH; JT, unpublished boxing MS.
98. IPBH.
99. Ibid.
100. Ibid.; JT, unpublished boxing MS.
101. JT, "Tully-Grams."
102. Grismer, *The History of Kent*, 93–94.
103. IPBH.

104. Robin Beamon collection.
105. ML.
106. IPBH.
107. "Johnny Kilbane in Great Demand," *Cleveland Plain Dealer*, Jan. 4, 1910.
108. IPBH.

7. Troubled in Heart

1. IPBH; ML.
2. *BM*, 317.
3. ML.
4. *BM*, 317.
5. IPBH.
6. ML.
7. Robert E. Pfleger, *Green Leaves: A History of the Davey Tree Expert Company* (Chester, Conn.: Pequot Press, 1977), 35, 48; IPBH.
8. Baseball-Reference.com, "Matthew Muldowney," http://www.baseball-reference.com/minors/player.cgi?id=muldowoo1mat.
9. Ralph Ellison, *Invisible Man* (New York: Random House, 1952), 7.
10. IPBH.
11. Ibid. See also "Boards in Ballwin, Missouri," July 2, 1910; July 9, 1910; and July 16, 1910.
12. IPBH.
13. Ibid.; "Boards in Danville, Illinois," *Davey Tree Surgeon's Bulletin*, July 23, 1910.
14. IPBH; James B. Holm, ed., *Portage Heritage* (n.p.: Portage County Historical Society, 1957), 562.
15. IPBH. See also "Boards in Richmond, Indiana," *Davey Tree Surgeon's Bulletin*, Aug. 27, 1910; Sept. 3, 1910; Sept. 10, 1910; Sept. 17, 1910; Oct. 1, 1910; Oct. 8, 1910; Oct. 15, 1910; Oct. 22, 1910; and Oct. 29, 1910.
16. JT, "Boards in Richmond, Indiana," *Davey Tree Surgeon's Bulletin*, Sept. 24, 1910.
17. IPBH.
18. JT, letter to the editor, *Davey Tree Surgeon's Bulletin*, Sept. 24, 1910.
19. Ibid.
20. IPBH.
21. JT, letter to the editor, *Davey Tree Surgeon's Bulletin*, Dec. 3, 1910.
22. IPBH.
23. Ibid.
24. Ibid.
25. *BM*, 319–20; See also IPBH.
26. ML.
27. Jim Tully and Florence May Bushnell, marriage license, court record, Portage County, Ohio, Oct. 14, 1910.
28. ML.
29. Florence May Bushnell, application for birth certificate, court record, Portage County, Ohio, May 1941.
30. JT, "Boards in Bowling Green, Kentucky," *Davey Tree Surgeon's Bulletin*, Nov. 19, 1910.
31. JT, "Boards in Birmingham, Alabama," *Davey Tree Surgeon's Bulletin*, Nov. 26, 1910; Dec. 3, 1910; and Dec. 10, 1910. See also JT, letter to the editor, *Davey Tree Surgeon's Bulletin*, Dec. 3, 1910.
32. IPBH.
33. Ibid.
34. Ibid.
35. JT to Jesse Lasky, June 26, 1927, draft, UCLA. Kilbane would avenge his loss by knocking out Rivers in a rematch that September. Bert Randolph Sugar, ed., *The Ring 1981 Record Book and Boxing Encyclopedia* (New York: Atheneum, 1981), 711.

8. Write or Starve

1. *SI*, 121; Lester A. Bushnell, "The Buckeye's Picnic at Long Beach," *Kent Courier*, undated clipping, Robin Beamon collection.
2. Early in Tully's career (after he contributed articles to the *Davey Tree Surgeon's Bulletin* under the name James A. Tully), he wrote as James Alexander Tully, and sometimes (though rarely) as Jimmy Tully. Later he settled on Jim Tully.
3. G. R. Adams to JT, Feb. 8, 1933, UCLA.
4. Ted Robinson, "Ted Robinson Writes of the Courier Poets," *Kent Courier*, Dec. 29, 1911.
5. ML.
6. Thomas Alton Tully, birth certificates index, court record, Portage County, Ohio, Aug. 3, 1911.
7. JT, "It Wasn't Tully," *Kent Courier*, Jan. 26, 1912.

8. See, in the *Kent Courier*, JT, "Let Me Live in the House by the Side of the Road," Jan. 19, 1912; "Memories," Feb. 2, 1912; "To Those Who Fail," Feb. 9, 1912; "If," Feb. 23, 1912; "A Tribute to John Shanley," March 15, 1912; "To the Women Who Bake Good Bread," March 29, 1912; "Byron," March 29, 1912; "The Years that the Locust Hath Eaten," April 5, 1912.

9. JT, "The Most Unforgettable Character I Ever Met," *Reader's Digest*, Jan. 1941, 13.

10. "Five Nationally-Known Authors Lived or Worked in City Area," *Mansfield News Journal*, July 2, 1944.

11. Kid Sperry to JT, March 1, 1942, UCLA.

12. *Mansfield News Journal*, March 1, 1942, clipping, UCLA.

13. Undated clippings and scrapbooks, UCLA; IPBH; JT, "The Old Home Town," *Kent Courier*, Aug. 23, 1912. The chronology presented here of Tully's wanderings as a tree surgeon, interrupted by his brief return to boxing under an alias, is pieced together largely from Tully's references in his unpublished autobiographical papers to outside events such as championship boxing matches.

14. IPBH.

15. Undated clippings and scrapbooks, UCLA.

16. Robinson, "Ted Robinson Writes of the Courier Poets."

17. IPBH.

18. Randy Roberts, *Jack Dempsey: The Manassa Mauler* (Baton Rouge: Louisiana State University Press, 1979), 12–14.

19. IPBH; Bert Randolph Sugar, ed., *The Ring 1981 Record Book and Boxing Encyclopedia* (New York: Atheneum, 1981), 476.

20. JT, unpublished boxing MS, UCLA.

21. Ibid.

22. *BM*, 337. An account of this fight may also be found in JT, "Ringside: The Story of Pugilism," unpublished MS, 1940, UCLA.

23. JT, "Ringside: The Story of Pugilism."

24. Sugar, *The Ring 1981*, 655.

25. JT, unpublished boxing MS.

26. JT, "Portrait of My Father," *Esquire*, Nov. 1939, 91.

27. IPBH.

28. Sara Haardt, "Jim Tully," *American Mercury*, May 1928, 88.

29. IPBH.

30. Jack London to JT, Oct. 7, 1913, UCLA; Rose A. Lie, "Career of a Former Barefoot St. Marys Boy," *St. Marys Evening Leader*, Nov. 9, 1914, reprinted from *Waukegan Daily Gazette*, Oct. 12, 1914.

31. Clarice Stasz, *American Dreamers: Charmian and Jack London* (New York: St. Martin's Press, 1988), 227.

32. Andrew Sinclair, *Jack: A Biography of Jack London* (New York: Holt & Rinehart, 1977), 191–92.

33. Jack London to JT, Oct.7, 1913, UCLA; Lie, "Career of a Former Barefoot St. Marys Boy."

34. Undated clippings and scrapbooks, UCLA; IPBH. In a later interview, Tully claimed to have visited London at his home in 1914 but offered no details. Undated clippings and scrapbooks, UCLA.

35. IPBH.

36. JT to George Nathan, July 4, 1941, CORN.

37. IPBH.

38. Patti Lynn, "Jim Tully, Authors Finds Valley Haven," *San Fernando Valley Times*, Feb. 1942, clipping, UCLA.

39. IPBH.

40. Robin Beamon collection.

41. JT, "My Literary Fight, Round by Round," *Literary Digest International Book Review*, undated clipping (1923), UCLA.

42. Sinclair, *Jack: A Biography*, 23.

43. John Perry, *Jack London: An American Myth* (Chicago: Nelson-Hall, 1981), 43.

44. IPBH.

45. Sinclair, *Jack: A Biography*, 238; JT to Alfred Dashiell, Feb. 8, 1927, SCRIB; JT to HLM, Feb. 22, 1927, HLMNY.

46. IPBH.

47. James Welch to JT, Jan. 2, 1928, UCLA.

48. *Waukegan Daily News*, undated clipping, UCLA.

49. Otto Eisenschiml, "The Orpet-Lambert Case," in *Chicago Murders*, ed. Sewell Peaslee Wright (New York: Duell, Sloan and Pearce, 1945), 85–118; Edward Henry

Smith, *Famous American Poison Mysteries* (London: Hurst & Blackett, [1926]), 275–87; "Orpet Acquitted of Girl's Murder," *NYT*, July 16, 1916.

50. James Welch to JT, Jan. 2, 1928, UCLA.

51. Eisenschiml, "The Orpet-Lambert Case."

52. Barry H. Rumack and Robert G. Peterson, "Clinical Toxicology," in *Casarett and Doull's Toxicology: The Basic Science of Poisons*, ed. John Doull, Curtis D. Klassen, and Mary O. Amdur, 2nd ed. (New York: Macmillan, 1980), 686.

53. JT, "Harlots," *Kent Courier*, undated clipping (about Feb. 1916), Robin Beamon collection; JT, "The Castle Built in Spain," *Kent Courier*, undated clipping (about Dec. 1916), Robin Beamon collection.

54. JT to George Derby, Feb. 11, 1930, CORN.

55. JT, "Tully-Grams," *Hollywood Tribune*, Sept. 18, 1939.

56. U.S. Public Records Index, vol. 1; *Social Security Death Index*, http://ssdi.rootsweb.ancestry.com/.

57. Robin Beamon collection.

58. IPBH.

59. JT to HLM, May 8, 1928, UCLA; Haardt, "Jim Tully."

60. IPBH.

61. JT, "California—an' Everything," *Kent Tribune*, March 25, 1920.

62. IPBH.

63. Carl Sandburg to JT, Jan. 25, 1921, UCLA.

64. Theodore Dreiser to JT, April 3, 1921, UCLA.

65. IPBH.

66. Burton Rascoe and Geoff Conklin, eds., *The Smart Set Anthology* (New York: Reynal & Hitchcock, 1934); Carl Dolmetsch, ed., *The Smart Set: A History and Anthology* (New York: Dial Press, 1966); Sidney Skolsky, "Tintypes," News Syndicate Co. (about 1931), CORN.

67. IPBH.

68. ML.

69. James O. Kemm, *Rupert Hughes: A Hollywood Legend* (Beverly Hills, Calif.: Pomegranate, 1997), 36, 38, 44.

70. Ibid., 81.

71. IPBH.

72. JT to George Derby, Feb. 11, 1930, CORN.

73. IPBH.

74. Kemm, *Rupert Hughes*, 195.

75. IPBH.

76. Kemm, *Rupert Hughes*, 195.

77. IPBH.

78. Divorce papers of Jim Tully and Florence Bushnell Tully, Oct. 25, 1923, UCLA.

79. Anonymous, 16-page typed MS about Tully, UCLA.

80. IPBH.

81. Rupert Hughes to JT, July 14, 1921, UCLA.

82. IPBH.

83. Rupert Hughes to JT, July 14, 1921, UCLA; Rupert Hughes to JT, Aug. 22, 1921, UCLA.

84. IPBH.

85. Harcourt to JT, Oct. 18, 1921, UCLA; JT to HLM, May 8, 1928, UCLA.

86. IPBH.

87. JT to Upton Sinclair, Nov. 16, 1921, UVA.

88. JT to HLM, May 8, 1928, UCLA.

89. JT to Upton Sinclair, Nov. 22, 1921, UVA.

90. JT to Upton Sinclair, Dec. 21, 1921, UVA.

9. Emmett Lawler

1. JDT to JT, Oct. 13, 1927, UCLA; JDT to JT, Sept. 31, 1927, UCLA.

2. *SI*, 57–58.

3. *EL*, 4.

4. "The Editor Recommends," *Bookman*, April 1922, 191.

5. M.M.C., "*Emmett Lawler*," *Saturday Review of Literature*, Aug. 5, 1922; *Freeman*, Sept. 6, 1922, 622.

6. Rupert Hughes, *NYT*, Feb. 26, 1922.

7. Upton Sinclair, "Two Unusual Books," *Appeal to Reason*, April 1, 1922.

8. "There Are Tears and Laughter in Jim Tully's Book," *Kent Tribune*, March 2, 1922.

9. Ralph Block, "Jim Tully—An Appreciation," *Kent Tribune*, March 23, 1922.

10. Introduction to JT, "Romance Dead

in Hoboland," *LAT,* June 18, 1922.
11. Hulbert Footner, *New York Evening Post Literary Review,* April 8, 1922, 559.
12. JT, "Portrait of My Father," *Esquire,* Nov. 1939, 91.
13. JT, "The Most Unforgettable Character I Ever Met," *Reader's Digest,* Jan. 1941, 13.
14. JT to HLM, Feb. 2, 1923, HLMNY.
15. JT to George Derby, Feb. 11, 1930, CORN.
16. JT to Jesse Lasky, June 26, 1927, draft, UCLA.
17. EL.

10. Hollywood Writer

1. JT, "The King of Laughter," unpublished MS, 1936–40, UCLA.
2. *DOZ,* 11.
3. Peter Hay, *MGM: When the Lion Roared* (Atlanta, Ga.: Turner, 1991), 12.
4. JT, "Passing Strangers," unpublished MS, 1922, UCLA.
5. IPBH.
6. JT, "The Most Unforgettable Character I Ever Met," *Reader's Digest,* Jan. 1941, 14.
7. HLM, *Prejudices: Fourth Series* (New York: Alfred A. Knopf, 1924), 139–40.
8. William Manchester, *H. L. Mencken: Disturber of the Peace* (New York: Collier Books, 1962), 62.
9. HLM, *The Diary of H. L. Mencken,* ed. Charles A. Fecher (New York: Alfred A. Knopf, 1989), vii.
10. William H. Nolte, *H. L. Mencken: Literary Critic* (Seattle: University of Washington Press, 1967), 88.
11. HLM, *Prejudices: A Selection,* ed. James T. Farrell (New York: Vintage Books, 1958), vii.
12. JT to HLM, April 27, 1922, UCLA.
13. "Jim Tully in Kent," *Kent Tribune,* May 18, 1922.
14. "Jim Tully out among the Movie People of Hollywood," *Kent Tribune,* July 21, 1921.
15. "Jim Tully in France," *Kent Tribune,* May 18, 1922.

16. "Jim Tully out among the Movie People."
17. Roger Di Paolo, "From Kent to the Battlefields of France," *Kent-Ravenna Record-Courier,* April 22, 1990; "Miss Nellie Dingley Dies in France," *Kent Tribune,* September 26, 1918.
18. IPBH.
19. OMH; IPBH. Tully may have become confused on the title. It appears as "The Memoirs of a Japanese Geisha Girl" in Sara Mayfield, *The Constant Circle: H. L. Mencken and His Friends* (New York: Delacorte Press, 1968), 121.
20. JT, "Three Famous Authors Talk with Jim Tully," *LAT,* Sept. 10, 1922.
21. Ibid.
22. JT, "When Lights Burn Low in Chinatown: The Whispering Shadows of Chinatown," *LAT,* Aug. 13, 1922.
23. JT to HLM, June 18, 1922, UCLA.
24. IPBH; JT, "Convicts Open Hearts to Novelist," *LAT,* Sept. 17, 1922.
25. IPBH. Article not seen.
26. JT, "The Circus Flea," *Argosy All-Story Weekly,* July 21, 1923.
27. Rupert Hughes to JT, Jan. 5, 1923, UCLA.
28. James O. Kemm, *Rupert Hughes: A Hollywood Legend* (Beverly Hills, Calif.: Pomegranate Press, 1997), 329.
29. JT, "A Declaration," *Smart Set,* Dec. 1923, reprinted in *The Smart Set Anthology,* ed. Burton Rascoe and Geoff Conklin (New York: Reynal & Hitchcock, 1934), 461.
30. HLM, *My Life as Author and Editor,* ed. Jonathan Yardley (New York: Alfred A. Knopf, 1993), 417.
31. *DOZ,* 99.
32. Divorce papers of Jim Tully and Florence Bushnell Tully, Oct. 25, 1923, UCLA.
33. IPBH; JT, "June Mathis' Struggle," *Story World,* Nov. 1924, 19.
34. JT, "Hollywood . . . The Last Carnival," *Who,* Nov. 1941, clipping, UCLA.
35. IPBH.
36. Willard Keefe, "Jim Tully Sings Hymn of Hate for Movie Critics and Faking," *New York Morning Telegraph,* Oct. 10, 1926.
37. JT to George Nathan, April 11, 1942, CORN.

38. JT, "My Interview with Elinor Glyn: The Noted Author of 'Three Weeks' as Vivisected by an American Realist," *Vanity Fair,* Feb. 1926, 40, 80, 92.

39. Sidney Wallach, "The King of the Vagabonds Talks on Jewish Hoboes and Intellectuals," *Jewish Tribune,* Oct. 14, 1927, UCLA.

40. IPBH.

41. *DOZ,* 11.

42. Ibid.

11. The Road-Kid and the Little Tramp

1. JT, "The King of Laughter" unpublished MS, 1936–40, UCLA; *DOZ,* 11.

2. Robert F. Moss, *Charlie Chaplin* (New York: Harcourt Brace Jovanovich, 1977), 11.

3. *DOZ,* 11.

4. Ibid.

5. JT, "Inside the Movies," *Kent Tribune,* July 11, 1918.

6. *DOZ,* 14.

7. Charlie Chaplin, *My Autobiography* (London: Bodley Head, 1964), 154.

8. David Robinson, *Chaplin: His Life and Art* (New York: McGraw-Hill, 1985), 101.

9. Groucho Marx, *Groucho and Me* (New York: Bernard Geis, 1959), 134.

10. Chaplin, *My Autobiography,* 154.

11. *DOZ,* 23.

12. Ibid.

13. Ibid.

14. Ibid., 14.

15. Ibid., 15.

16. JT, "The King of Laughter."

17. Ibid.

18. *DOZ,* 15.

19. Ibid., 15–35.

20. JT, "The King of Laughter."

21. Robinson, *Chaplin: His Life and Art,* 308.

22. JT, "The King of Laughter."

23. Ibid.

24. Charlie Chaplin, "My Impressions of Folk, Movies, and Edna Purviance," *True Confessions,* June 1924, 59, 94.

25. *DOZ,* 19.

26. Ibid., 20.

27. Walter Kerr, *The Silent Clowns* (New York: Alfred A. Knopf, 1975), 125.

28. Chaplin, "My Impressions," 59.

29. Robinson, *Chaplin: His Life and Art,* 337.

30. *DOZ,* 26.

31. Ibid.

32. Lita Grey Chaplin, *My Life with Chaplin: An Intimate Memoir,* with Morton Cooper (New York: Bernard Geis, 1966), 55.

33. *DOZ,* 27.

34. Chaplin, *My Life with Chaplin,* 58.

35. Robinson, *Chaplin: His Life and Art,* 337–38.

36. *DOZ,* 28.

37. Robinson, *Chaplin: His Life and Art,* 338.

38. *DOZ,* 27–28.

39. Robinson, *Chaplin: His Life and Art,* 343.

40. *DOZ,* 29–30.

41. Robinson, *Chaplin: His Life and Art,* 337.

42. *DOZ,* 23.

43. Ibid., 26.

44. Chaplin, *My Autobiography,* 328.

45. *DOZ,* 28.

12. Beggars of Life

1. "Jim Tully Brings out Second Book," *Kent Tribune,* Nov. 8, 1923.

2. "Tully's Latest Book Tells of Tramp Life," *Kent Tribune,* Aug. 7, 1924.

3. *BL,* 49.

4. Ibid., 54–55.

5. Ibid., 69.

6. Ibid., 90.

7. Ibid., 259–60.

8. Ibid., 62.

9. "Jim Tully, Hobo and Side-Door Pullman Passenger," *NYT,* Jan. 4, 1925.

10. R. A. Parker, *Literary Digest International Book Review,* Jan. 1925, 90.

11. S. Martin, *Saturday Review of Literature,* Nov. 8, 1924, 261.

12. HLM, "Brief Notices," *American Mercury,* Dec. 1924, 510.

13. O. D. Russell, *New York Evening Post Literary Review,* Oct. 25, 1924, 14.

14. *Springfield (Mass.) Republican,* Nov. 21, 1924, 14.

15. Nels Anderson, *The Hobo: The Sociology of the Homeless Man* (Chicago: University of Chicago Press, 1923).

16. Nels Anderson, "Raw Life," *Survey,* Dec. 1924, 289.

17. "Jim Tully's 'Beggars of Life,'" *Kent Tribune,* Nov. 20, 1924.
18. Glen Mullin, *New York Tribune,* Nov. 16, 1924, 10.
19. Harry Carr, "The Lancer," *LAT,* April 6, 1925.
20. *Outlook,* Nov. 5, 1924, 377.
21. Sara Haardt, "Jim Tully," *American Mercury,* May 1928, 83.
22. JT to HLM, August 25, 1927, HLMNY.
23. *BL.*
24. JT, "The King of Laughter," unpublished MS, 1936–40, UCLA.

13. One More Illusion

1. Sara Haardt, "Jim Tully," *American Mercury,* May 1928, 90.
2. "Embark on Marriage Seas; Jim Tully Marries Co-ed," *LAT,* Jan. 25, 1925; Ted Cook, *Los Angeles Examiner,* March 12, 1928.
3. Haardt, "Jim Tully."
4. Dawn Powell, *The Diaries of Dawn Powell: 1931–1965,* ed. Tim Page (South Royalton, Vt.: Steerforth Press, 1998), 48.
5. Ralph Parker, "Hollywood's Ogre," *Screen Secrets,* June 1928, 67.
6. IPBH.
7. ML.
8. Sidney Skolsky, "Tintypes," News Syndicate Co. (about 1931), clipping, CORN.
9. Haardt, "Jim Tully," 90.
10. Frank Scully, "Jim Tully," *Scribner's,* Aug. 1937, 52.
11. R. A. Forster, "Christ Hospital Slayer, after Ten Years in Prison, Given Pardon by Governor," *Cincinnati Times-Star,* Jan. 20, 1925.
12. Haardt, "Jim Tully," 82.
13. JT to HLM, Jan. 12, 1925, HLMNY.
14. JT to HLM, Jan. 26, 1925, tipped in to H. L. Mencken's copy of *Shanty Irish* at the Enoch Pratt Free Library, Baltimore.
15. JT, "The Failure of Jack London," *Story World,* Feb. 1925, 11.
16. "Tully Speaks to Clubwomen," *LAT,* Feb. 19, 1925; Myra Nye, "Jim Tully Heard," *LAT,* Feb. 19, 1925.
17. *DOZ,* 28.
18. Ibid.
19. Ibid., 31.
20. W. A. Swanberg, *Citizen Hearst* (New York: Charles Scribner's Sons, 1961), 375; David Robinson, *Chaplin: His Life and Art* (New York: McGraw-Hill, 1985), 347; Theodore Huff, *Charlie Chaplin* (New York: Arno Press, 1972), 201.
21. Charlie Chaplin, *My Autobiography* (London: Bodley Head, 1964), 342.
22. David Nasaw, *The Chief: The Life and Times of William Randolph Hearst* (Boston: Houghton Mifflin, 2000), 345.
23. JT to HLM, May 13, 1925, HLMNY.
24. Swanberg, *Citizen Hearst,* 375.
25. Nasaw, *The Chief,* 345.
26. Contract between Jim Tully and the Thomas H. Ince Corporation, May 1, 1925, UCLA.
27. *Johnstown (Pa.) Democrat,* June 8, 1925, clipping, UCLA.
28. *DOZ,* 38.
29. Ibid.
30. William Saroyan, *Places Where I've Done Time* (New York: Praeger, 1972), 124–25.
31. JT to HLM, May 26, 1925, HLMP.
32. Virginia Tully to Marna and JT, July 14, 1925, UCLA.
33. JT, "Hollywood's Rebel," *New Movie Magazine,* Aug. 1932, clipping, UCLA.
34. Robert Coleman, *New York Daily Mirror,* Sept. 13, 1925.
35. George Jean Nathan, *New York Morning Telegraph,* Sept. 5, 1925.
36. Alexander Woollcott, *New York Herald-Tribune,* Sept. 13, 1925.
37. Charlie Chaplin, letter to the drama editor, *New York Herald-Tribune,* Sept. 13, 1925.
38. JT, "Hollywood's Rebel."
39. JT, "Tully-Grams," *Hollywood Tribune,* July 24, 1939.
40. James Cagney, *Cagney by Cagney* (New York: Pocket Books, 1977), 43.
41. Ibid.
42. JT, letter to the drama editor, Sept. 15, 1925, clipping from unknown newspaper, UCLA.
43. *The American,* undated clipping, UCLA.
44. "Tully at Hobo College," *Chicago Post,* Nov. 13, 1925.
45. Roger A. Bruns, *The Damndest Radical: The Life and World of Ben Reitman,*

Chicago's Celebrated Social Reformer, Hobo King, and Whorehouse Physician (Urbana: University of Illinois Press, 1987), 206.

46. "Tully at Hobo College."
47. Bruns, *The Damndest Radical*, 205.
48. "Tully at Hobo College."
49. Bruns, *The Damndest Radical*, 206.
50. JT, "The Most Unforgettable Character I Ever Met," *Reader's Digest*, Jan. 1941, 14.
51. Alton Tully to Myrtle Tully, n.d. (probably Aug. 1937), UCLA.
52. JT, "The Most Unforgettable Character," 14.
53. "Jim Tully, Tramp Poet, Won Notice Here," *Cleveland Plain Dealer*, Nov. 27, 1925.
54. *Kent Tribune*, Dec. 3, 1925; undated clipping from unknown newspaper, UCLA; *This Week*, Dec. 10, 1925, clipping, Robin Beamon collection.
55. *Seattle Post-Intelligencer*, Nov. 25, 1925, clipping, UCLA.

14. Jarnegan

1. Donald Freeman to JT, Feb. 26, 1926, UCLA.
2. George Jean Nathan, *The Intimate Notebooks of George Jean Nathan* (New York: Alfred A. Knopf, 1932), 72.
3. Ralph Parker, "Hollywood's Ogre," *Screen Secrets*, June 1928, 65.
4. JT, "King Vidor," *Vanity Fair*, June 1926, 46.
5. JT, "A Napoleon of Shadows: An Estimate of Cecil B. De Mille, an Amazing Potentate of Filmdom," *Vanity Fair*, April 1926, 56.
6. JT, "Irving Thalberg," *Vanity Fair*, Oct. 1927, 71, 98.
7. Donald Freeman to JT, Dec. 29, 1927, UCLA.
8. James Quirk, *Photoplay*, June 1928, clipping, UCLA.
9. Parker, "Hollywood's Ogre," 65–66.
10. Ibid.
11. Clara Bow to JT, Nov. 2, 1927, reprinted in *LAT This Week*, clipping, Jan. 19, 1936, UCLA.
12. Parker, "Hollywood's Ogre," 67.
13. Ibid.
14. JT to George Nathan, Nov. 26, 1941, CORN.
15. Parker, "Hollywood's Ogre," 67.
16. *JARN*, 249.
17. JT to John Munson, Sept. 5, 1934, UCLA.
18. *DOZ*, 135.
19. Ibid., 136.
20. *JARN*, 130.
21. Ibid., 131.
22. Frank Scully, "Jim Tully," *Scribner's*, Aug. 1937, 51.
23. *DOZ*, 148.
24. Frank Scully, "Scully on Tully," *Screen Writer*, Aug. 1947, 8, UCLA.
25. JT to John Munson, Sept. 5, 1934, UCLA.
26. *DOZ*, 147.
27. Willard Keefe, "Jim Tully Sings Hymn of Hate for Movie Critics and Faking," *New York Morning Telegraph*, Oct. 10, 1926.
28. Quoted in ibid.
29. HLM, "The Library," *American Mercury*, Nov. 1926, 382.
30. See, for example, "The Lion-Tamer," *American Mercury*, Oct. 1925; "Without What?" *Vanity Fair*, Nov. 1925; "The Strong Woman," *Liberty*, March 13, 1926; "Whiteface," *Liberty*, April 10, 1926.
31. Finley Peter Dunne to JT, April 15, 1926, UCLA; Gene Tunney to JT, July 9, 1926, UCLA.
32. See, in *Vanity Fair*, "A-Bout with Jack Dempsey," Dec. 1925; "Famous Bruisers Remembered," April 1926; "Glances at Great Pugilists," June 1926; "Early American Pugilism," July 1926; "Famous Negroes of the Ring," April 1927; "Ringers of the Ring," May 1927.
33. JT to HLM, May 20, 1926, HLMNY.
34. JT, unpublished boxing MS, UCLA.
35. "Rialto Gossip," *NYT*, Aug. 22, 1926.
36. JT, "The Most Unforgettable Character I Ever Met," *Reader's Digest*, Jan. 1941, 14.
37. OMH.
38. Ibid. Years later, as McCarthyism swept the country, White denounced Robeson as a Communist.
39. JT, "The Most Unforgettable Character," 14.
40. Ibid.

15. Circus Parade

1. "Horace Liveright Gives a Party Afterwards," *New York Morning Telegraph*, Oct. 9, 1926, UCLA.
2. Langston Hughes, *The Big Sea* (New York: Alfred A. Knopf, 1940), 251.
3. Brooks Atkinson, "The Play; Pugilism a la Mode," *NYT*, Oct. 7, 1926.
4. Alexander Woollcott, *New York World*, Oct. 7, 1926.
5. Willard Keefe, "Jim Tully Sings Hymn of Hate for Movie Critics and Faking," *New York Morning Telegraph*, Oct. 10, 1926.
6. Contract with A&C Boni for Chaplin biography, Sept. 1, 1926, UCLA.
7. JT to Charlie Chaplin, Oct. 16, 1926, UCLA.
8. Joyce Milton, *Tramp: The Life of Charlie Chaplin* (New York: Da Capo, 1998), 281–82.
9. "Chaplin Files Suit to Halt Life Story," *NYT*, Jan. 8, 1927; "Chaplin Loses Suit Here," *NYT*, March 3, 1927.
10. *DOZ*, 40.
11. Ibid.
12. JT, "Charlie Chaplin: His Real Life-Story, Part One," *Pictorial Review*, Jan. 1927, 8.
13. Milton, *Tramp*, 281–82.
14. JT to Maxwell Perkins, March 29, 1927, SCRIB; contract with A&C Boni for *Circus Parade*, April 8, 1927, UCLA.
15. Maxwell Perkins to Ring Lardner, April 6, 1927, in *Ring around Max: The Correspondence of Ring Lardner and Max Perkins*, ed. Clifford Caruthers (DeKalb: Northern Illinois University Press, 1973), 106.
16. JT to HLM, Aug. 13, 1927, HLMNY.
17. Marna Tully to JT, telegram, Nov. 12, 1927, UCLA; JT to Harry Maule, Sept. 11, 1929, UCLA.
18. JT to HLM, March 23, 1927, HLMNY.
19. Carl Bode, *Mencken* (Carbondale: Southern Illinois University Press, 1969), 189.
20. Mark Twain, *Mississippi Writings: Tom Sawyer, Life on the Mississippi, Huckleberry Finn, Pudd'nhead Wilson* (New York: Library of America, 1982), 253.
21. *CP*, 30.
22. Marna Tully to JT, telegram, Nov. 7, 1927, UCLA.
23. JT to HLM, July 9, 1927, HLMNY.
24. JT to HLM, March 23, 1927, HLMNY; contract with Clarence Brown, Oct. 1927, UCLA.
25. Lewis Galantiere, "Jim Tully and the Underworld," *Arts & Decoration*, Oct. 1927, 102, 106.
26. Edwin Clark, "Spielers, Shillabers, Fat Ladies and Clowns; *Circus Parade* Is a Carnival of Low Life and Mixed Emotions," *NYT*, Aug. 7, 1927, BR5.
27. James Agee, *Letters of James Agee to Father Flye* (New York: George Braziller, 1962), 31.
28. Countee Cullen, *Opportunity*, Dec. 1927.
29. Langston Hughes to JT, Nov. 3, 1940, UCLA.
30. Francis J. Finn, SJ, "A Gallant Tradition," *St. Xavier Calendar*, July 1927, UCLA.
31. IPBH.
32. Charles Boni to JT, July 29, 1927, authors' collection.
33. "Backs Plan to Ease Book Censorship," *NYT*, Jan. 24, 1930.
34. *Brooklyn Eagle*, Jan. 16, 1930, clipping, UCLA.
35. JT, letter to the "Soap Box," *American Mercury*, Jan. 27, 1933.
36. JT to HLM, July 31, 1927, HLMNY.
37. "Filth in Books," *St. Marys Evening Leader*, Sept. 1, 1927.
38. "Jim Tully Writes 'Home,'" *St. Marys Evening Leader*, Oct. 1, 1927.
39. Ibid.
40. "Supporting Evidence," *St. Marys Evening Leader*, Nov. 5, 1927.
41. Eugene Whitmore, "Jim Tully's Fairy Tales," *Bookman*, Aug. 1928, 694.
42. *CP*, 8.
43. Whitmore, "Jim Tully's Fairy Tales," 695.
44. James Stevens, letter to the editor, *Bookman*, Aug. 17, 1928.
45. JT to William Saroyan, Nov. 20, 1938, authors' collection.
46. JT to HLM, Aug. 25, 1927, HLMNY.
47. JT to George Derby, Feb. 11, 1930, CORN.
48. Frank Wilstach to JT, Nov. 15, 1929, UCLA; news release, Dec. 9 (probably 1929), UCLA.

49. John O'Hara to William Maxwell, Aug. 28, 1960, in *Selected Letters of John O'Hara*, ed. Matthew J. Bruccoli (New York: Random House, 1978), 343.

16. Shanty Irish

1. JT, "'Peace to His Red Hot Soul' Is Jim Tully's Eulogy to Former Buddy," reprinted in *Kent Tribune*, Sept. 27, 1928.
2. "Death Takes Original of Tully's Character, 'Blackie' of 'The Circus Parade' Dies Friendless and Penniless in Columbus Lodging Home," *Kent Tribune*, Sept. 27, 1928.
3. Vincent Donovan to JT, Sept. 14, 1927, UCLA.
4. William Manchester, *H. L. Mencken: Disturber of the Peace* (New York: Collier Books, 1962), 268.
5. Sara Mayfield, *The Constant Circle: H. L. Mencken and His Friends* (New York: Dell, 1969), 120.
6. Ibid., 122. Mayfield's use of the word "cicerone" to describe Tully's role is a clever piece of wordplay. As a cicerone, Tully could be expected to guide his guest with the knowledge and eloquence of Cicero or Marcus Tullius Cicero, sometimes called Tully.
7. Sara Haardt, "Jim Tully," *American Mercury*, May 1928, 82.
8. JT to HLM, May 31, 1928, UVA.
9. The argument over Sara Haardt's profile is detailed in a series of letters (April to June 1928) written by H. L. Mencken, Upton Sinclair, and Jim Tully. HLMP.
10. JT to HLM, June 9, 1928, UVA.
11. Mary Craig Sinclair to HLM, June 11, 1928, UVA.
12. Upton Sinclair, "Jim Tully: A Study in Ingratitude," *Haldeman-Julius Monthly*, Aug. 1928.
13. F. Scott Fitzgerald to Ernest Hemingway, July 1928, in *Fitzgerald and Hemingway: A Dangerous Friendship*, ed. Matthew J. Bruccoli (New York: Carroll & Graf, 1994), 220.
14. *SI*, 1.
15. Ibid., 34.
16. Ibid., 30.
17. Ibid., 57.

18. Mark Twain, "Washoe.—'Information Wanted,'" in *Early Tales and Sketches*, vol. 1, *1851–1864*, ed. Edgar Marquess Branch and Robert H. Hirst, with the assistance of Harriet Elinor Smith (Berkeley: University of California Press, 1979), 369.
19. *SI*, 36.
20. Ibid., 263.
21. Mark Twain, *Following the Equator* (Hartford, Conn.: American Publishing Co., 1897), 132.
22. Richard Lalor Sheil, *Sketches of the Irish Bar* (1854; New York: Redfield, 1858), 41–64.
23. JT to George Derby, Feb. 11, 1930, CORN.
24. OMH.
25. *SI*, ix.
26. IPBH.
27. JT to HLM, Dec. 22, 1932, HLMNY.
28. *BM*, 11.
29. *SI*, 38.
30. Ibid., ii.
31. HLM to JT, July 17, 1928, HLMP.
32. Bruce Gould, "Books on Our Table," *New York Post*, Oct. 8, 1928.
33. T.S.M., *New Republic*, Dec. 1928, 26.
34. Percy Hutchison, *NYT*, Oct. 14, 1928, 4.
35. *Chicago Daily Tribune*, Oct. 20, 1928.
36. JT to HLM, May 17, 1929, UCLA.
37. JT to Maxwell Perkins, May 31, 1941, SCRIB.
38. *Irish Times*, Aug. 16, 1929, UCLA.
39. Upton Sinclair to JT, Oct. 29, 1928, UCLA.
40. Solicitation to "serve on a committee of writers who endorse Upton Sinclair's candidacy for governor of California," Sept. 18, 1934, UCLA; Upton Sinclair to JT, Sept. 25, 1934, UCLA; Upton Sinclair, *I, Candidate for Governor and How I Got Licked* (1934; Berkeley: University of California Press, 1994), 166.
41. Michael Gold, *New Masses*, Feb. 1929, 26.
42. "A Slobbering Idiot," *Irish Independent*, Aug. 5, 1929.
43. Gertrude Lawler to JT, Aug. 17, 1931, UCLA.
44. James T. Farrell, *Daily Maroon*, March 1, 1929, 3, quoted in Charles Fanning, *The Irish Voice in America: 250 Years of Irish-*

American Fiction (Lexington: University Press of Kentucky, 2000), 256.
45. JT to HLM, March 15, 1945, HLMNY.
46. Charles Beahan to JT, Aug. 24, 1934, UCLA.
47. Emory Elliott, *The Columbia History of the American Novel* (New York: Columbia University Press, 1991), 395.
48. *SI*, 116.
49. "'Man in Office' Is Blamed by Poet for Poor Films," *NYT*, Sept. 12, 1926.
50. Robert Nichols, "Gene Tunney: The Fighter as Artist," *Observer*, Oct. 3, 1926.
51. "Life among the Yeggs," *Manchester Guardian*, May 14, 1928; Brandt & Brandt, statement, June 9, 1928, UCLA.
52. Contract, Paramount Famous Lasky Corp. with Jim Tully and Maxwell Anderson, Feb. 3, 1928, UCLA; "Tully Sells Two Stories to Make One," *Washington Post*, March 4, 1928.
53. *New York Morning Telegraph*, June 20, 1928.
54. "Flashbacks and Fadeouts," *Washington Post*, Dec. 2, 1928.
55. "Jarnegan: A Rough and Profane Play," *NYT*, Sept. 25, 1928.
56. "JARNEGAN Indicts All of Hollywood Except Its Climate," *New York Herald-Tribune*, Sept. 25, 1928.
57. Steve Randisi, "From Silents to Shadows: A Last Interview with Joan Bennett," *Scarlet Street*, Winter 1993.
58. Burns Mantle, *The Best Plays of 1928–29* (New York: Dodd, Mead, 1929), 15.
59. "Death Takes Bennett, Once Matinee Idol," *LAT*, Oct. 23, 1944.
60. Barry Paris, *Louise Brooks* (New York: Alfred A. Knopf, 1989), 107.
61. JT to HLM, May 21, 1928, HLMNYP.
62. Paris, *Louise Brooks*, 217.
63. Ibid., 217, 221, 225.
64. Ibid., 221, 225, 222.
65. Nels Anderson to JT, Oct. 12, 1928, UCLA.
66. Sara Haardt to HLM, Dec. 8, 1927, in *Mencken and Sara: A Life in Letters*, ed. Marion Elizabeth Rodgers (New York: McGraw-Hill, 1987), 363.

17. Shadows of Men

1. JT to HLM, March 23, 1927, HLMNY.
2. H. F. Manchester, "Fear of Bread Line Still Dogs Jim Tully," *Boston Herald*, June 9, 1929.
3. OMH.
4. IPBH.
5. JT to HLM, Sept. 27, 1927, HLMP; JT to HLM, May 5, 1927, HLMNY.
6. JT to HLM, March 23, 1927, HLMNY.
7. JT to Alfred Dashiell, Sept. 27, 1927, SCRIB; Alfred Dashiell to JT, Oct. 4, 1927, SCRIB.
8. JT to HLM, Sept. 27, 1927, HLMP.
9. JT, "A California Holiday," *American Mercury*, Jan. 1928.
10. *SM*, 321.
11. JT to HLM, Nov. 9, 1927, HLMP.
12. Frank Scully, "Jim Tully," *Scribner's*, Aug. 1937, 54.
13. JT, "A California Holiday," *Monthly Record* (of the Conn. State Prison inmates), April 1940; H. Bruce Franklin, ed., *Prison Writing in 20th Century America* (New York: Penguin, 1998); Ruby Darrow to JT, Sept. 28, 1937; JT to HLM, Oct. 10, 1937, HLMNY; JT to HLM, Nov. 10, 1938, HLMNY; Nels Anderson to JT, Oct. 12, 1928, UCLA.
14. JT, "Two-Time Losers," *American Mercury*, March 1928.
15. JT to HLM, Sept. 16, 1927, HLMNY; Ernest Booth, "We Rob a Bank," *American Mercury*, Sept. 1927.
16. JT, "Jungle Justice," *American Mercury*, April 1928; JT to HLM, Dec. 2, 1927, HLMNY.
17. HLM to JT, Dec. 9, 1927, HLMP.
18. HLM to JT, Dec. 21, 1927, HLMP; HLM to JT, Jan. 5, 1928, HLMP.
19. JT to HLM, Jan. 21, 1929, HLMNY; JT to HLM, Jan. 31, 1929, HLMNY.
20. H. F. Manchester, "Fear of Bread Line Still Dogs Jim Tully," *Boston Herald*, June 9, 1929; HLM to JT, April 2, 192[9], HLMP.
21. JT, "Handicaps Challenge Me," *Your Life: The Popular Guide to Desirable Living*, Nov. 1937, 14–17, UCLA.
22. *SM*, 3.
23. Ibid., 120.
24. Gerald Green, "Back to Bigger," in

Proletarian Writers of the Thirties, ed. David Madden (Carbondale: Southern Illinois University Press, 1968), 36.

25. *Paterson (N.J.) Press Guardian*, March 6, 1929, UCLA.

26. *SM*, 282.

27. JT, "Souls Broken by Cocaine," *LAT*, Sept. 24, 1922.

28. *SM*, 196.

29. Ibid., 197.

30. Ibid., 199.

31. Ibid., 201.

32. Ibid., 207.

33. JT to HLM, Dec. 22, 1932, HLMNY.

34. JT to HLM, Jan. 26, 1925, Enoch Pratt Free Library, Baltimore.

35. *SM*, 293.

36. Ibid., 294.

37. Ibid., 304.

38. Ibid., 305.

39. Harry Maule to JT, July 30, 1929, UCLA.

40. HLM to JT, Oct. 7, 1927, HLMP; Harry Carr to JT, Aug. 5, 1929, UCLA.

41. *SM*, 327.

42. Bruce Catton, undated clipping, NEA Service, UCLA.

43. Harry Hansen, *NYT*, Jan. 19, 1930.

44. *New Yorker*, Jan. 11, 1930.

45. Donald Henderson Clarke, *New York Herald-Tribune*, Jan. 12, 1930.

46. *Time*, Jan. 20, 1930.

47. *Cleveland Plain Dealer*, Jan. 12, 1930.

48. "Jim Tully Writes Another Book," *St. Marys Evening Leader*, Jan. 25, 1930.

49. J.M., *New Republic*, Feb. 1926.

50. Doubleday, Doran, & Co. to JT, May 13, 1930, UCLA; Ardis Smith, "Vagabondia's Poet, Tully, Tramps a Bit on Filmland," *Buffalo Evening News*, Jan. 24, 1939, UCLA.

51. JT to Maxwell Perkins, May 31, 1941, SCRIB.

52. *Shadows of Men* reader's report, April 10, 1931, UCLA.

18. Beggars Abroad

1. "Jim Tully's Wife is Seeking Divorce," *Akron Beacon Journal*, June 12, 1928.

2. HLM to JT, June 12, 1928, letter transcript, HLMP.

3. JT to HLM, June 15, 1928, HLMNY.

4. Sidney Skolsky, "Tintypes," News Syndicate Co. (about 1931), clipping, CORN.

5. ML.

6. JT, "Ex-Follies Girl," *Illustrated Love Magazine*, March 1932, 3.

7. ML.

8. JT to HLM, Aug. 17, 1931, HLMNY.

9. JT, "Ex-Follies Girl."

10. Ibid.

11. ML; JT to HLM, Aug. 17, 1931, HLMNY.

12. ML.

13. "Hobo-Author Again Is Sued for Divorce," *Akron Beacon Journal*, Sept. 22, 1928.

14. "Jim Tully Answers Wife's Divorce Plea," *LAT*, Oct. 5, 1928.

15. "Film Director Faces Charge," *LAT*, Jan. 16, 1929.

16. "Tully Battle Will Be Bitter," *LAT*, Jan. 17, 1929; "Gas Overcomes Neilan," *NYT*, Feb. 11, 1929.

17. HLM to JT, April 2, 192[9], HLMP; *Sunday News*, May 26, 1929, UCLA.

18. Roscoe Fawcett to JT, April 3, 1929, UCLA.

19. Ben Lindsey to JT, May 24, 1929, UCLA.

20. Marna Tully to HLM, March 28, 1929, HLMNY.

21. Gasoline Bill Baker, "His Majesty Protests," *New York World*, March 31, 1929, UCLA; "Pretender Flayed by King of Hoboes," *Washington Post*, March 31, 1929.

22. Maury Graham and Robert Hemming, *Tales of the Iron Road: My Life as King of the Hobos* (New York: Paragon House, 1990), 156–57.

23. JT to HLM, April 5, 1929, HLMNY.

24. *Sunday News*, May 26, 1929, UCLA.

25. JT to George Nathan, June 21, 1927, CORN.

26. HLM to JT, May 18, 1929, HLMP.

27. Contract with Doubleday, Doran & Co. for *Beggars Abroad*, May 20, 1929, UCLA; *Sunday News*, May 26, 1929, UCLA.

28. *BA*, 1–2.

29. Ibid., 14.

30. Ibid.

31. *Sunday News*, May 26, 1929, UCLA.

32. *BA*, 14.

33. Ibid., 18.

34. Ibid., 61.
35. JT to Sadie Hunter, July 4, 1929, UCLA.
36. *BA*, 61.
37. Ibid., 63; JT to HLM, June 3, 1929, HLMNY; *Nottingham Evening News*, Feb. 26, 1930, UCLA.
38. *BA*, 63.
39. JT to HLM, June 3, 1929, HLMNY.
40. HLM to JT, June 15, 1929, HLMP.
41. Paul Theroux, *Fresh Air Fiend: Travel Writings, 1985–2000* (Boston: Houghton Mifflin, 2000), 26.
42. Alfred Knopf to JT, July 23, 1929, UCLA.
43. *BA*, 80–86.
44. Alfred Knopf to JT, July 23, 1929, UCLA.
45. JT, "It's Good to Have to Rough It!" *London Daily Chronicle*, June 18, 1929, UCLA.
46. *BA*, 87–88.
47. Ibid., 99.
48. Ibid., 92.
49. Ibid., 121.
50. Ibid., 130.
51. Ibid., 131.
52. JT to Sadie Hunter, July 4, 1929, UCLA.
53. JT to George Nathan, Sept. 27, 1929, CORN.
54. *BA*, 138.
55. Ibid., 139.
56. Ibid., 140.
57. *BA*, 209–10.
58. Ibid., 238.
59. Ibid., 224.
60. Ibid., 225.
61. Ibid., 230.
62. Ibid., 229, 231.
63. Ibid., 232.
64. Ibid., 259–60.
65. Ibid., 271.
66. *New York World*, July 8, 1929.

19. Blood on the Moon

1. HLM to JT, Aug. 7, 1929, HLMP.
2. Harold Freedman to JT, Aug. 13, 1929, UCLA.
3. Ben Lindsey to R. Holtby Myers, Aug. 24, 1929, UCLA.
4. JT to George Nathan, Sept. 27, 1929, CORN.
5. JT's attorney to JT, Jan. 15, 1930, UCLA; HLM to JT, Dec. 22, 1929, HLMP.
6. JT to HLM, n.d., 1930, HLMNY.
7. JT to George Nathan, Jan. 7, 1930, CORN.
8. "Divorces Jim Tully," *NYT*, Feb. 26, 1930.
9. JT to George Nathan, March 6, 1930, CORN.
10. HLM, *The Diary of H. L. Mencken*, ed. Charles A. Fecher (New York: Alfred A. Knopf, 1989), 50.
11. HLM, *A Mencken Chrestomathy* (New York: Alfred A. Knopf, 1949), 281–84.
12. JT, "John Gilbert," *Vanity Fair*, May 1928, 85.
13. Leatrice Gilbert Fountain, *Dark Star* (New York: St. Martin's Press, 1985), 152.
14. JT, "A Glance Backwards," *Hollywood: The Motion Picture Magazine*, April 1930, UCLA.
15. Frank Wilstach to JT, June 8, 1928, UCLA.
16. James Quirk to JT, Jan. 28, 1929, UCLA.
17. Anita Loos, *Kiss Hollywood Good-By* (New York: Viking, 1974), 29–30.
18. Fountain, *Dark Star*, 196.
19. Donald Freeman to JT, Dec. 29, 1927, UCLA.
20. Fountain, *Dark Star*, 152.
21. JT, "They Take It on the Chin!" *Screen Book*, July 1935, UCLA.
22. Fountain, *Dark Star*, 196; JT, "Fights of Hollywood," *Scranton (Pa.) Times*, Nov. 24, 1934, UCLA.
23. Sidney Skolsky, "Tintypes," News Syndicate Co. (about 1931), clipping, CORN.
24. John Burke, *Rogue's Progress: The Fabulous Adventures of Wilson Mizner* (New York: Putnam, 1975), 260–61.
25. JT, "Fights of Hollywood."
26. William Saroyan, *Places Where I've Done Time* (New York: Praeger, 1972), 125.
27. JT, "Fights of Hollywood."
28. Frank Scully, "Scully on Tully," *Screen Writer*, Aug. 1947, 8, UCLA.
29. *Akron Beacon Journal*, Feb. 11, 1930.
30. JT, "They Take It on the Chin!"
31. John Hernon to JT, telegram, Feb. 12, 1930, UCLA.

32. "Gilbert Pledges Trouble If He Meets Tully Again," *LAT,* Feb. 13, 1930.

33. "Shh! All's Quiet on Tully-Gilbert Front," *LAT,* Feb. 21, 1930; Rosalind Shaffer, "Tully Changes His Mind about Jack Gilbert," *Chicago Daily Tribune,* March 16, 1930.

34. John Gilbert to JT, Sept. 22, 1930, UCLA.

35. "Items from Studios and Theatres," *NYT,* March 30, 1930.

36. Edwin Schallert, "Gales Blow on Screen at Loew's," *LAT,* Nov. 8, 1930; Fountain, *Dark Star,* 199; John Douglas Eames, *The MGM Story* (New York: Crown 1976), 67.

37. "Flashbacks and Fadeouts," *Washington Post,* July 13, 1930.

38. Hubbard Keavy, "Screen Life in Hollywood," *Washington Post,* July 6, 1930.

39. Fountain, *Dark Star,* 199.

40. Skolsky, "Tintypes."

41. JT, "They Take It on the Chin!"

42. JT, "Almost an Actor," *New Movie Magazine,* Dec. 1930, UCLA.

43. Ibid.

44. JT, "They Take It on the Chin!"

45. JT, "Hollywood's Big Secret," *LAT,* Dec. 15, 1935.

46. JT, "Almost an Actor."

47. Nelson B. Bell, "Palace," *Washington Post,* Oct. 26, 1930.

48. Schallert, "Gales Blow on Screen."

49. Mae Tinee, "Sailor's Search for Love Ends in Shipwreck," *Chicago Daily Tribune,* Nov. 3, 1930.

50. Samuel Marx, *Mayer and Thalberg: The Make-Believe Saints* (New York: Random House, 1975), 148.

51. Mordaunt Hall, "The Screen," *NYT,* Dec. 13, 1930.

52. Quoted in Louis Cochran to Maxwell Perkins, April 16, 1942, SCRIB.

53. Frank Wilstach to JT, Nov. 10, 1930, UCLA.

54. Skolsky, "Tintypes."

55. Madeleine Matzen, "A Writer Must Make People Think," *Writer's Market,* May 1938, 7.

56. Saroyan, *Places Where I've Done Time,* 123–25.

57. "Group Here Scores Anti-Soviet Drive," *NYT,* March 16, 1930; "155 in the Arts Join Anti-Dry Body," *NYT,* March 17, 1930.

58. International Union of Revolutionary Writers to JT, radiogram, Feb. 29, 1932, UCLA.

59. Edna Ferber to JT, Oct. 8, 1930, UCLA.

60. "American Peace Mobilization Report," Dec. 23, 1940, Federal Bureau of Investigation, File No. 61–1498.

61. Marginalia in Tully's handwriting on his copy of Benjamin DeCassere, "A Self-Interview," *Contempo,* Sept. 15, 1931, UCLA.

62. Quoted in Louis Cochran to Maxwell Perkins, April 16, 1942, SCRIB.

63. Frederick James Smith to JT, March 21, 1930, UCLA; Frederick James Smith to JT, May 15, 1930, UCLA.

64. Frederick James Smith to JT, May 14, 1930, UCLA; Frederick James Smith to JT, telegram, March 28, 1930, UCLA.

65. JT to HLM, April 26, 1930, HLMNY; JT, "The Irish Are Dumb People," *Vanity Fair,* May 1930, 54; HLM to JT, May 16, 1930, HLMP.

66. George Britt, *New York World-Telegram,* June 9, 1931.

67. HLM to JT, May 1, 19[30], HLMP.

68. Upton Sinclair to JT, Nov. 10, 1930, UCLA.

69. Fred Moore to JT, Feb. 12, 1931, UCLA.

70. JT to HLM, n.d. (about May) 1930, HLMNY.

71. "Mrs. Stresesmann to Lecture Here," *NYT,* May 4, 1930.

72. Al Hill, *Easy Pickings* (New York: Brentano's, 1931); George Milburn, *The Hobo's Hornbook: A Repertory for a Gutter Jongleur* (New York: Ives Washburn, 1930); George Milburn to JT, Jan. 15, 1931, UCLA.

73. JDT to JT, Oct. 3, 1927, UCLA.

74. JDT to JT, Oct. 13, 1927, UCLA.

75. JDT to JT, March 8, 1930, UCLA; JDT to JT, March 24, 1930, UCLA; JDT to JT, April 14, 1930, UCLA.

76. JDT to JT, May 12, 1930, UCLA; JT, "The Irish Are Dumb People."

77. JDT to JT, May 19, 1930, UCLA.

78. *NYT,* Oct. 7, 1930.

79. HLM to JT, Oct. 31, 1930, HLMP.

80. JT to HLM, Nov. 7, 1930, HLMNY.
81. JT, "Why I Have Written," *Writer's Digest*, Nov. 1930, 21–23.
82. JT to HLM, n.d. (about Oct. 1930), HLMNY.
83. JT to Sadie Hunter, Jan. 17, 1931, UCLA. A dark or blood-red moon is mentioned several times in the Bible, notably Acts 2:20 and Revelation 6:12. And the Roman historian Suetonius claims that Emperor Domitian had a vision that foretold his assassination: "There will be blood on the moon tomorrow as she enters Aquarius, and a deed will be done for everyone to talk about." Suetonius, T*he Twelve Caesars*, ed. by James Rives, trans. by Robert Graves (New York: Penguin, 2007), 307. See also Michael R. Molnar, "Blood on the Moon in Aquarius: The Assassination of Domitian," *The Celator* (May 1995), 6–12.
84. Skolsky, "Tintypes."
85. JT to Sadie Hunter, Jan. 17, 1931, UCLA.
86. JT's attorney to Hugh Tully, March 25, 1931, UCLA.
87. Charles Davis to JT, Jan. 23, 1931, UCLA.
88. Alton Tully to Myrtle Tully, May 28, 1937, UCLA.
89. Claude Owen to JT, Jan. 18, 1927, UCLA.
90. Ibid.; Claude Owen to JT, Feb. 14, 1927, UCLA.
91. Florence Tully to JT, n.d., UCLA.
92. Alton Tully to JT, Dec. 2, 1930, UCLA.
93. "Probation Given Son of Writer," *LAT*, Nov. 19, 1931, UCLA.
94. Alton Tully to JT, March 28, 1931, UCLA.
95. George Britt, *New York World-Telegram*, June 9, 1931, UCLA.
96. William Myers, *New York World-Telegram*, June 13, 1931, UCLA.
97. JT to HLM, telegram, June 13, 1931, HLMNY.
98. JT to HLM, July 28, 1931, HLMNY.
99. JT, *Man of the New School* (Cincinnati: Greater Hotel Gibson, 1931), UCLA.
100. Alton Tully to JT, n.d., UCLA.
101. Alton Tully to JT, July 10, 1931, UCLA.
102. Alton Tully to JT, Oct. 9, 1931, UCLA.
103. Mr. Murphy to Ben Axley, Nov. 10, 1931, UCLA.
104. "Probation Given Son of Writer," *LAT*, Nov. 19, 1931, UCLA.
105. Alton Tully to JT, Dec. 6, 1931, UCLA; Alton Tully to JT, Dec. 10, 1931, UCLA.
106. Alton Tully to JT, Dec. 16, 1931, UCLA; Alton Tully to JT, Dec. 23, 1931, UCLA.
107. Alton Tully to JT, Dec. 23, 1931, UCLA.
108. Trilby Tully to JT, Nov. 12, 1931, UCLA.
109. Trilby Tully to JT, Dec. 26, 1931, UCLA.
110. HLM, *The Diary of H. L. Mencken*, 51.
111. Virginia Peterson Ross, *New York Herald-Tribune*, May 17, 1931.
112. Frederic F. Van de Water, *New York Post*, May 23, 1931.
113. Fanny Butcher, "Tully Finishes His Series on the Underworld," *Chicago Daily Tribune*, May 29, 1931.
114. Percy Hutchison, "When Jim Tully Was Hopping Outbound Freights," *NYT*, May 10, 1931.
115. Fred Marsh, "Tully Rounds It Out," *Nation*, Aug. 19, 1931.
116. Jack Bracken to JT, Feb. 25, 1932.
117. Esme Warde and John Senn, MGM reader's report on *Blood on the Moon*, May 1, 1931, UCLA.

20. Laughter in Hell

1. J. E. House, "On Second Thought," *New York Evening Post*, Jan. 27, 1932, UCLA.
2. Floyd Simonton, "Jim Tully's New Residence," *Hollywood Citizen-News*, n.d., clip attached to JT to HLM, Nov. 29, 1932, HLMNY.
3. JT to HLM, Dec. 15, 1932, HLMNY.
4. Simonton, "Jim Tully's New Residence."
5. Ibid.; *LAT*, May 6, 1932, clipping, UCLA; "Permits in Van Nuys Area Jump," *LAT*, Aug. 21, 1932.
6. JT to HLM, Nov. 18, 1932, HLMNY.
7. JT to Sadie Hunter, Jan. 17, 1931, UCLA.
8. JT to HLM, Feb. 4, 1940, HLMNY.
9. JT to Sara Haardt Mencken, Aug. 3, 1933, HLMNY.

10. HLM to JT, Dec. 8, 1932, HLMP.
11. HLM, *The Diary of H. L. Mencken*, ed. Charles A. Fecher (New York: Alfred A. Knopf, 1989), 51.
12. Gertrude Lawler to JT, Nov. 7, 1932, UCLA.
13. Foster Egner, "Tully Turns Tables: Vow to Visit Governor Made Good," *Cincinnati Post*, undated clipping, UCLA.
14. JT's secretary to Ben Lindsey, Aug. 16, 1932, UCLA.
15. JT to George Nathan, April 1, 1932, CORN.
16. *LH*, 166–67.
17. HLM to JT, n.d. (about July, 1932), HLMNY; "The Barrymores in Hollywood," *LAT*, June 12, 1932; "Studio Newsreel," *LAT*, March 2, 1932; Hugh Weir to JT, March 31, 1932, UCLA.
18. JT to George Nathan, April 1, 1932, CORN; Charles Bickford to JT, telegram, May 9, 1932, UCLA; Louella Parsons, *New York American*, March 23, 1932, UCLA.
19. Pat O'Brien, *The Wind at My Back* (Garden City, N.Y.: Doubleday, 1964), 185–86.
20. "Projection Jottings," *NYT*, Sept. 25, 1932.
21. "The Barrymores in Hollywood," *NYT*, June 12, 1932.
22. Ibid.; *Galveston (Tex.) Daily News*, April 24, 1932, UCLA.
23. JT to Sadie Hunter, June 11, 1932, UCLA.
24. HLM to JT, April 2, 1932, HLMP; HLM to JT, April 12, 1932, HLMP; HLM to JT, Aug. 1, 1932, HLMP.
25. JT to HLM, Aug. 6, 1932, HLMNY.
26. JT to HLM, Aug. 9, 1932, HLMNY.
27. HLM to JT, Aug. 11, 193[2], HLMP.
28. "Before the Cameras and the Microphone," *NYT*, Sept. 11, 1932.
29. JT to George Nathan, Sept. 23, 1932, CORN.
30. Don Lynch and Ken Marschall, *Titanic—An Illustrated History* (London: Hodder & Stoughton, 1997), 77.
31. "Mr. Tully's Let-Down," *NYT*, Oct. 23, 1932.
32. "Illiterature," *Time*, Oct. 24, 1932.
33. *Saturday Review of Literature*, Nov. 19, 1932.
34. "Chain Gang Story by Jim Tully Has Pat O'Brien in It," *Washington Post*, Jan. 15, 1933.
35. "New Cinema Offerings," *Washington Post*, Jan. 15, 1933.
36. Mordaunt Hall, "The Screen; A Chain-Gang Melodrama," *NYT*, Jan. 2, 1933.
37. JT to HLM, Jan. 23, 1933, HLMNY.
38. JT, federal income tax return, 1932, UCLA.
39. "Jim Tully, Ex-Hobo, off Train, Riding for Life," *Boston Advertiser*, May 29, 1932, UCLA.
40. JT to George Nathan, Feb. 4, 1932, CORN.
41. HLM, *The Diary of H. L. Mencken*, 50.
42. Ibid.
43. JT to George Nathan, June 17, 1932, CORN.
44. JT to HLM, July 6, 1932, HLMNY.
45. JT to George Nathan, June 17, 1932, CORN; JT to HLM, July 6, 1932, HLMNY.
46. JT to HLM, Aug. 6, 1932, HLMNY.
47. JT, "The Waif Who Threatens Garbo," *New Movie Magazine*, Feb. 1932, clipping, UCLA; JT, "Ex-Follies Girl," *Illustrated Love Magazine*, March 1932, UCLA; JT, "Ugly Mug," *New Movie Magazine*, March 1932, UCLA; JT, "A Man of the Mountains," *Rob Wagner's Script*, March 5, 1932, clipping, UCLA; JT, "How Fame Came to Janet," *New Movie Magazine*, April 1932, UCLA; JT, "A Whale of a Man," *New Movie Magazine*, June 1932, UCLA; JT, "Hollywood's Rebel," *New Movie Magazine*, Aug. 1932, UCLA; JT, "Alias the Monster," *New Movie Magazine*, Sept. 1932, UCLA; JT, "Goodbye, Paul!" *Rob Wagner's Script*, Sept. 17, 1932, UCLA; JT, "Jim Tully Announces the Return of Clara Bow," *New Movie Magazine*, Dec. 1932, UCLA.
48. JT to Frank Scully, July 9, 1936, carbon copy, authors' collection.
49. Leo Grin to Paul Bauer, e-mail, April 12, 2002.
50. *DOZ*, 192.
51. George Shaffer, "'First Wife' of Bern Missing; Suicide Feared," *Chicago Daily Tribune*, Sept. 10, 1932.
52. David Stenn, *Bombshell: The Life and Death of Jean Harlow* (New York: Doubleday, 1993); Samuel Marx and Joyce

Vanderveen, *Deadly Illusions: Jean Harlow and the Murder of Paul Bern* (New York: Random House, 1990).
53. JT to HLM, Sept. 12, 1932, HLMNY.
54. Ibid.
55. *DOZ*, 196.
56. Probation office to Alton Tully, April 20, 1932, UCLA; Dollar Steamship Lines to JT, April 29, 1932, UCLA.
57. Alton Tully to JT, Oct. 21, 1932, UCLA.
58. HLM, *The Diary of H. L. Mencken*, 51.
59. "New Plea Made by Suspect," *LAT*, Feb. 2, 1933; *LAT*, Feb. 17, 1933.
60. Alton Tully to JT, Jan. 9, 1933, UCLA.
61. HLM, *The New Mencken Letters*, ed. Carl Bode (New York: Dial, 1977), 281.
62. JT to HLM, Feb. 11, 1933, HLMNY.
63. JT to HLM and Sara Haardt Mencken, Feb. 17, 1933, HLMNY.
64. HLM, *A Second Mencken Chrestomathy*, ed. Terry Teachout (New York: Alfred A. Knopf, 1994), 450.
65. Pat Frayne, "Sports Comment," *San Francisco Call-Bulletin*, April 8, 1933.
66. Ibid.
67. Frank Scully, "Jim Tully," *Scribner's*, Aug. 1937, 51. For a variation of this, see: Frank Scully, "Jim Tully," *'Rogues' Gallery: Profiles of My Eminent Contemporaries* (Hollywood, Calif.: Murray & Gee, 1943), 251.
68. JT, "Yeggs," *American Mercury*, April 1933; JT to HLM, Nov. 29, 1932, HLMNY.
69. JT to George Nathan, March 14, 1933, CORN.
70. JT to HLM and Sara Haardt Mencken, Feb. 23, 1933, HLMNY.
71. HLM to JT, March 14, 1933, UCLA.
72. JT to George Nathan, March 14, 1933, CORN.
73. JT to HLM and Sara Haardt Mencken, March 29, 1933, HLMNY; HLM to JT, March 24, 1933, UCLA.
74. *New York American*, June 6, 1933, UCLA; JT to HLM, June 11, 1933, HLMNY.
75. ML.
76. JT, "Portrait of My Father," *Esquire*, Nov. 1939, 120.
77. ML.
78. Trilby Tully to JT, June 17, 1933, UCLA.

79. James Alexander Tully and Myrtle Zwetow, marriage certificate, June 26, 1933, UCLA.
80. JT to William Randolph Hearst, Sept. 9, 1933, UCLA.
81. JT, "W as in 'Always Wrong,'" *Rob Wagner's Script*, Sept. 9, 1933, 8.
82. "Chaplin Mourns for Tully, Bindle Stiff Gone Highbrow," *Akron Beacon Journal*, Sept. 23, 1933.
83. JT to Charles Chaplin, Oct. 2, 1933, UCLA. It's not clear if this letter was ever mailed.
84. JT to Rob Wagner, Oct. 7, 1933, UCLA.

21. Ladies in the Parlor

1. Alton Tully to JT, Oct. 26, 1933, UCLA.
2. Florence Tully to JT, Oct. 5, 1933, UCLA.
3. "Statement of Facts," legal papers about Alton Tully–Violet Robey, n.d., UCLA; "Tully to Face Attack Charge," *LAT*, Dec. 8, 1933; "Son of Tully to Face Trial," *LAT*, Dec. 13, 1933.
4. "Tully Gets Long Term in Prison," *LAT*, March 16, 1934.
5. *Los Angeles Herald Express*, Dec. 7, 1933, UCLA.
6. JT, "Frank Capra," *Rob Wagner's Script*, March 3, 1934; JT to Frank Capra, March 1, 1934, carbon copy, UCLA.
7. Frank Capra to JT, Jan. 18, 1934, UCLA.
8. JT to Alton Tully, Feb. 7, 1934, UCLA.
9. "Defendant Hits Story of Woman," *LAT*, Feb. 7, 1934, UCLA.
10. "Jury in Tully Case Locked Up," *LAT*, Feb. 8, 1934.
11. JT to Alton Tully, Feb. 9, 1934, carbon copy, UCLA.
12. "Charges by Woman Win Conviction," *LAT*, Feb. 9, 1934.
13. "Tully Files Motion for New Trial," *LAT*, Feb. 14, 1934; "New Trial Fight Set for Today," *LAT*, Feb. 23, 1934.
14. Alton Tully to JT, Feb. 24, 1934, UCLA.
15. Alton Tully to JT, Feb. 25, 1934, UCLA.
16. JT to Frank Capra, March 1, 1934, carbon copy, UCLA.

17. Ibid.
18. "Tully Gets Long Term in Prison."
19. "Tully's Son Gets Prison Term," *NYT,* March 16, 1934, UCLA.
20. Alton Tully to JT, March 21, 1934, UCLA.
21. Alton Tully to JT, April 4, 1934, UCLA.
22. JT to Sadie Hunter, April 5, 1934, UCLA.
23. "Young Tully Wins Writ," *LAT,* April 7, 1934.
24. William Greet to Steven Aguirre, April 6, 1934, UCLA; JT to George Nathan, April 24, 1933, CORN; JT, "Senor Diego Rivera," *Esquire,* Aug. 1934.
25. JT to George Nathan, April 24, 1933, CORN.
26. *DOZ,* 79; JT to George Nathan, April 24, 1933, CORN.
27. *DOZ,* 92.
28. Ibid., 93.
29. Robert Howard, *Fat Charley Makley and the Dillinger Gang: The Great American Crime Spree of 1933–34* (St. Marys, Ohio: Buzan Books, 2010), 73.
30. "Tully Meets Old Playmate in Death Row," *Akron Beacon Journal,* June 19, 1934.
31. Walter Winchell, *New York Daily Mirror,* July 2, 1934, UCLA.
32. *Chicago News,* July 16, 1934, clipping, UCLA.
33. G. Russell Girardin, *Dillinger,* with William Helmer (Bloomington: Indiana University Press, 1994), 240.
34. W. C. Fields as told to JT, "Over a Barrel," *Esquire,* Oct. 1934; Paul Muni with JT, "Glancing Backward," *Esquire,* Dec. 1934.
35. JT to HLM, July 16, 1934, HLMNY.
36. Merritt to JT, June 12, 1934, UCLA.
37. NANA to JT, telegram, July 17, 1934, UCLA; NANA to JT, telegram, July 18, 1934, UCLA.
38. JT, undated MS about San Francisco, UCLA.
39. JT to Jerome Gross, Aug. 12, 1934, UCLA.
40. JDT to Myrtle Tully, April 2, 1935, UCLA.
41. "New Trial Won in Tully Fight," *LAT,* Aug. 18, 1934, UCLA.

42. Alton Tully to Myrtle Tully, Aug. 24, 1934, UCLA.
43. "Date Set for Tully Attack Case Retrial," *LAT,* Sept. 27, 1934, UCLA; "Tully Retrial Date Deferred," *LAT,* Oct. 19, 1934, UCLA.
44. Alton Tully to JT, Dec. 17, 1934, UCLA.
45. JT to Buron Fitts, Oct. 23, 1934, UCLA.
46. John Wheeler to JT, Sept. 27, 1934, UCLA.
47. Edwin Hubble to JT, Oct. 26, 1934, UCLA.
48. Charles Beahan to JT, Aug. 24, 1934, UCLA; Rudy Vallee to JT, Oct. 28, 1934, UCLA. Tully tried for another six years to bring "God Loves the Irish" to the stage before finally abandoning the project. See Samuel French Co. to JT, Oct. 23, 1940, UCLA.
49. "Tulley [sic] Gets Six Months after Plea," *LAT,* Nov. 15, 1934; Alton Tully to JT and Myrtle, Nov. 29, 1934, UCLA.
50. Alton Tully to Myrtle Tully, Dec. 28, 1934, UCLA.
51. JT to HLM, April 8, 1929, HLMNY.
52. JT to HLM, Aug. 15, 1932, HLMP.
53. JT, *Ladies in the Parlor* MS, draft of Aug. 7, 1934, UCLA.
54. Gregory William Mank, *Karloff and Lugosi: The Story of a Haunting Collaboration* (Jefferson, N.C.: McFarland, 1990); JT to George Nathan, Dec. 23, 1924, CORN; David Boehm and JT, "The Raven," unpublished MS, Nov. 23, 1934, UCLA; Edwin Schallert, "Veloz and Yolanda Remain as Team in Spite of Attractive Individual Offers," *LAT,* Nov. 39, 1934.
55. JT to HLM, Feb. 28, 1935, HLMP.
56. JT to HLM, March 12, 1935, HLMP.
57. *New York Morning Telegraph,* May 22, 1935, UCLA.
58. JT to George Nathan, Feb. 12, 1935, CORN.
59. JT, *Ladies in the Parlor* MS, draft of Aug. 7, 1934, UCLA.
60. *LP,* 1.
61. R. W. Stallman, *Stephen Crane* (New York: George Braziller, 1973), 74.
62. *LP,* 125.
63. Ibid., 101.
64. HLM to JT, July 30, 193[5], HLMP.
65. HLM to JT, April 22, 1936, HLMP.

66. HLM to JT, April 5, 1935, HLMP.
67. Jae Greenberg to California bookstore, May 23, 1935, UCLA.
68. *Cinema Sound and Fury*, undated clipping (around June 1935), UCLA.
69. Ted Robinson, *Cleveland Plain Dealer*, June 2, 1935.
70. JT to HLM, June 13, 1935, HLMNY.
71. *New York Herald-Tribune*, June 16, 1935, UCLA.
72. Douglas Lurton to JT, June 22, 1935, UCLA.
73. *New York Herald-Tribune*, Aug. 13, 1935, UCLA.
74. JT to HLM, Aug. 19, 1935, HLMP.
75. Jae Greenberg to JT, June 24, 1935, UCLA.
76. Sydney Sanders to JT, July 1, 1935, UCLA.
77. JT to HLM, n.d. (about 1936), HLMNY.
78. "Tully Book 'Indecent,'" *NYT*, Aug. 17, 1935.
79. JT, "Are You Sitting in a Breeze?" *Rob Wagner's Script*, Aug. 24, 1935, 7.
80. William Saroyan, *Places Where I've Done Time* (New York: Praeger, 1972), 124; Jae Greenberg to JT, Aug. 29, 1935, UCLA.

22. Return to the Ring

1. Emma Lou Sayers, "Walrond Best of Race Scribes Says Jim Tully," *Pacific Coast News Bureau*, Jan. 27, 1927, UCLA.
2. Langston Hughes, *The Big Sea* (New York: Knopf, 1940), 251.
3. Langston Hughes, *I Wonder as I Wander* (New York: Hill and Wang, 1964), 303.
4. Arnold Rampersad, *The Life of Langston Hughes* (New York: Oxford University Press, 2002), 309.
5. Hughes, *I Wonder*, 304.
6. Ibid., 304–5.
7. Ibid., 305.
8. JT to Frank Scully, July 9, 1936, carbon copy, authors' collection.
9. Read Kendall, "Around and about in Hollywood," *LAT*, Aug. 15, 1935.
10. Hughes, *I Wonder*, 306.
11. Ibid.

12. JT to Frank Scully, July 9, 1936, carbon copy, authors' collection.
13. Henry Armstrong, *Gloves, Glory and God* (Westwood, N.J.: Fleming H. Revell, 1956), 122.
14. Hughes, *I Wonder*, 306; *DOZ*, 213.
15. Armstrong, *Gloves*, 79.
16. *DOZ*, 213.
17. Ibid., 219.
18. Frank Scully, "Jim Tully," *Scribner's*, Aug. 1937, 52.
19. *DOZ*, 221.
20. Hughes, *I Wonder*, 306; *DOZ*, 223.
21. Bert Randolph Sugar, ed., *The Ring 1981 Record Book and Boxing Encyclopedia* (New York: Atheneum, 1981), 612–13.
22. JT, "The Manly Art," *Esquire*, July 1934, 64.
23. JT, "The Valiant Joe E. Brown," *Screen Play*, April 1935, UCLA; JT, "The Life Story of Ginger Rogers," *Picturegoer Weekly*, April 27, 1935, UCLA; JT, "The Real Truth about William Powell," *Screen Book*, April 1935, UCLA; JT, "Let's Laugh at Life with W. C. Fields," *Screen Play*, June 1935, UCLA; JT, "Tough Guy," *Screen Book*, June 1935, UCLA; "Clark Gable's Last Dime," *Screen Play*, March 1935, UCLA; JT, "Gary Cooper—Still Ridin' to Town!" *Motion Picture*, Aug. 1935, UCLA; JT, "Barbara Stanwyck," *Screen Book*, Aug. 1935, UCLA; JT, "Early Struggles of Norma Shearer," *Picturegoer Weekly*, Aug. 17, 1935, UCLA; JT, "Tragedies of Hollywood," *Screen Book*, Sept. 1935, UCLA; JT, "The Amazing Robert Montgomery," *Screen Play*, Sept. 1935, UCLA; JT, "A Chorus Boy Makes Good," *Screen Pictorial*, Sept. 1935, UCLA.
24. Ruby Darrow to JT, May 29, 1953, UCLA; Charles Lavell to JT, April 9, 1935, UCLA.
25. "Governor Attacks Pleas for Slayer by 'Sob Sisters,'" *Washington Post*, March 24, 1935; Walter Winchell and JT, "On Broadway: Letter from Jim Tully," *New York Daily Mirror*, April 17, 1935; "Prison Killer Is Saved by Court after Pleas of Noted Writers Fail," *Oklahoma City Times*, Aug. 30, 1935.
26. JT to Frank Scully, July 9, 1936, carbon copy, authors' collection.
27. Jae Greenberg to JT, July 16, 1935, UCLA.

28. JT, "All or Nothing," unpublished MS, Sept. 1935, UCLA.
29. *San Francisco Examiner*, Sept. 23, 19[35], clipping, UCLA.
30. "Young Tully Faces Trial," *LAT*, Sept. 17, 1935.
31. "How Did Such a Man Remain out of Jail?" *Sacramento Bee*, Sept. 19, 1935; JT to HLM, Oct. 7, 1935, HLMNY.
32. "Young Tully Faces Trial," *LAT*, Sept. 17, 1935.
33. JT to HLM, Sept. 19, 1935, HLMNY; JT, letter to the editor, *Woodland (Calif.) Daily Democrat*, Sept. 27, 1935, UCLA.
34. JT to Frank Scully, July 9, 1936, carbon copy, authors' collection.
35. IPBH.
36. "Prison Term Imposed on Jim Tully's Son," *NYT*, Sept. 24, 1935.
37. HLM to JT, March 12, 1935, HLMP.
38. "Young Tully in San Quentin as No. 58114," *Los Angeles Evening Herald and Express*, Sept. 24, 1935.
39. JT, letter to the editor, *Woodland (Calif.) Daily Democrat*, Sept. 27, 1935, UCLA.
40. Frank Scully to JT, Sept. 16, 1935, authors' collection.
41. JT to Alton Tully, Nov. 27, 1935, UCLA.
42. Alton Tully to JT, Nov. 30, 1935, UCLA.
43. Alton Tully to JT, Jan. 3, 1936, UCLA.
44. JT to Walter, Nov. 29, 1935, UCLA.
45. JT to HLM, Aug. 3, 1937, HLMNY.
46. JT to HLM, Dec. 8, 1942, HLMNY.
47. "Court Bans Tully Book," *NYT*, Nov. 1, 1935.
48. HLM to JT, Sept. 3, 1935, HLMP.
49. Sydney Sanders to JT, Nov. 6, 1935, UCLA.
50. Jae Greenberg to JT, Nov. 16, 1935, UCLA.
51. "Naughty Books Make Nice Fire," *New York Daily Mirror*, Nov. 13, 1936.
52. Scully, "Jim Tully," 56.
53. JT to Maxwell Perkins, Dec. 5, 1935, SCRIB.
54. Jae Greenberg, royalty statement, *Ladies in the Parlor*, June 30–Dec. 31, 1935, UCLA.
55. Maxwell Perkins to JT, Dec. 9, 1935, SCRIB.
56. HLM to JT, March 10, 1936, HLMP; JT, "Animal Stars," *LAT*, March 1, 1936.
57. JT to HLM, March 6, 1936, HLMNY.
58. Irene Kuhn, "Jim Tully to Do Right by Jack Dempsey, the Realest Guy in Town," *New York World-Telegram*, April 20, 1936.
59. JT to Frank Scully, July 9, 1936, carbon copy, authors' collection.
60. JT to HLM, Oct. 7, 1935, HLMNY.
61. "Jim Tully Estate Sells for $27,500," *LAT*, Dec. 8, 1940; Halina Rekwart, "Jim Tulleys Find Oil on Ranch," *San Fernando Valley Times*, Aug. 12, 1941, UCLA.
62. "Tully to Write Dempsey Play," *LAT*, April 7, 1936.
63. Forest Monroe to JT, April 13, 1936, UCLA.
64. Contract with A&C Boni for *The Bruiser*, April 21, 1936; JT to HLM, April 25, 1936, HLMNY.
65. JT to HLM, June 28, 1936, HLMNY.
66. Sydney Sanders to JT, June 18, 1936, UCLA.
67. JT to HLM, July 25, 1936, HLMNY; HLM to JT, July 8, 1936, HLMP.
68. JT to HLM, July 25, 1936, HLMNY.
69. Ibid.
70. Frank Scully to JT, Aug. 4, 1936, authors' collection; JT, "From Waitress to Film Star," *Picturegoer Weekly*, June 13, 1936, UCLA; JT, "Twice a Waitress," *LAT This Week*, July 5, 1936, UCLA.
71. JT, "Harlow Will Never Grow Up," *Picturegoer Weekly*, July 4, 1936, UCLA.
72. JT to HLM, Aug. 4, 1936, HLMNY.
73. Jae Greenberg to JT, July 26, 1936, UCLA; Frank Scully to Jae Greenberg, Aug. 3, 1936, UCLA; JT to HLM, Aug. 4, 1936, HLMNY.
74. Jae Greenberg to JT, Aug. 7, 1936, UCLA.
75. HLM to JT, July 9, 1936, HLMP.
76. Frank Scully to Jae Greenberg, Aug. 3, 1936, UCLA.
77. Quoted in Jae Greenberg to JT, Aug. 7, 1936, UCLA.
78. Frank Scully to Jae Greenberg, Aug. 3, 1936, UCLA.

79. Morton Thompson, *Hollywood Citizen-News,* April 20, 1937, clipping, UCLA.
80. Jae Greenberg to JT, Sept. 4, 1936, UCLA.
81. HLM to JT, Aug. 11, 1936, HLMP.
82. HLM to JT, Nov. 20, 1936, HLMP.
83. Jae Greenberg to JT, Sept. 4, 1936, UCLA.
84. Jae Greenberg to JT, Oct. 15, 1936, UCLA.
85. Bennett Cerf to JT, Oct. 29, 1936, UCLA.

23. The Bruiser

1. *B,* 14.
2. Ibid., 27.
3. Ibid., 83.
4. E. C. Beckwith, "A Tale of the Ring," *NYT,* Nov. 15, 1936.
5. David Tilden, *Books,* Nov. 8, 1936, 24.
6. Frank Scully, *Rob Wagner's Script,* Nov. 14, 1936, UCLA.
7. Camarillo (California) State Hospital to JT, Aug. 6, 1941, UCLA.
8. JT to Maxwell Perkins, Nov. 13, 1941, SCRIB.
9. JT to George Nathan, Oct. 27, 1936, CORN.
10. JT to HLM, Nov. 14, 1936, HLMNY.
11. Frank Scully to JT, Nov. 9, 1936, authors' collection.
12. "Author Complains," *LAT,* Jan. 31, 1937.
13. Gene Tunney to JT, Oct. 18, 1938, UCLA.
14. JT and Walter Cohen, *The Bruiser* adaptation MS, Motion Pictures of Tomorrow, Jan. 1938, UCLA.
15. W. C. Fields to JT, Oct. 24, 1936, UCLA.
16. Nella Braddy to JT, Nov. 9, 1936, UCLA.
17. Alton Tully to Myrtle Tully, Nov. 23, 1936, UCLA.
18. Alton Tully to Myrtle and JT, Aug. 28, 1936, UCLA.
19. Alton Tully to Myrtle Tully, Oct. 23, 1936, UCLA.
20. Alton Tully to Myrtle Tully, Feb. 24, 1937, UCLA.
21. Alton Tully to Myrtle Tully, June 22, 1936, UCLA.
22. "Jim Tully's Son Gets 25 Years," *NYT,* Sept. 26, 1936; Alton Tully to Myrtle Tully, May 15, 1937, UCLA.
23. Alton Tully to Myrtle Tully, Dec. 28, 1936, UCLA.
24. Alton Tully to Myrtle Tully, June 16, 1936, UCLA.
25. IPBH.
26. Dr. Wilfred Curphey to JT, telegram, Dec. 27, 1936, UCLA.
27. JT, "Portrait of My Father," *Esquire,* Nov. 1939, 120; "Father of Jim Tully Dies," *St. Marys Evening Leader,* Dec. 29, 1936.
28. Ruth Allen to JT, Jan. 15, 1937, UCLA.
29. Sister Augusta to Anna Durr, Dec. 31, 1936, UCLA.
30. JT, "Portrait of My Father," 120.
31. JT to HLM, March 14, 1942, HLMNY.
32. JT, "Portrait of My Father," 120.
33. Mrs. Eva Basch to JT, Aug. 18, 1936, UCLA.
34. Alton Tully to Myrtle Tully, Jan. 22, 1937, UCLA.
35. Jae Greenberg to JT, Feb. 23, 1937, UCLA.
36. Jae Greenberg, royalty statement, *The Bruiser,* July 1, 1936–Nov. 30, 1937, UCLA.
37. George Tucker. "Man of Manhattan," *Fort Worth Star-Telegram,* Feb. 5, 1938.
38. Ibid.
39. HLM to JT, Dec. 16, 1936, HLMP.
40. HLM to JT, March 1, 193[7], HLMP.
41. Charles Beahan to JT, April 6, 1937, UCLA.
42. JT, "The Napoleon of Bruisers," *Ring,* March 1937.
43. JT to HLM, March 16, 1937, HLMNY; JT, "The King of Laughter," *Esquire,* June 1937.
44. See, in *Esquire,* "A Harvest Memory," Dec. 1936; "Case of Convict 1174," Feb. 1937, 4; "The King of Laughter," June 1937; "The Dying Hobo," April 1937. See also George Milburn, *The Hobo's Hornbook: A Repertory for a Gutter Jongleur* (New York: Ives Washburn, 1930), xv, 67.
45. JT to HLM, June 4, 1937, HLMNY; JT to HLM, Aug. 3, 1937, HLMNY.
46. Mary King to JT, June 10, 1937, UCLA.
47. JT to HLM, July 17, 1937, HLMNY; JT, "She Got Her Number!" *LAT,* Aug. 29, 1937; JT,

"She Pawned Her Poodle," *LAT*, Sept. 26, 1937; JT, "His Name Didn't Help!" *LAT*, Oct. 10, 1937.

48. "Scullys Give Irish Fete," *LAT*, March 20, 1938; Juana Neal Levy, "Scullys Serve Corned Beef," *LAT*, Feb. 2, 1938.

49. Frank Scully, "Jim Tully," *Scribner's*, Aug. 1937. See the reprint (with minor changes) in Frank Scully, *Rogues' Gallery: Profiles of My Eminent Contemporaries* (Hollywood, Calif.: Murray & Gee, 1943).

50. Madeleine Matzen, "A Writer Must Make People Think," *Writer's Market*, May 1938, 7, UCLA.

51. Carey McWilliams, *The Education of Carey McWilliams* (New York: Simon & Schuster, 1979), 48; Jay Martin, *Nathanael West: The Art of His Life* (New York: Farrar, Straus and Giroux, 1970).

52. Leonard Lyons, *Washington Post*, April 10, 1941.

53. *Johnstown (Pa.) Democrat*, June 8, 1925, UCLA.

54. JT to HLM, Sept. 3, 1938, HLMNY; W. Colston Leigh to Anna D., June 6, 1938, UCLA.

55. Virginia Oakey, *Roanoke Times*, Jan. 7, 1939, clipping, UCLA.

56. Inez Robb, "JT . . . Defies Columbia Univ. Req.," Jan. 21, 19[39], clipping, UCLA.

57. HLM to JT, Sept. 9, 1938, UCLA.

58. William Lengel to JT, June 30, 1938, UCLA; William Lengel to JT, July 6, 1938, UCLA; Ralph Daigh to JT, Aug. 19, 1938, UCLA.

59. Jae Greenberg to JT, Aug. 11, 1938, UCLA; JT, "Hollywood Decameron," unpublished MS, 1938, UCLA.

60. HLM to JT, Oct. 12, 1938, HLMP.

61. HLM to Alfred Knopf, Oct. 12, 1938, HLMNY.

62. HLM to JT, Nov. 4, 1938, HLMP.

63. Blanche Knopf to JT, March 13, 1939, UCLA; JT, "Children of Thieves," unpublished MS, 1938, UCLA; JT to HLM, March 28, 1939, HLMNY.

64. Sydney Sanders to JT, July 27, 1939, UCLA.

65. HLM to JT, July 28, 1939, HLMP.

66. JT to HLM, Oct. 27, 1939, HLMNY; HLM to JT, April 3, 1939, HLMP.

67. JT, "Tully-Grams," *Hollywood Tribune*, May 19, 1939, UCLA; HLM to JT, April 3, 1939, HLMP.

68. JT to HLM, May 20, 1939, HLMNY; JT, "Tully-Grams," *Hollywood Tribune*, June 2, 1939, UCLA.

69. Sidney Olson, "Dies, a Tough Texan, Can't Be Laughed off, Administration Finds," *Washington Post*, Oct. 30, 1938.

70. Martin Mooney, *Parole Scandal* (Los Angeles, Calif.: Lymanhouse, 1939).

71. JT, "Tully-Grams," *Hollywood Tribune*, Sept. 4, 1939, UCLA.

72. JT, "Tully-Grams," *Hollywood Tribune*, Aug. 28, 1939, UCLA.

73. Ibid.

74. Wendell Wilkie to JT, Nov. 25, 1940, UCLA.

75. Jay Robert Nash, ed., *Encyclopedia of World Crime* (Wilmette, Ill.: CrimeBooks, 1990), 1564.

76. JT to Sara Haardt Mencken, Aug. 3, 1933, HLMNY.

77. JT to William Randolph Hearst, Sept. 9, 1933, UCLA.

78. Ardis Smith, "Vagabondia's Poet, Tully, Tramp a Bit on Filmland," *Buffalo Evening News*, Jan. 24, 1939, UCLA.

79. Soviet consulate to JT, June 3, 1939, UCLA.

80. JT, "Tully-Grams," *Hollywood Tribune*, June 9, 1939, UCLA.

81. HLM to JT, June 16, 1939, HLMP.

82. JT to HLM, June 21, 1939, HLMNY.

83. JT to Marie Kuhn, June 28, 1939, Ohioana Library, Columbus.

24. Biddy Brogan's Boy

1. JT, "Portrait of My Father," *Esquire*, Nov. 1939, 90.

2. JT to HLM, March 14, 1942, HLMNY.

3. JT, "The Most Unforgettable Character I Ever Met," *Reader's Digest*, Jan. 1941, 9.

4. Ibid., 13.

5. Ibid., 11.

6. Alton Tully to JT, Sept. 23, 1941, UCLA.

7. JT to Maxwell Perkins, Jan. 21, 1940, SCRIB.

8. Maxwell Perkins to JT, Sept. 5, 1940, UCLA. See JT, "Gypsy Sister," in *70 Most Unforgettable Characters from Reader's Digest* (Pleasantville, N.Y.: Reader's Digest Association, 1967), 182–89.

9. JT to George Nathan, July 4, 1941, CORN.

10. King Features Argentina office to JT, Dec. 11, 1939, UCLA.

11. JT to HLM, Feb. 4, 1940, HLMNY. See JT, "The King of Laughter," unpublished MS, 1936–40, UCLA.

12. JT to HLM, Jan. 16, 1940, HLMNY.

13. Faustina Orner to JT, Jan. 17, 1940, UCLA.

14. JT to HLM, March 7, 1940, HLMNY; JT to HLM, April 21, 1940, HLMNY; JT to HLM, May 4, 1940, HLMNY; Perry Loring to JT, Sept. 16, 1940, UCLA; JT to HLM, Dec. 12, 1940, HLMNY.

15. JT, "Tully-Grams," *Hollywood Tribune*, Aug. 7, 1939, UCLA.

16. Ibid.

17. JT, "Tully-Grams," *Hollywood Tribune*, Sept. 18, 1939, UCLA.

18. R. H. Cowper to JT, Aug. 8, 1939, UCLA; Garriott to JT, Aug. 11, 1939, UCLA.

19. JT to HLM, Aug. 3, 1939, HLMNY; *San Fernando Valley Times*, Aug. 17, 1939, clipping, UCLA.

20. Leonard Lyons, "The New Yorker," *Washington Post*, April 22, 1940.

21. Louise Dresser to Newcom & Tully, Oct. 6, 1939, UCLA.

22. Newcom & Tully, federal income tax return, 1939, UCLA.

23. JT to HLM, Dec. 7, 1940, HLMNY.

24. "Jim Tully Estate Sells for $27,500," *LAT*, Dec. 8, 1940.

25. Alton Tully to Myrtle Tully, Aug. 28, 1940, UCLA.

26. Florence Tully to JT, May 28, 1940, UCLA.

27. JT to HLM, Aug. 4, 1941, HLMNY.

28. Trilby Tully Beamon to JT, postcard, Oct. 14, 1940, UCLA.

29. JT to HLM, Feb. 13, 1941, HLMNY.

30. Trilby Tully Beamon to Myrtle Tully, Oct. 14, 1941, UCLA.

31. Trilby Tully Beamon to Myrtle and JT, Oct. 8, 1941, UCLA.

32. Trilby Tully Beamon to Myrtle Tully, Oct. 27, 1941, UCLA.

33. Trilby Tully Beamon to Myrtle Tully, Nov. 10, 1941, UCLA.

34. "American Peace Mobilization Report," Dec., 23, 1940, Federal Bureau of Investigation, File 61–1498.

35. "The American Committee for Protection of Foreign Born Report," May 5, 1941, Federal Bureau of Investigation, FBI 100–1452.

36. JT, "Clark Gable," *Family Circle*, July 4, 1941.

37. JT to HLM, May 7, 1941, HLMNY.

38. JT to HLM, Aug. 4, 1936, HLMNY; JT, "Hollywood Decameron," unpublished MS, 1938, UCLA.

39. JT to Maxwell Perkins, May 7, 1941, SCRIB.

40. Maxwell Perkins to JT, May 13, 1941, SCRIB.

41. JT to Maxwell Perkins, May 15, 1941, SCRIB.

42. JT to HLM, May 15, 1941, HLMNY.

43. Maxwell Perkins to JT, June 26, 1941, SCRIB.

44. JT to HLM, June 13, 1939, HLMNY.

45. JT to Maxwell Perkins, Aug. 11, 1941, SCRIB.

46. JT to Maxwell Perkins, Sept. 11, 1941, SCRIB.

47. JT to HLM, Sept. 20, 1941, HLMNY.

48. Maxwell Perkins to JT, Oct. 9, 1941, SCRIB.

49. JT to HLM, Nov. 1, 1941, HLMNY.

50. Maxwell Perkins to JT, Nov. 19, 1941, SCRIB; JT to Maxwell Perkins, Dec. 2, 1941, SCRIB.

51. "Hollywood . . . The Last Carnival," *Who*, Nov. 1941, clipping, UCLA.

52. Maxwell Perkins to JT, Nov. 10, 1941, SCRIB.

53. JT to Maxwell Perkins, Nov. 13, 1941, SCRIB.

54. JT to George Nathan, Nov. 26, 1941, CORN.

55. HLM to JT, Aug. 12, 1942, HLMNY.

56. JT to Maxwell Perkins, Aug. 11, 1941, SCRIB.

57. JT to HLM, Aug. 19, 1941, HLMNY.

58. Ibid.; Clinton Duffy to HLM, Aug. 25, 1941, HLMNY.
59. JT to HLM, Aug. 19, 1941, HLMNY.
60. Alton Tully to JT, Sept. 6, 1941, UCLA.
61. Alton Tully to JT, Sept. 15, 1941, UCLA.
62. D. G. Schmidt to JT, July 22, 1941, UCLA.
63. Alton Tully to HLM, Nov. 22, 1941, UCLA.
64. JT to George Nathan, Dec. 6, 1941, CORN.
65. Alton Tully to HLM, Nov. 22, 1941, UCLA.
66. Alton Tully to Patrick Foley, Nov. 23, 1941, UCLA.
67. Myrtle Tully to Maxwell Perkins, Dec. 29, 1941, SCRIB; Hedda Hopper, "Let Anvils Ring!" *Washington Post,* Jan. 12, 1942.
68. Maxwell Perkins to JT, Feb. 11, 1942, SCRIB; JT to Maxwell Perkins, n.d. (about Jan. 16, 1942), SCRIB; Maxwell Perkins to JT, Jan. 20, 1942, SCRIB; JT to Maxwell Perkins, Jan. 27, 1942, SCRIB.
69. JT, "Great Salt Lake," UCLA; JT, "Guadalupe Peak: Along a Road in Texas," Standard Oil Company of California, UCLA.
70. JT to HLM, Feb. 16, 1942, HLMNY.
71. JT, "My Valley Neighbors," *San Fernando Valley Times,* Jan. 1942, UCLA.
72. HLM to JT, Feb. 24, 1942, HLMP; JT to Maxwell Perkins, Feb. 20, 1942, SCRIB.
73. JT to HLM, March 14, 1942, HLMNY.
74. HLM to JT, March 20, 1942, HLMP.
75. *BBB,* 123.
76. Ibid., 205.
77. Ibid., 124.
78. Ibid., 127. The actual quote is: "When your heart is broken, your bridges are burned: nothing matters any more. It is the end of happiness and the beginning of peace."
79. JT to HLM, March 26, 1942, HLMNY; JT to Maxwell Perkins, March 26, 1942, SCRIB.
80. Thomas Quinn Curtiss, "A Vagrant's Life," *NYT,* April 5, 1942.
81. Ibid.
82. Paul Jordan-Smith, "What I Liked Last Week: Ex-Hobo Tully Writes of 'Em," *LAT,* April 12, 1942.

83. *Philadelphia Record,* April 19, 1942, UCLA.
84. *San Quentin News,* Oct. 29, 1942, UCLA.
85. Lisle Bell, *New York Herald-Tribune,* April 5, 1942, UCLA.
86. *New York Post,* April 8, 1942, UCLA.
87. JT to Maxwell Perkins, April 15, 1942, SCRIB.
88. JT to HLM, Nov. 14, 1941, HLMNY.
89. JT to HLM, April 14, 1942, HLMNY.
90. Maxwell Perkins to JT, April 23, 1942, UCLA.
91. JT to Maxwell Perkins, telegram, April 23, 1942, SCRIB; Maxwell Perkins to JT, April 24, 1942, UCLA.
92. JT to Maxwell Perkins, April 27, 1942, SCRIB.
93. Maxwell Perkins to JT, May 1, 1942, SCRIB.
94. JT to Maxwell Perkins, May 5, 1942, SCRIB.
95. JT to HLM, June 20, 1942, HLMNY.
96. HLM to JT, June 26, 1942, HLMP.
97. Charles Scribner to Joseph Burris, Nov. 17, 1942, SCRIB.

25. The Last Division

1. "Attack Charge Jails Parolee," *LAT,* April 30, 1942; "Asserted Attack Victim Testifies," *LAT,* July 2, 1942.
2. "Judge Orders Trial on Attack Charge," *LAT,* May 7, 1942; "Public Defender Will Act for T. A. Tully," *LAT,* May 28, 1942.
3. Alton Tully to Myrtle Tully, Sept. 15, 1943, UCLA.
4. JT to Maxwell Perkins, May 11, 1942, SCRIB.
5. Bill McCann to Jim and Myrtle Tully, May 16, 1942, UCLA.
6. Vincent Donovan to John Dockweiler, May 25, 1942, UCLA.
7. "Public Defender Will Act."
8. "Thomas Tully Wins Acquittal," *LAT,* July 7, 1942.
9. A. A. Scott to Clinton Duffy, March 18, 1943, UCLA.
10. Myrtle Tully to HLM, July 8, 1942, HLMNY.

11. "Thomas A. Tully Returned to Prison," *LAT,* July 18, 1942.
12. Alton Tully to Myrtle Tully, Oct. 1, 1942, UCLA.
13. JT to HLM, July 25, 1942, HLMNY.
14. JT to HLM, Aug. 11, 1942, HLMNY.
15. JT to Maxwell Perkins, Nov. 10, 1942, SCRIB.
16. JT to HLM, June 20, 1942, HLMNY.
17. JT to HLM, Dec. 31, 1942, HLMNY.
18. Lee Furina to JT, June 10, 1937, UCLA; Dutton Co. to JT, Feb. 23, 1943, UCLA.
19. JT, review of *Bound for Glory,* Feb. 23, 1943, Woody Guthrie Archives.
20. JT to HLM, July 25, 1942, HLMNY; Encyclopaedia Britannica to JT, Sept. 24, 1942, UCLA.
21. HLM to JT, July 31, 1942, HLMNY.
22. JT, "John the Great," unpublished MS, Sept. 26, 1942, UCLA.
23. Edgar Lee Masters to JT, July 27, 1937, UCLA; JT to HLM, Aug. 3, 1937, HLMNY.
24. Irving Stone to JT, Feb. 21, 1940, authors' collection.
25. Irving Stone to Wesley Stout, March 22, 1940, carbon copy, authors' collection.
26. JT to HLM, Sept. 10, 1942, HLMNY.
27. Ted DuBois to JT, Sept. 8, 19[42], UCLA.
28. Richard Schrader, ed., *H. L. Mencken: A Documentary Volume* (Detroit: Gale, 2000), 254.
29. HLM to JT, March 30, 1943, HLMNY.
30. Irving Stone to JT, May 17, 1943, UCLA.
31. *NYT,* May 16, 1943, UCLA.
32. *New Yorker,* April 10, 1943, UCLA; *Saturday Review of Literature,* April 17, 1943, UCLA.
33. Ben Howden, "Jim Tully's Pen Brings Filmdom Figures to Life," *LAT,* April 4, 1943.
34. Rupert Hughes et al., invitation, April 7, 1943, UCLA; JT to HLM, April 10, 1943, HLMNY; "Lunched at the Author's Club," undated clipping (about March 1, 1943) from unknown newspaper, UCLA.
35. JT to HLM, Jan. 26, 1943, HLMNY.
36. JT to HLM, Jan. 27, 1943, HLMNY.
37. Myrtle Tully to HLM, Aug. 19, 1943, UCLA; War Department document on Myrtle Tully, Aug. 24, 1943, UCLA.
38. Leonard Lyons, "Loose-Leaf Notebook," *Washington Post,* April 14, 1943.
39. Leonard Lyons, "Times Square Tattle," *Washington Post,* May 1, 1943.
40. Patrick Byrnes to JT, bill, June 7, 1943, UCLA; JT to HLM, June 4, 1943, HLMNY.
41. Myrtle Tully to HLM, June 28, 1943, HLMNY; Myrtle Tully to Marie Kuhn, July 5, 1943, Ohioana Library, Columbus.
42. Myrtle Tully to HLM, Aug. 19, 1943, HLMNY.
43. Myrtle Tully to Marie Kuhn, July 5, 1943, Ohioana Library, Columbus; Patrick Byrnes to JT, bill, June 21, 1943, UCLA; John Sharpe to JT, bill, July 26, 1943, UCLA.
44. JT, "The Saga of the Big Dane," *Esquire,* Aug. 1943, 124.
45. Ted DuBois to JT, Aug. 6, 1943, UCLA.
46. War Department document on Myrtle Tully, Aug. 24, 1943, UCLA; Screen Office Employment Guild to Myrtle Tully, Sept. 1943, UCLA.
47. Bryan Tully Beamon, birth notice, Aug. 23, 1943, UCLA.
48. Alton Tully to Myrtle Tully, Sept. 15, 1943, UCLA.
49. HLM to JT, Aug. 27, 1943, UCLA.
50. JT to HLM, Aug. 19, 1943, HLMNY; HLM to JT, Aug. 27, 1943, UCLA.
51. Myrtle Tully to HLM, Sept. 30, 1943, HLMNY.
52. JT to Burt MacBride, March 20, 1944, UCLA; JT to HLM, April 3, 1944, HLMNY.
53. Myrtle Tully to HLM, Nov. 12, 1943, HLMNY; Myrtle Tully to HLM, Sept. 30, 1943.
54. JT to HLM, May 1, 1944, HLMNY.
55. *New York Herald-Tribune,* Sept. [n.d.], 1933, clipping, UCLA.
56. HLM to JT, Dec. 12, 1930, HLMP.
57. JT to Julian Boyd, Oct. 7, 1942, SCRIB.
58. HLM to Myrtle Tully, Oct. 7, 1943, UCLA.
59. JT to HLM, May [n.d.], 1944, HLMNY.
60. HLM to JT, May 29, 1944, HLMNY.
61. JT to HLM, June 15, 1944, HLMNY.
62. JT to John, June 2, 1944, UCLA; JT to HLM, April 28, 1943, HLMNY.

63. Elliott Macrae to JT, June 14, 1944, UCLA.
64. Elliott Macrae to JT, Oct. 31, 1944.
65. Burl Tuttle to JT, Nov. 4, 1944, UCLA; Jae Greenberg to JT, Dec. 28, 1944, UCLA; Maxwell Perkins to JT, Jan. 10, 1945, SCRIB.
66. JT to HLM, n.d., 1944, HLMNY.
67. JT to HLM, Sept. 13, 1944, HLMNY.
68. Ibid.
69. Ibid.; Alton Tully to JT, Feb. 9, 1945, UCLA; JT to Burt MacBride, March 20, 1944, UCLA; JT to Maxwell Perkins, Aug. 12, 1946, SCRIB.
70. Raymond Beamon to Myrtle and JT, June 3, 1945, UCLA.
71. Alton Tully to Myrtle and JT, Jan. 17, 1945, UCLA.
72. Alton Tully to Myrtle and JT, June 28, 1945, UCLA.
73. Myrtle Tully to HLM, May 1, 1945, HLMNY.
74. Trilby Tully Beamon to Myrtle and JT, Oct. 13, 1945, UCLA.
75. Clinton Sanders to JT, Oct. 31, 1945, UCLA.
76. HLM to JT, Dec. 30, 1946, UCLA.
77. "Jim Tulley [sic], Novelist, Goes to Sanitarium," *LAT*, Dec. 24, 1946.
78. W. C. Fields as told to JT, "Over a Barrel," *Esquire*, Oct. 1934, 54, 139; W. C. Fields, "Am I Laughing," carbon copy crediting JT and Frank Scully, UCLA; JT, "Let's Laugh at Life with W. C. Fields," *Screen Play*, June 1935, UCLA; JT, "Clowns Never Laugh," *LAT*, Sept. 6, 1936.
79. James Curtis, *W. C. Fields: A Biography* (New York: Alfred A. Knopf, 2003), 34–35; Robert Lewis Taylor, *W. C. Fields: His Follies and Fortunes* (Garden City, N.Y.: Doubleday, 1949), 46–49; Fields, "Over a Barrel"; Fields, "Am I Laughing"; Karl P. Mosher, "I Remember," Kent Historical Society, oral history, recorded circa 1984. Mosher also recalled that Fields left behind two trunks with Mosher's parents, the owners of the Central Hotel, as "a token of good faith" that he would settle his room and board when he reached New York. Several days later, when the Moshers opened the trunks, they were disappointed to see that the trunks contained nothing more valuable than a few lithograph posters for Fields's next engagement. "Fields," Mosher noted, "never sent for the trunks or paid what he owed."
80. Curtis, *W. C. Fields*, 42.
81. *Hollywood Reporter*, June 28, 1934, UCLA.
82. Curtis, *W. C. Fields*, 319.
83. Frank Scully, "Scully on Tully," *Screen Writer*, Aug. 1947, 8, UCLA.
84. Curtis, *W. C. Fields*, 478.
85. Ibid., 479.
86. JT to HLM, Dec. 27, 1946, HLMNY.
87. Ibid., attached note.
88. Scully, "Scully on Tully," 8.
89. Ibid.
90. Charles S. Warren, "Jim Tully Takes Wheel Chair Trip to Call on Sick Doctor," *Santa Monica Evening Outlook*, March 5, 1947, UCLA.
91. Myrtle Tully to HLM, Feb. 4, 1947, HLMNY.
92. Scully, "Scully on Tully," 8.
93. JT, death certificate, Cedars of Lebanon Hospital, Los Angeles, Calif., June 22, 1947, UCLA.
94. Scully, "Scully on Tully," 8.
95. HLM to Myrtle Tully, telegram, June 23, 1947, UCLA.
96. "Jim Tully . . . Died Sunday," *St. Marys Evening Leader*, June 23, 1947; Hugh Tully, death certificate, Temple City Convalescent Hospital, Temple City, Calif., Aug. 3, 1974.
97. "Jim Tully, 56, Dies," *NYT*, June 23, 1947.
98. *Providence Journal*, June 30, 1947, clipping, UCLA.
99. "Last Rites Said for Jim Tully," *LAT*, June 26, 1947.
100. *CP*, 153.
101. Scully, "Scully on Tully," 8.
102. "Last Rites Said."
103. Scully, "Scully on Tully," 10.
104. JT to Frank Scully, July 9, 1936, carbon copy, authors' collection.
105. Scully, "Scully on Tully," 8.
106. Thomas Quinn Curtiss, "A Vagrant's Life," *NYT*, April 5, 1942.
107. JT, epitaph (written for inclusion in Homer Croy, *The Last Word* [Hollywood, Calif.: privately printed, 1932]), UCLA.

Epilogue

1. Abner Warshaw to Myrtle Tully, bill, Sept. 5, 1946, UCLA.
2. "Tully Will Case Ends," *LAT,* Nov. 19, 1947; "Jim Tully Estate Goes to Widow," *LAT,* July 16, 1947.
3. "Jim Tully Will Contested," *NYT,* Aug. 2, 1947; "Will Suit Filed," *LAT,* Aug. 2, 1947.
4. "Tully Will Case Ends."
5. Robin Beamon to Paul Bauer, e-mail, Sept. 17, 2000.
6. Vincente Minnelli, *I Remember It Well,* with Hector Arce (London: Angus & Robertson, 1974), 222.
7. Frank Gerold, *Judy* (New York: Harper & Row, 1975), 281.
8. David Shipman, *Judy Garland: The Secret Life of an American Legend* (New York: Hyperion, 1992), 297–98.
9. Robin Beamon to Paul Bauer, e-mail, Sept. 17, 2000.
10. "Jim Tully Son, Wife Suicides," *New York Journal American,* April 19, 1950.
11. *Los Angeles News,* April 20, 1950, UCLA; "Author Jim Tully's Son Joins Wife in Suicide," *LAT,* April 20, 1950.
12. "Jim Tully Son, Wife Suicides."
13. "Author Jim Tully's Son Joins Wife."
14. "Jim Tully Son, Wife Suicides."
15. Ibid.; "Author Jim Tully's Son Joins Wife."
16. "Jim Tully Son, Wife Suicides."

Index

Abbott & Costello, 138
Adamic, Louis, 270
Adams, John Quincy (Whiteface), 65
Addams, Jane, 59
Adrian, Michigan, 61
"Advertising Poem, A" (Tully poem), 103
Agee, James, 180
Akron Beacon Journal, 81, 91, 104
Akron, Ohio, 69–70, 75, 81, 86, 88, 90–91, 92, 99, 104, 280
Akron Press, 81, 104
Albert & Charles Boni, 292, 303; *Beggars of Life*, 149, 302; *The Bruiser*, 261–62; Charlie Chaplin biography, 177, 179; *Circus Parade*, 178, 181, 302; *Jarnegan*, 162, 170, 281, 302; *Laughter in Hell*, 261, 281, 302; *Shanty Irish*, 187, 190, 302
Alexander the Great, 29
Alexandria Hotel (Los Angeles), 112, 119
Alfred A. Knopf, 198
Algonquin Hotel (New York), 131, 163, 175, 223
Algren, Nelson, 4
Allsop, Kenneth, 49
All-Story, 131
Almayer's Folly (Conrad), 2, 118
American Committee for Protection of Foreign Born, 280, 335
American Mercury, 163, 198, 231, 248, 272, 292; and Mencken, 133, 181, 250–51, 263, 272; and Nathan, 4; reviews of Tully's work, 152; Sara Haardt profile of Tully, 185–87, 222; Tully appearances in, 158, 173, 190, 196–201, 238
American Peace Mobilization, 280
American Tragedy, An (Dreiser), 181, 183
American Tragedy, An (1931 film), 231
Anderson, David D., 8
Anderson, Judith, 176

Anderson, Maxwell, 5, 149, 162–65, 304
Anderson, Nels, 9, 152, 195, 197
Anderson, Sherwood, 129, 130, 181, 232
Arbuckle, Roscoe "Fatty," 143, 256
Arizmendi, Alberto "Baby," 255
Arlen, Richard, 194–95
Armstrong-Carlton's (Hollywood restaurant), 141
Armstrong, Harry, 254–55
Armstrong, Henry (Henry Jackson), 254–55, 289
Arrowsmith (1931 film), 231
Ask the Dust (Fante), 270
Atkinson, Brooks, 176
Auglaize County, Ohio, 13, 14, 15, 20, 22, 23, 39, 46, 188
Austen, Jane, 59
Axley, Ben, 224

Babbitt (Lewis), 165
Backus, Johnny, 153
Baer, Max, 234, 238
Baird, Betty, 287
Ballwin, Missouri, 97
Baltimore, Maryland, 7, 8, 128, 184, 224, 237, 296
Balzac, Honoré de, 2
Bantam, 296
Barnum, P. T., 169
Barrymore, John, 235
Barrymore, Lionel, 194, 235
Basch, Eva Mae (Rogers), 268
Bates, Rosebud, 65
Battleship Potemkin, The (The Cruiser Potemkin) (1925 film), 240
Beahan, Charles, 192, 193, 303, 304
Beamon, Bryan Tully, 291
Beamon, Dana Rae, 293
Beamon, Raymond, 279, 291, 293, 299
Beamon, Robin, 299

Beaumont, Texas, 182
Beamon, Trilby Jeanne Tully (daughter of Jim Tully), 133, 239, 241, 243, 299; birth of, 115; children, 291, 293, 299; and father's estate, 299; marriage to Raymond Beamon, 279; relations with brother, Alton, 224, 243, 267, 287; relations with father, 224–25, 267, 278–80
Beckwith, E. C., 265
Bedford, Pennsylvania, 301
Beery, Wallace, 7, 194, 218–19, 235, 256, 278
Beethoven, Ludwig van, 237
Beggars Abroad (1930 book by Tully), 10, 214, 220, 222, 302; reviews, 221–22; travels for, 207–13
Beggars of Life (1924 book by Tully), 7, 8, 155, 158, 162, 165, 173, 280; as autobiography, 5, 8–10, 35, 51, 222, 248; cited, 2, 42, 44, 49, 55, 56, 58–59, 60, 150–51, 297; dedication, 5, 153–54; film version (see *Beggars of Life* [1928 film]); influence of, 4, 209, 296; popularity in the Soviet Union, 6, 203, 273; publication, 4, 131–32, 148–49, 179, 302; reviews, 9, 151–53, 181; stage version (see *Outside Looking In*); style and themes, 122, 148–51, 179, 180, 183, 187, 199, 222; title, 128; writing of, 122, 130
Beggars of Life (1928 film), 5, 193–95, 230, 304
Behn, Harry, 193
Bellows, George, 262
Bennett, Joan, 193
Bennett, Richard, 193–94
Bergman, Henry, 138, 145, 146
Berkeley, Martin, 273
Berlenbach, Paul, 165
Bern, Paul, 128, 135–36, 138, 234, 289; death of, 235–37, 289; friendship with Tully, 7, 127–28, 133, 134, 170–71, 198, 206, 207, 235; marriage to Jean Harlow, 235–36
Bertucci, Joe, 110, 111, 117, 118, 119, 130, 201
Bickford, Charles, 163, 164, 231, 234
Biddy Brogran's Boy (1942 novel by Tully), 27, 51; publication of, 284, 322; reviews of, 284–85, 297; sales, 285–86, 290; style and themes, 280, 283–84; writing of, 280–83
Birmingham, Alabama, 100
Black Boy (1926 play by Tully and Frank Dazey), 174, 176, 192, 214, 252, 303
Blake, Robert, 219
Blake, William, 210
Block, Ralph, 123, 134, 135
Blood on the Moon (1931 book by Tully), 6, 35, 37, 228; cited, 2, 10, 30, 34, 61, 68–69, 76, 78, 85, 99, 190, 225; publication of, 222–23, 302; reviews, 225–27; style and themes, 10, 51, 122, 222, 225; writing of, 222, 230
Blosser, Joseph (the "Faith Healer"), 36, 37

Blue Rain (Boyd), 264
Bogart, Humphrey, 292–93
Bombshell: The Life and Death of Jean Harlow (Stenn), 236
Bonaparte, Napoleon, 29, 98, 158
Bookman, The, 122, 182, 183
Books, 265
Booth, Ernest, 197, 198
Boroff, Bee, 35, 36
Boroff, Solomon "Sol," 34–37, 122, 225
Borzage, Frank, 169
Boston, Massachusetts, 12, 62, 181, 209
Boswell, James, 10, 259
Bound for Glory (Guthrie), 288–89, 292
Bow, Clara, 170, 234
Bowling Green, Kentucky, 100
Boxing Hall of Fame, 255
"Boy from the South, A" (Tully), 232
Boyd, Brendan, 264
Boyd, Eva, 300–301
Bracken, Jack, 78, 91, 227
Braddy, Nella, 266
Bridges, Harry, 246–47, 280
"Bright Eyes" (Tully), 158, 200, 292
Bronte, Emily, 57, 59
Bronte sisters, 59
Brooklyn Public Library, 181
Brooks, Louise, 5, 194–95
Broughton, John, 211
Brown, Clarence, 169, 171
Brown Derby (Hollywood restaurant), 6, 205, 216–18
Browning, Tod, 183
Brown, Joe E., 256
Brownlow, Kevin, 194–95
Bruiser, The (1936 novel by Tully), 6, 269; publication of, 261–62, 296, 302, 303; reviews of, 265–66; sales, 268, 271; style and themes, 51, 264–65; writing of, 256, 261, 262–63, 265
Bruns, Roger A., 51, 52, 165, 166
Buffalo, New York, 62, 87
Bukowski, Charles, 4, 270
"Bull Horrors" (Tully), 200
Bunyan, John, 35, 172
Bunyan, Paul, 183, 244
Burkan, Nathan, 177
Burnett, W. R., 270
Bushnell, Florence May. *See* Tully, Florence May Bushnell (first wife of Jim Tully)
Bushnell, Lester A., 102, 106
Butler County, Ohio, 14
Butler, June, 223–24
Byrn, Anna Gaitens (great-grandmother of Jim Tully), 12
Byrn, Charles (great-grandfather of Jim Tully), 12

Cabell, James Branch, 116, 128, 250
Cagney, James, 5, 164, 256
Cahn, Edward, 231
Cain, James M., 190, 292
Caldwell, Erskine, 270
"California Holiday, A" (Tully), 197, 201
California, SS, 208–9
Call of the Wild (London), 113
Cameron, Bob, 64
Cameron's World's Greatest Combined Shows, 63–64, 180
Cannon, "Uncle" Joe, 97
Canoga Park, California, 261, 278
Capone, Al, 5, 165, 246, 247, 277
Capra, Frank, 7, 242, 243, 281
Carewe, Edwin, 155–56
Carey, Harry, 171
Carnegie, Andrew, 77
Carondelet, Missouri, 255
Carr, Harry, 130, 153, 201
"Castle Built in Spain, The" (Tully poem), 115
Cather, Willa, 59, 128
Catton, Bruce, 202
Cavalier, 131
Cedars of Lebanon Hospital (Los Angeles), 296
Celina, Ohio, 247, 267
Central Hotel (Glasgow), 209
Central Hotel (Kent), 294, 338n79
Cerf, Bennett, 263
Chainmakers National Union, 246
Chambers, Whittaker, 273
"Champions Inside the Ropes" (unpublished Tully manuscript), 277, 304
Chandler, Raymond, 292
Chaney, Lon, 133, 134, 169, 170, 171, 216
Chaplin, Charles Spencer, Jr., 147
Chaplin, Charlie (Charles Spencer), 162, 164, 166, 169–70, 174, 181, 194, 295; and *Beggars of Life* dedication, 5, 153–54; conversations with Tully, 135–36, 139, 141, 146–47, 177–78; and death of Thomas Ince, 160; described by Tully, 135, 138–39, 140, 142, 159, 162, 178, 179, 271; early life and career, 136–38; efforts to suppress Tully's writing about him, 6–7, 177–78, 179; and Lita Grey, 144–46, 147, 178; making *The Gold Rush*, 139, 142, 143–47, 163; meeting Tully, 134, 135–36; relations with Tully, 138–39, 141, 146–47, 159, 162, 177–78, 240; reputation, 5, 6–7, 137, 138, 142, 181; screen image, 135, 137, 138; on Tully, 146–47, 162, 178, 240; Tully employer, 7, 8, 136–39, 141–47, 155, 156, 157, 159, 162, 168, 297; Tully writing about, 6–7, 177–78, 179, 220, 256, 269, 277, 289–90, 303
Chaplin, Sydney Earle, 147
Chapman, Paul, 8
Charbonneaux, Frances, 237
Charles Scribner's Sons, 178, 260, 280, 285, 286, 289, 302
"Charlie Chaplin Builds a House" (Chaplin article ghostwritten by Tully), 143
"Charlie Chaplin: His Real Life Story" (Tully articles), 177–78
Chatterton, Ruth, 271
Chicago Daily News, 103, 129
Chicago, Illinois, 28, 110, 115, 130, 194, 214, 245; home of sister, Virginia (Margaret), 48, 67, 69, 70–71, 74–75, 128–29, 194–95, 276–77; lectures, 165–66; Orpet trial, 113, 114; Paddy Croan's bar, 61; and Tully's road years, 47–48, 54–55, 56–60, 63, 67–69, 70–72, 74–75, 150, 225, 293; Virginia's death, 175, 204; visits with Virginia, 67, 70–71, 74–75, 128–29, 166, 174–75
Chicago Newsboys' Home, 56–57, 60, 63, 200
Chicago Post, 165, 166
Chicago Tribune (*Daily Tribune*), 45, 60, 191, 219, 226
"Children of Thieves" (unpublished Tully manuscript), 248, 272, 323
Chopin, Frederic, 212
Christ Hospital (Cincinnati), 157
Churchill, Winston, 138
Cicero (Marcus Tullius Cicero), 322n6
Cincinnati Enquirer, 85
Cincinnati, Hamilton & Dayton Railroad (the Dayton & Michigan), 39
Cincinnati, Ohio, 157–58, 207, 224, 230, 302; orphanage years, 2, 25–33, 43, 51, 58; and Tully's road years, 48, 58, 60–61, 63, 66–67, 181, 225
Circus, The (1928 Chaplin film), 178
Circus Fans Association, 183
"Circus Flea, The" (Tully), 131
Circus Parade (1927 book by Tully), 6, 122, 184, 192, 296, 297; as autobiography, 5, 8–10, 51, 64, 179, 222; cited, 49, 64, 65; criticism of, 181–83, 203, 234; film version planned, 183, 227; publication, 178, 179, 302; reviews, 180–81; style and themes, 179–80, 183, 187; William Gropper as illustrator, 198; writing of, 178, 179
City Lights (1931 film), 143
Clark, Earl, 197
Clarke, Donald Henderson, 202
Clark, Edwin, 4, 180
Clemens, Samuel Langhorne. *See* Twain, Mark
Cleveland Athletic Club, 87
Cleveland Blues, 78, 227
Cleveland, Grover, 27

INDEX

Cleveland, Ohio, 76, 85, 90, 101; boxing and boxers, 86, 87, 91, 92, 174, 278; visited by Tully, 87, 90, 92, 103, 166, 174
Cleveland Plain Dealer, 87, 91, 166; publishes Tully poems, 102–3, 116, 122; reviews of Tully's work, 202, 250, 285; Tully interviewed by, 92
Clift Hotel (San Francisco), 246
Clinton County, Ohio, 12
Clinton, Iowa, 55
Coleman, Robert, 163
College Humor, 159, 163
Colman, Ronald, 271
Columbia Institute, 221
Columbia University, 271
Columbus & Northwestern, 39
Columbus, Ohio, 75, 157, 172, 184
Comedy Theatre (New York), 175
Committee to Defend America by Keeping Out of War, 280
"Confession of a Japanese Geisha Girl" (Tully), 130
Confessions (St. Augustine), 259
Connelly, Marc, 171
Conrad, Joseph, 2, 51, 116, 118, 127, 129, 186
Convoy, Ohio, 34
Conway, Eddie, 86, 88
Cook, Thomas, 208
Cooper, Gary, 216, 256
Corbett, James J. (Jim), 37
Corelli, Marie, 2
Corot, Jean-Baptiste-Camille, 212
County Donegal, Ireland, 12
County Kildare, Ireland, 14
Covered Wagon, The (1923 film), 281
Coward-McCann, 222, 302
Crane, Stephen, 249
Crawford, Joan, 235
Croan, Paddy, 61
Crosby, Bing, 294
Cross Creek (Rawlings), 285, 286
Cruze, James, 169, 173, 281, 291; friendship with Tully, 7, 170, 171, 179, 246, 288; model for Jack Jarnegan, 170, 171–72
Cunard, Nancy, 193
Curtis, James, 294, 295
Curtis, LeLand, 234
Curtiss, Thomas Quinn, 284, 297
Cuyahoga Falls, Ohio, 78

Danaher, Anna Tully, 12, 16
Danaher, William, 16
Dannakersand, William, 19
Danton, Georges Jacques, 172
Danville, Illinois, 97
d'Arrast, H. d'Abbadie "Harry," 138, 146, 147, 159
Darrow, Clarence, 5, 256, 289

Darrow, Ruby, 197
Dashiell, Alfred, 197
Davenport, Iowa, 55
Davey, John, 95, 98
Davey, Martin L., 95, 97–99, 100–101
Davey Tree Expert Company, 9, 95–97, 100–101, 105, 153
Davey Tree Surgeon's Bulletin, 98–99
David Copperfield (Dickens), 124
David Round Company chain works (Cleveland, Ohio), 103
Davidson, Pete, 36–37
Davies, Marion, 160–61, 176, 177, 234
Davis, Bette, 193, 262
Davis, Father Eugene A., 31–32
Davis, Happy, 83–85, 89–90
Davis, Jeff, 207
Davis, Robert H., 131
Day of the Locust, The (West), 171
Days of Wine and Roses (1962 film), 163
Dayton & Michigan Railroad. *See* Cincinnati, Hamilton & Dayton Railroad
Dayton, Ohio, 12, 179
Dazey, Frank, 174, 176, 177, 303
Deadly Illusions: Jean Harlow and the Murder of Paul Bern (Marx and Vanderveen), 236
"Declaration, A" (Tully essay), 132–33, 134
Del Rio, Texas, 60
De Mille, Cecil B., 169
Dempsey, Jack, 89, 106–7, 159, 174, 223, 266, 269, 289; friendship with Tully, 5, 7, 53, 234, 257, 261
"Denis Darel" (unpublished Tully manuscript), 178, 303
Devine, Alice (the Moss-Haired Girl), 65
Diamond, Jimmy, 91
Diary (Pepys), 259
Diary of a Lost Girl (1929 film), 195
Dickens, Charles, 2, 28, 29, 124, 138, 150, 194, 210, 276
Dickson, William Jay (Goosey), 65
Dies, Martin, Jr., 272
Dietrich, Marlene, 269
Dillinger, John, 244–45, 247
Dingley, Nellie, 80–81, 88, 94–95, 99, 112, 130, 131, 225
Domitian, 327n83
Donner Party, 144
Donovan, Father Vincent, 184, 287
Donovan, William Joseph "Wild Bill," 184
Doran, George H., 120
Dos Passos, John, 129, 163, 244
Dostoyevsky, Fyodor, 2, 196, 259
Doubleday, Doran and Company, 198, 201, 208, 222, 302, 304
Double Indemnity (Cain), 292

Dowie Cult, 9, 60
Dowie, John Alexander, 60
Dozen and One, A (1943 book by Tully), 6, 303; publication, 289, 302; reviews, 289–90; sales, 291; writing, 289
Dracula (1931 film), 183, 193
Dracula (stage play), 174
Dracula's Daughter (1936 film), 193
Dreiser, Theodore, 4, 116, 128, 131, 181, 183, 232, 259, 280
DuBois, Ted, 291
DuBois, W. E. B., 252
Duffy, Clinton, 282
Dugan, Nitro, 63
Dunkineely, Ireland, 12
Dunne, Finley Peter, 174, 187
Dunn, Jimmy, 88
Durant, Will, 238, 259, 273
Durr, Anna Tully (sister of Jim Tully), 16, 23, 25, 43, 48, 163, 166, 222, 296

Earl, Robert Bruce, 97
Eastman, Max, 259–60
Easy Pickings (Hill), 221
Ebest, Ron, 8
Edwards, Henry P., 87
Ehrman, Lillian Mae, 252–54
Eight Men Out (1988 film), 264
Einstein, Albert, 138
Eisenschiml, Otto, 114
Eisenstein, Sergei, 240
Eliot, George, 2
Elliott, Emory, 192
Ellison, Ralph, 4, 96–97
Elmer Gantry (Lewis), 181
Elwood, Indiana, 54
Emmett Lawler (1922 novel by Tully), 6, 9, 127, 128, 162, 196, 222; cited, 35, 36, 37, 40; film version proposed, 124–25; publication, 3, 119–20, 123, 126, 212, 302; reviews, 122–23; style and themes, 3, 8, 51, 121–22, 124–25, 148, 149, 283; and Upton Sinclair, 115, 120, 123, 186; writing of, 110, 117, 118, 119, 123
Emmett, Robert, 212–13
Emperor Jones, The (O'Neill), 174
Encyclopedia Britannica, 289
Engels, Friedrich, 109
E. P. Dutton and Company, 288, 292
Erie Railroad, 77, 79, 92, 294
Erik Dorn (Hecht), 130
Esquire, 6, 41–42, 242, 245, 269, 272; boxing essay, 245, 256; Diego Rivera interview, 244; "The Dying Hobo" (poem), 269; James Cruze profile, 288, 291; "Portrait of My Father," 275
Evans, John, 82–83, 90, 91, 100

Fairbanks, Douglas, 137
Family Circle, 280
Fanning, Charles, 8
Fante, John, 270–71
Faraway Farm, 261, 278, 290, 291
Farewell to Arms, A (Hemingway), 4
Farrar, Straus and Giroux, 248
Farrell, James T., 8, 129, 187, 192
Faulkner, William, 7, 181, 188, 260, 270, 298
Fawcett, Roscoe, 207
Fawcett, William "Captain Billy," 130
Fecher, Charles A., 129
Federal Bureau of Investigation (FBI), 220, 280
Fenton, Frank, 270
Ferber, Edna, 220
Fields, W. C., 7, 8, 138, 245, 256; friendship with Tully, 266, 293–95
Findlay, Ohio, 87
Finnegans Wake (Joyce), 212
Finnerty, Slug, 85
Finn, Father Francis J., 67, 181
Fire in the Flint (White), 175
Firsts: The Book Collector's Magazine, 8
Fitts, Buron, 247
Fitzgerald, F. Scott, 7, 116, 129, 149, 163, 171, 260, 270, 282, 298; proposes boxing match between Tully and Hemingway, 187; Tully opinion of, 170, 259, 281
Flaubert, Gustave, 2
Flesh and the Devil (1926 film), 215, 216
Flynt, Josiah, 113; meeting with Tully, 67–69, 108, 249, 254
Footner, Hulbert, 123
Ford, John, 40, 172, 231, 269, 281
Forest Lawn Memorial Park (Glendale), 297
Fort, Garrett, 193, 304
Fort Wayne, Indiana, 37
Foss, Sam Walter, 297
Foster, Eddie, 89
Fountain, Leatrice Gilbert, 216–17, 218
Fowler, Gene, 262, 294
France, 130, 212
Francis, Owen, 270
Frankenstein (1931 film), 193
Franklin, H. Bruce, 8
Freaks (1932 film), 183
Freeman, The, 122
Freeman, Donald, 168, 169, 179, 216

Gable, Clark, 7, 216, 256, 280, 289
Gandhi, Mahatma, 138
Gans, Joe, 61, 84, 176–77, 225, 265
Garbo, Greta, 169, 215, 235
Garland, Judy, 299–300
Garnier, Jean, 300–301

Garson, Greer, 299
Gartz, Kate Crane, 115
Gaynor, Janet, 234
Geneva, Wisconsin, 15
Gerhardt, Curly, 89, 109
Germany, 195, 210, 240
Gershwin, George, 113
Get Shorty (Leonard), 171
Gibson Hotel (Cincinnati), 60, 224, 302
Gibson & Otts (Kent restaurant), 78
Gilbert, John, 173, 235, 297; fight with Tully, 6, 216–18; film with Tully, 218–19; Tully article on, 169, 215–16
Gilfoil, Laura, 29
Gillette, King, 110
Gill, Jack, 88
Girl of the Golden West, The (1923 film), 156
Gloves, Glory and God (Armstrong), 254
Glyn, Elinor, 133–34, 160
Glynnwood Cemetery, 24, 26
Glynnwood, Ohio, 20, 24, 25
"God Loves the Irish" (play version of *Shanty Irish*), 192, 214, 248, 303
Goldman, Emma, 165
Gold, Michael, 191, 203
Gold Rush, The (1925 film), 137, 139, 141, 142, 143–47, 148, 163, 178
Goldsmith, Oliver, 29, 51
Goldstein, Jonah, 251
Goldwyn, Samuel, 127
Gompers, Samuel, 103
Gone With the Wind (Mitchell), 271
Gone With the Wind (1939 film), 271, 280
Gorky, Maxim, 2, 51, 124, 175, 187, 212, 238, 259; Tully compared to, 4, 149, 181–82, 190, 284
Grand Hotel (1932 film), 235, 236
Grange, Red, 5
Grapes of Wrath, The (Steinbeck), 284
Grapes of Wrath, The (1940 film), 281
Grauman's Chinese Theater, 235
Grauman, Sid, 217
Graves, Robert, 193
"Graveyard that Moved, The" (Tully), 200
Great Britain, 129, 192–93, 210–12, 248
Greater Hotel Gibson. *See* Gibson Hotel (Cincinnati)
Greed (1924 film), 133
Greenberg, Jae, 250, 251, 256, 260, 262–63, 271, 292
Greenberg Publishers, 248, 250, 251, 262–63, 302, 303
Green, Gerald, 199
Greenwich Village Playbill Theatre (New York), 163, 164
Grey, Lita (Lillita McMurray), 144–46, 147, 178
Griffith, D. W., 126, 137, 169

Griffith Park, 109
Grimhaven (Tasker), 198
Guthrie, Woody, 4, 288–89, 292
"Gypsy Sister" (Tully), 277

Haardt, Sara, 185–87, 222
Haldeman-Julius Monthly, 187
"Half-Sister of the Lord" (unpublished Tully manuscript), 268, 269, 292, 303
Hall, Charles D., 138
Hammett, Dashiell, 4, 116, 270, 272
Hammond, Percy, 164
Haney, Eddie, 276
Hansen, Harry, 129, 179
Harcourt, Alfred, 120, 128
Harcourt, Brace and Company, 120, 126, 130, 131, 302
Harding, Warren G., 105–6
Hardy, Mary, 38
Hardy, Thomas, 2, 57, 129, 141, 259
"Harlots" (Tully poem), 115
Harlow, Jean, 235–36, 262
Harper & Brothers, 120
Harris, Frank, 116
Harris, Mildred, 178
Harvard Club, 271
Haviland, Ohio, 33
Hayden-Corbett chain works, 75, 184
Hays office, 143, 231
Hays, Will, 231
He Who Gets Slapped (1924 film), 133
Hearn, Lafcadio, 130
Hearst, William Randolph, 160–61, 177, 233–34, 239
Heartbreak House (Shaw), 284
Hecht, Ben, 114, 129, 130–31, 163
Helburn, Theresa, 252–54
Hemingway, Ernest, 7, 181, 198, 219; comparisons with Tully, 4, 251, 256, 260, 298; Fitzgerald suggests boxing match with Tully, 187; Tully opinion of, 259–60, 261, 296
Henry VII (king), 211
Hepburn, Katharine, 252
Hergesheimer, Joseph, 251
Hersholt, Jean, 290
Hindenburg, Paul von, 208
Hinds, George, 294
"Hinkey Dink" Kenna's Saloon (Chicago), 54
Hinkle, Ray, 8
His Glorious Night (1929 film), 216
Hiss, Alger, 273
History of the Chicago Police, The, 154
Hobo, The (Anderson), 152
Hobo College, 166
Hobo from St. Marys: A Tribute to Jim Tully, The (Hinkle), 8

Hobos of America, 207
Hobo's Hornbook, The (Milburn), 221
Holford, Clyde, 256
Hollins College (Roanoke), 271
Hollywood, California, 5, 117, 150, 167, 174, 184, 188, 193; depiction in *Jarnegan*, 5, 162, 171–73, 193–94; Tully coverage of, 5–7, 158–62, 163, 168–70, 177–79, 211, 234–35, 244, 256, 262; Tully opinions of, 125, 166, 168–70, 173, 239–40, 243, 253–54, 273, 281; Tully residences, 126, 128, 130, 131, 176, 186, 222, 228; Tully's presence in, 6, 7–8, 53, 133–34, 155–58, 168–70, 180, 215–18, 240, 269–70; Tully and studios, 110, 126–28, 133–34, 135–49, 180, 194–95, 218–19, 230–33, 248; visit by Sara Haardt, 185–87
"Hollywood Decameron" (unpublished Tully manuscript), 272, 280, 303
Hollywood Roosevelt Hotel (Hollywood), 290
Hollywood Tribune, 272
Hollywood Writers' Club, 177
Holy Rosary Church (St. Marys), 16
Hoover, J. Edgar, 273
Hopper, Hedda, 277
"House by the Side of the Road" (Foss), 297
House of the Dead, The (Dostoyevsky), 196
Howard, Robert E., 235
How Green Was My Valley (1941 film), 281
Hubble, Edwin, 248
Hughes, Howard, 117
Hughes, Langston, 8, 176, 181, 252–55, 265
Hughes, Rupert, 117; and *Beggars of Life* dedication, 153; friend and mentor, 117–20, 126, 131–32, 134, 136, 170, 290; review of *Beggars of Life*, 122–23
Hugo, Victor, 2, 29, 98
Hutchison, Percy, 191, 226
Huntington, Henry, 109
Huxley, Aldous, 116, 193
Hyams, Leila, 218
Hyde Park, London, 210

I Am a Fugitive from a Chain Gang (1932 film), 231
Ibsen, Henrik, 129
I Cover the Waterfront (Miller), 246
Idle Class, The (1921 film), 144
Immigrant, The (1917 film), 142
Ince, Elinor K., 161–62
Ince, Thomas H., 126, 159–62, 163, 177, 233, 303
Indiana State Prison, 244
Industrial Workers of the World, 220
Informer, The (1935 film), 281
Ingraham, Rex, 172
International Union of Revolutionary Writers, 239–40

Invisible Man (Ellison), 96–97
Invisible Man, The (Wells), 211
"I Passed by Here" (unpublished Tully manuscript), 9, 303. *See also* "Out of My Heart"
Ireland, 11–12, 14, 188, 189, 209, 212–13, 221, 231
Irish Independent, 191
Irish Potato Famine, 11–12
Irish Times, 191
Irish Voice in America, The (Fanning), 8
It Happened One Night (1934 film), 281
I Wonder as I Wander (Hughes), 253

Jackman's (Cuyahoga Falls), 78
Jackson, Henry. *See* Armstrong, Henry
Jannings, Emil, 169, 170
Jarnegan (1926 Tully novel), 6, 177, 192, 248, 261, 288, 296; cited, 171; publication, 162, 170, 302; reviews, 173, 181; stage version (see *Jarnegan* [play version of Tully novel]); style and themes, 5, 169, 171–73; writing of, 162, 171–73
Jarnegan (play version of Tully novel), 193–94, 195, 304
Jewish Memorial Hospital (New York), 300
John Barleycorn (London), 110
Johnson, Jack, 90, 176, 313n90
Johnson, Samuel, 210, 259
Jolson, Al, 255
Jones, Bobby, 5
Jones, James, 7
Jones, LeRoi (Amiri Baraka), 199
Joyce, James, 7, 116, 212, 221, 284
Jude the Obscure (Hardy), 141
Jungle, The (Sinclair), 115
"Jungle Justice" (Tully), 198, 199

Kahlo, Frida, 244
Karloff, Boris, 171, 234, 248
Karno, Fred, 137, 138
Kaufman, Al, 207
Kaufman, George S., 171
Kearney, Patrick, 231
Keaton, Buster, 138
Keats, John, 80, 102–3, 104, 122, 240
Keller, Helen, 265, 266
Kelly, Web "Spider," 86
Kennedy, William, 4
Kent Courier, 106; covering Tully's boxing matches, 86; publishes Tully poems, 103–4, 115
Kent Free (Carnegie) Library, 77, 79–81, 94, 99, 130, 225
Kent National Bank, 95
Kent Normal School (later Kent State University), 130, 166
Kent, Ohio, 115, 120, 123, 172, 293–94; chain factory, 2, 75, 77–78, 82, 91–92, 225, 227;

in 1907, 76–77; Tully arrival in, 75; Tully revisits, 129–30, 166; Tully's years in, 75–104
Kent Opera House, 77, 293
Kent State University, 79, 130
Kent Tribune, 115, 120, 123, 130, 136, 152
Kerouac, Jack, 4, 199, 270
Kerr, Deborah, 299
Kerr, Walter, 143
Ketchel, Stanley, 53, 90, 109, 223, 313n90
Keystone Company, 136–37, 143
Kid, The (1921 film), 142
Kilbane, Johnny, 86, 87–89, 101, 106, 108, 278, 314n35
Kilbane, Tommy, 313n96
Kildare, Owen, 75
Kim (Kipling), 57
"King of Laughter, The" (unpublished Tully manuscript), 277, 303
Kinsella, W. P., 264
Kipling, Rudyard, 57, 116
Knopf, Alfred, 210, 272
Koch, Charlie, 39, 48
Kriendler, Mack, 278

Ladies in the Parlor (1935 novel by Tully), 6, 51, 256, 262, 269, 271, 289–90; charged with indecency, 250–51, 260; criticism of, 250–51, 253; publication, 248, 302; reviews, 250; sales, 26–61; style and themes, 248–49; suppressed, 260; writing of, 248
Lake Erie & Western Railroad, 39, 47
Lake Tahoe, Nevada, 233, 234
La Marr, Barbara, 206
Lambert, E. O., 113
Lambert, Marion, 113–14
Laments for the Living (Parker), 4
Lardner, Ring, 129, 178
Las Encinas Sanitarium (Pasadena), 293
Lasky, Jesse L., 124–25
Last Mile, The (play), 219
Last Tycoon, The (Fitzgerald), 171, 281
Las Vegas, New Mexico, 267
Laughter in Hell (1932 book by Tully), 6, 51, 248; film version (see *Laughter in Hell* [1932 film]); Mencken opinion of, 231–32; publication, 261, 302; reviews, 232; style and themes, 230–31; title, 230; writing of, 230
Laughter in Hell (1932 film), 230–33, 304
Laurel & Hardy, 138
Lawler, Dennis (uncle of Jim Tully), 14, 21
Lawler, Gertrude (cousin of Jim Tully), 191, 229–30
Lawler, James (uncle of Jim Tully), 14, 229
Lawler, John (uncle of Jim Tully), 14–15, 22, 42, 63, 172, 188, 192

Lawler, Margaret (grandmother of Jim Tully), 14, 15, 20, 22, 38
Lawler, Maud "Moll" (aunt of Jim Tully), 14, 21–22, 23–24, 188
Lawler, Peter (uncle of Jim Tully), 14
Lawler, Sadie Axe (aunt of Jim Tully), 15, 23, 24, 274
Lawler, Thomas Albert (grandfather of Jim Tully), 14, 21, 22
Lawler, Tom (uncle of Jim Tully), 14, 15, 23, 24, 25
Lawson, John Howard, 218
Lee, Rowland V., 239, 290
Leigh Lecture Bureau, 162, 165, 271
Lenin, Vladimir, 244
Leonard, Elmore, 171
Letter, The (1940 film), 193
Levene, Sam, 193
Levinsky, King, 234
Lewin, Albert, 119, 171, 198, 239, 269, 280, 290
Lewis, Ed "Strangler," 244
Lewis, Furry, 4
Lewis, Sinclair, 4, 129, 162–63, 165, 181, 259, 290
Liberty, 159, 173, 177, 207
Liebling, A. J., 86
"Life of Charlie Chaplin" (unpublished biography by Tully), 177–79, 303
Life of Samuel Johnson (Boswell), 259
"Life of Thomas H. Ince, The" (unpublished biography by Tully), 159–62, 303
Life on the Mississippi (Twain), 150, 180, 183
Lima, Ohio, 37, 44, 46, 47, 67, 222, 245; boxing matches, 82–85, 87–88
Limelight (1952 film), 142
Lincoln, Abraham, 100
Lindbergh, Charles, 5
Lindsey, Judge Ben, 207, 208, 214, 256
Lippincott, 277
Literary Digest International Book Review, The, 132, 152, 159, 175
Little Rascals, The, 261
Liveright, Horace, 174, 176
Lloyd, Doris, 218
Lombard, Carole, 269
London Daily Chronicle, The, 210
London, England, 137, 170, 192, 193, 208, 214, 221, 302; Tully visits, 208, 209–11
London, Jack, 4, 115, 149, 198, 259, 273, 289; early Tully hero, 2, 7, 51, 73, 80; Tully corresponds with, 110–11; Tully disillusionment with, 7, 112–13, 116; Tully meets, 111–12; Tully writes about, 132, 158–59
Longacre Theatre, 193
Longfellow, Henry Wadsworth, 172
Lord Jim (Conrad), 127

Los Angeles, California, 159, 160, 173, 193, 200, 233, 237, 248, 250, 254–55, 270, 296; Olympics, 234; school system, 147, 222; Tully residences, 104, 106, 120, 293; Tully's second marriage, 155; Tully travels to, 60, 106, 108
Los Angeles Parks Department, 109
Los Angeles Times, 197, 201, 300; publishes Tully stories, 130, 200, 261, 269; reports on Tully, 153, 155, 254; review of *Way for a Sailor*, 219; reviews of Tully's work, 123, 266, 284, 290
Louis, Joe, 286
Lovecraft, H. P., 235
Lubitsch, Ernst, 169
Luck, William, 62
Lueders, William, 66–67
Luft, Sid, 300
Lugosi, Bela, 174, 248
Lygo, Mary, 69–74, 83, 95, 99, 131, 204–6, 234, 235

Macmillan, 260
Macrae, Elliott, 292
Maedchen in Uniform (1931 film), 240
Maggie: Girl of the Streets (Crane), 249
Mailer, Norman, 7, 297
Main Street (Lewis), 165
Making a Living (1914 film), 136
Makley, Charles "Fat Charley," 41, 48, 244–45
Maloney, Brother Jonathon, 63
Maltese Falcon, The (Hammett), 189
Mamaroneck, New York, 174
Manchester Guardian, 153
Manchester, William, 128, 185
Mankiewicz, Herman, 218
"Manly Art, The" (Tully), 245, 256
Mannix, Eddie, 218
Man of the New School (pamphlet by Tully), 224, 302
Mansfield, Ohio, 104
Manson, Eddie, 145
Mantle, Burns, 164, 194
Marion, Ohio, 104–6
Marion Star, 105
Mark Twain Hotel, 185, 219
Marsh, Fred, 226
Marx Brothers, The, 138
Marx, Groucho, 137
Marx, Karl, 109
Marx, Samuel, 219, 236
Masefield, John, 2, 51
Masters, Edgar Lee, 129, 289
Mathis, June, 133
Maugham, Somerset, 116
Maxwell, William, 183
Mayer, Edwin Justus, 119
Mayer, Louis B., 127, 128, 216, 242

Mayfield, Sara, 185
Mayor of Casterbridge, The (Hardy), 57
McCann, Bill, 287
McClure, "Spec," 294
McCourt, Frank, 4
McCoy, Horace, 270
McGilvrey, John E., 130
McGlynn, "Young" Tommy, 87
McGovern, "Terrible" Terry, 88
McGovern, "Young" Terry, 87–88
McKoy, Charles "Kid," 53, 197, 239
McLaglen, Victor, 231, 234
McMillan, Maura, 8
McMurray, Lillian, 144, 145, 147
McMurray, Lillita. *See* Grey, Lita
McNamara, J. B., 197
McPherson, Aimee Semple, 268, 292, 303
McTell, "Blind" Willie, 4
McWilliams, Carey, 270
Melville, Herman, 210
Mencken, H. L. (Henry Louis), 9, 124, 157, 191, 219, 220, 224, 234, 237, 269; correspondence with Myrtle Zwetow Tully, 291, 292, 296; correspondence with Tully, 9, 123, 131, 161, 174, 181, 183, 190, 191, 194, 196, 204, 207, 210, 214–15, 221–22, 229, 236, 251, 258, 263, 266, 271, 279, 281, 283, 285–86, 288–89, 292–93, 295; as editor of the *American Mercury*, 133, 152, 155, 158, 163, 185–87, 190, 196–98, 231, 238, 248, 250–51; friendship with Tully, 7, 123, 128–29, 134, 158, 179, 184–85, 196, 198, 204, 207, 229, 237, 250–51, 281, 289, 291–92; life and career, 7, 116–17, 128–29, 132–33, 185, 298; mentor to Tully, 123, 128, 158, 179, 189, 196–98, 208, 238, 262, 268–69, 281; publishes Tully articles and stories, 132, 158, 190, 196–98, 238; on Tully, 129, 181–82, 190, 225, 229, 273–74; Tully's admiration for, 116–17, 179, 289; on Tully's *Beggars Abroad*, 221; on Tully's *Beggars of Life*, 152, 158; on Tully's *Biddy Brogan's Boy*, 286; on Tully's *The Bruiser*, 263; on Tully's *A Dozen and One*, 289; on Tully's *Jarnegan*, 173; on Tully's *Ladies in the Parlor*, 248–50, 260; on Tully's *Laughter in Hell*, 231–33; Tully's literary champion, 4, 7, 129, 132, 152, 173, 272, 298; on Tully's *Shanty Irish*, 190; and Tully visits to Baltimore, 184, 237–38; and Upton Sinclair, 186–87
Menjou, Adolph, 142, 169
Mercer County, Ohio, 247
Meredith, Burgess, 194
Meridian, Mississippi, 62–63
Merton of the Movies (Wilson novel), 171
Merton of the Movies (Kaufman and Connelly play), 171
Merton of the Movies (1924 film), 171

"Message of Cheer, A" (Tully poem), 103
Metro-Goldwyn-Mayer (MGM), 127, 128, 133, 216, 218, 235, 236, 239, 299
Michael, Magda, 295
Milburn, George, 221, 270
Milestone, Lewis, 281
Miller, Max, 246–47
Millette, Dorothy, 236
Minnelli, Vincente, 299–300
Mississippi vagrancy law, 49–50
Mitchell, Joseph, 8
Mitchell, Margaret, 271
Mitchum, Robert, 4
Mix, Tom, 171, 234
Mizner, Wilson, 205, 217
Mobile, Alabama, 50
Modern Library, The, 263
Moliere, 212
Monsieur Verdoux (1947 film), 142
Montgomery, Robert, 256, 271
Mooney, Martin, 272–73
Mooney, Tom, 197
Moon Is Down, The (Steinbeck), 288
Moore, Fred, 220
Moran, Polly, 218–19
Morrell, Ed, 197–98
Mosher, Karl, 338n79
Mosquitoes, The (Faulkner), 181
Motion Picture and Television Retirement Home, 300
Mount Charles, Ireland, 12
Mount Wilson Observatory, 248
Muldowney, Matt, 95–97
Muni, Paul, 231, 233, 245
Munsey's, 131
Murray & Gee, 289–91
Murray, Tom (actor), 144
Murray, Tom (sailor), 291
Musso & Frank Grill (Hollywood), 141
Myers, Margaret Rider. *See* Tully, Margaret Rider "Marna" Myers (second wife of Jim Tully)
Myers, R. Holtby, 155
"My Impressions of Folk, Movies, and Edna Purviance" (Chaplin article ghostwritten by Tully), 142–43
"My Interview with Elinor Glyn" (Tully), 134
My Mamie Rose (Kildare), 75

Nagel, Conrad, 235, 236
Nana (Zola), 249
Nasaw, David, 160–61
Nathan, George Jean, 116–17, 128, 164, 168, 208; correspondence with Tully, 54, 214, 232, 266, 281; as editor of the *American Mercury*, 133; friendship with Tully, 7, 132, 134, 163, 234, 244, 248; Mencken description of, 132; on *Outside Looking In*, 163; on Tully, 4, 179, 251; Tully description of, 132–33
Nation, The, 226
Neilan, Marshall, 206–7
Nelson, Oscar "Battling," 108
Nelson, Robert, 203
Newcom & Tully, Inc., 261, 278
New Masses, The, 191
New Movie Magazine, 220
New Republic, 191, 203
New York Daily Mirror, 163
New Yorker, The, 183, 202, 278, 289
New York Evening Post Literary Review, 123, 152
New York Herald-Tribune, 163, 193, 202, 225, 250, 285
New York Morning Telegraph, 163
New York Newsboys' Home, 62
New York, New York, 8, 12, 70, 137, 160, 205, 221, 293, 294; Alton Tully's last residence, 300; attacks on *Ladies in the Parlor*, 250, 260; publishers, 7, 120, 124, 128, 131–32, 162, 181, 259–60, 263, 280; Rudolph Valentino's funeral, 215; theater, 61, 162–63, 164–65, 174, 193, 252, 304; and Tully's road years, 59, 62; Tully visits to, 128, 130–32, 163, 174–75, 178, 208–9, 223, 234, 238, 261, 278, 280
New York Post, 191, 225, 285
New York Society for the Suppression of Vice, 250
New York Times, The, 231, 250; review of Dazey and Tully's *Black Boy*, 176; review of film version of *Laughter in Hell*, 233; review of *Outside Looking In*, 163; review of stage version of *Jarnegan*, 193; review of Tully's *Beggars Abroad*, 221; review of Tully's *Beggars of Life*, 9, 151–52, 297; review of Tully's *Biddy Brogan's Boy*, 284; review of Tully's *Blood on the Moon*, 226; review of Tully's *The Bruiser*, 265; review of Tully's *Circus Parade*, 180; review of Tully's *A Dozen and One*, 289; review of Tully's *Emmett Lawler*, 122–23; review of Tully's *Laughter in Hell*, 232; review of Tully's *Shadows of Men*, 202; review of Tully's *Shanty Irish*, 191; review of *Way for a Sailor*, 219; on Tully, 4, 193, 296
New York Tribune, 153
New York World, 176
New York World-Telegram, 223
Nichols, Robert, 192–93, 302
Night Must Fall (1937 film), 271
Nolte, William H., 129
North American Newspaper Alliance, 245

O'Brien, Pat, 231, 304
Ocean, 131

Of Mice and Men (1939 film), 163
Of Mice and Men (Steinbeck), 272
O'Hara, John, 183
Ohio Authors and Their Books (Chapman), 8
Ohio Clemency Board, 157
Ohio Penitentiary, 22
Ohio River, 48, 58, 60
Ohio Southern railroad, 39
Oklahoma Red, 59, 151, 152, 163–64, 165, 194
Old Curiosity Shop, The (Dickens), 194
Older, Fremont, 196–97, 234
"Old Glad Hand, The" (Tully poem), 103
Old Mr. Flood (Mitchell), 8
Oliver Twist (Dickens), 124
"One Christmas, Years Ago" (Tully poem), 103
O'Neill, Eugene, 4, 51, 116, 163, 174, 187
"On Keats' Grave" (Tully poem), 102–3, 104, 122, 240
On the Road (Kerouac), 199
Opera House (Kent), 77, 293
Orpet-Lambert murder case, 9, 113–15
Orpet, William, 113, 130–31
Otis, Harrison Gray, 201
Outline of History (Wells), 211
Outlook, 153
"Out of My Heart" (unpublished Tully manuscript), 9, 272, 277, 303. *See also* "I Passed by Here" (unpublished Tully manuscript)
"Out to Old Lake Brady" (Tully poem), 80
Outside Looking In (play version of *Beggars of Life*), 5, 162–65, 193, 194, 231, 304
Overland Monthly Outwest Magazine, 132
Owasso, Michigan, 268
Oxford Book of English Verse, 271

Pabst, G. W., 195
Pagano, Jo, 270
Painesville, Ohio, 80
Palmer, Frederick, 179
Pandora's Box (1929 film), 195
Paramount Pictures, 193, 195, 220, 304
Parker, Dorothy, 4, 116, 251
Parker, R. A., 152
Parker, Ralph, 170
Parole Scandal (Mooney), 272–73
Parry, Harvey, 195
Parsons, Louella, 169
"Passing Strangers" (unpublished Tully manuscript), 127, 128, 130, 193, 303
"Passing Strangers" (proposed film), 193
Paul Bunyan (Stevens), 244
Paulding County, Ohio, 37
Pecord, Ollie, 89–90
Pennsylvania-Ohio railroad, 76
Peoria, Illinois, 45

Pepys, Samuel, 259
Pere Lachaise cemetery, 212
Perkins, Maxwell, 260, 292; correspondence with Tully, 203, 261–62, 277, 287; editor of *Biddy Brogan's Boy*, 280–83, 285–86; meetings with Tully, 178, 280
Perry, John, 113
Peter Cooper Library, 62
Philadelphia, Pennsylvania, 94, 295
Philadelphia Record, 284–85
Photoplay, 6, 159, 169
Pickford, Mary, 5, 137, 170
Pictorial Review, 177–78, 277
Pierpont, Harry, 245
Pilgrim's Progress (Bunyan), 35
Pittsburgh Newsboys' Home, 59
Pittsburgh, Pennsylvania, 59, 97
Pitts, Zasu, 169
Player, The (Tolkin), 171
Poe, Edgar Allan, 235, 248
Police Gazette, 89
"Porter's Estimate, The" (Tully poem), 103
"Portrait of My Father" (Tully), 275
Portrait of the Artist as a Young Man (Joyce), 284
Post, Josephine G., 57
Pound, Ezra, 116
Powell, Dawn, 156
Powell, William, 234, 256
Power, Tyrone, 269
Preble County, Ohio, 14–15
Price, Harry ("Blackie"), 10, 184
Prison Literature in America (Franklin), 8
Private Histories (Ebest), 8
Providence Journal, 296–97
Public Enemy, The (1931 film), 164
Purcell, Henry, 212
Purviance, Edna, 142, 144

Queen City Club (Cincinnati), 60–61
Quiet Man, The (1952 film), 40
Quirk, James, 169–70, 207

Racine, Wisconsin, 67, 72–74
Raging Bull (1980 film), 264
Raley, Jack, 42–43, 44
Ralston, Frank, 37, 38, 41
Rappe, Virginia, 143
Rapp, George, 45, 47
Rascoe, Burton, 183
"Rave Laferty" ("A Broadway Doctor"; unpublished Tully manuscript), 288, 292, 304
Raven, The (1935 film), 248, 303
Rawlings, Marjorie Kinnan, 285, 286
Reader's Digest, 276, 277, 281
Red and the Black, The (Stendhal), 127

Reed, John, 154
Reedy, William Marion, 116
Reeves, Alf, 138, 139, 141, 145, 162
Reitman, Ben, 52, 165–66, 288
Renew, Ellen, 107
Rhodes, Eugene Manlove, 117
Richmond, Indiana, 98, 100
Riesner (Reisner), Chuck, 138, 139, 141, 144, 145, 147, 162
Riley, "One-Lung," 199
Rinehart, Mary Roberts, 158
Ring, 269
"Ringside" (unpublished Tully manuscript), 289, 304
Rivera, Diego, 244, 289
Rivers, Joe, 101
"Road Girls" (unpublished Tully manuscript), 277
"Road Kids" (proposed Tully comic strip), 248, 304
Roanoke, Virginia, 271
Robert Holden & Company, 192, 193, 302
Robeson, Paul, 174, 175, 176
Robey, Violet, 241–43, 247–48
Robinson, David, 144–45, 146, 166, 250, 285
Robinson, Ted, 102–3, 122
Rob Wagner's Script, 242, 251
Rochester, Indiana, 74
Rogers, Ginger, 256
Rogers, Will, 295
Rogue's Gallery (Scully), 269
Roosevelt, Franklin Delano, 239, 273–74
Roosevelt, Theodore, 58–59, 210
Rose, Stanley, 266, 270
Ross, Billy, 31, 54–56, 256
Ross, Virginia Peterson, 225
Ross, Wirt, 255
Runyon, Damon, 7, 165, 238, 266, 289
Ruth, Babe, 5

Sacco, Ferdinando Nicola, 220, 235, 280
Sacramento Bee, The, 257
Salt Lake City, Utah, 60, 106–7
Samaria (Hearst yacht), 208–9
Samuel Goldwyn Producing Company, 126–27, 131, 133
"Samuel Gompers" (Tully poem), 103
Sandburg, Carl, 116, 129, 130
Sanders, Clinton, 293
Sanders, Sydney, 248, 262, 272
San Diego, California, 160, 161
San Diego Naval Base, 293
San Diego Sun, 246
San Francisco, California, 112, 143, 197, 224, 233, 237, 304; Tully visits to, 8, 107–9, 238, 245–46, 247
San Francisco Call-Bulletin, 234
San Francisco Call and Post, 196, 234

San Quentin (prison), 153, 220; and Alton Tully (son), 243–44, 258–60, 266, 277, 281–82, 288, 291; Jim Tully visits, 10, 131, 196–97, 201, 282
San Quentin News, 285
San Simeon, 233–34
Santa Monica, California, 55, 110
Santa Monica Evening Outlook, 295
Saroyan, William, 162, 217, 219, 251, 270, 289
Saturday Evening Post, 250, 289
Saturday Night Club, 237–38, 292
Saturday Review of Literature, The, 122, 152, 159, 232, 289–90
Savannah, Georgia, 14
Sayers, Emma Lou, 252
Sayles, John, 264
Schallert, Edwin, 219
Schmeling, Max, 238
"Schoolhouse on the Hill, The" (Tully poem), 103
Schreiner, Olive, 59
Schulberg, B. F., 169
Schulberg, Budd, 171, 270
Schultz, Johnny "Battling," 88–90, 265
Schuster, Max, 262
Scorsese, Martin, 264
Screen Play, 6
Screen Secrets, 170, 207
Screen Writer, The, 297
Scribner's, 67, 197, 269
Scully, Frank, 262, 265, 297; friendship with Tully, 7, 257, 259, 261, 269, 290, 297; on Tully, 4, 6, 10, 29, 157, 172, 197, 238, 269–70, 315–16
Seneca Chain Company (Kent), 2, 75, 77–78, 82, 91–92, 225, 227
Seneca Chain works (Mansfield), 104
Sennett, Mack, 7, 126, 136, 137, 169, 294
Shadows of Men (1930 book by Tully), 6, 51, 122, 222, 244; as autobiography, 8, 10, 63, 198; cited, 200; film version proposed, 203, 227; popularity in the Soviet Union, 273; publication, 198, 302; reviews, 199, 202–3; sales, 203; style and themes, 63, 198–202; title, 198; Tully opinion of, 63, 203; William Gropper as illustrator, 198; writing of, 196–98, 200
Shakespeare, William, 2, 29, 238, 259
Shanty Irish (1928 book by Tully), 6, 51, 122, 195, 222, 296, 297; as autobiography, 5, 8, 10, 17, 20, 22–23, 43, 189–90; and *Biddy Brogan's Boy*, 274, 280, 283, 286; cited, 11, 18, 20, 21 22–23, 28, 188, 189, 190, 192; editing of, 191; Mencken's opinion of, 190; play version (*see* "God Loves the Irish" [play version of *Shanty Irish*]); publication, 178, 302; reviews, 190–92; style and themes, 11, 17–18, 20, 21, 22, 187–90, 192, 198, 225; writing of, 178, 179, 187, 189–90, 221

Shaw, George Bernard, 129, 138, 155, 157, 212, 256, 284; interviewed by Tully, 7, 211
Shearer, Norma, 256
Sheik, The (1921 film), 215
Sheil, Richard Lalor, 189
Shepard, Juanita, 256–57
Shoeless Joe (Kinsella), 264
Shoulder Arms (1918 film), 139, 142
Silberberg, Mendel, 242
Simms, Artie, 87
Simms, Eddie, 85
Simon & Schuster, 248, 262
Sinclair, Johnny, 91, 174
Sinclair, Mary Craig, 187
Sinclair, Upton, 115, 116, 120, 123, 186–87, 191, 207, 220
Singleton, Father John S., 25–27
Sioux City, Iowa, 54
Sister of the Road: The Autobiography of Boxcar Bertha (Reitman), 288
Sketches of the Irish Bar (Sheil), 189
Slattery, Jimmy, 165
Smart Set, The, 116, 128, 132–33, 134
Smith, Al, 187
Smith, Frederick, 220
Smith, Vernie, 104–6
Snows of Kilimanjaro, The (Hemingway), 259
Southern Pacific Railroad, 146, 197
Soviet Union (Russia), 203, 238, 273
Sperry, Henry "Kid," 104
Spoon River Anthology (Masters), 289
Springbrook Brewery, 62
Springfield Republican, 152
Stalin, Josef, 238
Stallings, Laurence, 163
Stallman, R. W., 249
Stander, Lionel, 193
Stanley Rose Bookshop, 266, 270
Stanwyck, Barbara, 234, 256
Star Rover, The (Morrell), 198
Steffens, Lincoln, 273
Steinbeck, John, 4, 272, 286, 288
Stendhal (Marie-Henri Beyle), 127
Stenn, David, 236
Stevens, James, 183, 244
Stevenson, Robert Louis, 117
St. Joseph's Orphan Asylum (Cincinnati), 2, 25–34, 36, 43, 51, 54, 56–57, 58, 74, 225
St. Luke's Hospital (Chicago), 5, 57
St. Marys chain works, 40, 41, 42, 48, 67, 76
St. Marys Evening Leader, 181, 203, 296
St. Marys, Ohio, 15, 20, 37, 104, 123, 244, 245, 293; and boxing matches, 82, 83, 84, 86–87; history of, 13, 38–40; later visits, 67, 87; responses to Tully's books, 181–82, 203; similarities to Kent, Ohio, 78; in Tully's books, 5, 122, 187, 304; Tully's childhood and adolescent years in, 16, 23, 25–27, 31, 33–34, 38–51, 53, 57, 62, 182; as Tully's hometown, 1, 5, 29, 64, 76, 124, 191, 296
Stone, Irving, 289
Story of an African Farm, The (Schreiner), 59
Story of My Life, The (Keller), 265
Story of Philosophy, The (Durant), 259
Story World, 133, 158
St. Patrick's Church (Glynnwood, Ohio), 24, 25, 26
St. Paul's Cathedral (London), 211
Strade, Joe, 83, 84
Stratton-Porter, Gene, 128
Stroheim, Erich von, 133, 163, 169, 170, 171, 290
Stuart, Gloria, 231
Sturges, Preston, 292
St. Xavier's College (Cincinnati), 67, 181, 230
Suetonius, 327n83
Sullivan, Dan, 67
Sullivan, Gabriel "Gabe," 31, 54–55, 157–58
Sullivan, John L., 37, 289, 304
Sullivan (Macy), Anne, 266
Sun Also Rises, The (Hemingway), 181
Sutherland, Eddie, 138, 141, 142, 145, 147, 162
Swain, Mack, 142, 143, 145
Swanberg, W. A., 161
Swerling, Jo, 243
Syracuse, New York, 63

Tall Timbers (Toluca Lake), 228–29, 255, 278, 290
Talmadge, Constance, 234
Talmadge, Norma, 176
Tasker, Robert, 197–98
Teasdale, Sara, 206
Ten Days That Shook the World (Reed), 154
Tess of the D'Urbervilles (Hardy), 57, 141
"Test, A" (Tully poem), 116
Thalberg, Irving, 128, 133, 169, 170, 218, 219, 235, 273
"Thanksgiving Meal on the Farm, A" (Tully poem), 103
That Printer of Udell's (Wright), 110
Theroux, Paul, 210
Thirty-ninth Street Theatre (New York), 164
Thomas, Frank "Bright Eyes" ("Blink"), 63, 158, 200–201
Thompson, Boxcar Bertha, 165, 288
Thompson, Jim, 4
Thompson, J. V., 95–96
Thompson's Drug Store (Kent), 166
Thorne, Gordon, 70–71, 74
Tierney, "Chicago Jack," 82–85, 265
Tilden, David, 265
Time Machine, The (Wells), 211

Titanic (1997 film), 231
Titanic, RMS, 209, 232
"To a Dead Athiest" (Tully poem), 103
Tobacco Road (Caldwell), 284
"To Geo. W. Austin, on His 103rd Birthday" (Tully poem), 103
Togo, 109
Toledo, Ohio, 88–90
Tolkin, Michael, 171
Toluca Lake, California, 228–29, 255, 278, 294
"To Robert Nichols" (Graves), 193
Totheroh, R. H. "Rollie," 138, 144, 145, 147
Tower of London (London), 211
Tracy, Spencer, 278
Trader Horn (1931 film), 218
Trafalgar Square (London), 210
Tramp, The (1915 film), 142
Tropic Death (Walrond), 252
Truckee, California, 144–46
True Confessions, 130, 131, 134, 142, 143
Tully, (Thomas) Alton (son of Jim Tully): birth, 104; childhood, 104, 113, 115, 133, 186, 222–23, 267; criminal and legal problems, 223, 224, 237, 241–44, 247–48, 256–59, 287–88, 300–301; death, 301; employment, 223, 224, 237, 241, 288, 293; and father's estate, 299; incarceration, 223, 224, 242–44, 247, 248, 258–59, 266–67, 277, 278, 281–82, 288, 291, 293; marriage, 300; psychological evaluation, 282; relations with father, 19, 20, 27, 34, 35, 41, 42, 123, 179, 190, 221, 222, 247, 267–68, 274–76
Tully, Anna (aunt). *See* Danaher, Anna Tully
Tully, Anna (sister). *See* Durr, Anna Tully (sister of Jim Tully)
Tully, Catherine Byrn (grandmother of Jim Tully), 12–13, 37, 102
Tully, Charles "Charlie" (brother of Jim Tully), 296; birth and childhood, 15, 16; and chain works in Kent, 75, 79, 83; in Columbus, 184; sent to orphanage, 25–27; working on Indiana farm, 31, 41
Tully, Florence May Bushnell (first wife of Jim Tully), 106, 113, 119, 155; birth of children, 104, 115; divorce from Jim Tully, 133; financial support from Jim Tully, 131, 157, 279; health, 293; marriage to Jim Tully, 100; meeting and courtship with Jim Tully, 92, 99–100; relationship with Alton, 222–23, 243, 247, 287; relationship with Jim Tully after divorce, 241; relationship with Trilby, 279
"Tully-Grams" (Tully newspaper column), 272, 273, 277
Tully, Henry (brother of Jim Tully), 308n93
Tully, Hugh (brother of Jim Tully), 26, 222, 296; birth and childhood, 15, 16, 24; hostler for Spencer Tracy, 278; as jockey, 74, 90–91; rescuing brother from orphanage, 31–33; visits nephew in prison, 243; working in Adrian, Michigan, 61; working in Meridian, Mississippi, 62; working in Racine, Wisconsin, 67, 72, 74, 75; working in St. Marys, Ohio, 25, 33, 45–46, 48
Tully, Hugh (Old Hughie; grandfather of Jim Tully), 26; death, 37, 38; ditchdigger, 13; immigration to America, 12; influence on grandson, 2, 11, 61; lace peddler, 12, 71; move to St. Marys, 13; portrayal in *Blood on the Moon*, 225, 230; portrayal in *Shanty Irish*, 10, 11, 188–90, 191, 192, 283; wedding, 12
Tully, James Dennis (father of Jim Tully): ancestry, 2; appearance, 16, 188; childhood, 13; correspondence with Jim Tully, 15–16, 109, 121, 179, 221; death of, 267; death of Bridget Lawler, 24; drinking, 11, 38, 221, 276; emigration from Ireland, 12–13; employment, 13–14, 15, 163, 240; as father, 16, 17, 19, 20, 27, 34, 35, 41–42, 247, 268, 274–76, 279; and finances, 20, 38, 81, 118, 157, 163, 221, 222, 247, 275; marriage to Bridget Lawler, 14, 15, 221; opinion of Jim Tully's work, 123, 221; reading interests of, 2, 20; religious views, 20, 188, 267; temperament, 19–20, 86, 87, 188–89, 190, 274, 275–76
Tully, Jim (James Alexander, 1886–1947): as actor, 7, 218–19; ancestry, 2, 11–15, 20, 121, 188; appearance and dress, 1, 5, 16, 45, 54, 185, 217, 228, 231, 270, 271, 295; autobiographical aspects of work, 8–10, 121–22, 198, 232, 281, 285; birth, 15–16; at Boroff farm, 34–36; and boxing, 62, 81–91, 92, 95–97, 101, 104, 106–9, 174, 187, 211, 217–18, 234, 238, 245, 255–56, 261–66, 268, 269, 278; and capital punishment, 8, 192, 197, 201–2, 219, 256; censorship of work, 181, 183, 214, 231, 250–51, 260; as chain maker, 40–41, 48, 67, 72, 75, 77–79, 84, 86, 91–92, 104, 115, 184, 246; as Chaplin employee, 136–47, 159, 162; childhood, 16–32; and circus, xii, 37, 53–54, 63–65, 168, 173, 178–80, 182–83, 234; death of father, 267; death and funeral, 296–97; death of mother, 22–24; drinking, 42, 47, 61, 62, 105, 112, 206, 207, 210, 231, 237–38, 253, 290, 292; education, 3, 28–30; FBI file, 220, 280; grandchildren, 291, 293, 299; health, 56–57, 282–83, 288, 290–293, 295–96; interviewing style of, 234–35; jail and prison, 49–50, 55, 58–59, 63, 66–67, 158, 159, 165, 196–99, 219, 223, 244–45, 258, 272, 281, 293; as jockey, 90–91; as kitchen laborer, 48, 60, 67, 224; lectures, 156, 159, 162, 165–66, 220–21, 271;

Tully, Jim (cont.)
and libraries, 2, 36, 43, 57, 59, 62, 67, 73, 74, 75, 77, 79–80, 94, 99, 105, 107, 112, 116, 118, 150, 181, 210, 229, 234, 244, 271, 281; literary influences, 2, 7, 29, 51, 57, 67–68, 75, 110–12, 117, 118, 124, 127, 129, 186, 210, 259; literary reputation, 4, 7, 149, 158, 166, 235, 251, 284, 296–98; loneliness, 2, 16, 27–28, 34, 35, 45, 72, 73, 95, 125, 214, 270; as newsboy, 54, 56, 57, 59, 60, 62, 63, 200; as newspaper columnist, 272–73, 277–78; as newspaper reporter, 81, 104, 245–47; and orphanage, 2, 25–32, 36, 58, 68, 157, 225, 235, 256; philosophical views, 132, 219, 223, 258, 270, 273–74; as poet, 79, 80, 102–4, 106, 115, 116, 122, 149, 166, 240, 269; police, 50, 55–56, 58, 66, 77; political views, 219–20, 272–74, 280; poverty, xi, xiv, 1, 3, 22, 26, 27, 33–65, 43, 196, 210–11; racial views, 64–65, 174–75, 252–54; as railroad worker, 92–93; relationship with Alton, 222–23, 224, 237, 242–44, 247, 257–59, 266–67, 282, 288; relationship with Chaplin, xiv, 135–47, 153–54, 159, 162, 164, 170, 177–78, 179, 240, 271, 290; relationship with father, 19, 20, 27, 34, 35, 41, 42, 81, 123, 179, 190, 221, 222, 247, 267–68, 274–76; relationship with Florence Bushnell, 92, 99–100, 106, 119, 133, 222–23, 241, 279; relationship with Margaret "Marna" Myers, 155–56, 157, 195, 204–8, 214–15, 229, 269; relationship with Mary Lygo, 69–71, 74, 83, 95, 204–6; relationship with Mencken, 7, 123, 128–29, 134, 158, 179, 184–85, 196, 198, 204, 207, 229, 237, 250–51, 281, 289, 291–92; relationship with mother, xiii, 2, 16, 18, 22, 25, 27, 28, 121, 221, 274, 283; relationship with Myrtle Zwetow, 239, 244, 254, 269, 295, 296; relationship with Nellie Dingley, 80–81, 94–95, 99; relationship with Trilby, 133, 224–25, 267, 278–80; relationship with Virginia (Maggie), 1–2, 16, 25, 27, 31, 38, 41, 42, 43, 63, 71, 72, 74, 100, 104, 123, 128, 166, 174, 175, 205, 276–77, 283–84; religious views, 29, 30–31, 65, 123–24, 188, 189, 209, 219, 220, 269, 270, 276; as rubber worker, 92; sexuality, 37, 47, 94, 99, 156; as storyteller, 2, 61, 67, 114; studio work, 126, 127, 133–34, 218, 248; as taxi starter, 111–12; as teamster, 37, 41, 46, 56; temperament, 6, 10, 195, 204, 206, 228, 238, 244, 257, 269–70; travels as road-kid, 45, 46, 47–75; as tree surgeon, 3, 95–99, 100, 101, 104–6, 109–10, 112, 113, 117; wanderlust, 42–44, 46, 49, 57, 66; will and estate of, 299; writing aspirations, 1–2, 43, 57, 71, 73, 80–81, 87, 99, 118, 196, 261; writing habits, 79, 100, 171, 186, 221–22

Tully, Jim (James Alexander, 1886–1947), works. *See specific titles of works*
Tully, Margaret Becker (wife of Alton Tully), 300–301
Tully, Margaret Rider "Marna" Myers (second wife of Jim Tully), 195; divorce filings, 204, 206–7, 214–15; marriage to Jim Tully, 155–56; meeting and courtship, 155–56; remarriage, 229, 269; temperament, 155, 157, 195, 205, 206; travels with Jim Tully, 207–13
Tully, Maria (aunt), 12
Tully, Maria Bridget "Biddy" Lawler (mother of Jim Tully), 15; appearance, 16; birth, 14; childhood, 14; death, 22–24, 28, 276; marriage, 14; and Moll, 21–22; as mother, 15, 16; temperament, 2, 18, 20, 22, 25, 188, 221, 224
Tully, Margaret McGrorty (great-grandmother of Jim Tully), 12
Tully, Myrtle Zwetow (third wife of Jim Tully), 244, 253, 254, 267, 269, 278, 292; and Alton, 247, 248, 257, 266–67, 268, 282, 292, 293; appearance, 239; as caretaker for Jim Tully, 291, 293, 295, 296; death, 300; employment, 239, 261, 278, 290, 291, 299–300; marriage to Jim Tully, 239; meeting and courtship, 239; temperament, 239; and Trilby, 239, 267, 279–80, 299; will and estate, 299
Tully, Thomas Alton (son). *See* Tully, (Thomas) Alton (son of Jim Tully)
Tully, Tom (brother of Jim Tully), 38, 43; birth and childhood, 15, 16, 18, 24; death in Mexico, 71, 166; sent to orphanage, 25–27, 29; travels to Mexico, 41–42; working on Kentucky farm, 31
Tully, Trilby (daughter). *See* Beamon, Trilby Jeanne Tully (daughter of Jim Tully)
Tully, Virginia (born Margaret "Maggie"; sister of Jim Tully), 67, 163, 281; appearance, 16, 276; birth, 15; changes name to Virginia, 48; death, 175, 204, 283; death of mother, 23–24, 26; employment, 25, 69, 71; finances, 69, 71, 276; friendship with Mary Lygo, 69, 70–71, 74, 205; religious views, 100, 188–89, 276, 283–284; support for Jim Tully's aspirations to write, 1–2, 43, 71, 75, 81, 104, 123, 128, 148, 174, 276–77; as surrogate mother, 16, 25–26, 27, 31, 38, 41, 42, 45, 63, 71–72, 74, 100, 166, 276–77, 283; temperament, 69, 71, 166
Tunney, Gene, 174, 266
Turgenev, Ivan, 259
Twain, Mark, 8, 64, 180, 185, 188, 208; Tully's admiration for, 51, 186, 210
Twentieth Century Club (Toledo, Ohio), 88–89
Twenty Below (1928 play by Tully and Robert Nichols), 192–93, 302

Twenty-fifth Man, The (Morrell), 198
21 Club, 278
Two Arabian Nights (1927 film), 281
Tyndall, John, 189

Ulysses (Joyce), 212
Uniontown, Pennsylvania, 95, 106
Universal City, California, 133
Universal Pictures, 193, 231, 232, 303
University of Chicago, 9, 192
University of Southern California, 156
University of Washington, 166
University of Wisconsin, 113

Valentino, Rudolph, 5, 215, 216
Vallee, Rudy, 248
Vander, Dutch, 58–59
Vanderveen, Joyce, 236
Van de Water, Frederic F., 225–26
Vanity Fair, 179, 194, 292, 303; Tully appearances in, 6, 134, 168–70, 173, 174, 215–16, 221, 304
Van Wert County, Ohio, 16, 18, 34, 37
Vanzetti, Bartolomeo, 220, 235
Vidor, King, 169

Wagner, Rob, 177, 178, 240
Walnut Grove Methodist Church, 21, 188
Walrond, Eric, 252
Walsh, John, 189
Warner Brothers, 231, 262
War of the Worlds, The (Wells), 211
Washington, D.C., 58, 63, 65, 97, 103, 105, 233, 239
Washington, Fredi (Edith Warren), 174, 176
Washington Post, 218, 219, 233
Watch and Ward Society, 181
Watson "Blue Beard," 131
Waukegan, Illinois, 9, 113–14
Way for a Sailor (1930 film), 218–19
Wayne, John, 40
Weird Tales, 235
Welles, Orson, 194
Wellman, William ("Wild Bill"), 5, 149, 193, 194–95, 304
Wells, H. G., 7, 211–12, 221
Westminster Abbey, 211
West, Nathanael, 172, 270
Wetjen, Albert, 218
What Makes Sammy Run? (Schulberg), 171

What Price Glory? (Anderson and Stallings), 163, 164
Wheeler, John, 177, 178, 245–47
Wheeling and Lake Erie Railway, 78
"When Trilby Came" (Tully poem), 115
White, Walter, 175
White, William Allen, 179
Whitman, Walt, 139, 210
Whitmore, Eugene, 182–83
Wiggin, Kate Douglas, 128
Wilder, Billy, 292
Wilhelm II, Kaiser, 298
Wilkie, Wendell, 273
Willard, Jess, 89
Willeford, Charles, 4, 8
Wilson, Edmund, 284
Wilson, Harry Leon, 171
Winchell, Walter, 7, 197, 245, 256, 262, 277, 293
"Winds of Wonder" (unpublished manuscript by Tully), 281
Winesburg, Ohio (Anderson), 129
Wings (1927 film), 193, 194
Winter, Ella, 273
Wolfe, Thomas, 7, 260–61
Wolgast, Ad, 108–9, 265
Wolheim, Louis, 176
Woman of Paris, A (1923 film), 142, 144
Wood, Sam, 218
Woollcott, Alexander, 163, 176
Wright, Harold Bell, 110, 115, 116, 128, 148, 182
Writer's Digest, 132, 221–22
Wuthering Heights (Bronte), 57
Wyler, William, 193
Wyoming, Denna, 64, 65

Yankee Doodle Dandy (1942 film), 164
Yankee Stadium (New York), 238
Yeager, Cloyce, 87
Yearling, The (Rawlings), 285
Yeats, William Butler, 116
"Yeggs" (Tully), 238, 292
York, Pennsylvania, 300
Young Lonigan (Farrell), 8
Youngstown Vindicator, 103

Zion City, Illinois, 9, 60
Zola, Emile, 249
Zwetow, Myrtle. *See* Tully, Myrtle Zwetow (third wife of Jim Tully)

www.ingramcontent.com/pod-product-compliance
Lightning Source LLC
Chambersburg PA
CBHW030315100526
44592CB00010B/440